Holy Boldness

Holy Boldness

Women Preachers' Autobiographies and the Sanctified Self

Susie C. Stanley

THE UNIVERSITY OF TENNESSEE PRESS / Knoxville

First Edition.

This book is printed on acid-free paper.

Library of Congress Cataloging-in-Publication Data

Stanley, Susie Cunningham, 1948–
Holy boldness: women preachers' autobiographies and the sanctified self/Susie C. Stanley.
p. cm.
Includes bibliographical references and index.
ISBN 1-57233-199-2 (cl.: alk. paper)
1. Holiness churches—Clergy—Biography.
2. Women clergy—Biography.
I. Title.
BX7990.H62 S73 2002
287'.092'273—dc21 2002003610

To John

CONTENTS

ILLUSTRATIONS

PREFACE

This book traces a trajectory of women's spiritual autobiographies from Madame Jeane Marie Bouvier de la Mothe Guyon to Mary Bosanquet Fletcher and Hester Ann Rogers before turning to the primary focus of examining autobiographies authored by thirty-four American Wesleyan/Holiness women preachers. This book is an analysis of the autobiographies themselves rather than a collective biography. The autobiographies did not yield sufficient material to undertake this task. Following the Acknowledgements is a chart listing the American women along with bibliographical information on their autobiographies. I have included birthplace, birth date, denominational affiliation, and ordination when provided by the autobiographers. Also listed are primary areas of ministry. In addition, I have provided bibliographical information on the biographies that have been written on several women.

Because I am a church historian and theologian whose training and research interests include gender studies, particularly in the Wesleyan/Holiness movement, I could have analyzed the autobiographies strictly from a historical and theological perspective informed by feminist scholarship. Granted, such a feminist approach is evident in my work. Scholars such as Mary Beard and Gerda Lerner, and others who have followed their lead, have influenced my methodology.[1] Like them, I do not see women solely as victims of the ideology of woman's sphere, the belief that women's place was in the home. The women preachers in this study illustrate women's place as a force in history in spite of this ideology. I also have benefited from my Wesleyan/Holiness upbringing. I grew up hearing women preach. I was sixteen before encountering Christians outside my denomination who believed women had no place in church leadership. I refuse, though, to view the early years of the Wesleyan/Holiness movement as a utopian past to be recovered, because even as opportunities expanded for public ministry the doctrine of woman's sphere penetrated the church. Unfortunately, I have also evidenced instances in the Wesleyan/Holiness movement where women have not been supported in their call to ministry.

While historical perspective is valuable, I have also employed autobiographical criticism where it contributed to a deeper understanding of Wesleyan/Holiness women and the development of the sanctified self that enabled them to break free of the constrictions of woman's sphere and assume active leadership in the public sphere. By incorporating autobiographical theory, I have ventured beyond the boundaries of my areas of training. I have immersed myself in the critical literature of women's autobiographies, and because I am not used to swimming here, I sometimes felt like I was drowning. I realize that, unintentionally, I may fall short in my comprehension of particular aspects of autobiographical theory and trust that theorists will correct any misunderstandings they spot. My hope is that this study will inform theoreticians in terms of the religious context and the theological convictions that propelled these women into the public sphere. I wish to join in conversation with theorists by contributing theological insights, particularly regarding the role of sanctification in Wesleyan/Holiness women's understanding of self.

ACKNOWLEDGMENTS

John E. Stanley provided assistance above and beyond the call of duty, both as a professional colleague and a husband. He played a significant role throughout the process, from acquiring autobiographies via interlibrary loan to checking cities and dates where women preached. As a sounding board, he listened patiently as I wrestled with the meaning of sanctification for these women. He read the manuscript at various stages of completion, continually offering useful advice. John's unequivocal support of me and other women in ministry exemplifies the Wesleyan/Holiness movement's theology at its best.

Thanks also go to Cheryl Sanders, Catherine Wessinger, Wendy Dasler Johnson, and Nancy Hardesty, who furnished helpful suggestions early in the process. In addition, Wendy Dasler Johnson and Nancy Hardesty read the completed manuscript and offered numerous recommendations for improvement. Mandy Stanley read a draft of the manuscript and proposed changes. I am grateful to Gregory Schneider, Paul Chilcote, Patricia Ward, and Leon Hynson for providing assistance relating to their areas of expertise.

B. J. (Cyga) Gontkovsky, Christina (Brye) Boes, Monica Volante, and Tawndee Witter, work-study students at Messiah College, helped with sorting information for the database, and Jennifer Hay assisted with proofreading. Faculty services at Messiah College graciously typed the database of information from the autobiographies. Messiah College awarded a scholarship grant and appointed me to the C. N. Hostetter Jr. Chair of Religious Studies, which released me from teaching to complete the book.

CHART OF WESLEYAN/HOLINESS WOMEN AUTOBIOGRAPHERS

The following information is from women's autobiographies. The scarcity of information in many cases reflects the women's lack of concern for details. In terms of ministry, missions generally served two purposes: evangelism and social holiness. Likewise, door-to-door work often incorporated both components of ministry. Material in brackets is from biographies of the women.

Mary Still Adams

AUTOBIOGRAPHY: *Autobiography of Mary Still Adams or, "In God We Trust."* Los Angeles: Buckingham Bros., Printers, 1893.
BIRTH PLACE AND DATE: Macon County, Missouri; 1839
DENOMINATIONAL AFFILIATION(S): Methodist Episcopal Church
LICENSED/ORDAINED: Not Provided
TYPE(S) OF MINISTRY: Revivalist, Camp Meeting Preacher, Social Holiness Worker among Former Slaves

Mary Lee Cagle

AUTOBIOGRAPHY: *Life and Work of Mary Lee Cagle: An Autobiography.* Kansas City, Mo.: Nazarene Publishing House, 1928.
BIRTH PLACE AND DATE: 21 Sept. 1864
DENOMINATIONAL AFFILIATION(S): Methodist Episcopal Church, [New Testament] Church of Christ, Church of the Nazarene
LICENSED/ORDAINED: [Ordained in 1899 by New Testament Church of Christ]
TYPE(S) OF MINISTRY: Revivalist, Camp Meeting Preacher, Street Meeting Preacher, Church Planter, Pentecostal Church of the Nazarene Cofounder, District Evangelist
BIOGRAPHY: Robert Stanley Ingersol, "Burden of Dissent: Mary Lee Cagle and the Southern Holiness Movement" (Ph.D. diss., Duke Univ., 1989).

Mary Cole

AUTOBIOGRAPHY: *Trials and Triumphs of Faith.* Anderson, Ind.: Gospel Trumpet, 1914
BIRTH PLACE AND DATE: Decatur, Iowa; 23 Aug. 1853

CHART OF WESLEYAN/HOLINESS WOMEN AUTOBIOGRAPHERS (Cont'd)

DENOMINATIONAL AFFILIATION(S): Methodist Episcopal Church, South; Church of God (Anderson, Indiana)
LICENSED/ORDAINED: Not Provided
TYPE(S) OF MINISTRY: Revivalist, Camp Meeting Preacher, Supervisor of Mission Home

Sarah A. Cooke

AUTOBIOGRAPHY: *The Handmaiden of the Lord, or Wayside Sketches.* Chicago: T. B. Arnold, 1896.
BIRTH PLACE AND DATE: Olney Buckingham Shire, England; 10 Nov. 1827
DENOMINATIONAL AFFILIATION(S): Free Methodist
LICENSED/ORDAINED: Not Provided
TYPE(S) OF MINISTRY: Street Meeting Preacher, Mission Worker

Dora A. Dudley

AUTOBIOGRAPHY: *Beulah: or, Some of the Fruits of One Consecrated Life.* Revised and enlarged edition. Grand Rapids, Mich.: By the author, 1896.
BIRTH PLACE AND DATE: Not Provided
DENOMINATIONAL AFFILIATION(S): Not Provided
LICENSED/ORDAINED: Not Provided
TYPE(S) OF MINISTRY: Revivalist, Supervisor of a Home for Healing, W.C.T.U.

Jane Dunning

AUTOBIOGRAPHY: *Brands from the Burning: An Account of a Work among the Sick and Destitute in Connection with Providence Mission, New York City.* Chicago: Baker & Arnold, 1881.
BIRTH PLACE AND DATE: Not Provided
DENOMINATIONAL AFFILIATION(S): Free Methodist? (B. T. Roberts, founder of Free Methodist Church, wrote the preface to her autobiography.)
LICENSED/ORDAINED: Not Provided
TYPE(S) OF MINISTRY: Door-to-Door Worker, Mission Worker among the Poor

CHART OF WESLEYAN/HOLINESS WOMEN AUTOBIOGRAPHERS (Cont'd)

Zilpha Elaw

AUTOBIOGRAPHY: *Memoirs of the Life, Religious Experience, Ministerial Travels and Labours of Mrs. Zilpha Elaw, an American Female of Color: Together with Some Account of the Great Religious Revivals in America.* London: By the author, 1846. Reprint, *Sisters of the Spirit: Three Black Women's Autobiographies of the Nineteenth Century.* Ed. William L. Andrews. Bloomington, Ind.: Indiana Univ. Press, 1986.

BIRTH PLACE AND DATE: Pennsylvania

DENOMINATIONAL AFFILIATION(S): Society of Friends, Methodist Episcopal Church

LICENSED/ORDAINED: Not Provided

TYPE(S) OF MINISTRY: Revivalist

Susan [Norris] Fitkin

AUTOBIOGRAPHY: *Grace Much More Abounding: A Story of the Triumphs of Redeeming Grace During Two Score Years in the Master's Service.* Kansas City, Mo.: Nazarene Publishing House, n.d.

BIRTH PLACE AND DATE: Not Provided

DENOMINATIONAL AFFILIATION(S): Society of Friends, Association of Holiness Churches, Church of the Nazarene

LICENSED/ORDAINED: Recorded Society of Friends Minister, Ordained, Pentecostal Church of the Nazarene

TYPE(S) OF MINISTRY: Revivalist, Pastor

Julia Foote

AUTOBIOGRAPHY: *A Brand Plucked from the Fire: An Autobiographical Sketch.* Cleveland, Ohio: By the author, 1879. Reprint, *Sisters of the Spirit: Three Black Women's Autobiographies of the Nineteenth Century*. Ed. William L. Andrews. Bloomington, Ind.: Indiana Univ. Press, 1986.

BIRTH PLACE AND DATE: Schenectady, New York; 1823

DENOMINATIONAL AFFILIATION(S): Methodist Episcopal Church, African Methodist Episcopal Church

CHART OF WESLEYAN/HOLINESS WOMEN AUTOBIOGRAPHERS (Cont'd)

LICENSED/ORDAINED: [First woman ordained a deacon (1895) and second woman ordained an elder (1899) in the Methodist Episcopal Zion Church.] This information is from Bettye Collier-Thomas's book, *Daughters of Thunder: Black Women Preachers and their Sermons, 1850–1979* (San Francisco: Jossey-Bass, 1997), 59.
TYPE(S) OF MINISTRY: Revivalist

Mary A. Ettinger Glaser

AUTOBIOGRAPHY: *Wonderful Leadings.* Allentown, Pa.: Haines & Worman, Printers, 1893.
BIRTH PLACE AND DATE: Sandusky, Ohio; 1836
DENOMINATIONAL AFFILIATION(S): United Brethren
LICENSED/ORDAINED: Not Provided
TYPE(S) OF MINISTRY: Speaker on Divine Healing and Holiness

Emma [Warren] Irick

AUTOBIOGRAPHY: *The King's Daughter.* Kansas City, Mo.: Pedestal Press, 1973.
BIRTH PLACE AND DATE: Jewell County, Kans.; 24 Jan. 1888
DENOMINATIONAL AFFILIATION(S): Wesleyan Methodist Church, Church of the Nazarene
LICENSED/ORDAINED: Licensed (1907), Texas Holiness Association; Ordained (1911), Pentecostal Church of the Nazarene
TYPE(S) OF MINISTRY: Revivalist, Pastor, Camp Meeting Preacher, Church Planter, District Evangelist

Maude H. Kahl

AUTOBIOGRAPHY: *His Guiding Hand: An Autobiography.* Overland Park, Kans.: Herald and Banner Press, 1970.
BIRTH PLACE AND DATE: Indiana; 1885–87? (age 82 in 1968)
DENOMINATIONAL AFFILIATION(S): Not Provided
LICENSED/ORDAINED: Not Provided
TYPE(S) OF MINISTRY: Street Meeting Preacher, Revivalist, Pastor, Church Planter, Door-to-Door Worker

CHART OF WESLEYAN/HOLINESS WOMEN AUTOBIOGRAPHERS (Cont'd)

Jarena Lee

AUTOBIOGRAPHY: *Religious Experience and Journal of Mrs. Jarena Lee, Giving an Account of Her Call to Preach the Gospel.* Philadelphia: By the author, 1849.
BIRTH PLACE AND DATE: Cape May, N.J.; 11 Feb. 1783
DENOMINATIONAL AFFILIATION(S): African Methodist Episcopal
LICENSED/ORDAINED: Not Provided
TYPE(S) OF MINISTRY: Revivalist, Camp Meeting Preacher

Martha A. Lee

AUTOBIOGRAPHY: *Mother Lee's Experience in Fifteen Years' Rescue Work: With Thrilling Incidents of Her Life.* Omaha, Nebr.: By the author, 1906.
BIRTH PLACE AND DATE: Indiana; 18 Apr. 1842
DENOMINATIONAL AFFILIATION(S): Free Methodist
LICENSED/ORDAINED: Not Provided
TYPE(S) OF MINISTRY: Founded Mission Homes for Homeless, Children, and Pregnant Young Women

Almira Losee

AUTOBIOGRAPHY: *Life Sketches: Being Narrations of Scenes Occurring in the Labours of Almira Losee.* New York: By the author, 1880.
BIRTH PLACE AND DATE: New York; 1825
DENOMINATIONAL AFFILIATION(S): Methodist Episcopal Church
LICENSED/ORDAINED: Local Preacher's License, Methodist Episcopal Church
TYPE(S) OF MINISTRY: Revivalist, Camp Meeting Preacher, Founded Mission Homes for Children and Elderly Women, W.C.T.U.

Lela G. McConnell

AUTOBIOGRAPHY: *Faith Victorious in the Kentucky Mountains: The Story of Twenty-Two Years of Spirit-Filled Ministry.* Berne, Ind.: Economy Printing Concern, 1946. *Hitherto and Henceforth in the Kentucky Mountains; A Quarter of a Century of Adventures in Faith—The Year of Jubilee.* Lawson, Ky.: n.p., 1949. *The Pauline Ministry in*

CHART OF WESLEYAN/HOLINESS WOMEN AUTOBIOGRAPHERS (Cont'd)

the Kentucky Mountains or A Brief Account of the Kentucky Mountain Holiness Association. Louisville, Ky.: Pentecostal Publishing, [1942]. *The Power of Prayer Plus Faith.* n.p., 1952. *Rewarding Faith Plus Works.* n.p., 1962.

BIRTH PLACE AND DATE: Honey Brook, Pa.

DENOMINATIONAL AFFILIATION(S): Methodist Episcopal Church

LICENSED/ORDAINED: Local Preacher's License, Deacon (1924), and Elder (1926), Methodist Church

TYPE(S) OF MINISTRY: Revivalist, Camp Meeting Preacher, Pastor, Founder and President of Kentucky Mountain Holiness Association, Radio Preacher

Lizzie E. Miller

AUTOBIOGRAPHY: *The True Way: Life and Evangelical Work of Lizzie E. Miller (of Fairview, West Va.) Written by Herself.* Los Angeles: By the author, 1895.

BIRTH PLACE AND DATE: Fairview, W.Va.

DENOMINATIONAL AFFILIATION(S): Not Provided

LICENSED/ORDAINED: Not Provided

TYPE(S) OF MINISTRY: Revivalist, Camp Meeting Preacher, Church Planter, Participated in Temperance Crusade, W.C.T.U. Preacher

Abbie C. Mills

AUTOBIOGRAPHY: *Grace and Glory.* Los Angeles: By the author, 1907. *Quiet Hallelujahs.* Boston: McDonald & Gill, 1886.

BIRTH PLACE AND DATE: Orange County, N.Y.; 19 Feb. 1829

DENOMINATIONAL AFFILIATION(S): Presbyterian, Methodist Episcopal Church

LICENSED/ORDAINED: Local Preacher's License, Methodist Episcopal Church

TYPE(S) OF MINISTRY: Revivalist, Camp Meeting Preacher, W.C.T.U.

Lucy Drake Osborn

AUTOBIOGRAPHY: *Heavenly Pearls Set in a Life: A Record of Experiences and Labors in America, India and Australia.* New York: Fleming H. Revell, 1893.

BIRTH PLACE AND DATE: Stoughton, Mass.; 27 Oct. 1844

CHART OF WESLEYAN/HOLINESS WOMEN AUTOBIOGRAPHERS (Cont'd)

DENOMINATIONAL AFFILIATION(S): Congregational Church
LICENSED/ORDAINED: Received letter signed by several clergy before going to India
TYPE(S) OF MINISTRY: Revivalist, Camp Meeting Preacher, Door-to-Door Worker, Supervised Missionary Training School

Phoebe Palmer

AUTOBIOGRAPHY: *The Way of Holiness: Notes by the Way.* 50th American ed., 1867. Reprint, Salem, Ohio: Schmul Publishing, 1988.
BIRTH PLACE AND DATE: [New York City; 18 Dec. 1807]
DENOMINATIONAL AFFILIATION(S): Methodist Episcopal Church
LICENSED/ORDAINED: [No]
TYPE(S) OF MINISTRY: [Revivalist, Camp Meeting Preacher, Lay Theologian, Mission Worker among the Poor]
BIOGRAPHIES: Harold E. Raser, *Phoebe Palmer: Her Life and Thought* (Lewiston: Edwin Mellen Press, 1987). Charles Edward White, *The Beauty of Holiness: Phoebe Palmer as Theologian, Revivalist, Feminist, and Humanitarian* (Grand Rapids, Mich.: Francis Asbury Press of Zondervan Publishing House, 1986).

Mattie E. Perry

AUTOBIOGRAPHY: *Christ and Answered Prayer; Autobiography of Mattie E. Perry.* Cincinnati: By the author, 1939.
BIRTH PLACE AND DATE: Cheohee, S.C.; 15 May 1868
DENOMINATIONAL AFFILIATION(S): Methodist
LICENSED/ORDAINED: Not Provided
TYPE(S) OF MINISTRY: Revivalist, City Missionary among the Poor

Anna W. Prosser

AUTOBIOGRAPHY: *From Death To Life: An Autobiography.* Buffalo: McGerald Publishing, 1901
BIRTH PLACE AND DATE: Albany, N.Y.; 15 Oct. 1846
DENOMINATIONAL AFFILIATION(S): Not Provided, then Methodist
LICENSED/ORDAINED: Not Provided
TYPE(S) OF MINISTRY: Founded a Mission in the Slums, Door-to-Door Worker, W.C.T.U. Preacher

CHART OF WESLEYAN/HOLINESS WOMEN AUTOBIOGRAPHERS (Cont'd)

Emma J. Smith Ray

AUTOBIOGRAPHY: *Twice Sold, Twice Ransomed: Autobiography of Mr. and Mrs. L. P. Ray.* Chicago: Free Methodist Publishing House, 1926.

BIRTH PLACE AND DATE: Springfield, Mo.; 7 Jan. 1859

DENOMINATIONAL AFFILIATION(S): Free Methodist

LICENSED/ORDAINED: Not Provided

TYPE(S) OF MINISTRY: Revivalist, Street Meeting Preacher, Prison Ministry, Mission Worker in the Slums, W.C.T.U. Local President and Superintendent of Jail and Prison Work

Florence Roberts

AUTOBIOGRAPHY: *Fifteen Years with the Outcast.* Anderson, Ind.: Gospel Trumpet, 1912.

BIRTH PLACE AND DATE: Not Provided

DENOMINATIONAL AFFILIATION(S): Not Provided

LICENSED/ORDAINED: Not Provided

TYPE(S) OF MINISTRY: Revivalist, Street Meeting Preacher, Prison Ministry, Rescue Missionary, Supervised Mission Homes Including One for Prostitutes, W.C.T.U. Preacher

Julia A. Shellhamer

AUTOBIOGRAPHY: *Trials and Triumphs of a Minister's Wife.* Atlanta: Repairer Publishing, 1923.

BIRTH PLACE AND DATE: Not Provided

DENOMINATIONAL AFFILIATION(S): Free Methodist

LICENSED/ORDAINED: Licensed, Free Methodist

TYPE(S) OF MINISTRY: Revivalist, Street Meeting Preacher, Pastor, Church Planter, Supervised Mission

Amanda Smith

AUTOBIOGRAPHY: *An Autobiography: The Story of the Lord's Dealings with Mrs. Amanda Smith, The Colored Evangelist.* Chicago: Meyer & Brother, Publishers, 1893. Reprint, New York: Garland Publishing, 1987.

CHART OF WESLEYAN/HOLINESS WOMEN AUTOBIOGRAPHERS (Cont'd)

BIRTH PLACE AND DATE: Long Green, Md.; 23 Jan. 1837
DENOMINATIONAL AFFILIATION(S): African Methodist [Episcopal]
LICENSED/ORDAINED: Not Provided
TYPE(S) OF MINISTRY: Revivalist, Camp Meeting Preacher
BIOGRAPHY: Adrienne M. Israel, *Amanda Berry Smith,* Studies in Evangelicalism, no. 16. (Lanham, Md.: Scarecrow Press, 1998).

Hannah Whitall Smith

AUTOBIOGRAPHY: *My Spiritual Autobiography or How I Discovered the Unselfishness of God.* New York: Fleming H. Revell, 1903.
BIRTH PLACE AND DATE: Philadelphia; 1832
DENOMINATIONAL AFFILIATION(S): Society of Friends [Plymouth Brethren, Society of Friends]
LICENSED/ORDAINED: Not Provided
TYPE(S) OF MINISTRY: Camp Meeting Preacher, [Bible Teacher, Preacher, W.C.T.U., Suffrage Leader]
BIOGRAPHY: Marie Henry, *The Secret Life of Hannah Whitall Smith* (Grand Rapids, Mich.: Chosen Books of Zondervan Corp., 1984).

Jennie Smith

AUTOBIOGRAPHY: *From Baca to Beulah, Sequel to "Valley of Baca."* Philadelphia: Garrigues Brothers, 1880. *Incidents and Experiences of a Railroad Evangelist*. Washington, D.C.: By the author, 1920. *Ramblings in Beulah Land: A Continuation of Experiences in the Life of Jennie Smith.* Philadelphia: Garrigues Brothers, 1886. *Ramblings in Beulah Land: A Continuation of Experiences in the Life of Jennie Smith. No. 2.* Philadelphia: Garrigues Brothers, 1888. *Valley of Baca: A Record of Suffering and Triumph.* Cincinnati: Press of Jennings and Pye, 1876.
BIRTH PLACE AND DATE: Vienna, Ohio; 18 Aug. 1842
DENOMINATIONAL AFFILIATION(S): Methodist Episcopal Church
LICENSED/ORDAINED: Not Provided
TYPE(S) OF MINISTRY: Revivalist, Camp Meeting Preacher, Railroad Evangelist, Participated in Temperance Crusade, W. C.T.U. National Superintendent of Railroad Dept.

CHART OF WESLEYAN/HOLINESS WOMEN AUTOBIOGRAPHERS (Cont'd)

Sarah Sauer Smith

AUTOBIOGRAPHY: *Life Sketches of Mother Sarah Smith: "A Mother in Israel."* Anderson, Ind.: Gospel Trumpet, 1902. Reprint, Guthrie, Okla.: Faith Publishing House, n.d.
BIRTH PLACE AND DATE: Summit County, Ohio; 20 Sept. 1822
DENOMINATIONAL AFFILIATION(S): Lutheran, Church of God (Anderson, Indiana)
LICENSED/ORDAINED: Not Provided
TYPE(S) OF MINISTRY: Revivalist

Maggie Newton Van Cott

AUTOBIOGRAPHY: *The Harvest and the Reaper: Reminiscences of Revival Work of Mrs. Maggie N. Van Cott: The First Lady Licensed to Preach in the Methodist Episcopal Church in the United States.* New York: N. Tibbals & Sons, Publishers, 1876.
BIRTH PLACE AND DATE: New York City; 25 Mar. 1830
DENOMINATIONAL AFFILIATION(S): Methodist Episcopal Church
LICENSED/ORDAINED: Licensed by Methodist Episcopal Church
TYPE(S) OF MINISTRY: Revivalist

Elizabeth R. Wheaton

AUTOBIOGRAPHY: *Prisons and Prayer; or, A Labor of Love.* Tabor, Iowa: M. Kelley [1906].
BIRTH PLACE AND DATE: Wayne County, Ohio; 10 May 1844
DENOMINATION AFFILIATION(S): Methodist Episcopal Church
LICENSED/ORDAINED: Not Provided
TYPE(S) OF MINISTRY: Revivalist, Street Meeting Preacher, Prison Evangelist

[Mollie] Alma [Bridwell] White

AUTOBIOGRAPHY: *The Story of My Life and the Pillar of Fire.* 5 vols. Zarephath, N.J.: Pillar of Fire, 1935–43.
BIRTH PLACE AND DATE: Lewis County Ky.; 16 June 1862
DENOMINATIONAL AFFILIATION(S): Methodist Episcopal Church, South, Methodist Episcopal Church, Pillar of Fire

CHART OF WESLEYAN/HOLINESS WOMEN AUTOBIOGRAPHERS (Cont'd)

LICENSED/ORDAINED: Ordained (1902), Pillar of Fire

TYPE(S) OF MINISTRY: Camp Meeting Preacher, Revivalist, Street Meeting Preacher, Founder of Pillar of Fire, Radio Preacher, Women's Rights Advocate

BIOGRAPHY: Susie C. Stanley, *Feminist Pillar of Fire: The Life of Alma White* (Cleveland, Ohio: Pilgrim Press, 1993).

Emma M. Whittemore

AUTOBIOGRAPHY: *Mother Whittemore's Records of Modern Miracles.* Toronto: Missions of Biblical Education, 1931.

BIRTH PLACE AND DATE: Not Provided

DENOMINATIONAL AFFILIATION(S): Presbyterian

LICENSED/ORDAINED: Not Provided

TYPE(S) OF MINISTRY: Door-to-Door Worker, Founded Missions for Prostitutes

Celia Bradshaw Winkle

AUTOBIOGRAPHY: *The Preacher Girl: A Thrilling Story.* St. Petersburg, Fla.: By the author, 1967.

BIRTH PLACE AND DATE: Southeastern Ohio

DENOMINATIONAL AFFILIATION(S): Methodist; Pilgrim Holiness? (A Pilgrim Holiness general superintendent wrote the foreword of her autobiography.)

LICENSED/ORDAINED: Not Provided

TYPE(S) OF MINISTRY: Revivalist

INTRODUCTION

Expanding the Canon of Women's Autobiographies

This text represents the first comprehensive effort to recover the autobiographies of Wesleyan/Holiness women preachers and to use autobiographical and feminist theory to analyze them. To determine the role their religious convictions played in their ability to carry out their public ministries, I investigated the sanctified self these women revealed in their writings. These narratives deserve inclusion in the canon of women's autobiography because they document how women's religious experience of sanctification emboldened them to leave woman's private sphere and move into public ministries.

Rose Norman contended that "few white American women published spiritual autobiographies in the 19th century."[1] This book challenges her erroneous assumption by introducing previously unknown spiritual autobiographies that will expand our understanding of Christian spirituality in the nineteenth and twentieth centuries. The canon of women's autobiographies remains incomplete because a significant number of autobiographies authored by women preachers in the Wesleyan/Holiness movement are missing.

Estelle Jelinek identified three types of women who authored autobiographies in the late nineteenth century: writers, pioneers who traveled West, and feminists and reformers. A fourth category, Wesleyan/Holiness women preachers, must be added to complete the list. A preliminary bibliography of Wesleyan/Holiness women clergy included more than seventy-five autobiographies. Most of them are absent from the canon of American autobiographies. For instance, Robert E. Sayre's overview of American autobiographies in 1981 included no Wesleyan/Holiness women. Subsequently, the following African American Wesleyan/Holiness women have been added to the canon: Jarena Lee, Julia Foote, Zilpha Elaw, and Amanda Smith.[2] Undoubtedly, William L. Andrews must receive credit for recovering the autobiographies of the first three women because he reprinted them in *Sisters of the Spirit* in 1986.[3] These African American autobiographies have reached a broad audience and have provided a significant contribution to the fields of American Christianity and African American studies. Autobiographical theorists, as well as historians, have extensively examined these books. With respect to the study of Wesleyan/Holiness women preachers' autobiographies, those by African American women have become normative due to their availability. For this reason, the study of Wesleyan/Holiness women preachers is not subject to the general assessment voiced by feminist critic Deborah McDowell that the experience of white women often became the standard for early feminist theorists: "Seeing the experiences of white women, particularly white middle-class women, as normative, white female scholars proceeded blindly to exclude the work of Black women writers from literary anthologies and critical studies."[4] To the contrary, in the case of Wesleyan/Holiness women, Black women have been the norm. White women have remained outside the scope of canonical consideration. Most feminist scholars and autobiographical theorists have been unaware that there were white women preachers who shared the experience of sanctification described by African American women. This study remedies the omission.

In all, I analyze five autobiographies by African Americans and twenty-nine by white women. The autobiographies range in length from thirty-six pages to five volumes. In addition to the four African American women preachers listed above, I include the autobiography of Emma Ray, an African American preacher who ministered in Washington and Kansas. Her narrative has never been analyzed prior to this study. Some white Wesleyan/Holiness women have been the subject of biographies or dissertations, but none of their autobiographies have been critically examined by autobiographical theorists.

Jelinek is not the only scholar unacquainted with Wesleyan/Holiness women's autobiographies. Phoebe Davidson revealed a similar unfamiliarity. She did, however, leave open the possibility that such spiritual autobiographies might exist: "Very probably the spiritual narratives of white women are buried somewhere—in odd attics and library archives that no one has gotten around to exploring."[5] Actually, all the autobiographies used in this study are available through interlibrary loan.[6] Scouring attics and archives would, no doubt, bring to light many additional contributions to the canon. Despite the wealth of primary material available, no feminist or autobiographical critic has analyzed these autobiographies. Likewise, no one engaged in Wesleyan/Holiness studies, to my knowledge, has contributed to the emerging field of autobiographical theory.[7] It is safe to assume that a majority of Wesleyan/Holiness adherents themselves are unacquainted with most of these women, much less their writings. This is the first endeavor to undertake the recovery of these resources.

While Wesleyan/Holiness women's autobiographies have, for the most part, been overlooked for placement in the canon of women's autobiographies, they are often missing from the historical canon as well. In 1998 Brenda Brasher asserted, "With little exception, conservative Protestant congregations exclude women from the central leadership role of senior pastor." She qualified her statement in a footnote: "This exclusion is not absolute. Conservative Pentecostal congregations historically have been some of the most receptive to female leadership."[8] Many others have assumed, incorrectly, that women preachers were extremely rare outside Pentecostalism and recent mainline Protestantism and have no knowledge of the long tradition of Wesleyan/Holiness women preachers.

The sociologists who collaborated to produce *Women of the Cloth* documented the story of women clergy in the nine denominations having the highest number of women clergy within mainline Protestantism.[9] Several years before *Women of the Cloth* appeared, a 1976 survey reported 1,801 women clergy in these denominations while the number reported for Wesleyan/Holiness groups was 4,131.[10] By limiting their study to mainline denominations, the authors of *Women of the Cloth* told only a small portion of the story of ordained women.[11] Subsequent research, conducted by the authors of *Clergy Women,* corrected the omission by including women from four Wesleyan/Holiness denominations.[12]

The additions to the trajectory of women's autobiography that I am proposing represent the tip of the iceberg in terms of the actual number of women preachers active in the Wesleyan/Holiness movement between the early nineteenth century and the mid-twentieth century. It is impossible to determine how many women were ordained, because in many cases clergy records are nonexistent. Also, the majority of women preachers did not write autobiographies. For instance, even though The Salvation Army boasted more than one thousand women officers in 1896, no Salvation Army women published their autobiographies. However, Diane Winston has offered evidence that Salvation Army women did write diaries, quoting from the diary of Ensign Margaret Sheldon, who served near the front lines during World War I. Women included in my study documented the activities of The Salvation Army by frequently noting their cooperation with urban ministries sponsored by the organization. For instance, Abbie Mills gave a Bible study at a Salvation Army meeting. Elizabeth Wheaton led a meeting for The Salvation Army. Sarah Cooke worked with The Salvation Army in Indianapolis in 1895. She described Catherine Clibborn, the oldest daughter of Salvation Army founders, William and Catherine Booth: "On no other woman's face I

Abbie C. Mills, author of *Grace and Glory* (Los Angeles: By the author, 1907) and *Quiet Hallelujahs* (Boston: McDonald & Gill, 1886).

had ever looked upon, had I seen so much of the apostolic power." Julia Shellhamer encouraged women to work with The Salvation Army locally if they could not initiate their own ministries. On one occasion, The Salvation Army contributed financially toward a mission home led by Martha Lee. Florence Roberts referred to The Salvation Army several times. The Salvation Army also influenced Wesleyan/Holiness women and their ministries. Emma Ray remembered conducting street meetings, "singing like the Army."[13] Also imitating The Salvation Army, Alma White adopted uniforms for her group's members and conducted meetings on street corners. Thus, although no published autobiographies of Salvation Army women are extant, thousands of them performed numerous ministries throughout the country.

The autobiographers included in this study mentioned the existence of other Wesleyan/Holiness women preachers as well. Some women traveled with female coworkers, as documented in chapter 6. Others listed women preachers who were friends or acquaintances. Writing in 1907, Abbie Mills recited a litany of the names of women preachers she encountered as she traveled from camp meeting to camp meeting.[14] She listed at least twenty-four women, most of whom are unknown today. Evangelist Lizzie Smith's name appeared most frequently. Mills recorded that Lizzie Smith held daily meetings at the Ocean Grove, New Jersey, camp meeting and also preached at Mountain Lake Park, where she had led services for twenty years. Others named by Mills included Lucy Meyer and Jenny Fowler Willing, who are familiar to Methodist scholars. Carrie Judd Montgomery, another acquaintance of Mills, was prominent in the faith healing movement. While Mills was, by far, the most prolific name-dropper, other narrators added several names to the roster of women preachers who are unknown today. Amanda Smith spoke of hearing Laura Bowden, who "was then in her prime of power. How the Lord did use her testimony and exhortation to the saving of many, young and old." Jennie Smith heard a Mrs. Lathrope preach at Ocean Grove in 1878. Susan Fitkin dedicated her autobiography to Rev. M. Emily Ellyson, "the friend of my youth, and companion in the Master's Vineyard . . . whose beautiful life of faith and devotion to Jesus has been a constant source of inspiration to me."[15] Reverend Ellyson wrote the one-page introduction to Fitkin's autobiography, but her name is missing from Fitkin's narrative. Women officers in The Salvation Army, along with women preachers mentioned by their colleagues in the autobiographies under consideration in this study, show that the thirty-four autobiographers in this study represent a small proportion of the Wesleyan/Holiness women engaged in professional ministry.

The Trajectory of Women's Spiritual Autobiographies

The term *autobiography* has been traced back to 1786. Despite its relatively recent addition to our vocabulary, a trajectory of autobiographical writing has been mapped through the centuries. Augustine's *Confessions* (circa 400) generally begins the list of autobiographies written in the Western world. Autobiographical theorists have thoroughly analyzed Augustine's work. As a cartographer of the trajectory of women's autobiographical writings, however, I must begin the trajectory with Perpetua's firsthand account of the persecution she experienced under Septimius Severus in 202–3 because she was a Christian.[16] Perpetua's story was lost to subsequent centuries until rediscovered in the seventeenth century. Wesleyan/Holiness women were unacquainted with Perpetua, yet their writing style and content corresponded to her narrative rather than Augustine's. Unlike Augustine, Perpetua did not have the luxury of reflecting on her life as a Christian; instead, she provided a brief recitation of persecution leading up to her death.

During the medieval period, several mystics authored spiritual autobiographies, including Julian of Norwich, Catherine of Sienna, Margery Kempe, and Teresa of Avila. Julian's account of her religious experience, *Revelations of Divine Love,* appeared in 1393. Margery Kempe, a contemporary of Julian, once visited her cell in Norwich, England. Kempe authored the first autobiography written in English in 1438. Like Perpetua's, it was lost for many years, but it was rediscovered in 1934.

Quaker women, also in England, authored spiritual autobiographies. While the Anglican Church was the state religion, Quakers, and later John Wesley's Methodists, were among those known as dissenters because they dissented from the practice and beliefs of the Church of England, which was the official state-sponsored religion. Quaker women published almost ninety confessions and journals between 1650 and 1725.[17]

I initiate my analysis with Madame Jeane Marie Bouvier de la Mothe Guyon's autobiography, following the lead of Wesleyan/Holiness women who later began their autobiographical trajectory with Guyon. For inspiration, Wesleyan/Holiness adherents continue to read her autobiography and her other books that remain in print. When I mentioned to a Wesleyan/Holiness layperson that I was researching a seventeenth-century mystic, she immediately asked if it was Guyon. When I answered in the affirmative, she told me she had read her autobiography.

The trajectory continues with autobiographies of women who were friends and associates of John Wesley. I chose to include Mary Bosanquet Fletcher and Hester Ann Roe Rogers in my autobiographical trajectory because Wesleyan/Holiness women most frequently quoted these colleagues of Wesley. It is not surprising that Wesley's followers authored autobiographies, since he encouraged them to share their religious experiences in class meetings. These testimonies were often written down and published. Because of the emphasis on experience as a valid source of theology, narrative for Wesleyans became an important means of sharing one's spiritual quest.

Tracing the trajectory in the United States, Catherine Brekus discovered "twenty women preachers who published their . . . memoirs during their lifetimes" between 1740 and 1845.[18] None of these twenty authors indicated an awareness of the women who preached before them in the colonies during the First Great Awakening. While Wesleyan/Holiness women preachers were cognizant of Madame Guyon and their Methodist foremothers in England, they, too, seemed unacquainted with their predecessors in the United States. Women preachers today, including Wesleyan/Holiness women, for the most part are unacquainted with their precedents in the Wesleyan/Holiness movement. This study seeks to close one gap in the trajectory of women preachers' autobiographical writings by adding a significant number of previously unstudied Wesleyan/Holiness autobiographies.

Criteria for Choosing the Autobiographies

There are several criteria for inclusion in my Wesleyan/Holiness autobiographical canon. First, women had to be Wesleyan/Holiness or believers in sanctification, the defining doctrine of the Wesleyan/Holiness movement. Second, they must have engaged in public ministry in the United States. The experience of sanctification emboldened these women to challenge the ideology of woman's sphere. Public ministries were not limited to pulpit preaching. Some women preached in jails, on trains, in rescue homes, or at camp meetings. Several of the women also ministered outside the country (Amanda Smith, Mattie Perry, Alma White, Elizabeth Wheaton, and Lucy Drake Osborn), but I have restricted my discussion to their ministries in the United States. I did not include foreign missionaries, whose social contexts would be extremely diverse. Third, I chose autobiographies available via interlibrary loan, so they would be accessible to others.

Last, I must say that literary merit was not a criteria for inclusion. I will not be assessing the literary value of the autobiographies under consideration. Most of these autobiographies would be rejected for canonical status from a literary standpoint. As the canon of autobiographies has expanded to include autobiographies of women, the tendency has been to establish an exclusive list of literary classics; however, Margo Culley has advised scholars to "resist the temptation to establish a canon of 'great books' by women and to stop there." Though most of the autobiographies I analyzed would fail the "literary merit" litmus test, Florence Roberts, for one, noted her shortcomings in this area but claimed a higher purpose in writing: "Dear readers, I am well aware that this book, judged from a literary point of view, would be regarded as a failure; but I make no pretensions as a writer, nor do I entertain any aspirations for literary fame. My sole object in endeavoring to present faithfully a few experiences of my brief years of service for the Master is to warn many who are in danger." Perhaps most of the other authors in this group would have made a similar assessment of their work.[19] However, they deserve inclusion in this canon of women's autobiographies because they are the only sources available which tell the story of Wesleyan/Holiness women preachers who rejected the constructions of self that society sought to impose upon them.

Attributes of the Autobiographies

Wesleyan/Holiness women's narratives resemble spiritual autobiographies authored during the medieval period rather than contemporary autobiographies. Wesleyan/Holiness women were more at home with the premodern mind-set than with the tenets of modernity. They placed experience above reason and acknowledged a supernatural world that exists alongside the natural world. Authors focused on the events that contributed to their spiritual growth. They described their religious experiences of conversion and sanctification while devoting the majority of their writing to chronicling their public ministries, sometimes simply providing a travelogue of locations where they ministered.

Wesleyan/Holiness women writers did not have access to Perpetua's third-century account of her persecution. However, there are numerous similarities between the two in style and content, notwithstanding the centuries that separate Wesleyan/Holiness women's autobiographies from Perpetua's narrative. Perpetua wrote a straightforward account of her experience with little reflection. She exerted prophetic spiritual authority that other Christians recognized. She did not mention the Holy Spirit in her account, but the anonymous author of the introduction, probably Tertullian, referenced the power of the Holy Spirit, documented in Acts 2, where Peter quoted the prophet Joel to justify the speaking of men and women at Pentecost. Tertullian, Perpetua's contemporary, was a member of the Montanist movement at one time. Montanists stressed the role of the Holy Spirit in the Christian's life and questioned the emerging ecclesiastical hierarchy in what became known as the Roman Catholic Church. Importantly, they also recognized the spiritual leadership of women. Tertullian spoke of the Holy Spirit's distribution of gifts, which included prophesying. Tertullian also recorded the details of Perpetua's martyrdom following her narrative. Visions did not play a major role in the spiritual lives of later Wesleyan/Holiness women, but several, like Perpetua, did describe mystical visions. Perpetua also struggled with conflict over her responsibilities as a mother but ultimately chose God as her priority. Had she agreed to offer a sacrifice for the emperor, her life would have been spared. Just as colleagues often provided affirmations of Wesleyan/Holiness women's ministries, the anonymous commentator described Perpetua just prior to her martyrdom as having a "shining countenance and calm step, as the beloved of God, as a wife of Christ."[20]

Historians may be disappointed by the lack of historical details included in this study. Evidently, the women were not interested in providing basic biographical information about themselves, thus making a collective biography infeasible. This is particularly frustrating to a historian such as myself, who wishes they would have included more facts about themselves. Because of their lack of attention to the particulars of their lives, it is impossible to state how many women remained single, how many married, or how many were widowed. For this reason, I employ the names they used as authors throughout this study. Likewise, it is impossible to determine how many women had children and the number of children they had. For many women, the level of education they achieved is also unknown. More than likely, most did not attend college, much less seminary. Emma Whittemore and Jane Dunning represent the extreme position, since they offered no biographical information whatsoever about themselves in their books. Whittemore focused on people to whom she had ministered, while Dunning primarily included conversion accounts and extensive vignettes of people she visited. These two books are included because they provide extensive information on the public social ministries of two Wesleyan/Holiness women. Sometimes women even omitted important personal history, such as date of birth and information regarding their ordination. For instance, Mary Lee Cagle provided few dates in her narrative and neglected to mention her ordination, while Susan Fitkin never revealed her husband's first name.

I will not attempt to reconstruct women's lives since most of them did not provide enough factual information to accomplish this task. Obviously, this was not their intent. I do not stress biographical details in the text because they seemed insignificant to the subjects of my study and, in most cases, they were missing from their narratives. Only on a few rare occasions do I succumb to my historical impulses and provide biographical information on women that is not included in their autobiographies.

In many cases, however, we know nothing about the women other than the information they provided in their autobiographies. Minimal secondary literature exists to provide biographical facts to fill in the blanks. For example, nothing is known of Jarena Lee's life outside of her autobiography, including the date and location of her death. While her narrative has been analyzed extensively, no one has discovered additional information about her life. I found references to Julia Foote in an unpublished journal of D. S. Warner, the founder of the Church of God (Anderson, Indiana). They preached together at least twice.[21] Crucial information such as this would derive from serendipitous discoveries. To provide biographies of these women is out of the question in many instances. It would require a sleuth examining denominational magazines and newspaper articles in towns where women preached to recover further details of their preaching activities. Even this task would be difficult because women often provided the names of towns where they preached but not the states or the dates.

Paralleling the lack of historical data, the authors did not engage in self-analysis for the most part. Hannah Whitall Smith and Phoebe Palmer are the exceptions. Their books, *My Spiritual Autobiography, or How I Discovered the Unselfishness of God* and *The Way of Holiness: Notes by the Way,* respectively, most clearly meet the expectation that the purpose of spiritual autobiography is to reflect theologically. Smith explained: "It is of the processes leading to this discovery [of the unselfishness of God] by my own soul that I want to tell."[22] Since Smith and Palmer focused almost solely on their spiritual development in these books, I incorporate them in the discussion of theology in chapter 4. Palmer's spiritual autobiography, in particular, served as a road map in the quest for sanctification for many of the women in this study.

Hannah Whitall Smith and Phoebe Palmer are undoubtedly the most well-known white women in this study. They wrote numerous other books. Biographies document their lives and extensive ministries. While my historical inclination would be to include information on their important public ministries from their other books and biographies, I have withstood the temptation for the most part. I have restricted myself primarily to their autobiographies since autobiographical analysis is my primary purpose here. I encourage readers to consult the biographies listed in the chart included before the introduction for further information on these pivotal women.

In the following chapter, I will briefly outline the theology embraced by Wesleyan/Holiness women and summarize feminist and autobiographical theory, which I will be using to analyze their autobiographies. Chapter 2 provides information on Madame Guyon, who begins the autobiographical trajectory for Wesleyan/Holiness women. Even though Madame Guyon was a Roman Catholic mystic, Wesleyan/Holiness women identified with her quest for perfection. Guyon's autobiography yields enough biographical information to reconstruct her life. In this chapter, as in future chapters, I begin with a discussion of theology followed by the public ministries made possible by the theology the women embraced. Without the theological basis, women would not have engaged in public ministries.

Chapter 3 concentrates on Mary Bosanquet Fletcher and Hester Ann Roe Rogers, prominent workers with John Wesley in England. Also relying on their writings, this chapter summarizes their theology and their ministries. Chapter 4 examines the self through the theological lens of sanctification as understood by nineteenth- and twentieth-century Wesleyan/ Holiness women in the United States. The sanctified self was an empowered self that broke through the invisible barriers of woman's private sphere and ministered in the public realm. While chapter 4 focuses on the self, or *auto,* aspect of autobiography, chapters 5, 6, and 7 consist of the *bio,* or biographical, aspect.

Chapter 5 summarizes both the affirmation and the opposition Wesleyan/ Holiness women experienced. While their churches for the most part encouraged them, they faced resistance from opponents in other churches and from society at large. Chapters 6 and 7 document the ministries of Wesleyan/Holiness women. While they would not have made the distinction between evangelistic and social holiness ministries, I have done so for the sake of organization. The last chapter addresses the *graphy* of autobiography, examining the gender-marked writing of these women and their precise rationale for writing. They wrote explicitly to offer testimony to the fact that sanctification enabled them to undertake the challenge of moving outside the confines of woman's sphere and to perform public ministries.

Textual Note

The texts of Madame Guyon, Mary Bosanquet Fletcher, and Hester Ann Roe Rogers were all altered in some way by editors. The edition of Madame Guyon's autobiography used here does not include information from the last seven years of her imprisonment. That material was discovered and published in 1992. Wesleyan/Holiness autobiographers did not have access to information about this period of Guyon's life, so I have used an earlier version of her autobiography, which, more than likely, they did read. Also, Hester Ann Roe Rogers's and Mary Bosanquet Fletcher's autobiographies were edited after they died. Henry Moore compiled Fletcher's memoirs, yet he insisted in the preface that "the whole of these Memoirs are from Mrs. Fletcher's pen." While Moore did not add to Fletcher's memoirs, he deleted or condensed duplicate information or material he deemed of little interest and made her sentences more concise. On two occasions, Moore injected paragraphs in the text that were clearly identified as editorial comments.[23] E. Davies used quotation marks to indicate Rogers's writing and to distinguish it from his observations and comments, which he sprinkled throughout her autobiography. While Fletcher's autobiography is listed as being "compiled and edited" by Moore, and Rogers's was "condensed and combined," they should not be confused with biographies. The women's words are clearly evident. It is extremely unfortunate that the two editors did delete portions of Fletcher's and Rogers's autobiographies. While the work of Moore and Davies diminished the value of Fletcher's and Rogers's writing as autobiographies, their narratives still provide crucial information on these women's lives that otherwise would not have been available to Wesleyan/Holiness adherents. Through their autobiographies, they served as role models and influenced future generations of women and men.

While Rogers's and Fletcher's writings appeared after their death, many American women self-published their autobiographies, giving them total control over their writing. They did not have to please an editor or publisher. To my knowledge, only one woman, Mary Lee Cagle, had assistance with her writing. This was obvious in a few extraneous comments the ghostwriter injected in the narrative, such as, "It was beautiful to see her undying devotion for her husband," and "but Sister Cagle often says that when the impossible is before her is the time when God gives her the most faith."[24]

In several cases, I had to make a choice regarding which edition of autobiographies to use. Heeding Katherine Bassard's argument "for the centrality of the longer and more densely written *Journal,*" I used the version of Jarena Lee's autobiography she published sixteen years following the earlier account, which Andrews reprinted in *Sisters of the Spirit.* Abbie Mills published two records of her life. The shorter version was appended to a devotional book, *Quiet Hallelujahs.* I have quoted this source only for information that is unique to it. Alma White wrote *Looking Back from Beulah* in 1902 and from 1919 to 1934 she authored the six-volume *The Story of My Life and the Pillar of Fire.*[25] Instead of utilizing these volumes, I consulted the five-volume revision of *The Story of My Life and the Pillar of Fire* that she published between 1935 and 1943.

While the subtitle "Autobiography of Mr. and Mrs. L. P. Ray" implies that Emma Ray and her husband coauthored their autobiography, that is not the case. She copyrighted the book in 1926 and the dedication concludes with "the author" instead of "the authors." Lloyd P. Ray's contribution to the book was merely a six-page testimony.[26]

Some women relied solely on their memories for their autobiographical material.[27] Others made extensive use of journals or diaries, in some cases quoting from them directly or inserting significant portions from them in their narratives.[28] Women often incorporated articles and sermons in their autobiographies. Sometimes they identified these items; on other occasions they simply interrupted the flow of the narrative with excerpts from their preaching. In several cases, women added correspondence with friends or included letters of recommendation. Written between 1849 and 1973, the American narratives as a whole do not reflect a major change in content or in context with respect to preaching audiences and the opposition women faced.

CHAPTER ONE

Wesleyan Theology and Feminist and Autobiographical Theory

This book addresses at least two audiences. Many in the first audience, those interested in women's autobiographies and women's studies, may not be familiar with the theological roots of the Wesleyan/Holiness movement. For these readers, there is a brief introduction to the experience and doctrine of sanctification, the primary individuals who promoted the doctrine, and denominations in the Wesleyan/Holiness movement. Sanctification was an experience that changed Wesleyan/Holiness women's self-understanding, empowered them to challenge the claim that woman's sphere was in the private realm of domesticity, and motivated them to serve in the public sphere by preaching. The second audience, church historians and others already acquainted with sanctification, may want to skip this section and move to the summary of feminist theory and autobiographical theory in the following sections. In terms of feminist and autobiographical theory, it is argued here that sanctification fosters a graced autonomous self that enabled women to act as public religious leaders in ways impossible prior to their experience of sanctification.

The Historical Roots of Sanctification

John Wesley founded Methodism in England during the eighteenth century. The lackadaisical attitude toward religion exhibited by his Christian contemporaries disturbed Wesley, an Anglican priest. Initially, Wesley's followers in England maintained their ties to the Church of England but met in class meetings and bands committing themselves to the development of a holy life that increasingly reflected the example of Christ. Their opponents soon referred to them using the derogatory term *Methodist* because they adhered to a strict schedule or method for maturing as Christians. While Wesley is known for articulating the doctrine of perfection, which is the result of sanctification, the doctrine did not originate with Wesley. He was widely read and his theology incorporated the wisdom of the early Church fathers and the mystics as well as biblical passages. His *Plain Account of Christian Perfection* (1777) includes excerpts from his sermons, writings, and hymns relating to perfection.[1] It is more a scrapbook of information collected over a period of twenty-seven years than a systematic explanation of the doctrine of perfection. However, it still functions as the general guide to Wesley's understanding of this doctrine, and it will be used as the resource in this study for Wesley's views of perfection.

Wesley described sanctification as a distinct experience that followed conversion. One's sanctification occurred instantaneously and was both preceded and followed by gradual growth in grace. While Wesley most often stressed growth in the process of perfection, his statements also allowed for the immediate attainment of perfection. Rather than being ambivalent about whether perfection occurred instantaneously or gradually, Wesley recognized that both possibilities were conceivable. Wesley contended that perfection could take place now and could be received merely by faith. Wesleyan/Holiness believers in the United States, though, most often chose to stress the instantaneous aspect of perfection rather than Wesley's emphasis on growth. Wesley, as well as his theological heirs in the Wesleyan/Holiness movement, believed in free will, maintaining that humans could choose to accept God's offer of both conversion and sanctification by faith.

Wesley accepted Augustine's view of original sin, in that all humans possessed inbred or inward sin inherited from Adam and Eve. One result of sanctification was the removal or cleansing of inbred sin. A Calvinist version of holiness emerged in England about one hundred years after Wesley. Known as Keswick, or "the higher life," this understanding of holiness affirmed suppression of original sin rather than cleansing. Also, the Keswick position did not allow for an instantaneous attainment of holiness but only spoke of it in terms of a process.

According to Wesley, along with the removal of inbred sin, another outcome of sanctification was "pure love reigning alone in the heart and life—this is the whole of Scriptural perfection." Referring to love, Wesley wrote that "there is nothing higher in religion; there is in effect, nothing else." He did not allow the concept of love to remain in the abstract realm. Repeatedly, he quoted Luke 10:27: "Thou shalt love the Lord your God with all thy heart, and with all thy soul, and with all thy strength and with all thy mind; and thy neighbor as thyself." It was clear to Wesley that loving God meant loving one's neighbor. Actions on behalf of others resulted from love. In summary, sanctification, as articulated by John Wesley and his theological heirs, is a distinct second work of grace following conversion in which the heart is cleansed of inbred sin and filled with God's love.[2]

Methodist preachers who traveled to the American colonies disseminated the doctrine of perfection or holiness, following Wesley's admonition to "spread scriptural holiness throughout the land." John Peters summarized the presence of Methodists in colonial America: "The data appear to support the conclusion that American colonial Methodism in its standards and—more importantly—in its preaching made the doctrine of Christian perfection one of its characteristic features."[3] The Methodist Episcopal Church organized as a denomination in the United States in 1784. Its first discipline or list of doctrines encouraged all members to seek perfection. Numerous bishops throughout the nineteenth century continued to support the doctrine.

At a revival in a Methodist church in New York City, Sarah Lankford embraced holiness, a synonym for perfection, in 1835. Lankford initiated a weekly meeting that focused on holiness for women from two Methodist churches. Her example inspired her sister, Phoebe Palmer, who began seeking the experience for herself. Shortly thereafter, Palmer's search resulted in a clear testimony of holiness. When Lankford moved in 1837, Palmer assumed the leadership for the Tuesday Meeting for the Promotion of Holiness. Initially limited to women, men sought admittance to the meetings, and soon Methodist bishops as well as religious leaders from other denominations joined laypeople at the meetings.

Palmer's reputation grew, and she preached at more than three hundred camp meetings and revivals. The appellation "mother of the Wesleyan/Holiness movement" is apt. Theologian Thomas Oden has referred to Palmer as "one of Christianity's most important lay theologians, male or female." She popularized the doctrine of holiness and promoted it to a broad audience through her prolific writing and preaching. Palmer's *Way of Holiness,* her spiritual autobiography, outlined her theology of holiness and chronicled her successful quest for holiness, which became known as the "shorter way."[4] Selling 100,000 copies, *Way of Holiness* and other writings, along with her preaching, eventuated in Palmer's recognition as the primary proponent of the doctrine in the early years of the Wesleyan/Holiness movement, and her understanding of holiness became standard.

The doctrine of holiness initially flourished within Methodism primarily due to Palmer. However, church leaders within other denominations, such as Baptists, Congregationalists, Episcopalians, and Presbyterians, embraced and promoted the doctrine as well. Members of these denominations also attended holiness camp meetings sponsored by Methodists. In 1867 a camp meeting in Vineland, New Jersey, resulted in the founding of the National Camp Meeting Association for the Promotion of Holiness. The leadership primarily consisted of Methodist clergy, although anyone was welcome to attend.

The atmosphere was ecumenical. Social outreach programs that emerged within the movement tended to be ecumenical as well. Ministries to the poor, prostitutes, and alcoholics accepted workers from various denominations. In many cases, denominational affiliation was unimportant. Some women, such as Emma Whittemore, affiliated with two or more groups at the same time.

The Wesleyan/Holiness movement traces its roots to these camp meetings and social outreach activities that originated in the United States during the nineteenth and early twentieth centuries. Indeed, the name Wesleyan/Holiness is a descriptive term identifying the organizations and churches that emerged primarily from Methodism and continued to advocate the doctrine of holiness promoted by John Wesley. Two denominations originated when African Americans left Methodism due to prejudicial treatment. The African Methodist Episcopal Zion Church traces its roots to a 1796 split from a Methodist Episcopal congregation in New York City. The African Methodist Episcopal Church began in Philadelphia when members left a local congregation for the same reason. Initially operating as an African American church within the Methodist Episcopal denomination, the group became independent in 1816.

Two groups, the Wesleyan Methodist Connection of America (1843) and the Free Methodist Church (1860), also left the Methodist Episcopal Church prior to the Civil War. Among other differences with the mother church, they rejected what they perceived to be Methodism's lukewarm opposition to slavery.[5] More groups began to emerge by the latter decades of the nineteenth century as individuals became convinced that contemporary Methodism was abandoning the doctrine of holiness. Methodist leadership, on the other hand, decried the organization of groups independent of their control. The Church of the Nazarene consists of several mergers of holiness groups concluding in 1908. The Church of God (Anderson, Indiana) is a distinctly come-outer movement. Early leaders began inviting Christians to come out of their existing denominations in the early 1880s and form a truly holy, pure group. Methodists as well as members of other denominations responded to the call, creating a movement that was more diverse than the other Wesleyan/Holiness groups. The Salvation Army traces its roots to a mission cofounded by Catherine and William Booth in England when they left Methodism in 1865. The first Salvation Army workers arrived in the United States in 1880. The three last-named groups are the largest within the Wesleyan/Holiness movement in the United States today. Many smaller groups emerged as well. One was the Pentecostal Union (later renamed the Pillar of Fire) founded by Alma White in 1901.

A few women in this study are from the broader holiness movement, and they remained members of the Methodist Episcopal Church (now the

United Methodist Church) or other mainline denominations. Lucy Drake Osborn, for one, was Congregational and Emma Whittemore was Presbyterian, yet both women embraced the Wesleyan/Holiness theology of sanctification. Abbie Mills also was Presbyterian. She testified: "It was Bible holiness that I had obtained and not a blessing that belonged to Methodists alone." However, she did eventually join the Methodist Episcopal Church.[6] These women serve as reminders that neither Methodists nor their heirs can assert sole ownership of the doctrine. I use the term Wesleyan/Holiness in a broader sense to encompass these women who experienced and preached Wesley's doctrine of holiness but were not always affiliated with Wesleyan/Holiness denominations.

Several women neglected to mention their denominational membership altogether, possibly reflecting its lack of significance to them. I have not included Wesleyan/Holiness women who later joined the Pentecostal movement, which emerged at the beginning of the twentieth century. While there are many similarities between Holiness and Pentecostal women, the particular context of Pentecostalism and the specific theology that defined Pentecostalism requires a separate study.

The Theological Basis for Affirming Women Preachers—Sanctification and Egalitarian Primitivism

The doctrine of sanctification played a major role in transforming Wesleyan/Holiness women's understanding of self, making it possible for them to transcend the constructions of self imposed on them by various forces in society. Phoebe Palmer testified to the death of self. Palmer quoted Scripture, substituting a female pronoun to indicate that she had appropriated this verse as her own in her third-person explanation of what happened to the self in the process of sanctification. She "'reckon[ed] her self dead indeed unto sin, but alive unto God through Jesus Christ our Lord'; to account herself permanently the Lord's, and in verity no more at her own disposal, but irrevocably the Lord's property, for time and eternity." Her substitution of the feminine pronoun in this verse is highly unusual. Later, switching to the first person, she described the consequences of her action: "my heart was emptied of self, and cleansed of all idols, from all filthiness of the flesh and spirit, and I realized that I dwelt in God, and felt that He had become the portion of my soul, my All in All."[7]

Palmer's view of self related to her theology of what happened to the self in sanctification. Gregory Schneider is one of the few scholars who has explored the understanding of the self among Methodists. Schneider quoted from an 1816 article that incorporated Gal. 2:20: "I must pass through the agonies of self-mortification, I must be crucified with Jesus Christ that I may live with him. The old man must die in me, that the new man may be raised up in all his vigor and strength."[8] Death of self signified the death of the "old man," which was replaced by the "new man." Believers spoke of the "crucified self," which was, in fact, superceded by the sanctified self.

Various aspects of the spiritual self will be considered in more depth in the discussion of sanctification in chapter 4, but suffice it to say briefly at this point that the spiritual self in Wesleyan/Holiness theology is a sanctified self empowered by the Holy Spirit to engage in public religious activities, including preaching. Referring specifically to Methodist women, Schneider observed that the quest for sanctification eventuated in a "confidence in a self that was no longer a woman's own self, but God's, and that, nevertheless, felt freer and more authentic than she had ever felt simply on her own." The transformation of the self in Methodism served in a positive manner to justify women's limited public involvement in church activities. Methodists encouraged women to testify at their informal meetings but balked when it came to ordaining women. Schneider further concluded that the transformation resulting from the death of the natural self "did not in itself obviate their [women's] institutionalized inferiority and dependence." The Methodist Episcopal Church would not ordain women, in part because of their reliance on priestly rather than prophetic authority. The Methodist Episcopal Church did make the concession of issuing preaching licenses to women between 1869 and 1880, but when Anna Howard Shaw and Anna Oliver requested ordination in 1880, the church hierarchy denied them ordination and also revoked all licenses they had issued to women. Schneider concluded: "It [holiness] freed women to claim their own moral and spiritual identity, it also granted such selfhood only on the paradoxical condition of self-denial. Insistence on self-denial tended to keep women confined to their traditional domestic sphere, however widened in significance that sphere had become."[9] It remained for the Wesleyan/Holiness movement to extend the public involvement of women. The death of self as a result of Christian religious experience was not unique to holiness theology but can be traced to Scripture, as noted above in Palmer's description. The mystical tradition within the Roman Catholic Church also focused on the death of self. Wesleyan/Holiness women were aware of this trajectory, primarily through the writings of Madame Guyon. Within the Wesleyan/Holiness movement, the belief in the death of self resulting in a new self was foundational rather than an offshoot of the movement. It was not a fringe doctrine promoted by a few. The mystical view of the death of self represented mainstream Wesleyan/Holiness understanding of the doctrine.[10]

In addition to the emphasis on sanctification, Wesleyan/Holiness believers were primitivists who sought to emulate the faith and practices of the early church as documented in the New Testament. Richard Hughes has identified three expressions of primitivism: experiential, ecclesiastical, and ethical. I have added a fourth type, egalitarian primitivism, to his typology.[11] A primitivist does not necessarily embrace all forms of primitivism. For instance, a denomination that identifies with ecclesiastical primitivism may not necessarily condone experiential primitivism. Likewise, not all primitivists endorse women preachers. Wesleyan/Holiness adherents are egalitarian primitivists who affirmed women preachers because they saw that the Bible documented women's leadership and public ministry in the early church. They sprinkled their defenses of women preachers with verses from the Bible that verified the important role of women in the early church. A favorite passage was the account of Pentecost in Acts 2, where men and women who were filled with the Holy Spirit preached in Jerusalem after Jesus' earthly ministry had ended. These verses attest that the Holy Spirit was no respecter of persons; therefore, it did not discriminate between the sexes. Pentecost was the scriptural event that fulfilled the prophecy of Joel as recorded in the Hebrew Bible: "I will pour out my Spirit upon all flesh, and your sons and your daughters shall prophecy" (Acts 2:17). Pentecost was a significant occurrence in terms of Wesleyan/Holiness self-understanding. Wesleyan/Holiness adherents sought to restore to contemporary women the prominent place they had filled in the life of the early church. Women's autobiographies included this primitivist emphasis. Mary Cole, writing in 1914, referred to Acts 2:4 ("They all spake as the Spirit gave them utterance") to bolster her case that "all" included the women present and that "their speaking as the Spirit gave utterance [was] the act of a minister in preaching." Likewise, to justify her own preaching, Julia Foote noted in 1879 the presence of women at Pentecost who were filled with the Holy Spirit.[12] Pentecost became the precedent for prophetic authority by which the authority of the Holy Spirit superceded human authority and validated women preachers.

Wesleyan/Holiness believers emphasized prophetic authority, which derives from the Holy Spirit, who gifts both women and men for service in the church. The Holy Spirit enables women as well as men to fill positions of responsibility. Prophetic authority contrasts with priestly authority, in which the authority to minister originates with the ministerial office itself. Priestly authority is conferred when an individual assumes a ministerial office rather than coming directly from the Holy Spirit to individuals.

Wesleyan/Holiness adherents were not the first egalitarian primitivists to recognize prophetic authority. The Montanists, a Spirit-filled Christian movement that began in the second century, likewise believed that power came directly from God with no need of human intervention. Montanus and two of his prominent disciples, Priscilla and Maximilla, believed they were mouthpieces of the Holy Spirit. Elaine Huber in 1985 documented prophetic authority within the Montanist movement, using the phrase "authority of inspiration" as a synonym for prophetic authority: "Movements claiming the authority of inspiration necessarily gave primacy to the Spirit. And Spirit-filled movements are, by definition, open, flexible and inclusive. Because it is impossible to limit the Spirit, or legislate the question of who will be its recipients, charismatic movements always present a potential threat to formal ecclesiastical structures."[13] While she was describing the Montanist movement, Huber could have been defining the Wesleyan/Holiness movement.

Christians have exercised prophetic authority throughout church history, from the early church, to the Montanists, to the women mystics throughout church history to Wesleyan/Holiness women. Medieval historian Carolyn Walker Bynum noted in 1982 that medieval women mystics exercised prophetic authority: "The mysticism of thirteenth-century women is therefore an alternative to the authority of office. It is an alternative that is fostered by the presence of institutions within which a female religious culture can develop. It is fostered also by a theology that emphasizes God as accessible in intimate union and comprehensible in human images, yet, just [and] powerful."[14] Phoebe Palmer provides an excellent example of a woman who exerted prophetic authority because she was never ordained by the Methodist Episcopal Church. Despite her lack of priestly credentials from her denomination, people recognized the prophetic authority that she exhibited in her ministry. Rev. A. Lowrey, a eulogist, commented on Palmer's credentials: "Her license came from no subordinate source. She was accredited from on high. Her authority and credentials were conferred by the Holy Ghost. She was set apart and gifted as a gentle leader . . . She was vested with a remarkable power to produce immediate results. Nor were these fruits evanescent. They were lifelong and permanent."[15] While not using the term *prophetic authority,* Reverend Lowrey clearly defined this understanding of authority, particularly when he credited the Holy Ghost or the Holy Spirit as being the source of Palmer's authority.

Wesleyan/Holiness men adopted a primitivist outlook to promote the ministry of women. Luther Lee, a founder of the Wesleyan Methodist Connection in 1843, contended: "All antiquity agrees that there were female officers and teachers in the Primitive Church." Likewise, B. T. Roberts in 1891 employed primitivism to justify his support of women clergy: "In the New Testament church, woman, as well as man, filled the office of Apostle, Prophet, Deacon or Preachers, and Pastor. There is not the slightest evidence that the functions of any of these offices, when filled by a woman, were different from what they were when filled by a man. Woman took a part in governing the Apostolic church."[16] Roberts, a founder of the Free Methodist Church, was unable to win all of his ministerial colleagues over to his position. Roberts advised his opponents on this issue: "Men had better busy themselves in building up the temple of God instead of employing their time in pushing from the scaffold their sisters, who are both able and willing to work with them side by side."[17] Despite the initial reluctance of the Free Methodists, egalitarian primitivism obviously benefited most Wesleyan/Holiness women because it provided a precedent for their public ministries.

Wesleyan/Holiness women found themselves in a theological culture that was highly unusual for its day because, while Wesleyan/Holiness denominations accepted women preachers, the general climate within most churches with the exception of Quakers was extremely hostile to women preachers. Most Christian groups refused to ordain women during the nineteenth and early twentieth centuries. Later, between 1956 and 1977, several mainline denominations removed prohibitions on ordaining women. The United Methodist Church (1956), Presbyterian Church (USA) (1956), Evangelical Lutheran Church in America (1970), and the Episcopal Church (1977) are among this group. Many, including the Roman Catholic Church, Orthodox churches, and most fundamentalist churches, continue to forbid the ordination of women. The Southern Baptist Convention, the largest Protestant denomination in the United States, reaffirmed its opposition to women pastors in 2000 by adding the following to their faith and message statement: "The office of pastor is limited to men as qualified by Scripture."[18]

Since most leaders in the Wesleyan/Holiness movement endorsed women's preaching, women did not face insurmountable institutional barriers to preaching as did women in other denominations. This supportive atmosphere played a positive role in making it possible for women to hear and respond to God's call for them to preach. They were in an environment that affirmed that God called women to preach. Margo Culley observed that women who look in a mirror do not truly see themselves but visualize themselves "through the imagined (or real) gaze of another." As Wesleyan/Holiness women looked in their mirrors, they could see themselves as preachers because they perceived themselves through the eyes of others who not only envisioned them as preachers but who actively helped them actualize the image. In her study of Puritan women, Ann Taves described a "socially constructed reading of God's will."[19] In the Wesleyan/Holiness movement, the socially constructed reading of God's will acknowledged that God calls women to public ministry.

Wesleyan/Holiness authors unabashedly stated their understanding of God's will for women by authoring defenses of women's right to preach. Luther Lee preached on the biblical text Gal. 3:28 at the ordination of Antoinette Brown in 1853: "The text fixes no limits, prescribes no bounds, names no places, occasions, subjects or duties, but affirms in general and unqualified terms, that there is neither male nor female, but that all are one in Christ Jesus, and this is done by way of proclaiming the abrogation of the Mosaic law, and it of necessity places males and females upon an equal platform of rights under the gospel." Phoebe Palmer based her case in *The Promise of the Father* on Jesus' promise that God (the Father) would grant power from heaven (Luke 24:49) to Jesus' followers. This promise was fulfilled, she claimed, for both men and women who preached at Pentecost. Catherine Booth, cofounder of The Salvation Army, wrote the tract *Female Ministry* in 1859, in which she agreed with Palmer that God used men and women at Pentecost. In *Ordaining Women,* B. T. Roberts minced no words in his affirmation of women clergy: "The Gospel of Jesus Christ, in the provisions which it makes, and in the agencies which it employs, for the salvation of mankind, knows no distinction of race, condition, or sex, therefore no person evidently called of God to the gospel ministry, and duly qualified for it, should be refused ordination on account of race, condition, or sex." William Godbey, the noted holiness evangelist, authored the pamphlet *Woman Preacher* in 1891, concluding with this judgment: "The soul of a man must be wonderfully small, who, actuated by ignorance, prejudice, or egotism, would lay the weight of a straw on the dear sisterhood, whose hearts the Lord has touched, and whose lips he has anointed with a live coal from heaven's altar."[20]

In some cases, the endorsement of women preachers extended to sanctioning women's activity in the political realm as well. For instance, B. T. Roberts advocated suffrage for women. E. E. Shellhamer, a Free Methodist evangelist and husband of Julia Shellhamer, likewise supported women's rights: "But God took a 'rib' from near Adam's heart that she should be loved and protected by him; that she should run by his side, and be equal with him, and that his rights should be her rights."[21]

Wesleyan/Holiness adherents maintained that Christianity and, more specifically, sanctification promoted women's equality. Not everyone agrees with this contention. Some feminists issue a blanket rejection of Christianity. In their view, Christianity never benefits women. For instance, Carolyn Heilbrun, a prominent feminist theorist, alleged that whether deferring to a man or putting "God or Christ in the place of a man; the results are the same:

one's own desires and quests are always secondary."[22] Heilbrun did not consider the fact that perhaps women's pronouncements that God called them to preach allowed them to fulfill their personal desires and quests by claiming God's authorization of their public activities. She did not acknowledge the fact that by putting God "in the place of man," women were circumventing male control over their lives. As far as Heilbrun and others are concerned, Christianity can only inhibit the development of a woman's self. In actuality, though, Christianity cannot be dismissed so easily. Granted, some individuals and groups have used Christianity to thwart women's pursuit of self-worth. No one can deny this historical fact. Yet, Christianity has also exerted a liberating influence on women. Contemporary feminist theologian Elizabeth Johnson noted the positive correlation between a close relationship between God and autonomy: "Nearness to God and genuine autonomy grow in direct rather than inverse proportion. That is, God is not threatened by the active independence of the creature nor enhanced by its diminishment but is glorified by the creature's flourishing in the fullness of its powers. The nature of created participation in divine being is such that it grants creatures their own integrity, without reserve."[23] Wesleyan/Holiness women illustrate Johnson's contention that women experience autonomy as their relationship with God becomes closer and they mature as Christians.

Psychologist Sandra Lipsitz Bem has advocated the abolition of androcentrism, yet she examined biblical texts through androcentric lenses. The clearest example of this is her distorted interpretation of Gen. 1:26–27, where she alleged "only Adam is unambiguously said to be created in God's image." However, "man" in the passage she referenced is obviously generic, since in the latter part of verse 27, "male and female he created them" amplifies the prior phrase "in the image of God he created him." Skipping God's command to both man and woman in verse 28 to rule the earth together, Bem's androcentric lenses again cause her to miss the implications of the creation of men and women jointly in God's image. Bem also assumed that the serpent's choice to tempt Eve in the Garden of Eden "emphasizes the definition of woman as an inferior departure from the male standard." Wesleyan/Holiness women such as Alma White cast aside androcentric lenses as they examined the Bible. For instance, White claimed that woman was "the stronger citadel" rather than the weaker one, because the serpent approached her first rather than risking losing her after deceiving the man. Egalitarian lenses enabled Wesleyan/Holiness women to acknowledge that God created both men and women in God's image and that God gave both joint dominion over all the earth.[24]

Autobiographical theorist Julia Swindells has warned against the possibility that criteria established by feminist theorists might serve as a barrier to enlarging the canon of women's autobiographies. Her concern was that older autobiographies would be rejected in favor of those written by women during the contemporary second wave of feminism beginning in the 1970s.[25] A parallel concern is that Wesleyan/Holiness women's autobiographies might be rejected for inclusion in the canon because of some scholars' aversion to the positive accounting of the role of Christianity in their lives. A negative view of Christianity, I hope, will not prevent the women's autobiographies I am introducing from being added to the canon, along with the several Wesleyan/Holiness African American women's narratives that already have found their place there.

Those who have analyzed the writings of African American women recognize the positive role of Christianity in their lives. For instance, Carla Peterson perceived: "Christianity functioned both as a central belief system and as a source of personal and political empowerment." Nellie McKay agreed that "religious faith meant self-empowerment . . . Their faith gave them the self-assurance they needed to search out the positive identity that other circumstances in their lives denied."[26] While African American women would have contended that the power came from the Holy Spirit rather than from themselves, self-assurance was a result of their faith.

Kimberly Rae Connor's study of conversion among African American women revealed numerous instances of the beneficial role of Christianity in their lives. In terms of the positive impact of Christianity, she concluded: "Conversion created a sense of individual value and personal vocation that contradicted the dehumanizing forces of slavery and helped Blacks to assert and maintain a sense of personal value, of ultimate worth, and often inspired them to challenge the system of slavery itself." In the broader context of American racism, the culture of the early African American community "of which the religion was an essential part, defended African Americans against personal degradation, bolstered their self-esteem, gave them courage, confidence, and autonomy, and prepared them for conversion into selfhood." Connor summarized her position: "Religion, in other words, cooperated in their efforts to authenticate themselves." While Connor did not examine the doctrine of sanctification, her positive assessment of Christianity and its function in affirming the self complements my contention that sanctification likewise benefits women's development of self.[27]

African American women explicitly credited Christianity with their high view of self. Nellie McKay has accurately summarized that "other scholars have ably demonstrated that the rhetorical aims of early Afro-American autobiographical narrative focused on the authentication of the Black self in a world that had denied that self humanity." In 1849 Jerena Lee recorded that this authentication sometimes took place as a result of her preaching. On one occasion she met an old man who told her he did not believe "the coloured people had any souls." After her sermon, he had changed his mind.[28]

The racial pride of one of my subjects, Amanda Smith (b. 1837), predated the Christian Black Power movement, which originated in the late 1960s. She identified herself by the color of her skin: "I was of the royal black." Smith did not desire to be white. Speaking for herself and other Blacks, she declared: "We who are the royal black are very well satisfied with [God's] gift to us in this substantial color." She continued: "I, for one, praise Him for what He has given me." Smith justified her title to royalty by declaring her acquaintance with God, the King of Kings. Zilpha Elaw bluntly acknowledged racism, writing in 1846: "the pride of a white skin is a bauble of great value with many in some parts of the United States, who readily sacrifice their intelligence to their prejudices, and possess more knowledge than wisdom." She provided an overview of the biblical basis for defying racism: "The Almighty accounts not the black races of man either in the order of nature or spiritual capacity as inferior to the white; for He bestows his Holy Spirit on, and dwells in them as readily as in persons of whiter complexion: the Ethiopian eunuch was adopted as a son and heir of God; and when Ethiopia shall stretch forth her hands unto him (Ps. 68:31), their submission and worship will be graciously accepted . . . Oh! that men would outgrow their nursery prejudices and learn that 'God hath made of one blood all the nations of men that dwell upon all the face on the earth.' Acts xvii. 26."[29]

Sue Houchins and Williams Andrews are among the autobiographical theorists who have uncovered the positive ramifications of the doctrine of sanctification in the lives of African American women preachers. Houchins explicitly credited sanctification for empowering Black women. "Obviously, once a woman was bold enough to demand and receive assurance of her sanctification from God, her courage was boundless, and she was empowered to believe that her story was significant enough to repeat across the land as well as to defy and to combat the political forces of slavery (racism, in general) and sexism."[30] While *sexism* and *racism* were not specific words in their vocabulary, African American women who believed in sanctification experienced both sexism and racism and overcame them by relying on the power of the Holy Spirit.

Houchins also noted the relationship between holiness or perfection and power for medieval women mystics:

> The dictated texts of Christina of Markyate and Margery Kempe's lives and the book of contemplations or *Showings* by Julian of Norwich numbered among the earliest examples of the autobiographical form in English. These women sought to document in their

> self-writing their quests for perfection through mystical union and the concomitant rise to a sense of empowerment to demand a space in medieval society where, like the black women revivalists of subsequent centuries, they could "function as persons of authority," could resist the pressures of family and society, thereby rejecting the politics of gender, and could achieve legal and structural support from the church for their work as spiritual advisors, teachers, and occasional preachers.[31]

Houchins compared these medieval women with sanctified Black women, contending that both groups manifested a relationship with God that freed them "to reject the gender roles of their respective societies." She acknowledged that some scholars refused to see the similarity between the religious experience of medieval mystics and African American women revivalists. However, she maintained that both groups of women shared an "emphasis on the workings of the Spirit in the inner life, on the psychology of spiritual response, and on an intimate experience of Jesus."[32] In each case, women, even though separated by centuries, challenged gender role expectations that sought to prevent them from exercising prophetic authority.

William Andrews highlighted the positive consequences of sanctification for the women whose autobiographies he included in *Sisters of the Spirit.* He credited sanctification for making possible "feminist activism within Christianity." He explained: "Lee, Elaw, and Foote undoubtedly knew that to their critics, their spiritual self-reliance smacked of prideful individualism at worst, womanly waywardness at best. Nevertheless, they portrayed themselves as serenely confident, as a result of their 'sanctification' by the Holy Spirit, they had ample sanction for acts that many, especially men, would judge as rebelliously self-assertive and destructive of good order in the church."[33] Andrews clearly identified sanctification as the source of the empowerment of these African American preachers and realized the role of the Holy Spirit in authorizing their public ministries.

While Houchins and Andrews accurately situate Black women within a religious context that emphasized sanctification, they are apparently unaware that many white women shared the same experience of sanctification and empowerment. While analysis of the role of sanctification in women's lives has concentrated on Black women, this was not unique to African American Christian experience. Research on white women whose experience paralleled that of their African American sisters has been minimal.[34]

Despite the evidence to the contrary as summarized above, Virginia Brereton insisted that sanctification in itself has a negative impact on the development of a woman's self. Since my thesis is that sanctification has a positive impact on the self-understandings of Wesleyan/Holiness women, it is imperative to address this negative perspective. It appears that Brereton's adverse assessment arises from a misunderstanding about the consequences of holiness or sanctification.

Brereton's disapproval of holiness is caustic: "Nor is it difficult to comprehend the disgust which holiness teachings would elicit in those who have worked for and called for greater autonomy and self-reliance for women." She maintained that holiness teaching "has also accentuated the kinds of character traits that if embraced would keep women docile and yielding. The sanctified person—like the converted person, only more so—is supposed to be unassertive, selfless, serene, and slow to complain." Despite her bias, in one case Brereton inadvertently highlighted a positive aspect of sanctification. She incorrectly identified Maggie Newton Van Cott's sanctification by referring to it as her conversion, which "resulted in exuberance and a loss of inhibiting self-consciousness."[35] Rather than allowing Van Cott's testimony of holiness to temper her dismissal of sanctification, Brereton mislabeled it. While the theology of the death of the self appears on the surface to support Brereton's judgment that sanctified women are selfless, nevertheless the empowered self that resulted from this experience undermines this assumption. The other character traits she associated with sanctification, particularly unassertiveness, hardly describe Wesleyan/Holiness women preachers. Brereton failed to consider the new empowered self that replaced the carnal nature or the old self in sanctification.

Mary Cole's behavior at a camp meeting in Kansas is illustrative. Rather than announcing who would preach ahead of time at Church of God (Anderson, Indiana) camp meetings, all the preachers sat on the platform. Whoever felt led to preach would stand and walk to the pulpit at the appointed time. On this particular occasion, Cole noticed that another preacher whom she felt should not preach made a move toward the pulpit. She recalled that "it came to my mind that if I wanted to obey the Lord and to keep my promise I must act quickly. I asked the Lord to exercise his control and to give me the needed opportunity to obey. He did, and I preached the sermon that day."[36] To do so, she literally had to race across the platform and beat the other pastor, a man, to the pulpit. Further illustrations counteracting the assessment that Wesleyan/Holiness women were unassertive and lacked self-reliance will be considered in chapter 6.

Brereton also pointed out that holiness language utilizes a "rhetoric about extreme dependence on a male Person" to support her case that holiness is harmful for women's self-esteem. She did concede, however, that "the fact that the utter dependence is upon God rather than upon human males alters the usual dynamics of female submission."[37] In fact,

Mary Cole, author of *Trials and Triumphs of Faith* (Anderson, Ind.: Gospel Trumpet, 1914).

sanctification creates a significant change in the dynamics of submission. Sanctified women were no longer subject to society's constraints or male authority but relied on God's authority to challenge efforts to thwart their public ministries.

Brereton dismissed sanctification as a doctrine that was harmful to women. Her assessment disregarded the perspective of the women themselves and of theorists mentioned above as well as the evaluation of scholars such as sociologist Gordon Melton, who has contended that the Wesleyan/Holiness movement was "among the important forces working for the general elevation of women in the social structures of nineteenth century America, and the single most important force within the large religious community opening space for women to exercise power and hold positions previously reserved for men alone." The movement's emphasis on the doctrine of sanctification accounted for this distinction. Autobiographical theorist Liz Stanley, commenting on the role of sanctification specifically in the lives of African American women preachers Zilpha Elaw, Julia Foote, and Jarena Lee, credited the doctrine for "provid[ing] women a route into a public life and also an unanswerable legitimation straight from God for their conduct in doing so." Likewise, Phebe Davidson recognized the place of sanctification in opening up opportunities for public ministry to women, which, of necessity, took them away from their homes and families.[38] This study likewise demonstrates that the autobiographies of Wesleyan/Holiness women preachers also reveal that sanctification was a liberating and empowering experience.

Feminist Theory

This examination of autobiographies utilizes aspects of feminist theory and autobiographical theory as well as a theological analysis, and it advocates the approach of feminist literary critic Annette Kolodny: "As I see it, our task is to initiate nothing less than a playful pluralism, responsive to the possibilities of multiple critical schools and methods, but captive of none, recognizing that the many tools needed for our analysis will necessarily be largely inherited and only partly of our own making."[39]

According to Sidonie Smith and Julia Watson, numerous theorists insist that "privileging the oppression of gender over and above other oppressions effectively erases the complex and often contradictory positionings of the subject." In many cases, this warning is apt. However, in the present study, gender is the dominant category. Women's right to preach was not challenged on racist grounds; rather, women encountered arguments based on narrow constructions of gender. Opposition was due to sexism, not racism—although issues relating to race are not ignored here; they are incorporated in the text. African American and white women shared similarities in their experiences as preachers, and this study confirms Elizabeth Elkin Grammer's analysis of the spiritual autobiographies of four African American women and three white women. She found that "more often than not, however, the politics of gender overshadows those of race in these spiritual autobiographies."[40] The aim here is to avoid essentializing the experiences of all Wesleyan/Holiness women, whether white or African American, but, at the same time, to acknowledge similarities where they do exist.

Employing gender as an analytical tool is vital to this study. Gender is a foundational consideration in feminist theory. The Personal Narratives Group in 1989 provided a concise summary of the relationship between

ꟷer and female experience: "The fact that human experience is gendered ꟷ central to the radical implications of feminist theory. That recognition of the impact of gender and an insistence on the importance of the female experience have provided the vital common ground for feminist research and thought. Feminist theory emerges from and responds to the lives of women. The recovery and interpretation of women's lives have been central concerns of feminist scholarship from the earliest pioneering works to the present. Listening to women's voices, studying women's writings, and learning from women's experiences have been crucial to the feminist reconstruction of our understanding of the world."[41] This study applies feminist theory to Wesleyan/Holiness women whose lives and experience, except for several African Americans, have not yet been examined.

Elaine Showalter observed that feminist theory values women's experience as opposed to "scientific criticism [which] struggled to purge itself of the subjective." The feminist emphasis on experience corresponds with the theology of the Wesleyan/Holiness movement, which affirms the role of experience in religious knowledge in contrast to some other Christian traditions that reject experience and endorse reason as the primary path to conversion. Phoebe Palmer illustrated this distinction when she emphasized the importance of experience: "That which is learned by *experience* is much more deeply written upon the heart than what is learned by mere precept."[42] The Wesleyan quadrilateral consisting of experience, tradition, Bible, and reason succinctly summarizes the sources of authority in the Wesleyan/Holiness movement. They are not equally important. The Bible is the primary source of theological authority, followed by experience. Tradition and reason have a place, but they play lesser roles compared to Scripture and experience. Because they were encouraged to share their personal religious experiences in various church settings, Wesleyan/Holiness women appeared to be unintimidated when it came to recording their experience in autobiographical form.

While *gender* is often popularly used as a synonym for one's sex, male or female, its specialized meaning refers to roles that are culturally assigned on the basis of sex. I use *gender* to denote this more precise definition. There are at least two schools of thought regarding gender. Essentialists maintain that innate differences between the sexes determine roles that cannot be altered. In the Christian context, those who ascribe to essentialism speak of roles as being God-given or ordained by God. Others hold that gender roles are socially constructed—that is, created by a given society. The discussion of constructions of gender as opposed to essentialism represents a variation of the nurture versus nature debate, with the former holding that gender roles result from the way we are nurtured, while essentialists take the position that differences between the sexes are attributable to nature and therefore are innate.

The cult of true womanhood, with its doctrine of woman's sphere, was a nineteenth-century expression of essentialism. Barbara Welter, in her classic 1976 article, described the cult of true womanhood, drawing on prescriptive literature in both women's and religious magazines written between 1820 and 1860.[43] The ideology of woman's sphere endorsed and promoted domesticity, the belief that woman's place was in the home. Domesticity was one component of the cult of true womanhood. The Victorian woman at the hearth, maintaining a safe haven for husband and children, symbolized domesticity.

The restrictions of woman's sphere held contradictory implications for nineteenth-century African American women. Black women generally worked outside the home. The boundaries stretched for them, but employment outside the home for these mostly working-class women did not include preaching from the pulpit. On the other hand, many African Americans nevertheless subscribed to the tenets of domesticity, viewing it as evidence of achieving middle-class status. They also saw it as a means of overcoming negative stereotypes initially perpetuated by proponents of slavery. Shirley Yee explained: "The strength and complexity of negative sexual imagery about black women, however sexist, gave the idea of 'true womanhood' deep significance, racial as well as sexual, for free blacks. Acceptance of these notions reflected an understandable desire to erase the stereotypes that had been developed to justify their subjugation and attain a sense of independence. But championing for themselves 'ideal' roles and stereotypes that supposedly characterized 'free' women and men, free black men and women found themselves trading one set of stereotypes for another."[44] The African American women in this study did not succumb to the temptation to achieve status solely characterized by domesticity.

In her 1993 book, *The Lenses of Gender,* Sandra Lipsitz Bem defined the lenses of gender as the "hidden assumptions about sex and gender" present in society. Rejecting essentialism, Bem identified "mutually exclusive scripts for being male and female" as artificial distinctions. Although Bem did not consider Wesleyan/Holiness women preachers, they fall within her category of "those who resist the gender lenses and thereby construct a gender-subversive identity" by engaging in an activity that their culture has designated for men only. Wesleyan/Holiness women refused to look through the lenses society prescribed for them. While outlining ways in which Christianity grinds the lens of androcentrism, Bem appeared unfamiliar with Christianity's role in providing another vision that undermined this culturally constructed lens.[45]

Following Bem and others, I align myself with the constructionist view of gender. This coincides with Wesleyan/Holiness theology, which maintains that people have free will. We determine our own destiny just as society determines gender roles. I agree with theorist Liz Stanley, who challenged essentialism from a historical perspective: "Feminism is predicated upon a constructionist and indeed deconstructionist view of gender that *a priori* rejects essentialism . . . For as long as there has been feminism it has been devoted to the dismantling of essentialist views of sex and the insistence on the social construction of gender."[46]

Deconstruction of this sort is not a recent activity undertaken by contemporary feminists. In the nineteenth century, Sarah Grimké's and Elizabeth Wilson's understanding of gender roles attested to the truth of Liz Stanley's statement. Male clergy had castigated Grimké and her sister Angelina in 1837 for their public denunciation of slavery, accusing them of stepping outside woman's sphere. Writing the following year, Grimké defined her understanding of the origin of woman's sphere: "Our views about the duties of men and the duties of women, the sphere of man and the sphere of woman, are mere arbitrary opinions, differing in different ages and countries, and dependent solely on the will and judgment of erring mortals." Writing in 1849, Elizabeth Wilson agreed with Grimké's conclusion that the concept of woman's sphere was humanly created and not ordained by God despite efforts in religious and secular magazines to credit God with its creation. Grimké, Wilson, and Wesleyan/Holiness women challenged roles based on gender without the benefit of current feminist terminology to describe their enterprise. They engaged in identical arguments and resisted similar constructions of gender. They confirm Stanley's 1992 declaration that "the complexities of the categories 'women' and 'men' are not reserved knowledge for theoreticians/researchers."[47] These women reached their conclusions based on personal experience.

Wesleyan/Holiness women preachers were "gender non-conformists" who explicitly defied their society's construction of gender.[48] Historian Janet Wilson James mistakenly referred to several Wesleyan/Holiness women preachers, including Amanda Smith, Mary Cole, and Alma White, as "traditionalists in their concept of woman's place."[49] Public preaching, in itself, undermines the assertion that Wesleyan/Holiness women preachers were traditionalists. Their preaching flagrantly challenged traditional notions of woman's sphere since the pulpit was the literal symbol of the male domain. They clearly disregarded the advice of Sarah Josepha Hale, the editor of the popular *Ladies Magazine* who warned her nineteenth-century readers: "It is only in emergencies, in cases where duty demands the sacrifice of female sensitiveness, that a lady of sense and delicacy will come before the public, in a manner to make herself conspicuous."[50] Given this cultural climate, which persisted throughout the nineteenth and twentieth centuries, and now into the twenty-first, Wesleyan/Holiness women preachers relied on God to empower them when they confronted and overcame these ideological obstacles and preached.

Wesleyan/Holiness women not only acted on their convictions but also documented their public activities in their autobiographies. Their ministries and their writing undermined the social construction of gender based on the essentialist premise that women, either by nature or by God's design, could not preach. As Felicity Nussbaum has stated: "In short, autobiographical writing, published and private, serves as a location where residual and emergent notions of gender and class clash to replicate and challenge reigning notions of identity."[51] Wesleyan/Holiness women wrote autobiographies explicitly to spotlight their preaching and other public activities. They challenged essentialism head-on by offering their experience as an antidote to inhibiting gender expectations.

Autobiographical theorist Sidonie Smith contended that examination of the self must consider the role of gender, which "has always constituted *a,* if not *the,* fundamental ideological system for interpreting and understanding individual identity and social dynamics." Simone de Beauvoir first described the gendered self from a philosophical perspective in *The Second Sex.*[52] While Wesleyan/Holiness women did not incorporate a philosophical or psychological understanding of self in their writings, they were clearly describing a spiritual self that transcended gender roles. Christianity fostered the notion of a nongendered soul that made possible the potential of spiritual equality, as articulated in Gal. 3:28b: "There is neither male nor female for you are all one in Christ Jesus." However, women still had to contend with the gendered self as they applied the equality inherent in their souls to equality in their public activities. The gender-subversive self made possible by sanctification enabled women to challenge their opponents. Rather than serving an essentialist agenda by affirming the status quo for women, the doctrine of sanctification made it possible for women to break through the barriers of woman's sphere. The understanding of sanctification became gendered when women appropriated the power of the Holy Spirit to challenge the restraints placed on them solely because they were women.

Wesleyan/Holiness theology, with its emphasis on prophetic authority and the empowerment of the Holy Spirit made possible by sanctification, offered a social ethic for women that enabled them to question the ethic of domesticity, which the ideology of woman's sphere reinforced. Challenging woman's sphere was a formidable task. Elizabeth Wilson in 1849 revealed the price for exceeding the boundaries of woman's sphere: "To be accused of appearing out of their sphere, is excruciatingly painful. Their sphere of action is so circumscribed, and hence this sensitiveness; they revolve in an egg-shell, and if any of them appear a hair's-breath out of their prescribed orbit, they are assailed with so much virulence, contumely, and vulgar sarcasm, that it is only some daring spirits who will attempt it."[53] Wesleyan/Holiness women had access to spiritual power on which they relied to escape woman's sphere.

Power was a central element of Phoebe Palmer's doctrine of holiness. She recollected an instance where "holy boldness seemed to seize me" and described the experience as being "assisted by a power beyond myself." She attributed this power to the Holy Spirit. Applying the phraseology of Françoise Lionnet, the Holy Spirit's power superceded the power behind "the essentializing tendencies that perpetuate exploitation and subjection on behalf of those fictive differences" between the sexes. Promulgators of the ethic of domesticity insisted woman's place was in the private arena of the home. Wesleyan/Holiness women, empowered by the Holy Spirit, superceded the power behind the ethic of domesticity when they preached and engaged in other public ministries. The act of preaching transcended the restricted roles that the advocates of the ideology of woman's sphere sought to impose on women. Marjorie Procter-Smith's observation that the Shakers played an "emancipatory function" by enabling "women to transcend existing social restraints" could also apply to the Wesleyan/Holiness movement.[54] The confining boundaries of woman's sphere could not contain Wesleyan/Holiness women preachers who appealed to a higher authority to break through the invisible barriers intended to inhibit their activities. The ethic of empowerment, making possible the expansion of women's role, effectively opposed the ethic of domesticity by authorizing women to cross the invisible boundaries of woman's sphere. See chapter 6 for specific examples of Wesleyan/Holiness women's successful challenge to the doctrine of woman's sphere.

While these Wesleyan/Holiness women highlighted their public careers in their autobiographies, in contrast, women activists and writers who also wrote autobiographies at the turn of the twentieth century did not stress their public lives. Estelle Jelinek discovered that many feminists and reformers minimized their public lives in their autobiographies. For example, Elizabeth Cady Stanton slighted her activism as a suffragist in her autobiography *Eighty Years and More: Reminiscences, 1815–1897*. She referred her readers to *The History of Woman Suffrage* for a record of her public achievements, "thereby banishing to the margins of her 'woman's' text the story of agency and autonomy." Jelinek observed that women writers who authored autobiographies also minimized their public activities and did not use their autobiographies as a platform to denounce woman's sphere.[55] In contrast to Stanton and literary autobiographers, Wesleyan/Holiness women confidently and without apology concentrated on the public aspects of their lives in their narratives.

Wesleyan/Holiness women rejected notions of the self imposed on them by their culture. Were they feminists? Showalter defined feminist women's writing as "*protest* against [the] standards of art and its views of social roles" and "*advocacy* of minority rights and values, including a demand for autonomy."[56] Given this definition, Wesleyan/Holiness women were feminists. However, this was not a self-descriptive term. One reason was that the word *feminism* was not coined until the end of the nineteenth century. However, even Alma White, the most vociferous proponent of women's rights among this group, chose not to refer to herself as a feminist when she wrote in the twentieth century. While their agendas were decidedly feminist, Wesleyan/Holiness women did not embrace the term itself.

Autobiographical Theory

Defining *autobiography* remains a contested activity. Rather than joining the debate, I will adopt William Spengemann's definition: "However various critics have defined autobiography, their ability to recognize one has always depended on some evidence that the writer's self is either the primary subject or the principal object of the verbal action." James Olney dated the advent of theoretical and critical literature about autobiographies to 1956. The focus on gender in autobiographies is more recent, beginning in 1980 with Estelle Jelinek's *Women's Autobiography* and Domna Stanton's *Female Autograph* in 1984. Feminist theory informs autobiographical theory. The two are not mutually exclusive. For instance, the examination of the *bio,* or biographical component of autobiography, includes a focus on the forces that influence gender: "'women' cannot be studied in isolation from the forces that shape gender relationships in any social formation." Among historians, Wilhelm Dilthey, a philosopher of history, particularly valued the contribution of autobiographies to the historical enterprise, going so far as to identify autobiography as "the germinal cell of history."[57] Librarians classify autobiography under biography, which is itself a subheading of history.

Some theorists, however, emphasize the fictional nature of autobiographies, maintaining that the autobiographical self is a fabrication. Sidonie Smith claimed: "Because the autobiographer can never capture the fullness of her subjectivity or understand the entire range of her experience, the narrative 'I' becomes a fictive persona." Phrases such as "fictive persona" and "autobiographical fictions" seem to deny the historical value of autobiography. Janel Mueller contended: "As an appreciable body of theory and criticism dealing with first-person writing continues to make clear, there is never an equation to be drawn between an author as an actual historical person and the 'I' of that author's text."[58]

The supposition that autobiography is fiction jars historical sensibilities. Liz Stanley's clarification helps: "A concern with auto/biography shows that 'self' is a fabrication, not necessarily a lie but certainly a highly complex truth; a fictive truth reliant on cultural convention concerning what 'a life' consists of and how its story can be told both in speech and, somewhat differently, in writing. But this does not mean that such writings have no points of connection with the material realities of everyday life; it rather emphasizes how complex this relationship is and that neither realism nor a total rejection of it will do." An autobiographer can never fully discern or reveal herself through her writing. The self she exposes is not a mirror image of the actual self. At best, the autobiographer provides glimpses of her self-understanding. To speak of autobiography as fiction recognizes the reality that it is impossible to portray the self exactly as it is. Nancy K. Miller explains: "Every inscription of the self is an approximation and a projection; as matter of details, shadows, adjustment, and proportion—an *arrangement* of truths." Bella Brodzki and Celeste Schenck, likewise, challenged the assumption that "autobiography is a transparency through which we perceive the life, unmediated and undistorted."[59] While recognizing that the self described by Wesleyan/Holiness authors can never be identical to the actual self, their autobiographies are extremely important because their portrayals of the sanctified self revealed the basis for their involvement in the public sphere as religious workers

The *bio* component of autobiography is crucial because it reveals an individual's life and the context in which it is lived. I am not rejecting a historical approach, but have broadened the analysis by incorporating theoretical insights relating to *auto* and *graph.* According to Elizabeth Elkin Grammer: "To read 'autobiographically' with an emphasis on auto (self) and graphe (writing) is not to exclude bio (life), but to consider how these texts reveal their authors and their lives."[60] The analysis in the following chapters draws on the tools of autobiographical theory to address all three components: self, life, and writing, in that order. Regrettably, many Wesleyan/Holiness autobiographers neglected to discuss important biographical events such as their marriage or if they had children. That omission precludes a thorough biographical examination of the narratives. The main focus of this study is the sanctified self described in women's autobiographies and the public ministries that the sanctified self made possible.

Needless to say, autobiographical theory and historical analysis overlap. My thinking resonates with Liz Stanley, who recognized the pivotal place of *bio:* "'Bio,' the narration of the material events of everyday life, is the crucial element in theorizing and understanding both 'auto' and 'graph.'" Some theoreticians, such as Estelle Jelinek, are not interested in incorporating *bio* in their analysis. Jelinek chose to focus instead on "literary characteristics of the autobiographies, not on women as people." Albert E. Stone, however, stressed the need to value history above literature: "I remain uneasy over the tendency to treat autobiography chiefly as a branch of imaginative literature and thus to stress artistic creation over the equally complex processes of historical recreation, ideological argument, and psychological expression. *Life* is the more inclusive sign—not *Literature*—which deserves to be placed above the gateway to the house of autobiography."[61] While I attempt to avoid privileging *bio,* I do not disregard it because of its important contribution to understanding the sanctified self.

Context is an aspect of *bio* that is critical to this study. Context provides an interpretive framework for understanding the vital role of sanctification in women's construction of self. Felicity Nussbaum contended "the self is an ideological construct that is recruited into place within specific historical formations rather than always present as an eternal truth." Religious and secular cultures provide the context for examining the self. Women did not formulate their understandings of self in a vacuum; rather, the self emerged and developed in response to definitions proposed by the cultures in which they lived. Jill Conway correctly contended, "Our culture gives us an inner script by which we live our lives." Wesleyan/Holiness women found themselves with two scripts that were in conflict with each other. The sanctified self defied what Sidonie Smith referred to as "culturally prescribed norms of female identity" promoted by a broader societal context.[62] The sanctified self cannot be isolated and scrutinized solely within its religious context because in some ways it was a reaction to the self that society sought to impose on women. The cultural forces that helped shape the self for women have been explored in depth.[63] However, prior to this study, the role of the sanctified self and its displacement of the societal view of self for women has been undertaken by only a few scholars who were researching the lives of several Wesleyan/Holiness African American women. In chapter 5, I briefly identify the gendered self promoted by societal culture. My primary focus, however, will be on the religious culture that supported women as they directly challenged this restrictive view of woman's self.

While autobiographical theory addresses the *bio* component of autobiographies, I am primarily indebted to autobiographical theory for its discussion of the *auto,* or self. My focus is on the spiritual self, the self in relation to God. Specifically, I am analyzing the sanctified self. I explore how women perceived the self and particularly how the doctrine of sanctification transformed the understanding of self.

It is ironic that the doctrine of sanctification promotes a theology of the death of self, yet women wrote autobiographies accentuating the individual self and its achievements. The paradox should be obvious but many refuse to acknowledge it. If Wesleyan/Holiness women believed the literal death of self was the end result of sanctification, they would not have penned autobiographies. Speaking of nineteenth-century women, Sidonie Smith observed: "In daring to write about herself for public consumption, the autobiographer already transgressed cultural boundaries, straying beyond the boundaries of a 'selfhood' situated at the very margins of cultural action, meaning, and discourse into another's territory at the center of culture."[64] Wesleyan/Holiness women asserted a sanctified self that enabled them to transcend cultural boundaries by authoring their narratives.

In terms of *graphy,* I include the autobiographers' rationale for why they wrote. Wesleyan/Holiness women frequently addressed their readers explicitly, making the connection between writer and reader obvious. I seek to avoid the temptation to mold women into my contemporary ideal and attempt to respect each author's outlook rather than attributing my views to them. Linda Anderson recognized the paradox that exists between criticism and autobiography: "For a feminist criticism of autobiography could well be attempting to speak for–about those very discourses where women might best be seen as speaking for themselves." For this reason, I allow the women, for the most part, to speak for themselves by including a large number of direct quotations. In this way, the authors' voices can be heard along with my interpretation of their words. The Personal Narratives Group cautioned that "personal narratives cannot be simply expropriated in the service of some good cause, but must be respected in their integrity." They also acknowledged "the need to recognize both the agenda of the narrator and that of the interpreter as distinct and not always compatible."[65] In this case, the agendas of both the narrators and the interpreter overlap because, like them, I advocate women clergy. However, the women do not always measure up to twenty-first-century expectations of feminism. Again, I have attempted to allow them to speak for themselves without forcing them into a contemporary mold I have created.

Wesleyan/Holiness women's autobiographies are gender marked. Unlike men, they had to justify their preaching and other public religious activities precisely because they were women. While not specifically referring to these women, Felicity Nussbaum could have been speaking of them when she wrote in 1989: "I am arguing here that women's autobiographical writing, organized within prevailing discourses, helped to shape and resist the dominant cultural constructions of gender relations and to substitute alternatives." The Wesleyan/Holiness movement sanctioned a spiritual self that empowered women rather than enslaved them within the confines of woman's sphere. Robert E. Sayre wrote regarding slave narratives: "A necessary step in anyone's liberation from stereotypes and injustice is the moment when he or she asserts his or her own rights and values against those imposed from without. This is the discovery of self, and it is what has made autobiography such an important ideological weapon, not only in the abolitionist era but in the civil rights era, and to many other groups and causes."[66] Wesleyan/Holiness women constitute a group that appropriated autobiography as a weapon in the fight for their own liberation. While the autobiographers would not have used the phrase "political tool," they were appropriating autobiography, in part, as a political tool to justify their religious activities in the public arena. I promote their agenda by employing their writings to justify and promote the continued involvement of women in professional ministry.

As an interpreter of these autobiographies, it is impossible to divorce myself from my own context. Alistair Thomson stressed that "the life-history of the researcher shapes the research agenda and research approaches." Feminist scholarship recognizes that objectivity is impossible. Adrienne Rich reflected on the style of her book *Of Women Born* in a new introduction she wrote for the 1987 edition: "But this approach [employing personal testimony mingled with research and theory] never seemed odd to me in the writing. What seems odd is the absentee author, the writer who lays down speculations, theories, facts, and fantasies without any personal grounding."[67] I have not incorporated my personal testimony explicitly in the manuscript. However, my own support of women clergy, no doubt, led me to ask questions and select material that would result in a decidedly different book in contrast to a book covering the same narratives written by someone opposed to women preachers.

It is my responsibility as a feminist interpreter to acknowledge my own context and agenda. The Personal Narratives Group recognized that "the expectations and understandings that the interpreter herself brings to the life story are themselves an essential element in the contextualization of personal narratives." I am not a disinterested student of Wesleyan/Holiness women preachers. I am ordained in the Church of God (Anderson, Indiana). My feminism is a direct outgrowth of my own history in the Wesleyan/Holiness tradition. In a brief comparison of Wesleyan theology and Christian feminism, Randy Maddox concluded that Wesleyanism, more so than the Reformed, Catholic, or Lutheran traditions, "presents to Christian feminists a theological tradition with which they will find strong affinities and on which they can build." Since 1992, I have been executive director of Wesleyan/Holiness Women Clergy, International, which is an organization that sponsors biannual conferences for women in ministry and women preparing for ministry. The group publishes materials and maintains a web site to support and encourage women clergy.[68]

My agenda is explicitly political because, like Julia Swindells, I see autobiography as a political tool that women used to subvert constructions of gender that inhibited them. Swindells utilized autobiography to "identify and change educational and cultural processes, where these operated against oppressed and powerless groups."[69] I employ autobiographies in this study as a tool to challenge the very churches that initially enabled and fostered women's ministries but now often discourage women from engaging in professional ministry. With the exception of The Salvation Army, the percentage of Wesleyan/Holiness women clergy has declined drastically over the years. Wesleyan/Holiness groups have fallen short of the ideal they espoused and often practiced during the early decades of their existence.

My purpose in analyzing Wesleyan/Holiness autobiographies reflects Kathryn K. Sklar's understanding of history: "History is important because it seizes the power of definition over what *has been done* and this very deeply affects our sense of what *can be done*."[70] By describing their sanctification and subsequent empowerment, Wesleyan/Holiness women preachers appropriated autobiography as a tool to sanction their public activities. One of my goals is to illumine a usable past that can serve as a foundation for a renewed appreciation for the doctrine of sanctification and its role in fostering a self that is autonomous and empowered to act in ways that were impossible prior to the experience of sanctification.

CHAPTER TWO

Madame Guyon

An examination of the Wesleyan/Holiness trajectory of women's autobiographies must begin with Madame Guyon's autobiography, which served as the forerunner of Wesleyan/Holiness women's spiritual autobiographies. Scholars have noted the quest for holiness documented in the spiritual autobiographies of medieval mystics. For instance, Eleanor McLaughlin summarized the searches of Lioba, Christina of Markyate, and Catherine of Siena. She recognized the positive relationship between holiness and power in their lives: "The effectiveness of these women was rooted in their holiness. Power out of holiness." Their pursuit of holiness resulted in empowerment. McLaughlin attributed the ability of these women to move "beyond the limitations of biology and social convention" to the doctrine of holiness.[1] Rather than these other autobiographies, however, the writings of Madame Guyon captured the attention of Wesleyan/Holiness adherents.

A Holiness Saint

Madame Jeane Marie Bouvier de la Mothe Guyon (1648–1717) was a French Roman Catholic mystic associated with the development of quietism, although this was not a term she used. Patricia Ward provided a concise description of quietism, a seventeenth-century school of spirituality: "Quietism emphasized the abandonment of the self to God, annihilation of the will in union with God, pure love, and a form of inner prayer."[2]

At first glance, it might seem odd to trace the trajectory of Wesleyan/Holiness women's spiritual autobiographies to Guyon; however, her writings and her pursuit of perfection provided a model for John Wesley and his followers. J. Agar Beet, an early-twentieth-century author, recognized a "profound agreement" and "a similarity of phrase" between quietists such as Guyon and John Wesley, suggesting "he learned this great truth of holiness, in part, from them." Likewise, Darius Salter, referring primarily to Guyon, has maintained that "the radical 'death' and 'crucifixion' language used by Wesley and the American exponents of entire sanctification was not unlike the spiritual descriptions of the seventeenth-century European Mystics."[3]

Wesley praised Guyon: "She was undoubtedly a woman of a very uncommon understanding, and of excellent piety." However, Wesley did not issue an uncritical endorsement of Guyon's theology. He published an extract of Guyon's autobiography in his Christian library, in which he printed "the gold without the dross," contending the selection would be helpful for those "going on to perfection." While Wesley shared Guyon's commitment to experiential piety, Wesley faulted Guyon for placing experience above the Bible as the primary source of theological authority. Despite his critique, Wesley praised Guyon: "Upon the whole, we may search many centuries before we find another woman who was such a pattern of true holiness."[4] Wesley lifted up Guyon as a model for his followers to emulate. Wesleyan/Holiness women followed her example of holiness and the active life she pursued.

No doubt influenced by Wesley's endorsement, Guyon's reputation extended to the United States. Patricia Ward noted the appropriation of Guyon's writings by Wesleyan/Holiness believers: "Madame Guyon was claimed as a predecessor and spiritual model because her experience was deemed identical to the 'sanctification' or 'deeper life' of popular Protestant piety." Thomas Upham, a Congregational professor at Bowdoin College who experienced sanctification under the ministry of Phoebe Palmer, was a primary figure in popularizing Guyon in the United States. He authored a biography of Guyon in 1847 that underwent thirty-seven editions. He contributed to the high regard of this mystic, particularly among Wesleyan/ Holiness believers. In his compilation of Phoebe Palmer's life and letters, Richard Wheatley attested to Guyon's ongoing popularity in 1881: "The mystical piety of Madame Guyon is widely and deeply influential today; as much so, perhaps as at any previous epoch in the history of the Church."[5]

George Scott Railton and B. T. Roberts presented Madame Guyon's ministry as a model for Wesleyan/Holiness women to imitate. The Salvation Army published Railton's pamphlet on Guyon in the United States in 1885. Railton, a leading theologian in The Salvation Army, summarized Guyon's life and ministry, incorporating extensive quotations from her autobiography. He concluded with a plea that women follow her example of promoting "the great salvation from all sin," since more doors were now open to women: "God has swept from before you all that can prevent your standing before the thousands of the city just as men have done. You are no longer kept like some little child looking on in the back-ground whilst others lead and are led to victory." Roberts mentioned Guyon twice in *Ordaining Women,* including her among the many examples he offered to bolster his thesis favoring the leadership of women in the church.[6] Both Railton and Roberts encouraged Wesleyan/Holiness women to follow the example of Guyon's public ministry.

Guyon's enduring influence among Wesleyan/Holiness believers in the United States is evident. Clara McLeister and J. O. McClurkan each included her in their compilations of short biographies of prominent Christians published by Wesleyan/Holiness presses. McLeister, writing in 1920, contrasted her positive appraisal of Guyon with a negative assessment of Catholicism: "The black mantle of Roman Catholicism smothered all true Divine life in the hearts of its devotees . . . In such an age Madame Guyon groped her way to such eminence of holiness that even in this day of marvelous light she stands among the foremost of saintly characters." Both McLeister and McClurkan underlined the fact that opposition to Guyon was due, in some part, to the fact that she was a woman. McLeister quoted Guyon: "It [the world] could not bear that a woman should thus make war against it, and overcome." Likewise, McClurkan cited a reference where Guyon attributed opposition to her sex. Similar to Wesley, McClurkan praised Guyon but included a qualification: "Possibly she stressed penance and mysticism rather too much, but for a profoundly holy life, manifesting itself in utter annihilation of the self-life, she had few equals." Jennie Fowler Willing authored a three-part series at the turn of the twentieth century entitled "Madame Guyon the Mystic" in *Guide to Holiness,* a major holiness journal. Like McLeister, Willing incorporated anti-Catholic sentiments in her articles, but she also commended Guyon for "carrying her benefactions to hundreds of poor families, and great spiritual blessing to thousands of souls." Guyon remained popular in Wesleyan/Holiness circles in the twentieth century as already indicated by the writings of McLeister. Also, Bessie Goldie Olson authored a pamphlet about Guyon in 1946 while God's Revivalist, a Wesleyan/Holiness publisher, reprinted an abridged version of her autobiography into the 1970s. Various editions of Guyon's autobiography remain in print. Melvin Dieter, historian of the Wesleyan/Holiness movement, observed in 1996 that Guyon "remain[s] on the active list of holiness saints."[7] Despite their anti-Catholic bias, Wesleyan/Holiness authors acknowledged the importance of Guyon's life as a woman whose commitment to holiness enabled her to conduct public ministries.

Comments by Wesleyan/Holiness women autobiographers also reflect Guyon's popularity. In her autobiography, Hannah Whitall Smith reported reading extracts from Guyon's writings and also followed Guyon as her model in terms of dealing with opposition. Lela McConnell, likewise, compared her spiritual experience with Guyon's. Lucy Drake Osborn and Julia Shellhamer visited the Bastille while in Paris and noted that Guyon had been imprisoned there. Sarah Cooke sprinkled her autobiography with direct quotations from Guyon. She expressed dismay when her autobiography of Guyon was among the possessions destroyed in the Chicago fire of 1871.[8]

Members of the Wesleyan/Holiness movement throughout its history have shared an affinity with Guyon's quest for holiness. Lizzie Miller listed Guyon along with Mary Fletcher and Hester Ann Rogers, contemporaries of John Wesley, who "were not only Christians but public workers for God." Lucy Drake Osborn sought to emulate Guyon's religious experience. Osborn wrote of mystical encounters when "self was lost to sight" and the soul is "quiet and peaceful."[9] Miller and Osborn both claimed Guyon as their spiritual mentor.

Madame Guyon's Mystical Theology

Like other mystics, Guyon stressed experience as a primary source of knowledge about God. This emphasis, no doubt, contributed to problems with her Roman Catholic superiors because it made the understanding of God available to all laity without the mediation of priests. Once, she berated herself for following the advice of M. Bertot, her spiritual director at the time, rather than trusting her own experience. While not joining an order as a nun, she made personal vows of chastity, poverty, and obedience, "covenanting to obey whatever I should believe to be the will of God, also to obey the Church, and to honor Jesus Christ in such a manner as he pleased."[10] Revealingly, she listed personal experience *before* the authority of the church. This bold assertion of autonomy, from a layperson, surely roused the ire of those church leaders to whom she was accountable. This reliance on self-discernment is surprising in light of her theology of the death of the will, which will be discussed later.

For Guyon, experience clearly outranked reason as well as church tradition as a source of theology: "Why should any amuse themselves, in seeking reasons for loving Love itself? Let us love without reasoning about it, and we shall find ourselves filled with love, before the others have learned the reasons which induced to it. Make trial of this love, and you will be wiser in it than the most skillful philosophers." According to Guyon, in love as in everything else, experience instructs better than reasoning.[11]

Guyon's aversion to reason was evident in her statement stressing the importance of prayer: "The only way to heaven is prayer; a prayer of the heart, which every one is capable of, and not of reasonings which are the fruits of study." Guyon advocated inward prayer, "that sweet interior correspondence," and authored *Short and Easy Method of Prayer* to promote it. After practicing inward prayer she found it impossible to say repetitive vocal prayers, which were the norm within Catholicism. Her emphasis on continual inward prayer placed her at odds with ecclesiastical authorities who promoted vocal prayers. Guyon engaged in inward prayer not only in private but in public, where she sometimes became unaware of what was going on around her. She described her experience of prayer: "There was made in me, without the sound of words, a continual prayer, which seemed to me to be the prayer of our Lord Jesus Christ himself; a prayer of the Word, which is made by the Spirit, that according to St. Paul, 'asketh for us that which is good, perfect, and conformable to the will of God.' Rom. xiii 26–27." Guyon stressed the importance of prayer, not only for the seeker but also for the converted. Prayer was the link to "the fountain of living water." She ranked prayer above "ecstasies [and] transports or visions," which were "more subject to illusion or deceits from the enemy."[12]

Contrary to many Catholics who believed merit and public confession produced conversion, Guyon insisted that prayer led to conversion. While Augustine's theology exerted a tremendous influence among Catholics, as well as later Protestants, Catholics rejected his doctrine of predestination, holding to their church's original affirmation of human free will with regard to salvation. Guyon agreed with her church's avowal of free will, commenting "I cannot bear to hear it said, 'we are not free to resist grace.'" As for God's part, God granted grace in response to the request made by an individual.[13]

Guyon described the circumstances of her own experience at age nineteen:

> At length, God permitted a very religious person, of the order of St. Francis, to pass by my father's habitation . . . He saw there was something for him to do, and imagined that God had called him for the conversion of a man of some distinction in that country; but his labors there proved fruitless. It was the conquest of my soul which was designed . . . I told this good man, "that I did not know what he had done to me, that my heart was quite changed, that God was there; for from that moment he had given me an experience of his presence in my soul; not by thought or any application of mind, but as a thing really possessed after the sweetest manner."[14]

It is impossible to determine if Guyon's religious experience as a young woman corresponded with Wesleyan/Holiness women's understanding of conversion. More than likely, her Roman Catholic context precludes a close parallel.

Likewise, terminology becomes problematic when attempting to describe Guyon's understanding of spiritual maturity. *Sanctification* was not a term that she used in her autobiography. Yet *sanctification* frequently appeared in translated abridgements of her autobiography available to Wesleyan/Holiness women in the nineteenth and twentieth centuries. Since the intent is to explore the relationship between Guyon and Wesleyan/ Holiness women, my focus is on the language Wesleyan/ Holiness women encountered when they read her narrative.

It is easy to see why Wesleyan/Holiness women identified with Guyon. Even though Guyon did not use the phrase "perfect love," as did John Wesley and his followers, she emphasized that love played a role in the purification process, which gave rise to pure love. Guyon testified: "This love of God occupied my heart so constantly and so strongly, that I could think of nothing else, as indeed I judged nothing else worthy of my thoughts." Also, Guyon never called sanctification a second work of grace, as was common among Wesleyan/Holiness adherents, but her description fits this understanding: "Souls are received into grace, as soon as the cause of sin ceases; but they do not pass into the Lord himself, till all its effects are washed away. If they have not courage to let him in his own way and will, thoroughly cleanse and purify them, they never enter into the pure divinity of this life." She called this experience by several names, including perfection, which she defined as being in "entire conformity with Jesus Christ."[15]

Guyon did not emphasize the Holy Spirit's part in purification and perfection as did Wesleyan/Holiness theology. Nevertheless, she made it clear that the Holy Spirit did play a role: "Oh, Holy Spirit, a Spirit of love, let me ever be subjected to thy will, and, as a leaf is moved before the wind, so let me be moved by thy Divine breath. As the impetuous wind breaks all that resists it, so break thou all that opposes thy empire." Guyon acknowledged that the Holy Spirit empowered her: "I found there was nothing which I was not fit for, or in which I did not succeed . . . I well knew that I had but meagre capabilities, but that in God my spirit had received a quality which it had never had before. I thought I experienced something of the state which the apostles were in, after they had received the Holy Ghost." The Spirit inspired her when writing letters dealing with business matters and responding to her critics. Likewise, the Spirit guided her religious writing. She "felt his immediate impulse" and wrote quickly to keep up with the Spirit's dictation. The Holy Spirit also provided her with words of counsel, in one case when she was conversing with the bishop of Geneva.[16] Guyon did not develop her understanding of the Holy Spirit beyond these brief references.

Rather than emphasizing the role of faith in purification, Guyon spoke of suffering as being executed by God, which culminates in purification. Wesley criticized Guyon for her focus on suffering instead of faith, calling it her "capital mistake" because it was not scriptural.[17] Suffering was a significant aspect of her spiritual growth. She desired suffering and spoke of the joy that suffering generated. The death of self results from the "silent path of suffering for Christ, and to be united to him, through the mortification of all that was of nature in me, that my senses, appetites and will, being dead to these, might wholly live in him." For Guyon, mortification described an asceticism that incorporated deprivation and denial of the flesh. She confessed: "I still continued to use many severe mortifications and austerities." To Guyon, pain was a necessary component of spiritual growth: "So eager was I for the cross, that I endeavored to make myself feel the utmost rigor of every mortification and felt them to the quick."[18] The quest for holiness advocated by Wesley and his Wesleyan/Holiness heirs did not include physical suffering.

Wesley and his spiritual descendants believed that sanctification is both a crisis experience and a lifelong process. Guyon agreed: "And here I may remark, that though the state of my soul was already permanent in newness of life; yet this new life was not in that immutability in which it has since been. To speak properly, it was a beginning life and a rising day, which goes on increasing unto the full meridian; a day never followed by night; a life which fears death no more, not even in death itself." Guyon reported, "I found myself every day more transformed into [Christ]." She claimed that it was a "fixed state" but explained that one can still "decline or fall," allowing for free will. But it is "fixed and permanent, compared with the states which have preceded it, which were full of vicissitudes and variations." "My passions (which were not thoroughly mortified) revived, and caused me new conflicts." She described herself at one point "as being in the lowest stage of perfection." Guyon was perhaps referring to herself when she mentioned a woman who felt she was "at the summit of perfection" but then discovered "she was yet very far from it."[19] Guyon's description of the holy life paralleled Wesley's, thus making it easy for his later Wesleyan/Holiness followers to adopt her as a model for imitation.

Guyon spoke of purification while Wesleyan/Holiness adherents generally used the term *cleansing*. Most Wesleyan/Holiness adherents affirmed that cleansing occurred in an instant at sanctification. Guyon disagreed, maintaining that purification is ongoing. Her description, though, indicated a crisis moment that inaugurated the process. Guyon mentioned "superficial impurity, which remains to be done away, and which one may compare to refined but tarnished gold. It has no more need to be purified in the fire, having undergone that operation; but needs only to be burnished."[20]

Guyon described the process of purification: "[God] destroys that he might build; for when he is about to rear his sacred temple in us, he first totally razes that vain and pompous edifice, which human art and power had erected, and from its horrible ruins a new structure is formed, by his power only." The phrase "horrible ruins" is more than likely a reference to her sinful human nature. Purification culminates in "perfect life . . . raised above nature, as before I had been depressed under its burden." "It is an internal burning, a secret fire, sent from God to purge away the fault, giving extreme pain, until this purification is effected." She sought "mortification of all that was of nature in me, that my senses, appetites and will being dead to these might wholly live in him."[21] For Guyon, perfection entailed overcoming the sinful human nature.

According to Guyon, it is the "impure and selfish soul" which is transformed by purification:

> In regard to thoughts or desires, all was so clean, so naked, so lost in the divinity, that the soul had no selfish movement, however plausible or delicate; both the powers of the mind and the very senses being wonderfully purified. Sometimes I was surprised to find that there appeared not one selfish thought. The imagination, formerly so restless, now no more troubled me. I had no more perplexity or uneasy reflections. The will, being perfectly dead to all its own appetites, was become void of every human inclination, both natural and spiritual, and only inclined to whatever God pleased, and to whatever manner he pleased.[22]

Purification occasioned the death of the soul, which she also referred to as the death of the will. While the soul was "full of its own judgment, and its own will before," it "now obeys like a child, and finds no other will in itself." "I have no will of my own, but purely the love and will of [God] who possesses me." Guyon offered the biblical basis for her understanding of the death of the self: "Whosoever will lose his life for my sake shall find it; and whosoever will save his life shall lose it." Guyon testified: "Jesus was then living in me; and I lived no more." She also exclaimed: "How very straight is the gate which leads to a life in God! how little one must be to pass through it, it being nothing else but death to self! But when we have passed through it, what enlargement do we find!" As the following three statements indicate, Guyon spoke of the death of the soul, the death of the will, and the death of the self separately: (1) "The soul, by death to itself, passes into its divine object." (2) "The will, being perfectly dead to all its own appetites, was become void of every human inclination." (3) "I thus died to self, in order to live wholly in thee." It is unclear how she related soul, will, and self. Subsequent promoters of sanctification were comfortable speaking of the death of self as a condition of perfection, but the death of the will was another matter. When Thomas Upham advocated the death of the will and union with God as a third work of grace following sanctification, Phoebe Palmer admonished him, claiming that this view had no foundation in the Bible. Despite Palmer's censure, one subsequent Wesleyan/Holiness woman reported a mystical experience lasting four hours. During this time, Lucy Drake Osborn

Lucy Drake Osborn, author of *Heavenly Pearls Set in a Life: A Record of Experiences and Labors in America, India, and Australia* (New York: Fleming H. Revell, 1893).

affirmed that she was "in a state of union with God." She explained: "My will seemed to flow naturally with the divine, as when you put water into a glass it takes the shape of the glass." On several occasions, Jennie Smith also employed mystical language when she recorded that she "sank deeper into the divine will."[23]

Osborn's testimony echoed Guyon's belief that when the individual's soul, or will, has died, union with God is possible. This conviction is generally associated with mysticism. Drawing from her own experience, Guyon described union with God. The union is "so great with the good will of God, that my own will seemed entirely lost." Guyon also claimed that her will gave up its place to God. "There seemed, indeed, to be no will left in me but thine only. My own disappeared and no desires, tendencies or inclinations were left, but to the one sole object of whatever was most pleasing to thee, be it what it would. If I had a will, it was in union with thine, as two well tuned lutes in concert,—that which is not touched renders the same sound as that which is touched; it is but one and the same sound, one pure harmony."[24] It is *two* lutes, however, that make music, not one. Notwithstanding her claim of union with God, Guyon acknowledged her separate self in this figure of speech.

Guyon offered another metaphor for union with God that obliterated human identity: "It seemed to me, as if it was wholly and altogether passed into its God, to make but one and the same thing with him, even as a little drop of water, cast into the sea, receives the qualities of the sea. Oh, union of unity, demanded of God by Jesus Christ for men, and merited by him! How strong is this in a soul that is become lost in its God! After the consummation of this divine unity, the soul remains hid with Christ in God." In a third comparison, she again appropriated water imagery to explain the soul's relation to God:

> It is certain then that the soul, by death to itself, passes into its divine Object; and this is what I then experienced. I found, the farther I went, the more my spirit was lost in its Sovereign, who attracted it more and more to himself. And he was pleased at first that I should know this for the sake of others, and not for myself. Indeed he drew my soul more and more into himself, till it lost itself entirely out of sight, and could perceive itself no more. It seemed at first to pass into him. As one sees a river pass into the ocean, lose itself in it, its water for a time distinguished from that of the sea, till it gradually becomes transformed into the same sea, and possesses all its qualities; so was my soul lost in God, who communicated to it his qualities, having drawn it out of all that it had of its own. Its life is an inconceivable innocence, not known or comprehended of those who are still shut up in themselves or only live for themselves.[25]

Guyon did not reconcile the conflicting metaphors of a self as a lute playing a duet with God's lute versus the self as a drop of water lost in the sea, which represented God.

Guyon differentiated her permanent union with God from temporary experiences reported by other mystics: "This happy loss is not like those transient ones which ecstasy operates, which are rather an absorption than union, for the soul afterwards finds itself again with all its own dispositions. But here she feels that prayer fulfilled—John xvii.21: 'That they all may be one as thou Father art in me, and I in thee; that they also may be one in us.'"[26]

The purification process led to annihilation, which Guyon described as the attainment of nothingness. Wesleyan/Holiness women preferred the phrase "death of self" to annihilation. The only woman in this study to use the word *annihilation* was Zilpha Elaw, who recorded an instance in her life when "self seemed annihilated." Guyon cried to God, "Let me be thy victim! Spare nothing to annihilate me." In doing so, she explained that her longing was "to be more reduced, and to become, as it were, nothing." Guyon claimed to have achieved this state and advised her readers to seek the death of self choosing "to enter into the most profound nothingness."[27]

In addition to nothingness, other characteristics of the annihilated soul are the infilling of charity or love, the death of pride and passion, perfect indifference, and passivity. Charity replaced that which was annihilated:

> This loss is called the annihilation of the powers, for although in themselves they still subsist, yet they seem annihilated to us, in proportion as charity fills and inflames, it becomes so strong, as by degrees to surmount all the activities of the will of man, subjecting it to that of God, in such sort that when the soul is docile, and leaves itself to be purified, and emptied of all that which it has of its own, opposite to the will of God, it finds itself by little and little, detached from every emotion of its own, and placed in a holy indifference wishing nothing but what God does and wills.
>
> When the will of the creature entirely submits to that of the Creator, suffering freely and voluntarily—and yielding only a concurrence of the divine will (which is its absolute submission)—suffering itself to be totally surmounted and destroyed, by the operations of love; this absorbs the will into itself, consummates it in that of God, and purifies it from all narrowness, dissimilitude and selfishness.[28]

She concluded her discussion, "And finally the powers are all concentrated and lost in pure love." Guyon described the results of this process as "the central union or unity—because that by means of the will and love, all are reunited in the center of the soul in God, our ultimate end."[29] Wesley's emphasis on love paralleled Guyon's belief that love was the goal of a Christian.

The annihilated soul is also devoid of pride and passion: "As it is pride which dies the last in the soul, so it is passion which is last destroyed in the outward conduct. A soul thoroughly annihilated or dead to itself finds nothing of rage left . . . But when annihilation is perfected all passion is gone, for it is incompatible with this state." Along with the absence of pride and passion, annihilation of the will resulted in "perfect indifference." Guyon described the soul in the state of entire resignation: "Outwardly, its life seems quite common; inwardly, it is wholly resigned to the divine will."[30]

Last, her annihilated self enabled Guyon to perceive herself passively as God's instrument: "I felt that what I spoke flowed from the fountain, and that I was only the instrument of him who made me speak." God deserved the credit or the blame; she was not responsible. "I am only a poor nothing. God is all-powerful. He delights to operate, and exercise his power by mere nothings." While it might appear that annihilation of the will culminated in a loss of freedom, Guyon reported the opposite: She was "set wholly at liberty."[31] This passive instrument also contrasts with the metaphor of the lute, quoted above, in which two lutes (Guyon's and God's) played music rather than one. Despite her contradictory language, Guyon modeled an active woman liberated to do God's work in the public arena. This was the example followed by Wesleyan/Holiness adherents who likewise shared much of her theology, along with her commitment to public service.

Madame Guyon's Indefatigable Ministries

Wesleyan/Holiness women found inspiration not only in Guyon's theology but also in her ministries, partly because they also faced opposition and shared similar ministries despite the centuries that separated them. Guyon modeled a woman with a strong sense of self despite her use of the word *annihilation*. She actively resisted all efforts to silence her. Enemies attempted to thwart her active ministries by tarnishing her reputation or by resorting to other means, but she persisted.

Guyon was born 18 April 1648 at Montargis in France. As a child, she attended various convent schools sponsored by Ursuline, Dominican, and Benedictine sisters. Shortly after turning fifteen, Guyon married a man twenty-two years her senior. After twelve years of marriage, Guyon's husband died on 21 July 1676. She reported that upon hearing the news of her husband's death, she cried: "Oh, my God, thou hast broken my bonds, and I will offer thee a sacrifice of praise." One wonders if her response reveals as negative a view of her marriage as it seems to modern ears. Left a widow with three children, Guyon assumed the business affairs for her family. She credited God for giving her the wisdom that resulted in a reputation "of being a skillful woman."[32]

After getting her finances in order, Guyon began contemplating a move to Geneva because she was concerned for the souls of its inhabitants. In an interview with the bishop of Paris, she informed him of her plan "to go into the country, to employ there my substance, to erect an establishment for all such as should be willing truly to serve God, and to give themselves unto him without reserve."[33] The bishop approved her plan, telling her that a group of New Catholics were starting a ministry to convert Protestants at Gex, near Geneva, and she could join them there. She reminded the bishop that her calling was to Geneva and not Gex, but he replied she could commute from one city to the other. Leaving her children was a hardship to her, and she ultimately decided to take her five-year-old daughter with her. She gave six months' annuity to the New Catholics she would be joining at Gex and departed for that city in 1681. Once in Gex, she gave the group the balance of her income. Despite her significant financial support, the New Catholics joined those who later persecuted her. Between her time at Gex and her return to Paris in 1686, Guyon lived at Grenoble and visited several other cities.

Guyon had initiated ministries on behalf of the poor as a young girl. During the years of her marriage, she continued to assist the poor, seeing that "the very best at my table was distributed among them." She listed specific activities on their behalf: "I went to visit the sick, to comfort them, to make their beds. I made ointments, dressed their wounds, buried their dead. I privately furnished tradesmen and mechanics where-with to keep up their shops. My heart was much opened toward my fellow-creatures in distress; and few indeed could carry charity much farther than our Lord enabled me to do, according to my state, both while married and since." Sometimes, she kept sick poor people in her home so she could care for them. Following the winter of 1680, she distributed ninety-six dozen loaves of bread every week from her home. She also employed poor boys and girls.[34] Particularly aware of the temptations facing young women, she saw that girls learned a livelihood so they did not need to resort to prostitution. Two hundred years later, Wesleyan/Holiness women performed many of these same ministries.

Guyon also had launched her ministry of spiritual counsel before leaving France. She wrote: "I longed indeed to contribute to the conversion of wandering souls, and God made use of me to convert several families before my departure." She was instrumental in the conversion of three Barnabites, members of a small religious order. Guyon became acquainted with Father La Combe, a superior with this order whom she met through an introduction from her brother, Father La Mothe. The bishop of Geneva eventually appointed La Combe as Guyon's spiritual director. She recounted a meeting with Father La Combe: "He told me he had remarked in my countenance a deep inwardness and presence of God, which had given him a strong desire of seeing me again. And God then assisted me to open to him the interior path of the soul, and conveyed so much grace to him through this poor channel, that he has owned to me since, that he went away changed into quite another man."[35] This encounter offers insight into her ministry. The depth of Guyon's spirituality was obvious to others who sought her for guidance in developing their own spiritual maturity, and she was not shy about reporting it.

Guyon voiced her concern for the spiritual condition of others in terms of her desire for the perfection of souls. Speaking of La Combe she declared that the Lord showed her that she would be instrumental in his "destruction of the old man" and that she also would direct others on this spiritual path. At one point, she reported that the Lord had revealed to her that her relationship with La Combe was like that between a mother and son since she was farther along in the spiritual journey. As her influence spread, some of La Combe's friars followed his example in "advancing toward perfection."[36] Even though she never used the phrase, Guyon asserted prophetic authority when she exercised spiritual influence over friars and others who held priestly authority. Her authority came directly from God rather than from the church hierarchy.

Guyon received confirmation of her calling from several sources. Father La Combe had written her that God had revealed to him "great designs" for her. During a trip to Paris before leaving for Gex, she visited a church and sought out a confessor. She began and ended her retelling of the conversation with the confessor by observing that this encounter surprised her. The confessor initiated the discussion: "I know not who you are, whether maid, wife or widow; but I feel a strong inward motion to exhort you to do what the Lord has made known to you, that he requires of you. I have nothing else to say." Guyon replied: "Father, I am a widow who have [*sic*] little children. What else could God require of me, but to take due care of them in their education?" The confessor responded to her defense of women's role as a mother: "I know nothing about this. You know if God manifests to you that he requires something of you; there is nothing in the world which ought to hinder you from doing his will. One may have to leave one's children to do that." Guyon reflected on the conversation: "I loved my children much, having great satisfaction in being with them, but resigned all to God to follow his will." She was willing to arrange for others to care for her children so she could fulfill God's will.[37]

Guyon also acknowledged two women who encouraged her and, in addition, played an influential role in her spiritual development. One was a Benedictine prioress, Genevieve Granger. Guyon respected Mother Granger and found it easy to confide in her: "She was the only person I could be free to open my state to . . . I placed an extreme confidence in Mother Granger. I concealed nothing from her, either of my sins or my pains. I would not have done the least thing without telling her." Granger advised Guyon regarding modesty of dress and the austerities she could practice.[38]

The second woman was the marchioness of Prunai, with whom Guyon established a "strong friendship and intimate union of spirit," comparing their relationship to that between two sisters. Guyon described her close friend: "This lady is one of extraordinary piety, who had quitted the splendor and noise of the Court, for the more silent satisfaction of a retired life, and to give herself up to God." When opposition first emerged in Gex, the marchioness offered Guyon asylum at her home in Turin.[39]

Encouraged by the support she received from various quarters, Guyon's evangelistic efforts extended across a wide spectrum of society. Many people sought out Guyon for advice on how to develop a deeper spiritual life. She counted numerous nuns and ecclesiastical leaders among her followers, as well as other groups of individuals: "I could not describe the great number of souls which were then given me, as well maids as wives, priests and friars. But there were three curates, one canon, and one grand-vicar, who were more particularly given me." The bishop of Geneva was among her disciples after she arrived in Gex. Roles were reversed as the bishop confessed to Guyon "his own deviations and infidelities . . . He was so clearly convinced, and so much affected, that he could not forbear expressing it. He opened his heart to me on what God had required of him . . . Every time, when I spoke to him, he entered into what I said, and acknowledged it to be the truth." In Marseilles, another ecclesiastic "open[ed] his inward state" to Guyon, receiving from the Lord "all that was necessary for him, from whence he was filled with joy, and thankful acknowledgements to God." Another bishop who profited from Guyon's ministry was the bishop of Verceil. She reported that he "conceived as strong a friendship for me as if I had been his sister; and his only pleasure, amidst his continual occupations, was to come and pass half an hour with me in speaking of God."[40] These examples also illustrate recognition of Guyon's prophetic authority and her willingness to share her spiritual leadership in her autobiography.

Guyon maintained that she possessed the gift of discernment, which assisted her as she counseled with those, whatever their place in society, who sought her advice. She remembered that she first was aware of this gift when working with a nun. Subsequently, at Grenoble, she used this gift in helping others: "I felt myself invested, all of a sudden, with the apostolic state, and discerned the conditions of the souls of such persons as spoke to me, and that with so much facility, that they were surprised at it, and said one to another, 'that I gave every one of them the very thing they had stood in need of.'"[41]

News of Guyon's ministry spread by word of mouth. At Grenoble, she generally spent from 6 A.M. until 8 P.M. "speaking of the Lord" to those who consulted her. Sometimes she was so busy that there was no time to eat. Her heavy schedule belies the stereotype of the quietist who spent all her time in passive communion with God. Guyon's continued concern for the poor and those who were ill also contradicts this misconception about her quietism. Along with her ministry of providing spiritual advice, she was influential in establishing several hospitals.[42] Wesleyan/Holiness women who followed Guyon likewise combined a concern for the soul as well as for the body.

Guyon found time in her crowded schedule to record her religious insights on "the interior path of faith, under the comparison of torrents, or of streams and rivers." This text was printed at Grenoble by a counselor of the Parliament, who read it and thought it would be beneficial to others. This publication was probably the *Short and Easy Method of Prayer,* which detractors believed was sufficient reason to banish her from the city. She listed "two little printed books" along with her commentaries on the Bible among her writings. She related the process of writing the commentaries: "When I began I was impelled to write the passage, and instantly its explication was given me, which I also wrote, going on with inconceivable expedition, light being poured in upon me in such a manner, that I found I had in myself latent treasures of wisdom and knowledge which I had not yet known of."[43] This statement reveals a positive view of self that, despite claims of annihilation, seemed far from "dead."

Not every church leader welcomed Guyon's ministry. Several rejected Guyon's prophetic authority and sought to diminish her spiritual influence. Guyon's views on inward prayer, expressed verbally and in writing, contributed to the opposition she faced. Rejecting Guyon's prophetic authority, some friars told a poor woman who had come under Guyon's influence that "it was only for churchmen to pray, and that she was very bold to practice it."[44]

The fact that she was female contributed to the antagonism against Guyon. She disclosed that the superior and master of the novices of one order of friars "declared against me, without knowing me; and were grievously chagrined that a woman, as they said, should be so much flocked to, and so much sought after." According to Guyon, "they had contempt for the gift which was lodged in so mean an instrument."[45] Guyon's sex embittered her adversaries while jealousy further fueled their sexism.

One bishop who came to Guyon's aid was the bishop of Meaux, who confirmed her calling late in her life. After reading an earlier version of her autobiography, he commented "that he had found therein such an unction as he had rarely done in other books, and that he had spent three days in reading it, with an impression of the presence of God on his mind all that time." Besides his hearty endorsement of her autobiography, the bishop of Meaux also researched ecclesiastical histories and reported "we may see that God has sometimes made use of laymen, and of women to instruct, edify, and help souls in their progress to perfection."[46] The bishop defended her right to engage in public religious activities. Despite the friendship and endorsement of the bishop of Meaux and others, her opponents, nevertheless, continued to denounce her.

Some enemies sought to tarnish Guyon's reputation by associating her theological views with Molinos, who had run afoul of the Inquisition. The job of the inquisitors was to root out and punish any who appeared to deviate from orthodox Roman Catholic belief. Among other charges, Guyon's opponents convinced the king that she corresponded with Molinos. Guyon responded that she had never heard of Molinos until these allegations were made. As a result of the false association, Guyon revised her writings to distance them from Molinos's teachings: "I had written them at a time when the affairs of Molinos had not broken out, I used the less precaution in expressing my thoughts, not imagining that they would ever be turned into an evil sense."[47]

Opposition came from several other sources. The bishop of Geneva, who had initially befriended her and benefited from her spiritual counsel, turned against her. Guyon observed that he was easily swayed by others and suggested that he along with other confessors was jealous because of her popularity. The bishop was the source of rumors that romantically linked Guyon and Father La Combe, her spiritual director, by writing letters denouncing her to various cities, including Paris and Grenoble. Guyon did not divulge the contents of these letters other than to disclose that the bishop alleged that she had traveled to Turin to pursue La Combe. The bishop further enlisted his nephew to visit from house to house in Grenoble, spreading rumors in an attempt to tarnish her reputation.[48]

Rather than standing by her, Guyon's relatives openly renounced her. They were indeed among her staunchest adversaries. Upon her return to Paris, her brother, Father La Mothe, enlisted by the bishop of Geneva, led the attack against Guyon and Father La Combe. La Mothe willingly joined Guyon's detractors since he was incensed that his sister had not given him a pension from her income as he had expected and because she sometimes refused his advice. La Mothe joined the bishop of Geneva and others who plotted to falsely accuse Guyon and La Combe of impropriety at Marseilles. The ruse included counterfeiting a letter from someone in Marseilles to the archbishop of Paris that outlined their alleged scandalous behavior. The author of the letter purported to have witnesses who would corroborate the story. The rumors and accusations should have subsided when Guyon revealed that Father La Combe had never been to Marseilles in his life. In this instance, though, the truth did not squelch the falsehoods: "Every imaginable device was used to terrify me by threats, forged letters, and by memorials drawn up against me, accusing me of teaching erroneous doctrines, and of living a bad life and urging me to flee the country to escape the consequences of exposure." Disparaging stories regarding the two proliferated despite the fact that he lived approximately 375 miles from Guyon and had only made three visits to see Guyon as her confessor.[49]

Guyon's efforts to prove their innocence were unsuccessful. Additional false stories abounded. Guyon recounted that "envious people wrote against me, without knowing me. They said I was a sorceress, that it was by a magic power I attracted souls, that everything in me was diabolical; that if I did some charities, it was because I coined, and put off false money." Confessors in Grenoble insinuated that penitents had "a great affection" for her, implying that the affection was not platonic. Other letters diagnosed her as "mad" and a "monster of pride."[50]

Authorities confined Guyon at St. Mary's convent in January 1688. They demanded that she turn over her writings on the Bible, but she refused to do so unless she was released. Guyon became acquainted with Fénelon after leaving St. Mary's. Archbishop Fénelon, also a quietist, is the person most often associated with Guyon today. They first met each other because Fénelon was a friend of her son-in-law's family. Fénelon agreed with her theology to the extent that Guyon asserted that "no one more fully imbibed my sentiments than he."[51]

When her theological views again came under suspicion, Guyon "wrote a work to facilitate their examination, and to spare them as much time and trouble as I could, which was to collect a great number of passages out of approved writers, which showed the conformity of my writings with those used by the holy penmen." Guyon compiled this defense at her inquisitors' request.[52]

Guyon wrote her autobiography in obedience to a demand from her spiritual director. She had apparently written a short autobiography but had been ordered to burn it and begin again. Addressing her spiritual director in several places, she reminded him that she incorporated extended discussions of matters such as the relationship with her husband and her persecution only because he had ordered her to include everything about her life. She recognized, though, that it was impossible to write an all-encompassing autobiography since it was inconceivable that she could remember everything.[53] While not explicitly making the point, Guyon acknowledged that the portrayal of her self would be incomplete. She wrote that she expected the director to destroy her book after he and others had benefited spiritually from her writings.

Guyon's direct comments to other potential readers, however, indicated her desire to minister more broadly through her writing: "For you, my dear children, if my chains and my imprisonment in any way afflict you, I pray that they may serve to engage you to seek nothing but God for himself alone, and never to desire to possess him but by the death of your whole selves; never to seek to be something in the ways of the Spirit, but choose ye to enter into the most profound nothingness." In a later selection, she again addressed readers as her children: "I shall say something of the interior dispositions I was then in, and I shall think my time well employed, if it serves you who are willing to be of the number of my children, and if it serves such as are already my children, to induce them to let God glorify himself in them after his manner, and not after their own. If there be anything which they do not comprehend, let them die to themselves, and they will find it much easier to learn by experience than from anything I could say; for expression never equals experience."[54] Wesleyan/Holiness women considered themselves Guyon's children and not only followed her theological example where it agreed with Wesley but also authored autobiographies outlining their own theology and the public ministries that flowed from it.

Guyon was arrested again in December 1694 and sent to the convent at Meaux for six months. She was jailed at Vincennes in 1695 and finally at the infamous Bastille from 1698 to 1703. Guyon credited God for enabling her to endure the ongoing persecution she faced: "His invisible hand supported me; else I had sunk under so many probations." Guyon covered this period of her life in a few pages, concluding her autobiography with this disclaimer: "I shall not speak of that long persecution, which has made so much noise, for a series of ten years imprisonments, in all sorts of prisons, and of a banishment almost as long, and not yet ended, through crosses, calumnies, and all imaginable sorts of sufferings. There are facts too odious on the part of divers persons, which charity induces me to cover." When released from the Bastille, authorities banished Guyon to the city of Blois, where she died on 9 June 1717.[55]

While quietism generally is associated with passivity, this trait may only be appropriately applied to Guyon in the sense that she passively waited before God in prayer. Her life and ministry cannot be characterized as passive. She actively responded to what she understood to be God's will: that she expand her ministry through spiritual counseling and writing. She sought to meet the needs of the poor. When persecuted, she did not passively accept her plight. Instead, she fought back, defending herself against false accusations and malicious rumors. Rather than quietly accepting the judgment of her opponents, she prepared a written justification of her theology. In this way, she also served as a prototype for her Wesleyan/Holiness daughters.

CHAPTER THREE

Mary Bosanquet Fletcher and Hester Ann Roe Rogers: Methodist Women in England

British Trajectory

Mary Bosanquet Fletcher (1739–1815) and Hester Ann Roe Rogers (1756–1794), as well as Madame Guyon, were women listed by Lizzie Miller, an American Wesleyan/Holiness evangelist, as public workers for God.[1] Both Rogers and Fletcher were significant co-laborers and close personal friends of John Wesley, who frequently corresponded with them. While Fletcher and Rogers did not mention Guyon in their own writings, subsequent Wesleyan/Holiness women traced a trajectory of women in public ministry that extended from Guyon to these English women. Wesleyan/Holiness women read and valued the autobiographies of Fletcher and Rogers because they provided models and inspiration for readers who chose to be ministers rather than being confined to the private sphere. Hereafter, rather than attempting to use their maiden names when discussing their lives or writings before marriage, I will consistently use their married names for the sake of clarity, except in specific references to their marriages.

Historian Earl Kent Brown recovered information on forty-five Methodist women who were class and/or band meeting leaders and twenty-seven women preachers who were contemporaries of John Wesley. They, along with other British Methodist women, wrote journals that incorporated information regarding their public ministries. Rogers's and Fletcher's books remained in print throughout the nineteenth century. In fact, Fletcher's autobiography was so popular that it appeared in twenty editions by 1850.[2] Likewise, publishers in both England and the United States reprinted Rogers's narrative numerous times.

Jennie Smith, Anna Prosser, and Lucy Drake Osborn were among the American Wesleyan/Holiness women who read Rogers and Fletcher for guidance in their quest for sanctification. Mary Cole and Almira Losee also read their autobiographies, while Sarah Cooke reported she was "wonderfully helped" by reading the lives of these two women. Cooke included Rogers's and Fletcher's narratives in a short list that she highly recommended: "I know of no books, outside of the Bible, like these autobiographies." Cooke specifically reported that she missed her copy of Fletcher's autobiography, which was destroyed, along with Guyon's autobiography and other belongings, in the 1871 Chicago fire. Lizzie Miller included Rogers in a list of Christians whose "holy lives stimulated me to do good and be useful every day." Zilpha Elaw visited Leeds while in England, designating it as "a place rendered memorable to the Methodist societies by the labours of Mrs. Fletcher, whose ministry the Lord so signally blest with the communications of His Spirit."[3]

Jennie Fowler Willing, who wrote a regular column on women in *Guide to Holiness* magazine, contributed four articles on Fletcher in 1900. In one article, she stressed the importance of Fletcher's writing as well as Rogers's book and a few other books distributed by Methodist itinerant ministers to establish their converts in the faith. Willing admonished: "If I can induce a hundred of our *Guide* readers to get each a copy of the *Life of Mary Fletcher*, and put it into the hands of as many young people as will read it, this writing will not be in vain."[4]

Phoebe Palmer attested to the popularity of Rogers's autobiography: "From childhood, I have perused and reperused the Memoirs of Hester A. Rogers; and having with thousands of others, communed with her through her writings in the narration of her early and later trials and triumphs." Rogers's writings, and to a lesser extent Fletcher's narrative, had an immense impact on the development of Palmer's theology.[5]

Fletcher and Rogers engaged in ministries normally considered outside the realm of women's appropriate behavior, and their lives and their writings justified their public activities. Felicity Nussbaum, a feminist political critic who is one of the few theorists to explore eighteenth-century British Methodist autobiographies, maintained: "Conversion narratives in the eighteenth century, especially those written within the Methodist camp, thus take on an ideological framework that acquires paradigmatic force to affect and even determine the way people perceive and inscribe reality." Wesleyan/Holiness women read Fletcher's and Rogers's narratives and noticed a reality they could emulate. This is particularly true in the case of Fletcher, who provided an alternate reality that portrayed a woman who expanded her role by preaching in public. Palmer quoted Fletcher in *The Promise of the Father*, her defense of women preachers. Likewise, Jarena Lee referred an opponent to Fletcher's example when he claimed that women preachers were a recent development. Sarah Cooke also identified

Fletcher as a woman God called to ministry.[6] Wesleyan/Holiness women consciously followed Fletcher's lead in pursuing a public role as preachers.

Apparently, literary theorist Carolyn Heilbrun was unaware of the tradition of autobiographies written by women within the Methodist tradition when she authored *Writing a Woman's Life* in 1988. She bemoaned the fact that women have no "alternative stories" that might function as scripts for them to follow if they wanted to choose unconventional lives.[7] Wesleyan/Holiness women of the nineteenth and twentieth centuries had access to autobiographies written by their foremothers in the faith who had embraced a public path not taken by most of their contemporaries. Journal writing was a natural outgrowth of the emphasis on testimony within Methodist class meetings in England in the eighteenth century. Members shared their spiritual journeys orally in small groups. John Wesley instructed his followers to write journals, so it is not surprising that many left extensive accounts of their lives, some of which were published after their death.[8] Spiritual autobiography was a direct outgrowth of Methodist class meetings and worship since exhorters centered on their religious quest, formulating an oral account of their lives that could later be written down.

Methodists along with Quakers, Baptists, and smaller groups, such as the Fifth Monarchists and Diggers, comprised the religious dissenters in England during the eighteenth century. During Wesley's lifetime, members of Methodist societies maintained their affiliation with the Church of England. They dissented from their church's lack of emphasis on Christian piety and maturity by attending additional services sponsored by Methodists. One distinguishing characteristic of dissenting groups was their general acceptance of women preachers. By far, the largest number of women preachers were Quakers. Historian Rebecca Larson calculated that there were "thirteen hundred to fifteen hundred women ministers active in the transatlantic Quaker community during the first three-quarters of the eighteenth century."[9] Methodist women joined Quaker women and other dissenters who assumed a public role in the religious arena in England.

Methodist women worked with John Wesley in various capacities. The trajectory for women's public involvement commenced in the class meetings, obligatory gatherings where everyone, male or female, was encouraged to testify and pray. Today's equivalent of class meetings are growth and support groups sponsored by local congregations. Those who were more mature spiritually attended band meetings on a voluntary basis. Women led classes that consisted of women and men and bands segregated by sex. Wesley initially opposed women preachers but gradually modified his position based on both theological and pragmatic grounds. In Wesley's estimation, the success of women such as Sarah Crosby (1729–1804) justified and legitimated women's increased public activity. Crosby led a class that grew to two hundred members. Even so, Wesley originally advised Crosby not to think of herself as a woman preacher but told her to limit her speaking to simply sharing what was in her heart, reading from his *Notes* on the Bible or from a sermon prepared by someone else. Eight years later, in 1769, he wrote Crosby that she could pray or exhort but should not take a text or speak for more than five minutes. Wesley made a distinction between preaching and exhorting: preaching was stating and applying the meaning of the Bible, while exhorting took place after the sermon, during which time the exhorter coaxed the congregation to respond to the message. By 1771 Wesley removed the last barrier and permitted women to preach. Historian Paul Chilcote documented that Mary Fletcher wrote a letter that year that influenced Wesley's change of heart. Chilcote described Fletcher's letter as "the first serious defense of women's preaching in Methodism."[10] Preachers working under Wesley were either men ordained by the Church of England or lay preachers, both men and women.

Joyce Quiring Erickson itemized the contents of the journals written by Rogers and Fletcher. They consisted of "a composite of conversion narrative, spiritual autobiography, and hagiographic commentary, included in a single volume that includes first-person narrative, diary entries, letters, and third-person accounts of events."[11] They were not biographies. Fletcher chronicled her life in narrative form until 1781. At this point, the text switched to a journal format that overlapped the autobiographical material somewhat, beginning with 1772. The book concluded with a firsthand account of Fletcher's final illness and death written by a friend, Miss Tooth, and "a Review of Her Character," penned by the editor. Approximately 40 percent of Rogers's book consisted of "spiritual letters," to use her editor's phrase.

Earl Kent Brown described the journals of Fletcher, Rogers, and others: "They were not written as autobiography or to communicate to others. They were, in general, written as a spiritual exercise—to recall to the writer the grace of God working in her life. Some of them, like Mrs. Fletcher and Mrs. Rogers, included a great deal of narrative about day-to-day activity and concerns along with their spiritual meditations." Contrary to Brown's assessment, Fletcher may have initially written as "a spiritual exercise," but she ultimately intended for her writings to survive her. She assumed her papers would be edited after her death because she left explicit instructions in reference to one conflict that she documented: "O let not one word of this be left out."[12] Perhaps a factor contributing to the popularity of Fletcher's and Rogers's autobiographies was the very fact that they included narrative along with an accounting of their spiritual journeys.

Sanctification

For both Hester Ann Rogers and Mary Fletcher, the doctrine of sanctification was of paramount interest. Rogers wrote extensively on sanctification while Fletcher chronicled her ongoing spiritual journey as a sanctified Christian. Their preoccupation with sanctification reflected the emphasis John Wesley placed upon this doctrine. As contemporaries of Wesley, Rogers and Fletcher shared his understanding of the doctrine of sanctification. Like Wesley, they also were inconsistent in their use of terms. While sanctification refers to the process that leads to perfection or holiness, Wesley and his followers often used the terms interchangeably. The following discussion reflects an attempt to be clear about whether the women are talking about the process of sanctification or the goal of holiness. Concurring with Wesley's view, Fletcher and Rogers contended sanctification was a second work of grace, made possible by faith. It involved the removal of inbred sin and resulted in pure love. Fletcher's ministry, in particular, reflected Wesley's emphasis on the Christian's responsibility to love one's neighbor by meeting the needs of the poor.

Fletcher defined the result of sanctification as Christian perfection, "a heart simplified by love divine, and kept each moment, by faith, from the pollution of sin." She testified that she was sanctified during the Methodist revival of 1761 and 1762, when "an earnest desire was stirred up in many hearts, after full salvation," another term for holiness. Fletcher believed that faith was necessary on the seeker's part in order to achieve this blessing. At the moment of sanctification, Fletcher reported: "I felt a calmness overspread my spirit, and by faith I laid hold on Jesus as my full Saviour." Rogers quoted from Wesley's sermon "The Scripture Way of Salvation" to bolster her case for the role of faith in sanctification. Rogers also acknowledged the role of free will by insisting that believers needed to cooperate with God. Faith is "the only instrument" required, since, according to Acts 26:18, "we are sanctified by faith in Jesus."[13]

Following Wesley, Rogers initially believed that Christians had to wait until close to death to achieve holiness, the goal of sanctification. However, she ultimately came to the conclusion, as did Wesley, that it could be attainable earlier in this life. She quoted 1 Thess. 5:23 ("Now the very God of peace sanctify you wholly") as scriptural support for this conviction that Christians could achieve holiness long before their death. In correspondence with Wesley, Rogers referred to a sermon he delivered that confirmed her belief that the process of sanctification did not have to be long and drawn out. During Rogers's quest for sanctification, she reported that Satan assailed her by suggesting that her prayer seeking sanctification would be a mockery. After overcoming this hurdle with God's help, she further related that Satan tried a different tack, suggesting she had not been converted long enough. In a last-ditch effort, Satan claimed she would lose the experience if she had it. This did not prove to be the case, but Rogers admitted that while she never lost the experience of holiness, her witness of perfect love was not always clear.[14]

While the seeker's role was to have faith, God's role in sanctification was the removal of inbred sin, which Rogers described as "the strong man, and all his armor of unbelief and sin" and "God's foes in that heart." According to Rogers, sanctification destroys the root of all sin. The result of sanctification is heart holiness or full salvation. In place of inbred sin, Rogers reported that God's "whole image [was] stamped on my heart."[15]

When Fletcher was sanctified, she experienced a sense of purity that was indescribable. As a result of sanctification, she now had a clean heart. She did not mention the removal of inbred sin in her testimony of sanctification, but this is implied by her use of the words *purity* and *clean heart.* She made a few brief references to inbred sin elsewhere in her journal. With regard to sanctification, she also quoted the Bible verse, "I will thoroughly purge away thy dross and take away all thy tin." For Fletcher, purification was not completed at the moment of sanctification but was a continuing process. She wrote: "The Spirit of God is a spirit of sanctification, purifying the heart. I do feel it is working that in me." This belief in a gradual process of purification contrasted with Rogers's view that the death of sin was instantaneous.[16]

Rogers explained to a seeker that while faith is the instrument of sanctification, "faith lays hold of the blood of Christ, as the procuring cause of our holiness, and which *alone* cleanseth from all sin." Rogers employed several metaphors to describe the removal of inbred sin in a letter to a Miss Loxdale: "Behold rivers of living waters gushing out of your Redeemer's wounds,—water that will wash your inbred sin away. Is not the Holy Ghost waiting to apply the efficacious blood, and make you white as snow?"[17]

Like Guyon, Fletcher and Rogers spoke of annihilation or the death of self. They appropriated this language to describe the purification that accompanied sanctification. Fletcher professed that sanctification annihilated the self and contended that Christians "must become a whole burnt sacrifice." Those "most emptied of self . . . and most fully prepared to receive and reflect the image of Christ should eternally bear the highest resemblance to their Lord." Fletcher concluded that "nothing could bring honour to God, but our becoming nothing, that he might be all in all!" Fletcher prayed continually: "Lord, break me in pieces! Melt me down, and let me flow, and more fully take the mould divine!" Rogers, similarly, related sanctification to the death of self: "But O! how precious do I now prove the experience of these words, 'I am crucified with Christ; nevertheless I live; yet not I, but Christ liveth in me."

She wrote of her experience: "Yea, Lord, my soul is delivered of her burden. I am emptied of all; I am at thy feet, a helpless, worthless worm; but I take hold of thee as my fulness!"[18] Fletcher and Rogers agreed with Guyon that the self must die. The death of self did not signify passivity on the part of these women but rather enabled them to fulfill public roles as women who claimed God's endorsement of their activities. The British women's view differed from Guyon, though, in that they never mentioned mortification or self-induced suffering as a means of seeking sanctification.

Fletcher explained how sanctification related to perfection: "I saw sanctification in a clearer light than ever. It is to be perfectly ingrafted into the vine; to have no impediment remaining to hinder the flow of the sap, and while the soul thus abide by faith it brings forth much fruit, and experimentally knows the meaning of those words of St. John, *He that abideth in Him sinneth not.*" She admitted, though, that in her case: "I know I do taste of pure love, but I do not abide in Jesus, therefore I do not bring forth much fruit."[19]

Fletcher referred to perfection as perfect love with God. It was "love made perfect." Rogers also spoke of her intimate communion with God in terms of love: "I am conquered and subdued by love. Thy love sinks me into nothing . . . I am now one with God; the intercourse is open; sin, inbred sin, no longer hinders the close communion, and God is all my own!" God's love replaced inbred sin. She also spoke of a longing to be "dissolved in love." Rogers used similar mystical language in a letter to a seeker: "[God] is preparing your heart for his perfect love: he is emptying you of self that you may be swallowed up in him."[20]

Fletcher, too, employed a mystical metaphor when she explained her relationship with God: "Being taken into Christ, as a drop of water, into the ocean, I lose myself in him." While she did not attribute her language to Madame Guyon, the similarity is striking. As discussed earlier, Guyon described her union with God "even as a little drop of water, cast into the sea, receives the qualities of the sea." Further, Fletcher utilized mystical language when she reported a dream in which Christ called her to minister to the rich and poor alike: "It seemed to me I sunk down before him as if I were sweetly melting into nothing." Another time, she spoke of her heart being "melted into love!" The close relationship or union with God enabled these women to claim God's authority when they engaged in public ministries.[21]

Ministries

Mary Fletcher's Anglican parents opposed her affiliation with Methodists. Her first contact with Methodism occurred at age six when she conversed with a Methodist servant. In her early teens, she met another Methodist, Mrs. Lefevre, who was a friend of the family. Initially, Fletcher's parents were unaware that Mrs. Lefevre was a Methodist. Reflecting the influence of Methodists, Fletcher refused to attend plays with the family and began wearing plain clothes as a teenager. Devout members of the Church of England, her parents resented her rejection of their lifestyle and expressed concern that she would persuade her two younger brothers to adopt her views. When she refused to promise to keep her convictions to herself, Fletcher and her parents decided that it was best for her to leave home. She had received an inheritance from her grandmother that she then used to support herself.[22] The estrangement, occurring when Fletcher was twenty-two, was not absolute, yet tension persisted within the family.

In 1763 Fletcher began an orphanage with the assistance of Sarah Ryan, also a Methodist, in the home at Leytonstone that had been willed to her. She credited Ryan with the "resolution and diligence" to carry out the plans for the orphanage, and they became close co-workers. Fletcher called Ryan "the friend of my soul" and claimed their "hearts were united as David and Jonathan's." The motive for their work was love. This was one means of fulfilling Jesus' admonition to "love thy neighbor as thyself" (Luke 10:27), which Fletcher believed was a natural result of sanctification. She explicitly stated her goal was "to save their bodies from misery, and their souls from eternal destruction." She was a primitivist in that her aim was to follow the biblical example of female deacons in the early church who lodged strangers, cared for children, and performed good works. Altogether, she and Ryan ministered to thirty-five children and thirty-four adults at the home. Fletcher's care for the poor included making medicines and clothes for them. She consciously followed the pattern of August Francke, the prominent Pietist who had established an orphanage in 1695 at Halle, located in the area now known as Germany. After five years, she transferred her ministry to Yorkshire and worked there for thirteen years until her marriage. Like Guyon, Fletcher's interest in the poor persisted following her marriage and throughout her life.[23]

Fletcher led both classes and bands and also preached. She was fortunate to have early models of female preachers. As a teen, she had heard Sarah Crosby preach, and in a Methodist revival several years later she commented that both men and women preached. Fletcher received her call to preach in a dream. Jesus stood before her and spoke to her, saying: "I will send thee to a people that are not a people, and I will go with thee. Bring them unto me, for I will lay my hand upon them and heal them. Fear not, only believe!" She inaugurated her preaching ministry at weekly public meetings at the orphanage, where she "read a chapter, and sometimes spoke from it." In her first actual sermon in 1773 she spoke on Nebuchadnezzer, a king mentioned in the Hebrew Bible. This is the first recorded instance of preaching by a Methodist woman that included the scriptural text. She reported after preaching: "The Lord gave me freedom of speech." Her prayer before preaching a sermon was to have full liberty, "such as was given at the out-pouring of the Spirit on the day of Pentecost," when both women and men preached. She also recorded that she sensed God's power when preaching. Fletcher's experience of full liberty and power when preaching reflected her egalitarian primitivism because she explicitly compared it to the biblical event of Pentecost recorded in Acts 1–2. She continued to feel God's liberty and power even when she was in declining health near the end of her life.[24] There were no constraints, either personal or cultural, that held Fletcher back when she preached.

Soon Fletcher's preaching engagements necessitated that she travel away from home. She reported the opposition she faced. In 1775, one man "was sure I must be an impudent woman; no modest woman, he was sure, could proceed thus." An audience of two thousand to three thousand heard her preach at Huddersfield. Fletcher responded to opposition there: "If I have a word to speak from [God], He will make my way. If not, the door will be shut. I am only to shew the meekness of wisdom, and leave all to God." About a week following her engagement in Huddersfield, she mused: "I have been more abundantly led to reflect on the difficulties of the path I am called in." Following this statement, Fletcher offered three reasons why she spoke of giving a meeting rather than explicitly saying she was preaching: "First, it is less ostentatious. Secondly, it leaves me at liberty to speak more or less as I feel myself led. Thirdly, it gives less offence to those who watch for it."[25] Fletcher was pragmatic. Even though she was actually preaching, her alternative language reflected her attempt to avoid drawing negative attention to herself as a woman preacher.

Despite the caution in the language she used to describe her work, opponents suggested that she join the Quakers since they already had many women preachers, claiming that "here nobody can bear with you." Fletcher replied: "Though I believe the Quakers have still a good deal of God among them, yet, I think the Spirit of the Lord is more at work among the Methodists." Then, she made her final point: "Besides, I do nothing but what Mr. Wesley approves."[26]

Felicity Nussbaum contended that Methodist women were "largely untroubled, at least in public texts, with the desire to resist patriarchal church leaders on the questions of women's preaching." Fletcher's approach confirms Nussbaum's observation. She saw no need to argue her case since she had Wesley's endorsement. She also knew she was in God's favor since God continually granted her liberty and freedom in preaching, a fact she noted frequently. Moreover, she specifically spoke of being "conscious of the Lord's approval" while preaching.[27] This reflected her reliance on prophetic authority which came directly from God.

Later in life, Mary Bosanquet married and entered into joint ministry at Madeley with her husband, Rev. John Fletcher. He was a close associate of John Wesley and, like Wesley, was an ordained priest in the Church of England. Reverend Fletcher initiated the courtship in June 1781 by writing her a letter confessing he had had "a regard" for her for twenty-five years. She had first mentioned him in her diary years earlier, before founding the orphanage with Sarah Ryan. Even though at that time Bosanquet was committed to remaining single, she did speculate that marriage to Reverend Fletcher might be "rather an help than an hindrance to my soul." One wonders why it took twenty-five years for them to reveal their affection for each other. Shortly after declaring himself, Reverend Fletcher traveled to Yorkshire to visit Bosanquet and remained for a month. The two decided to marry, with the wedding taking place on 12 November 1781. The new wife wrote that she was more than happy with her mate: "I have such a husband as is in every thing suited to me. He bears with all my faults and failings in a manner that continually reminds me of that word, *Love your wives as Christ loved the church*. His constant endeavor is to make me happy; his strongest desire, my spiritual growth." After only three years of marriage, Reverend Fletcher died 14 August 1785. She noted thereafter every anniversary of his death and every wedding anniversary in her journal. One year she recorded her ongoing grief: "My wound continually bleeds."[28]

Before his death, the Fletchers had built a chapel in Madeley, where Methodists were assured a pulpit. She preached in that chapel and recorded preaching from sixty to ninety minutes to crowds in various other locations. Fletcher continued her ministries for thirty years after her husband's death. Even after age began to slow her down, she was preaching five services a week in 1814, a year before her death at age seventy-six. She conceded that she was weak but reported she could still preach loud enough for everyone to hear.[29]

Hester Ann Roe Rogers's name did not appear in Mary Fletcher's published autobiography. However, Rogers reported meeting her when traveling with Reverend Fletcher and Mrs. Crosby.[30] This was before the Fletchers married. Unfortunately, Rogers was silent regarding their conversation or her first impressions.

Hester Ann Rogers was known for her piety. Her life exemplified the holiness that Methodists sought to emulate. While she did not preach, she did lead Methodist classes and bands, called on the sick, and corresponded with those seeking sanctification. At one point, she conducted two classes,

Sarah A. Cooke, author of *The Handmaiden of the Lord, or Wayside Sketches* (Chicago: T. B. Arnold, 1896).

one with thirty-eight members and one with thirty-six, as well as a class of young girls. Rogers's path to Methodism was a difficult one. Like Fletcher, her family disapproved. Rogers's mother threatened to disown her if she even listened to Methodists, but her daughter persisted. When she experienced conversion, Rogers cast her lot with the Methodists. Once disowned, she could not do hard labor to support herself, so as a compromise she became a servant in her own home in November 1774. This punishment lasted eight months. Threats and reproofs failed to have their desired effect, and Rogers remained a Methodist.[31]

Rogers and John Wesley first met in her hometown of Macclesfield on 1 April 1776. She reported: "He behaved to me with parental tenderness." Wesley, age seventy-three at the time, encouraged the young woman, now twenty, during an hour-long conversation. After their meeting, Wesley continued to write encouraging letters to Rogers.[32]

Hester Ann Roe married Rev. James Rogers, a widower, on 19 August 1784. Roe and his first wife had been friends, and Roe cared for Mrs. Rogers following childbirth until her death soon afterward. Anticipating her death, the first Mrs. Rogers had approved of the future union between her husband and Roe. Following their marriage, Rogers assisted her husband, who pastored in Dublin and Cork before his assignment in London. Reverend Rogers credited his wife for adding approximately two thousand members to the Methodist Society in Dublin while they worked there. Hester Ann Rogers died in childbirth at age thirty-nine.[33]

The autobiographies of Fletcher and Rogers, who worked closely with John Wesley, provided alternative stories for Wesleyan/Holiness women who modeled their active religious lives after these foremothers. While Carolyn Heilbrun rightfully claimed that most women had no such stories, Wesleyan/Holiness women inherited stories of women who engaged in public ministries and served as models for imitation. Fletcher and Rogers provided precedents by successfully challenging restrictive gender roles. Their writings also played a crucial role in the spiritual growth and theological understanding of Wesleyan/Holiness women who knew the value of autobiographies from their own experience. Writing in 1896, Sarah Cooke reported that others shared her appreciation of the spiritual significance of these autobiographies: "In traveling, I often meet with Christians of deep experience, who received their first religious light, especially on holiness, through the lives and writings of . . . Mrs. Fletcher, Mrs. H. A. Rogers, and others."[34] Perhaps Cooke hoped to provide inspiration to others through her own autobiography.

CHAPTER FOUR

Sanctification: Autobiography as Testimony

Many Wesleyan/Holiness women confessed their reliance on the autobiographies of Hester Ann Rogers and Mary Fletcher as they formulated their theology, particularly the doctrine of sanctification. The similarities become obvious in this chapter, which focuses on the experience of sanctification as expressed by Wesleyan/Holiness women in their autobiographies. At the outset, it is crucial to remember that these women were lay theologians who, for the most part, lacked a college education. Like a majority of their male counterparts, they were not seminary trained. They were not outlining a systematic theology. Rather, they based their theological understanding on their personal experience as it was confirmed in the Bible and by the experience of others. Drawing heavily on the writings of Phoebe Palmer, sometimes intentionally and sometimes indirectly, these women appropriated her formula for sanctification. This chapter highlights Palmer's understanding of holiness as stated in *The Way of Holiness* (1867) and illustrates the indebtedness that Wesleyan/Holiness women owed Palmer for their own theology of holiness.

The *auto* component of autobiography concerns the self and its representations. Wesleyan/Holiness women did not engage in protracted reflection on the self. For the most part, their writings contained very little introspection. The primary explicit consideration of self took place within discussions of sanctification. In examining the self with respect to sanctification, my interest is the spiritual self, the self in relation to God. I am not analyzing the psychological understanding of self, but rather emphasizing the spiritual self as understood by the women themselves. The spiritual self was not restricted to Sunday morning and then left behind in the sanctuary. Instead, it permeated all areas of life. The autobiographers' description of the spiritual self in their narratives utilized language familiar to others in the Wesleyan/Holiness movement. It was not unique. The spiritual journey of those who believed in sanctification consisted of three stages in the development of the self: the sinful self, the saved self, and the sanctified self. Sermons depicted the heart at each phase of the spiritual quest. Lela McConnell, herself an evangelist, reported that her colleague, Miss Archer, used pictures of colored hearts on canvas in her "Three Hearts Lesson": "First, the black heart of sin; then, the red heart which was the saved heart covered by the Blood, but yet with the root of carnality in it; and last, the white heart, representing the clean, sanctified heart."[1] Two types of sin characterized the sinful self before it encountered Christ: it commits sin and it is sinful by its very nature. The saved self has been converted, or saved, from the actual sins a person has committed. A radical difference existed between the saved self and the sanctified self, which is purified through the removal of the sinful, or carnal, nature, the second form of sin. Some women spoke of the self being crucified as a result of sanctification. For most of these women, the self that is sinful by nature and coexists with the saved self died at sanctification. The sanctified self was a transformed self as evidenced by such language as the old man being crucified and replaced by the new man or new creation as a result of sanctification. *Old man* and *new man* were generic terms defining the self before and after sanctification.

The implications of the sanctified self extended far beyond the theological ramifications of the removal of the sinful self. Sanctification required total consecration of one's life to God. While consecration could be interpreted as self-sacrifice, in actuality women were consecrating themselves to God and not sacrificing themselves to their families or to authorities who opposed their public ministries. Giving first place to God sometimes required that women put their families second. It also meant that women answered to God and not to the men who sought to silence them. Consecration to God superceded both familial obligations and human authority. Sanctification also endowed women with the power of the Holy Spirit, which enabled them to fulfill God's calling on their lives when it contradicted society's claim that women's only responsibility was to their families. Empowerment of the Holy Spirit equipped women to overcome any opposition they faced, whether it was based on prescribed gender roles or a faulty interpretation of Scripture that reinforced gender roles. Rather than thwarting their "desires and quests," to use Heilbrun's phrase, sanctified women fulfilled them. Believers extended the egalitarian nature of holiness, claiming that holiness eliminated racial prejudice as well as prejudice based on sex. The sanctified self offered both white and African American Wesleyan/Holiness women an autonomy that enabled them to break out of any obstacles they faced as they carried out their public ministries. Undoubtedly, sanctification played a positive role in these women's lives.

The Saved Self

Before examining sanctification as Wesleyan/Holiness women described the doctrine, it is necessary to discuss conversion or salvation, which is a prerequisite to sanctification. Whether one is an Arminian or a Calvinist plays a major role in determining one's understanding of conversion. Wesleyan/Holiness women embraced Arminian theology, which stresses free will in that God gives people the option to choose or reject God's grace, which is offered freely to everyone. This view corresponds to John Wesley's position that humans must participate in the process of salvation. Wesleyan theologian Randy Maddox has recently called this "responsible grace" because "it internalizes Wesley's conviction that our requisite co-operation is only possible in *response* to God's empowering." The individual plays an active role in this view of conversion. In contrast, according to traditional Calvinist doctrine, God predestines or predetermines who will be converted or saved. The individual's role is passive because Calvinists believe God's grace is irresistible. God has made the decision for everyone. While Phebe Davidson did not use theological labels, she illustrated the difference between Arminianism and Calvinism when relating Jarena Lee's quest for conversion: "Lee had rejected the role of the prey of God and become instead his avid pursuer."[2] In theological terms, Lee rejected the passive posture dictated by the Calvinist doctrine of predestination and became an active seeker of conversion, reflecting the Arminian conviction that individuals possess free will.

The distinctions between Calvinism and Arminianism with respect to free will became blurred somewhat due to the popularity of revivalism in the nineteenth century when many Calvinists moved away from a rigid position on predestination and began to allow room for human free will. Thus, the few women in this study who came from Congregational or Presbyterian churches, which traditionally advocated Calvinist theology, nevertheless spoke of their experience in terms of free will. Most women worshiped in churches that advocated free will, requiring them to play an active role in seeking their conversion. Lizzie Miller and Lucy Drake Osborn's testimonies illustrated the active nature of conversion. As she walked to school one morning, the words came to Lizzie Miller: "Why not decide now, to be a Christian." Lucy Drake Osborn remembered: "I chose Christ and eternal life and dropped on my knees."[3] This initial activism played a part in preparing women to assume active roles in church and society.

It has been impossible to reduce the circumstances of Wesleyan/Holiness women's conversion accounts to a formula. Dora Dudley, Jane Dunning, and Maude Kahl neglected even to share the story of their conversion in their spiritual narratives. While most women understood conversion as forgiveness of sins, Quaker Hannah Whitall Smith was an anomaly in that preoccupation with her sins was not a factor leading to her conversion. Instead, "It was simply and only that I had become aware of God, and that I felt I could not rest until I should know Him." She attributed this lack of concern about sin to the fact that she was a birthright Quaker, and Quakers contended that members "were already born into the kingdom of God, and only needed to be exhorted to live up to our high calling." Elizabeth Wheaton and Julia Shellhamer were more representative. They spoke of being "convicted of sin." Others confessed their sins as they prayed for conversion.[4]

For Wesleyan/Holiness women, conversion did not occur at a particular age, location, or follow a predictable pattern. While the majority who provided their age at conversion were in their teens, several reported earlier conversions with the youngest conversion occurring at age eight. A few, such as Hannah Whitall Smith and Maggie Newton Van Cott, became Christians as adults. Conversions took place in numerous locations. Some were solitary and some resulted from the efforts of siblings, while most occurred in a public church setting. As indicated above, the crisis came to Lizzie Miller on the way to school. She prayed, "Jesus do teach me what I shall do to be thine." Instead of continuing to school, she returned home. While praying on bended knee, the following words came to her: "They that seek the Lord shall not want any good thing." Her conversion took place when she accepted God's promise. Writing in the third person, Maggie Newton Van Cott reported her solitary conversion as an adult: "One morning, while on the way to the office, and crossing Fulton-street ferry, she heard plainly the voice of her Savior, saying, 'You must decide *to-day. Now* is the accepted time; behold, now is the day of salvation. Why longer delay?' Suddenly, as if awakening from a dream, with her heart trusting, praying, believing, she cried out, 'Lord, if thou wilt accept the sacrifice, I from this moment give thee my body and soul. I will be wholly thine, and, by thy grace, I will never turn back.' That moment she stood on the pavement in front of old John Street Methodist Episcopal Church, and from heaven light streamed in upon her soul. She was soundly powerfully converted." While Van Cott's conversion was dramatic, Susan Fitkin experienced conversion while reading the Bible alone.[5]

Although mothers traditionally bore the responsibility for the spiritual training of their children, when conversion resulted from the efforts of a family member, it was generally a sibling. Mary Cole's oldest brother counseled her prior to her conversion. Likewise, it was Sarah Smith's brother and Sarah Cooke's sister who urged them to become Christians.[6] As is becoming apparent, the conversions of these women varied, not only as to whether they ever wrote of it, but also as to their age and circumstances.

The church settings where women were converted varied remarkably. Abbie Mills's conversion took place at an informal prayer meeting. Others became Christians while praying at the altar in front of the church following a regular service. Revivals, special church services designated for the conversion of sinners, resulted in the conversion of several women. Hannah Whitall Smith's conversion took place during the Prayer Revival of 1857–58. Throughout the country, millions of people gathered daily for prayer over their lunch hour. Smith joined the crowds one day and her quest ended.[7]

The location of Emma Whittemore's conversion was perhaps the most unusual. One evening, she and her husband visited Jerry McAuley's mission in the New York slums. Motivated by curiosity, they went to hear McAuley, a converted thief, preach. They were wealthy, so their attire stood in stark contrast to that of the regular worshipers who surrounded them. When they came forward to pray, McAuley instructed them to kneel at the bench, which served as an altar, with the other seekers, whom Whittemore described as "river-thieves, drunkards, gamblers and abandoned women of the streets" who were "scantily-clad, unclean, vicious-looking men and women."[8] In this unlikely setting, the humbled Whittemores became Christians. Their subsequent ministry was among the very people with whom they had rubbed shoulders at the makeshift altar.

For some women the search for conversion ended quickly, while for others the pursuit extended over a prolonged period of time. Martha Lee's testimony places her in the first category. She attended a holiness meeting in the home of Mrs. E. D. Furness. While such meetings generally focused on the doctrine of holiness rather than conversion, it was here that Lee prayed: "Oh Lord, if there be such a salvation, and I believe there is, give it to me." Then, as she professed, "Scarcely were the words out of my mouth, ere the Lord came, bringing such a flood of joy, peace, and glory, that those in the room felt the Divine Presence. I sprang to my feet, tears streaming down my face, and with shouts of joy, feeling that God had given me just what I asked Him for." Lee's response ensured that everyone attending the meeting became aware of her conversion. In contrast, Abbie Mills's conversion occurred as the result of unspoken prayer. No one knew she had been converted. Emma Ray fell on her knees at the church altar, praying: "Yes, Lord, have mercy on me and I will serve you all my life." She rose to her feet declaring publicly, "I am saved."[9] Lee, Mills, and Ray were converted quickly.

Others found conversion more difficult. Amanda Smith prayed three times before her conversion occurred. Almira Losee knelt at the altar ten

Emma Ray, author of *Twice Sold, Twice Ransomed: Autobiography of Mr. and Mrs. L. P. Ray* (Chicago: Free Methodist Publishing House, 1926).

different times before claiming conversion. Alma White sought conversion for several years, hoping someone would explain how it could be achieved. Phoebe Palmer, however, spent the longest time seeking assurance of her conversion. She first claimed conversion at age four. She doubted her experience, though, measuring it by the specific testimony of others. A major concern was that she could not precisely date the event in her life.[10] She continued to doubt until shortly before her sanctification, more than twenty years later.

It may have taken a lengthy period of time for some women to claim conversion, but, once professed, they generally did not doubt their experience. After her ten-year search for conversion extending from age sixteen to twenty-six, Hannah Whitall Smith never experienced doubt as to her relationship to God. Likewise, Martha Lee and Zilpha Elaw were never troubled with doubt. Amanda Smith prayed: "Lord, I believe Thou hast converted me, but give me the evidence, so clear and definite that the Devil will never trouble me on that line again." God answered her prayer: "Though I have passed through many sorrows, many trials, Satan has buffeted me, but never from that day have I had a question in regard to my conversion. God helped me and He settled it once for all." Susan Fitkin testified to a "sky-blue conversion, which the devil was never able to make me doubt." On the other hand, one person admitted to questioning her experience. Almira Losee reported: "Many painful doubts arose as to the genuineness of my conversion, seeing the old propensities [to sin] proved such a trial to me."[11] Losee was an exception to the more typical certitude concerning conversion.

A vision accompanied conversion for two of the women. While reading on the afternoon of 13 September 1896, Florence Roberts saw a cross, which she compared to a giant opal with rays of light penetrating her. An indescribable being next appeared who encouraged her to "come!" An awareness of her sin preceded Roberts's positive response to the being's entreaty. Alma White remembered her experience immediately prior to her conversion at a revival service when she was sixteen: "Suddenly I lost consciousness and felt I was carried away to hell. Black demons were all about me in this awful place, and lost men and women were weeping and wailing and gnashing their teeth. Some of the latter had bodies like serpents and heads like human beings, and vice versa."[12]

In accounts of their conversions, women often recorded the conversation that occurred at the time. Sometimes, the dialogue was with the person counseling them. Other times, it was between themselves and Christ who was encouraging them or the Devil who was dissuading them from becoming a Christian. Sarah Cooke maintained that in response to her prayer, "The Lord revealed himself to me as my Savior, saying to my inmost being, 'Thy sins, which are many, are all forgiven.'" A few blamed the devil or Satan for hindering their efforts. While Almira Losee cried, "I believe," Satan whispered: "It is false; you *do not* believe." Jesus triumphed and she was converted. As Mary Cole sought salvation, she related that the devil tried to confuse her. Again, Jesus prevailed.[13]

Some women provided specific details relating to their conversion. Several furnished the day, month, and year it occurred. Jarena Lee remembered that the preacher's sermon text on the evening she was converted was Acts 8:21. Mary Lee Cagle recalled that the congregation was singing "Oh, Mourners, Will You Meet Me?" the night of her conversion. A former school teacher invited Lela McConnell to the altar to pray, resulting in her conversion. Others, previously quoted, reported precisely the words of their prayers of petition. On the other hand, Hannah Whitall Smith had no recollection of anything that was said at the prayer service where she was converted.[14]

The circumstances surrounding women's conversions varied dramatically. Age, location, length of time seeking conversion, and individual responses did not follow a set pattern. The consistent theme that appears throughout the accounts is that conversion results when individuals exert their free will to seek it. Another conviction shared by all Wesleyan/Holiness women is that conversion is not an end in itself but is the requirement necessary prior to seeking sanctification.

The Sanctified Self

Many Christian traditions collapse conversion and sanctification into one experience, believing that sanctification is a process initiated at conversion. Wesleyan/Holiness women never equated the two. Almira Losee spoke of conversion and sanctification as "the two grand epochs of my life." Alma White succinctly defined the two terms: "Justification [conversion] and sanctification are both instantaneous works of grace, actual sins being forgiven in the first work, and original sin being taken out of the heart in the second." Florence Roberts explained sanctification: "Perhaps my reader does not know the interpretation of that word, 'sanctification.' Briefly, it refers to a second blessing, following justification, or the forgiveness of sins; a second work of grace, whereby the nature becomes purified and kept free from sin by the operation and power of God's Holy Spirit—now the indwelling presence." Susan Fitkin offered a concise description of sanctification when she wrote of her desire "to be sanctified wholly, cleansed from inherited sin, the old man cast out, the carnal nature destroyed, and to be baptized with the Holy Ghost and fire."[15] Roberts and Fitkin were referring to the same person of the Trinity since the Holy Spirit and the Holy Ghost are synonymous.

As reflected above, sanctification was the primary term Wesleyan/Holiness women used to refer to the religious experience that followed conversion. They also employed holiness as a synonym. However, to sanctify means to make holy, so, technically, sanctification results in holiness. Most adherents, though, following the example of John Wesley as well as Mary Fletcher and Hester Ann Rogers, used the terms interchangeably, making it extremely difficult to determine when they were referring to the process of sanctification or the goal of holiness. Phoebe Palmer utilized the following list of synonyms in *The Way of Holiness:* full salvation, promise of the Father, entire consecration, perfect love, rest of perfect love, way of holiness, the blessing, and rest of faith. A few other phrases, such as "living in Canaan," "promise of the Father," "baptism of the Holy Ghost," and "the double cure," appeared infrequently in other narratives. Second blessing and second work of grace were other designations that indicated explicitly that sanctification was a distinct experience following conversion, the first blessing, or first work. Hannah Whitall Smith informed her readers that Presbyterians referred to "The Higher Life" or "The Life of Faith" but assured them that "by whatever name it may be called, the truth at the bottom of each name is the same, and can be expressed in four little words, 'Not I, but Christ.'"[16] Even though she was a Quaker who believed in sanctification and not a Presbyterian, she preferred the phrase "the life of faith," which she described in *The Christian's Secret of a Happy Life,* a popular devotional book that remains in print. Even though Smith used a phrase that was uncommon among other Wesleyan/Holiness advocates, it denoted her experience of sanctification that she understood in Wesleyan terms.

While my focus is the Wesleyan/Holiness doctrine of sanctification, a Calvinist emphasis emerged in England in 1874 that came to be known as Keswick, named after the location where the first meetings were held. Hannah Whitall Smith and her husband, who had been deeply influenced by the Methodist formulation of the doctrine, were primary figures in the foundation of this movement. The key difference between the Methodist and Keswick formulations of the doctrine related to inbred sin. While most Wesleyan/Holiness adherents maintained that sanctification eradicated inbred sin, Keswick believers held that inbred sin was suppressed. Writing in 1949, Lela McConnell referred to this viewpoint: "Some are willing to be deluded by Satan and take the erroneous theory of Repression, saying that inbred sin cannot be cleansed out, but must be kept suppressed." While suppression of inbred sin as opposed to the eradication of inbred sin distinguished the Calvinist and Wesleyan doctrines of sanctification after 1874, the difference was less clear earlier in the century. Camp meetings were ecumenical gatherings where Christians from many diverse groups came together under the banner of holiness, which was in actuality John Wesley's formulation of the doctrine. In some cases, the distinction remained blurred later as well. Writing in 1926, Emma Ray reported hearing a woman who was a member of a United Presbyterian church, which is Calvinist, preach "that the baptism of the Holy Spirit was the promise of the Father, and He could fill us with Himself and cleanse us from all unrighteousness."[17]

Phoebe Palmer's Shorter Way

Phoebe Palmer played a principal role in popularizing and promoting John Wesley's doctrine of sanctification in the United States during the nineteenth century. Her language helped shape the experience of her spiritual sisters and brothers in the Wesleyan/Holiness movement. Specific references to Palmer along with statements that reflected Palmer's influence appeared frequently in autobiographies by Wesleyan/Holiness women. For instance, Abbie Mills related in 1886 that she had read Wesley's *Plain Account of Christian Perfection* as well as Palmer's *The Way of Holiness* and *Faith and Its Effects,* another book by Palmer, in order to understand the doctrine. Mills and Amanda Smith counted Palmer among their friends and visited the Tuesday Meeting for the Promotion of Holiness held in Palmer's home in New York City. Mary Cole also mentioned reading *Faith and Its Effects,* while Sarah Cooke read *Entire Devotion,* a third book by Palmer on holiness. In addition, Jennie Smith benefited from Palmer's writings.[18] While others may not have come in direct contact with Palmer personally or through her writings, her theology of holiness permeated sermons by holiness preachers and her language found its way into other women's autobiographies.

Palmer's emphasis on the shorter way constituted an adaptation of Wesley's position because Wesley recorded experiences of his contemporaries for whom the blessing of holiness came only after a prolonged quest. As noted in the introduction, Wesley believed that growth both preceded and followed the experience of sanctification. Palmer eliminated the growth period prior to sanctification and wrote and preached that a Christian could be sanctified immediately upon consecrating her life to Christ and believing in Christ's promise that consecration was the action necessary to achieve sanctification. While Palmer's theology bypassed the period of growth a Christian underwent before sanctification, both she and Wesley contended that the experience of sanctification itself is received merely by faith and given instantaneously.

While authorship of the map outlining the shorter way is generally attributed to Palmer, this innovation in fact did not originate with her. As documented earlier, Hester Ann Rogers also experienced sanctification immediately as a result of her faith. It was not a long, drawn-out process. Palmer contended that one did not have to engage in endless soul searching or pleading with God before the blessing of holiness could be received. She encouraged a seeker: "I am sure this long waiting and struggling with the powers of darkness is not necessary. There is a shorter way." This had been her own experience. Writing in the third person, Palmer recorded that as soon as she expressed faith in God's ability to make her holy, "the Lord . . . led her astonished soul directly into the 'way of holiness.'"[19]

Palmer's shorter way also reflected the revivalist atmosphere of mid-nineteenth-century America. Evangelists preached that conversion could be had for the asking. Believers in holiness concluded that sanctification could be achieved in the same way. Almira Losee echoed this view when she asked: "Why struggle to submit? Why wrestle for hours? If that or any other act of our own brought the light, the power, then I would say, Yes, struggle on and *into* the blessing. But why contend with Jehovah? Why not yield at once, and let him sweetly reveal himself without any contending?"[20]

Like conversion, the quest for sanctification required the seeker to play an active role. Abbie Mills spoke of sanctification as a choice. Echoing Hester Ann Rogers's viewpoint, Phoebe Palmer had written, referring to herself again in the third person: "she had been but a co-worker with God in this matter." Palmer, following John Wesley, outlined two steps, consecration and faith, which constituted the way to sanctification, both of which required action on the seeker's part. Departing from Wesley, she incorporated altar language, emphasizing that one must consecrate everything "on the altar of Christ." "Gracious intentions, and strong desires, she was convinced, are not sufficient to bring about these important results; corresponding *action* is also necessary; the offering must be *brought* and believingly *laid upon the altar,* ere the acceptance of it *can* be realized. In this crucifixion of nature, the Spirit helpeth our infirmities, and worketh mightily to *will*—but *man must act.*"[21] Echoing both Wesley and Rogers, Palmer stressed the individual's role in achieving sanctification. She added another step, though, which involved symbolically laying one's all on the altar of Christ. This activity was not restricted to women. Men, too, lay their all on the altar as they sought sanctification. However, the ramifications for women were different.

Quoting Matt. 23:19, Palmer claimed "the altar sanctifieth the gift" when she spoke of consecration, the first step toward sanctification. While altar terminology became identified with Palmer's theology and is considered her trademark contribution to understanding this step leading to sanctification, this aspect of Palmer's theology did not originate with her either. David Bundy credited Madame Guyon as a source for the altar theology Palmer preached. Hester Ann Rogers, who had used the identical phrase with the same supporting Scripture, also influenced Palmer.[22] Palmer popularized altar language others, before her, had introduced. Basing their understanding of sanctification on Palmer's theology, Sarah Cooke and Dora Dudley were among those who used altar language with reference to their own consecration preceding sanctification. Like Palmer, Lela McConnell in 1946 quoted Matt. 23:19, concluding "the altar is Jesus and we are the gift."[23] Mary Still Adams, writing in 1893, reported the words of the person who had counseled her. Apparently informed by Palmer's theology, the adviser set forth how sanctification was achieved: "The altar

Christ sanctifies the gift, and if you have put all onto the altar the work is already accomplished. You have complied with God's requirements; God will and has done his part."[24]

Placing all on the altar illustrated the active role individuals played in seeking sanctification. The gift that was to be laid on the symbolic altar of Christ was comprehensive, requiring complete consecration. Abbie Mills realized she had "to present my all to God a living sacrifice." Lela McConnell specified that consecration encompassed a complete offering of "your friends, your time, your earthly store, your family." Sarah Cooke's list differed somewhat from McConnell's: "All had been laid on the altar—husband, dress, reputation, all yielded; everything with self, a living sacrifice." Often, consecration was a difficult process. Women struggled and agonized as they sought to consecrate everything to God. It must have been particularly hard to consecrate husband and children to God, because this went against the convention that family members should have first priority in a woman's life. Giving God first place undermined the belief that women should devote their lives wholly to their families. As indicated by Cooke's enumeration, consecration included sacrificing self by symbolically laying self on the altar.[25] Even though consecration could be construed as self-sacrifice, women were not sacrificing themselves for their families but for God. Consecration to God required women to make an active choice, a decision that placed them in direct conflict with their culture, which expected them to be willing to sacrifice everything for their families.

For most women, sacrificing all on the altar of Christ was a one-time event that preceded sanctification and never had to be repeated. This is one conviction that deviated from Phoebe Palmer's articulation of the doctrine of sanctification. She believed that one must continually keep all on the altar to remain sanctified. Lela McConnell was an exception to the norm in that she agreed with Palmer. McConnell also regarded consecration as an ongoing process: "Keep all on the altar constantly by confiding in the promises of God. Should you find at any time that you have taken something off the altar, put it back instantly."[26] Her viewpoint reflected the belief in human free will. After consecrating one's all on the altar of Christ, these two women believed it was possible, at any time, to remove something from the altar.

Consecration was the first active step toward sanctification, but, as previously pointed out, the second active step was faith. The seeker must believe God's promise that she would be sanctified after totally consecrating her all to God. Palmer followed John Wesley, who preached that faith results in sanctification. She defined faith as "taking God at His word." To doubt God's ability to sanctify was the "sin of unbelief." Jane Dunning and Anna Prosser also spoke of the simple faith that was necessary in order to achieve sanctification. Julia Foote asked, "How is sanctification to be obtained?" and answered her own question: "Faith is the only condition of sanctification." Even though altar language is absent in Foote's explanation, she did not ignore the step of consecration. She defined appropriate faith as "a faith that dies out to the world and every form of sin; that gives up the sin of the heart; and that believes, according to God's promise, he is able to perform, and will do it now—doeth it now." Rather than simply defining sanctification, she concluded her discussion with a plea to the reader, "Why not yield, believe, and be sanctified now—now while reading?"[27]

Women did not understand sanctification as an accomplishment of human effort alone. While consecration and faith required women's active participation, they never lost sight of the fact that God's role was essential. Like Phoebe Palmer, women perceived themselves as co-workers with God. It was God who sanctified them. On the way to holiness, they had to walk the two steps of consecration and faith. But it was God who accepted their consecrated lives and rewarded faith. Sanctification involved both divine and human dimensions.

Women did not always distinguish between the members of the Trinity in their writing. Palmer wrote of both God and the Holy Spirit as agents of sanctification. Others emphasized the role of the Holy Spirit or the Holy Ghost, a term Christians also used in reference to the third person of the Trinity. Holy Spirit is more frequently used today. Almira Losee waited for the baptism of the Holy Ghost and the resultant sanctifying of her soul by the Holy Ghost. Lela McConnell credited the Holy Ghost for cleansing her carnal heart. Abbie Mills recorded three aspects of the Holy Spirit's work. First, the Holy Spirit worked "within, urging me to enter the Canaan of perfect love." The Holy Spirit did this by revealing the things of God to her. Second, the Holy Spirit not only called her to choose the experience of sanctification, but it also played a role in the cleansing or purifying process by "consum[ing] the dross, and refin[ing] that which was not to be destroyed." Last, Mills reported that the Holy Spirit "abiding in my purified heart, would enable me to keep the commands of God."[28] Whether relying on God or the Holy Spirit, sanctification required divine assistance and could not be achieved by human means. Mills's reference to consuming the dross indirectly echoed Mary Fletcher's emphasis on Isa. 1:25 ("I will thoroughly purge away thy dross and take away all thy tin"), which Fletcher quoted frequently when she explained the process of sanctification. Mills knew she could not achieve purity by her own effort, but at the same time she recognized that consecration required her to take the initiative. These women reported that holiness occurred as a result of divine action whether undertaken by God or the Holy Spirit.

After attaining sanctification, Phoebe Palmer stressed that one must testify to the experience in order to maintain it. Palmer initially feared this requirement: "The duty of making confession with the mouth had stood before her of all duties the most formidable; but she now formed the resolution, that if she should literally die in the struggle to overcome nature, she would be a martyr in the effort, rather than that Satan should triumph." Needless to say, Palmer won the battle with God's help. Mary Cole accepted Palmer's emphasis on the necessity of consecration and faith in order to achieve sanctification. She also followed Palmer's admonition to testify and shared her experience with others shortly after claiming sanctification. Lela McConnell admonished her readers: "Frequently testify to what the Lord has done for you in two works of grace distinctly. If you shut the damper of publicly confessing and praising Jesus you will soon smother the fire of sanctification." Cole and McConnell along with Sarah Cooke were among the few authors who explicitly connected the preservation of sanctification with public testimony.[29] In light of Palmer's stress on the necessity of public testimony, I had expected that many women would list mandatory testimony as a rationale for public preaching. However, this was the exception rather than the norm.

When recounting their quest for sanctification, women revealed their conviction that they were on speaking terms with both God and the Devil. In Lizzie Miller's case, the voice of God seemed audible, while Almira Losee wrote that her conversations were mental rather than audible. Miller prayed: "'Dear Father in heaven, when all nature tells me of true peace and happiness, why is it that I am so cast down and miserable?'" She remembered: "An audible voice whispered in my ear: 'Fast and pray today.' It was so distinct that I looked around to see if it were possible that anyone could have entered the room unobserved. No one being present, I at once realized it to be the voice of God and immediately obeyed." Losee said that the Tempter questioned her motives as she sought sanctification. After her successful pursuit of sanctification, the "subtle enemy" approached her again, asking: "What are you going to do in regard to *professing* this definitely *as* sanctification?" Losee mentally responded: "Why, stand as Jesus' witness." The Devil persisted: "The next morning, on waking, the first thought was, (and it seemed as if some one was actually jeering and scorning,) 'So you think you are *sanctified,* eh? Yes, indeed, how presumptuous in the extreme, you sanctified,' said in such sneering tones that I at once discovered the voice of the evil one."[30] Reflecting their premodern mind-set, women reported vivid experiences and conversations with both God and the Devil because to them the supernatural and natural worlds overlapped.

Other women reported roadblocks on the way to holiness. Susan Fitkin sought the experience and had claimed it by faith several times. She even preached on the doctrine but remained unsatisfied as to her own experience. During one service, she "did battle with the enemy," who chided her, suggesting people would assume she had backslid if she went forward to the altar to pray for sanctification. The Enemy's efforts to dissuade her were unsuccessful, and she claimed sanctification at the conclusion of the service. Julia Shellhamer and Lela McConnell also claimed to withstand successfully the Devil's temptations, which would have derailed their search for sanctification.[31] Tracing the trajectory of women's spiritual autobiographies, their experience paralleled that of Hester Ann Rogers, who also overcame temptations.

With the help of the Holy Spirit, Phoebe Palmer resisted mental temptation, which to her exemplified Satanic subtlety. When the Enemy taunted her, suggesting that sanctification was merely the effort of her own will, she said that the Holy Spirit assured her, "It has all been the work of the Spirit." Sarah Cooke, Sarah Smith, and Jarena Lee also engaged in a three-way conversation between themselves, God, and the Devil. As Cooke pondered the sanctified women surrounding her at the camp meeting altar, the Lord asked: "Are you willing to pay the price?" Cooke knew that full consecration meant adopting the plain dress of those around her: "Common calico, a little linen collar, bonnets the plainest that could be made; no bow, no feather, no lace, no flower." As Cooke considered this sacrifice, the Devil said: "You would look just like an old washer-woman." Despite the taunts, Cooke ultimately chose sanctification. Sarah Smith recorded the conversation just prior to her sanctification. God said, "Are you willing to work for Me?" Then the Devil interceded in its attempt to dissuade her from seeking sanctification: "If you promise to work for God you will have to leave home, and your husband will not let you go." Smith recalled that "the death-struggle commenced," but the victory ultimately was God's and hers. During her quest for sanctification, Jarena Lee heard a voice whispering in her heart, "Pray for sanctification." She did and no sooner was her prayer answered than she heard another voice saying, "No, it is too great a work to be done." She attributed this second comment to Satan, but his words were counteracted by another spirit saying, "for the witness—I received it—*thou are sanctified!*"[32] These women understood their mystical experiences to be encounters with God and Satan. Women believed the consequences of their decisions in these duels between God and Satan were crucial to their spiritual growth. With God's help, they maintained victory over the mental conversations during which Satan tempted them.

While everyone agreed on the two steps of consecration and faith, which comprised the shorter way to sanctification, the immediate emotional reaction to sanctification varied. Mary Fletcher and Hester Ann Rogers did not address the role of emotion in sanctification. Phoebe Palmer initially encountered difficulty completing the shorter way because she believed that emotion should accompany the achievement of sanctification. She ultimately came to the conclusion that she had to accept God's gift by faith without expecting an emotional response to confirm it. Jennie Smith took the same route as Palmer: "I was able to place all upon the altar, as I had never done before. I laid hold of the promises by naked faith, without any feeling." At first, Lucy Drake Osborn doubted she had achieved sanctification because she lacked emotion. But then, an evangelist counseled her: "If you have a book and I tell you if you will give it to me I will take it, just as sure as I am a person of my word if you hand it to me I take it. God says, 'If first there is a willing mind it is accepted.' You say you are willing to be His: are you accepted?" Osborn answered: "Why, I am accepted whether I ever feel it or not!" Osborn realized that "when God said I was accepted, if I did not say it I was making Him a liar." Like Palmer and Osborn, Abbie Mills felt no emotion at that "never-to-be-forgotten moment." After several unsuccessful attempts, Susan Fitkin claimed sanctification by faith, even if she never experienced any feeling. Alma White also testified that her sanctification took place without any emotion at the time. Anna Prosser relied solely on faith: "I must believe it because God says so, apart from feelings or emotion of any kind." She criticized those who insisted on an emotional response before claiming sanctification.[33] These statements echoed Palmer's argument for the efficacy of faith alone without an emotional confirmation. While some stereotype women as being primarily emotional, Palmer's emphasis on faith as intellectual belief that sanctification has occurred defies the affective stereotype.

Hannah Whitall Smith allowed for both the felt presence and absence of emotion at the moment of sanctification, depending on a person's personality. She attributed the lack of overpowering emotions at her own sanctification to the fact that her nature was unemotional. She explained: "To me it came with intellectual conviction and delight, to more emotional natures it came, with emotional conviction and delight, but in both cases the truth was the same, and it was the truth, not the emotion, that set the soul free."[34]

Some women did recall an emotional experience at some point after their sanctification. This was the case for Lucy Drake Osborn, but she maintained that even if emotion was absent at sanctification or even after sanctification, she remained sanctified. Emma Ray, like Osborn, initially lacked the emotion others exhibited at sanctification but claimed the experience by faith with no feeling. Subsequently, however, as she lay reading, "All of a sudden it seemed that a streak of lightning had struck over the corner of the house, and it struck me on the top of my head, and went through my body from head to foot like liquid fire, and my whole body tingled. I tried to rise and was so weak I fell back upon the lounge." She was too weak to stand, but "there came another dash of glory through my being and a voice inside of me said, 'Holy.'"[35] Osborn and Ray, who claimed sanctification without an accompanying emotional corroboration, ultimately experienced a feeling that they associated with their sanctification. The role of emotion in Wesleyan/Holiness women's sanctification was not homogeneous. Some experienced no emotion. For others, emotion accompanied sanctification, while for a third group emotion followed sanctification.

John Wesley spoke of confirmation in terms of receiving the witness of the Holy Spirit, which verifies one's sanctification. The witness of the Spirit was one aspect of Wesley's understanding of sanctification, which Palmer and many other Wesleyan/Holiness women did not emphasize. However, several Wesleyan/Holiness women did mention receiving the witness of the Holy Spirit, which confirmed their sanctification. Julia Shellhamer claimed "a calm, sweet assurance possessed me which was the witness of the Spirit." Lela McConnell quoted Heb. 10:15, "the Holy Ghost also is a witness to us," to justify her belief in this verification of sanctification. Osborn believed in the witness of the Holy Spirit following sanctification. Likewise, Ray spoke of the witness of the Holy Spirit.[36]

While Ray's mystical encounter with God following her sanctification was unusual, several other women related experiences accompanying sanctification that can only be categorized as mystical. Phoebe Palmer's experience of sanctification occurred at the moment she believed: "her very existence seemed lost and swallowed up in God; she plunged, as it were, into an immeasurable ocean of love, light and power."[37] Elizabeth Wheaton remembered:

> After wrestling in prayer until about three o-clock in the morning, I seemed held by an invisible power, pure and holy, and was so filled with awe that I feared to speak or move. Soon I heard a wonderful sound, soft, sweet and soothing, like the rustle of angels' wings. Its holy influence pervaded my whole being, a sound not of earth, but distinctly audible in both myself and the sister who was in the same room! I listened enraptured. I feared it was death, and my breath grew shorter and shorter. I did not move nor open my eyes. Presently Jesus stood before me, and O the wonderful look of love—so far above the love of mortals, so humble, meek and pleading! In the tender voice of the Holy Spirit came these words: "Can

Elizabeth R. Wheaton, author of *Prisons and Prayer; or, A Labor of Love* (Tabor, Iowa: M. Kelley, [1906]).

you give up all and follow me? Lay your weary, aching head upon my breast. I will never leave you nor forsake you. Lo, I am with you always even unto the end of the world." I was enabled by the Holy Spirit to say, "Yes, Lord Jesus." I knew it was Jesus. When I said, "Yes, Lord," the power of God fell upon me, soul, and body, and I was bathed in a sea of glory. When I had recovered from my rapture, Jesus had vanished as silently as He came; but the blessing and power remained.[38]

Susan Fitkin described a similar mystical experience: "Then suddenly the chapel roof seemed to be cleft asunder; the heavens were rent; and shafts of heavenly light like sunbeams shot down directly into my heart, filling and thrilling my soul." Fitkin's words are similar to those penned by Teresa of

Avila, a medieval nun. In Teresa's mystical vision, she reported seeing an angel with a "long golden spear and at the end of the iron tip I seemed to see a point of fire. With this he seemed to pierce my heart several times so that it penetrated to my entrails. When he drew it out, I thought he was drawing them out with it and he left me completely afire with a great love for God."[39] It is impossible to assess if the similarity between the two visions is a coincidence or if Fitkin's language reflected an awareness of Teresa of Avila and her mystical encounter with God.

Once the individual consecrated herself totally to God and believed, sanctification occurred instantaneously, whether or not it was accompanied by emotion. Mattie Perry referenced Acts 26:18 and explained: "It is instantaneous the moment we meet God's conditions, and believe it, that moment the work is done. It is a gift of God. There is a moment when we receive it. It is instantaneous." Mary Lee Cagle "at once sought and obtained the blessing" within three days after "she got the light of holiness." Others engaged in a prolonged struggle before meeting the two qualifications, consecration and faith. For some, the search lasted for several days. For others, the pursuit extended into weeks or months. Sanctification eluded Sarah Smith for several years, and Alma White spent at least ten years as a seeker before finally claiming the experience by faith.[40] Whether the quest itself was short or long, once women met the two conditions of consecration and faith, they believed that sanctification took place immediately.

Sanctification Resulted in Inward and Outward Purity

One of the most controversial aspects of the doctrine of sanctification was the claim, initially made by John Wesley, that sanctification removed inbred sin. Conversion resulted in the forgiveness of actual sins while Wesley and his followers asserted sanctification uprooted inbred sin or the sinful nature that persisted despite conversion. Another synonym for inbred sin was carnality. Martha Lee spoke of the destruction of her "carnal nature" at sanctification. Lela McConnell identified carnality as the flesh. In *The Way of Holiness,* Phoebe Palmer wrote of "being cleansed from all unrighteousness [and] from all filthiness of the flesh and spirit" when she was sanctified.[41] While Palmer did not use the term *inbred sin,* her statement assumes the meaning of the term.

Wesleyan/Holiness women generally believed that one's inbred sin was eradicated at the moment of sanctification and that the cleansing process occurred instantly. This resulted in a clean heart where God could abide. This corresponded to Hester Ann Rogers's emphasis more so than Mary Fletcher's. Purity became associated with the Wesleyan/Holiness view of sanctification because of the emphasis on cleansing the heart of inbred sin. Alma White discovered: "At last my soul was robed in the garments of purity . . . my heart was now cleansed from inbred defilement." Jane Dunning described the "heart-purity" of a woman she had counseled: "At length the all-cleansing touch was given. Her soul had been much drawn out in prayer all day for *purity of heart.* She said the Spirit fell on her, and seemed to go through both soul and body."[42] Essentialists who promoted the notion of the cult of true womanhood in the nineteenth century claimed that women were purer than men by nature. No Wesleyan/Holiness women accepted this false dichotomy. They sought purity through sanctification with the same intensity as men. They did not accept the theory that women were naturally purer than men, simply because they were women.

Abbie Mills employed a metaphor to explain the removal of inbred sin: "The ground, covered with short stubs where the underbrush had been cut away, reminded one of the remains of the carnal mind, and when I saw a brother trying to clear the ground in front of his tent and, moreover, hacking at a tough root, I thought that was the way many tried to get rid of inbred sin. But such attempts are more futile in the spiritual realm than in the case mentioned. The Lord has made a straight way for his people wherein they shall not stumble, and he will lead them there when they consent to the cleaning, uprooting, clearing processes of the Holy Spirit. Praise the Lord!"[43] References to eradication of inbred sin often utilized "root" language when referring to God's removal of sin from the heart.

Following John Wesley, the Wesleyan/Holiness understanding of inbred sin derived from Augustine (354–430), one of the most influential theologians of the Christian church. Prior to Augustine, Christians believed in the goodness of human nature. They held that all babies are born innocent. Augustine's theory of original sin ultimately prevailed, replacing the earlier consensus. Augustine introduced the idea that, as a result of Adam and Eve's sin in the Garden of Eden, all humans are depraved, inheriting a sinful nature. In Augustine's estimation, babies are born with original sin, which is transmitted through the passion of procreation. Mary Cole's (b. 1853) view reflected Augustine's opinion that sin is directly transmitted from one generation to the next when she described "that depraved nature, the sin-principle inherited from the fall of Adam." Although the term *inbred sin* presumes the inheritance of sin, Cole and Phoebe Palmer were the only women to use language that explicitly connected the origin of inbred sin to the fall of Adam.[44] Amazingly, no woman traced inbred sin to Eve, who has often been blamed throughout church history as the source of sin. Wesleyan/Holiness women accepted Augustine's doctrine; although, for the most part, they did not refer to it as original sin or discuss the source of inbred sin.[45]

While Augustine's view of original sin became a key component of the Wesleyan/Holiness doctrine of sanctification, he would have been horrified at the notion that original sin could be eradicated from an individual through God's power. He maintained that original sin was a permanent condition of humanity. In opposition to Augustine, Wesleyan/Holiness believers contended that the experience of sanctification eradicated inbred sin, and the Christian was understood then to be "cleansed from all sin."[46]

Generally, Wesleyan/Holiness women used the term *inbred sin* as a comprehensive expression. They did not spend a significant amount of space elaborating on its specifics, and only a few accounts listed aspects of inbred sin that were cleansed at sanctification. Alma White explained: "Sensitiveness is burned out; lust, pride, envy, impatience, jealousy, strife, self-seeking, and the desire for the good opinions of others have to go when the fiery baptism purifies the heart." Lela McConnell defined "strife, ill will, pride and anger" as symptoms. After recounting a personal experience with racism, Julia Foote asked in her narrative: "O Prejudice! thou cruel monster! wilt thou ever cease to exist?" She answered her question, "Not until all shall know the Lord, and holiness shall be written upon the bells of the horses—upon all things in earth as well as in heaven. Glory to the Lamb, whose right it is to reign!" It is unclear whether she anticipated the termination of prejudice as a result of holiness to occur in human history or in heaven, although the latter seems more likely. Amanda Smith alluded to the fact that prejudice persisted even in sanctified individuals. She reflected: "Some people don't get enough of the blessing to take prejudice out of them, even after they are sanctified." This is further evidence that sanctification involves a process of growth. Amanda Smith's criteria for white missionaries' eligibility for service in Africa included that they be "wholly sanctified to God, so that all their prejudices are completely killed out, and their hearts are full of love and sympathy."[47] Sanctification involved a social component with the removal of prejudice.

Julia Shellhamer specifically identified fear as another attribute of inbred sin. She prayed for "complete deliverance from the fear of man," which she had been told was a trait of carnality.[48] Defining fear as a sin seems particularly suited to women who had every reason to be apprehensive about testifying publicly. Undoubtedly, some Wesleyan/Holiness men also were fearful, but the obstacles in their way did not include a hostile and disapproving culture. As with the elimination of racial prejudice, replacing fear with confidence was a social aspect of sanctification.

Wesleyan/Holiness theologian Diane Cunningham Leclerc has recently argued that relational idolatry defined Phoebe Palmer's doctrine of original sin. Leclerc explained relational idolatry as "inordinate love for others" or putting others before God. For Palmer, laying all on the altar included her children and her husband. This did not mean that she would no longer love them, but rather that love for them would not surpass her love for God. Other women also associated relational idolatry with inbred sin. The two were not identical, however. Relational idolatry was one evidence of inbred sin along with other characteristics noted above. Lela McConnell symbolically placed friends and family on the altar of Christ. Sarah Cooke also laid her husband on the altar as she consecrated her life to God. During her pursuit of sanctification, Cooke feared that her non-Christian husband would disapprove. As she continued her quest, the Holy Spirit reminded her of a major hindrance: "If I loved any earthly relation more than Jesus my Lord, I was not worthy of Him; giving me the foreshadowing of the hundred-fold in this life, and also of the persecution that would follow." Cooke's statement is the most straightforward declaration of the consequences of the sin of relational idolatry. Julia Shellhamer also confessed to relational idolatry: "It was killing to carnality but the Lord was helping his child to die out to her parents."[49] It appears she was afraid of praising God out loud in her father's presence. Dying out to parents meant she would no longer be intimidated or fearful of their disapproval if she testified. God's will came first, not relatives'.

The focus thus far has been on inward purity, which was a primary concern for Wesleyan/Holiness believers. However, they also emphasized outward evidences of purity as well when they spoke of avoiding what they called worldliness. This should not be misunderstood as an escape or retreat from the world itself, as was the case for solitary mystics who avoided any contact with the world in their effort to achieve holiness. The examination of women's ministries in chapters 6 and 7 illustrates that sanctified women did not flee the world but encouraged others to become holy and sought to make the world holy, too. The term *worldliness* encompassed two primary categories. One related to clothing, jewelry, and accessories, while the other embraced worldly pleasures that included attending theaters and other entertainment, playing cards, reading novels, dancing, and singing secular music. Worldliness implied fancy clothing and other adornments and activities that took one's focus off Christ.

As indicated earlier, Sarah Cooke's sanctification experience hinged on her willingness to "pay the price" and forsake fancy clothing, which she had to lay on the altar. To achieve sanctification, she had to "be crucified to the world." For others, the decision to adopt a plainer wardrobe followed sanctification. Anna Prosser and Julia Foote quoted Rom. 12:2, "Be not conformed to this world," when speaking of the need for inner and outer holiness. The verse continues, "but be transformed by the renewing of your mind." Foote rejected the argument of those who limited the application of this verse to the mind, arguing, "But, if the mind be renewed, it must affect the clothing." Nonconformity was a consistent theme. Women used the same language with reference to outer holiness as they did for inner holiness or holiness of heart. Prosser wrote of being "crucified to the world," quoting Gal. 6:14. She also confessed to the realization that her purse was not "on the altar" as long as "yards of needless trimming were purchased for every dress and also considerable expense upon hats and gloves which might be avoided and thus the work of God advanced."[50]

While a majority of Wesleyan/Holiness women simplified their wardrobes in order to avoid worldliness in the area of dress, there were other reasons, too. While Prosser contended that the money saved could be applied to God's work, Dora Dudley provided yet another rationale for plain dress. She believed not only that it was more acceptable to God, but also that wearing plain clothing would enable her to minister more effectively among the poor. Abbie Mills gave up fashionable dress because it was unhealthy.[51] Women's corsets often were tied so tightly that they constricted a woman's internal organs, making it difficult to breathe. In this case, outward purity resulted in freedom from physical restrictions imposed by fashion.

Lucy Drake Osborn warned against the danger of becoming too preoccupied with one's clothing: "I adopted great plainness of dress, verging on such a severe rigidity as to involve me in great bondage over what I might and might not wear . . . if we have gone to an extreme in one direction, we are quite liable to go to the opposite. This is what I did." She remembered talking to young people about the liberty Christians have in Christ and realizing the inconsistency between her comments and the severe outfit she was wearing. "The thought presented itself that my outside appearance did not suggest liberty, for I certainly looked like a straight-jacket. I became convicted. It was somewhat of a trial to change, but I did it, believing it was God's will, and still endeavoring to maintain the simplicity of dress enjoined by the Gospel." Mattie Perry also warned against "becoming somewhat narrow on the dress question."[52]

Other accessories to be eschewed included feathers, flowers, flounces, and jewelry. Maggie Newton Van Cott literally placed her rings on "the altar of God." Elizabeth Wheaton joined Van Cott in forgoing rings. Alma White contended: "Where no change of sentiment is seen in regard to the wearing of gold and worldly apparel the genuineness of one's profession may be seriously questioned." She rejected "fancy dress" and followed the lead of The Salvation Army by adopting uniforms for herself and the members of her mission branches. Distinctive uniforms clearly delineated her members from the world around them. Other women adopted clothing similar to the plain dress of the Quakers. Amanda Smith began dressing Quaker style for economic reasons prior to her sanctification. While many sanctified women in the United States forsook worldly attire as a result of sanctification, in England Hester Ann Rogers had made this decision prior to her conversion, while Mary Fletcher's choice came before her sanctification.[53]

Women placed less emphasis on other aspects of personal appearance as well. Dora Dudley and Mary Lee Cagle mentioned forsaking makeup. For Dudley, this decision followed a difficult struggle: "I argued with the Spirit, I have always considered it a part of my toilet; I cannot give it up." This was particularly difficult for Dudley, because prior to her decision to forsake makeup she had supported herself financially through the sale of makeup. Cagle's resolution to stop curling her hair reflected her intention to avoid worldliness.[54] The desire to separate oneself from the world in these ways reflected a determination to avoid anything that might be construed as not putting God first in their lives.

Nonconformity to the world included renouncing numerous activities as well as simplifying one's wardrobe and spending less time on one's appearance. Some of these standards seem archaic today, and many current Wesleyan/Holiness believers do not follow this model of nonconformity. Sarah Smith admonished: "God's people . . . do not conform to this world, have no desire to go to fairs, church frolics, shows, dances, secret orders, and such like." Julia Foote wrote: "Dear reader, do you engage in the ensnaring folly of dancing? . . . Does dancing help to make you a better Christian?" Julia Shellhamer advised parents to keep "worldly music" from entering their homes because of its power to mold character, quoting Scripture to bolster her argument: "Whatsoever ye do, do all to the glory of God." Playing cards was rejected as a "pernicious amusement." Reading novels and attending the theater joined the list of proscribed activities. Florence Roberts warned of the consequences of worldly behavior. She blamed novel reading, attending shows, and dancing, along with wearing fancy dress, on the downfall of two women who had become prostitutes.[55] Roberts neglected to explain the connection between these activities and prostitution.

Alma White identified secular employment as a worldly activity to be abandoned. Christians who joined her group, the Pillar of Fire, had to resign from their jobs: "God has commanded the Pillar of Fire to break every yoke and to let the oppressed go free. He wants people in a position to offer themselves and their services wholly to His work, and this cannot be done without breaking with the world and getting out of ungodly business entanglements."[56] Pillar of Fire members were expected to devote all their time to the ministries of the group, and members lived together in mission branches to avoid entanglement with the world.

Women understood consecration to include every aspect of their lives, from their clothing to their leisure activities. Mary Glaser warned against reducing religion to issues of clothing, but she did see a relationship: "I do most sincerely believe that when the heart is full of the love of Jesus, it cannot and will not at the same time love the vanities of the world." According to Lucy Drake Osborn, if an activity did not "benefit others or myself in the divine life," she abstained from it.[57] While, in retrospect, one can accuse these women of perhaps adopting a "Christ against culture" stance, or the sanctified self against the world, one can commend them for constructing selves that challenged society's rather than merely reflecting their culture.

Sanctification Resulted in the Death of the Sinful Self

Wesleyan/Holiness women believed that sanctification resulted in purity that obliterated prejudice, relational idolatry, and any other sins that abided in their hearts after conversion. Hester Ann Rogers, and Phoebe Palmer following her, quoted Rom. 6:11—"Reckon yourselves, therefore, to be dead indeed unto sin." Women described the death of self that transpired at sanctification and resulted in purity. Abbie Mills spoke of sanctification as "consenting to self-crucifixion," which acknowledged the active role of the individual, while Mattie Perry "died the deeper death to self" at her sanctification.[58]

To a feminist critic, the notion of the death of self initially appears to offer no positive potential for a woman's development of a strong sense of self. It seems to reinforce constructions of gender that assert the inferiority of women. However, despite a few isolated pronouncements to the contrary, women did consciously possess a self after sanctification, a self radically different from the presanctified self. What died was the sinful or carnal self, which was replaced by the sanctified self, a self empowered to contest cultural expectations based on sex and race. Sanctification resulted in a new construction of the self, a self no longer plagued by self-doubt or fear. If Wesleyan/Holiness women truly believed the self had died at sanctification, they would not have documented the activities of the sanctified self by authoring autobiographies.

What constituted the self according to Wesleyan/Holiness authors? Lela McConnell defined carnality as "self in opposition to God." She contended that the old man was the sinful nature: "our old man is crucified with [Christ], that the body of sin might be destroyed." Anna Prosser illustrated the paradox existing as a result of the belief in a crucified self that makes possible a sanctified self. She equated the self with the carnal or sinful nature that was destroyed in the moment of sanctification: "I saw by the illumination of the

Holy Ghost as clearly as the noon-day that my depraved, fallen, carnal nature (the self-life) and yours, dear reader, positively expired there just as truly as Jesus did; that when God says, 'Ye are dead,' He certainly means your very self, the wretched 'I' which has been your worst enemy, your most subtle foe . . . Could it be a finished work if it had left me with the same carnal nature with which I was born? And what is the carnal nature if it is not 'self'?" Prosser believed that just as Christ died and was buried, "I was actually buried with him, and oh, what a source of satisfaction to know that I, that detestable 'I' never came up again! . . . The 'old man' was left in the grave, and out of his ashes came up the pure, clean, 'new man,' which after God is created in righteousness and true holiness.' (Eph. 4:24) A new creation indeed!" The "old man" denotes the carnal nature while the "new man" is the sanctified self. While Prosser claimed the "wretched I" was crucified, in actuality the sinful self died resulting in a pure "new man," or new self. According to Prosser, after the "old usurper 'self' is cast out," the Holy Spirit "then place[s] Jesus on the throne within you, for there will be no rival there to dispute his sway any more." She further addressed the death of self: "I saw that the believer is as truly dead to 'self'— that hideous monster—as he is to his transgressions, his inbred sin and his sicknesses through the finished work of Christ. I saw that it was not a figure of speech, as I had supposed, but an accomplished fact long ago upon Calvary's cross." Again, the self that has died was the sinful self. Prosser assured her readers that the death of self was permanent: "Now with regard to this important question which at once arises in every mind as soon as the death of self is presented, viz: 'Will it not rise and trouble us again?' Satan will surely do his best to drive us from our strong position, and will tempt us with the same old feelings over and over again, trying to make us doubt God's Word, which assures us that we are dead." She rejected any notion that the Christian must die to self daily, emphasizing her point: "Self forever slain! Self so extinct that the memory of it has perished."[59] The crucifixion of the sinful self, of the "old man," was a necessary step in the sanctification process that enabled women to possess a sanctified self, or "new man," which was unafraid to participate in the public arena.

This view that the sinful self needed to be crucified corresponded with John Wesley's perspective. He claimed that Gal. 2:20—"I am crucified with Christ; nevertheless I live; yet not I, but Christ liveth in me"—described "deliverance from inward as well as outward sin." Several women quoted Gal. 2:20 as the biblical explanation for what happened to them at sanctification. The "new man" who replaced the "old man" was filled with Christ's presence. What is dead is the sinful or carnal self. Amanda Smith experienced God's presence filling up the vacuum in her soul as "a pleasant draught of cool water." She defined sanctification as "God in you." Elizabeth Wheaton and Maggie Newton Van Cott used the same language, claiming that in sanctification, they were emptied of self and filled with the Holy Spirit. Mary Glaser and Jennie Smith spoke of the death of self enabling them to follow God's will.[60] In this sense, sanctification brought one's self into alignment with God. If it was God's will for them to preach, who were they to refuse the call? They had God's authorization for their public activities.

Sarah Cooke, like Anna Prosser, understood her sanctification as "a death unto sin—*a new creation!*—that the 'strong man armed' had been cast out, and Jesus all enthroned within." Rather than eliminating self, sanctification resulted in a new creation. Mary Glaser advised her readers: "But remember, we must first empty our vessels of everything that is sinful, before this great blessing can be ours. We must just turn this old vessel upside down to get this old self out, and step out of self and then Christ will come in and take possession of His house to reign as King." While not acknowledging a new sanctified self, Glaser implied this by writing of the "old self." Lizzie Miller spoke of the death of the self at sanctification: "How much I felt my utter unworthiness before the infinite glory of the blessed Redeemer. In the light of that hour I became convinced as never before that I was nothing and I bless God, the conviction grew upon me that I know my nothingness, and that Christ is all and in all to me." Dora Dudley likewise understood that "self must be put out of sight, and nothing but Jesus must be seen." While not declaring a sanctified self that replaced the old man, Miller and Dudley in the act of writing autobiographies documented the presence and activities of sanctified selves. Autobiography, by its very nature, reveals a self. These sanctified women fall within the Christian mystical tradition. Mystics sought to lose themselves in God and yet when they testified to that loss, paradoxically, they asserted a self. As discussed in chapter 2, Madame Guyon held that the individual will was annihilated as it united with God, but her autobiography testified to an extremely strong sense of self in that she forcefully challenged her opponents. Lucy Drake Osborn's description of a mystical encounter with God could have been copied from the account of a medieval mystic. Osborn wrote: "Upon the soul, as it went deeper into the bosom of God, was produced a ravished, charmed state; that is, if I can speak of myself at all, for at such times self was lost to sight. For heart-work I never knew anything to be compared to this experience. Such depth and richness of the affections! It seems a divine enchantment."[61] Osborn's mystical experience was the exception rather than the rule among Wesleyan/Holiness women. Lizzie Miller and Dora Dudley were the only other women who spoke in terms of nothingness of the self following sanctification, but they did not describe an actual encounter such as

Osborn's. For the majority of women, a "new man" or new creation interacted with Christ. The goal of sanctification was to become more like Christ.

While modern scholars analyze the socially constructed self, Wesleyan/Holiness women understood the sanctified self as being divinely constructed. They would not agree with literary critics who claim the self is constructed in the act of writing autobiography. Wesleyan/Holiness women believed they were merely reporting the transformation of self that had already occurred as a result of experiencing sanctification. Women who maintained that sanctification resulted in the crucifixion of the sinful self would vehemently renounce any focus on the individual self. However, they appeared blind to the obvious paradox that they authored autobiographies that documented the activities of the sanctified self. In actuality, it was the crucifixion of the sinful self that made possible the sanctified self, which was empowered by the Holy Spirit to preach in the public realm. Despite the denials of self-construction, the act of writing was a literary expression of what they perceived to be divinely transformed selves. Their understanding of self that they described had emerged from their experience of sanctification.

Sanctification Resulted in Perfection Understood as Maturity and Love

Probably the most problematic synonym for sanctification is perfection. Abbie Mills was one of the few women in this study to use this alternate term. She quoted the Scripture verse "Be ye therefore perfect, even as your Father which is in heaven is perfect" and wondered prior to her sanctification how she could measure up to this standard. She realized that the Holy Spirit would enable her to keep God's command to be perfect. Mills sought "complete victory" over sin as a result of sanctification. Other women experienced "full emancipation" or said they were no longer "slave[s] of sin" but had thrown off "the old yoke of bondage."[62] These comments imply the ability to live without sinning.

While Abbie Mills professed to understand perfection better after reading John Wesley and Phoebe Palmer, these theologians themselves were not always clear in their explanations of the term. Sometimes, Wesley defined perfection by asserting that humans would no longer commit sin once they were sanctified. In other references, he contended that sanctified individuals could make mistakes or commit transgressions, but they were still perfect because he did not interpret these actions as sin.[63] Wesley emphasized intentionality. If Christians' intentions were pure, but they inadvertently committed wrongdoing, this was not sin in Wesley's estimation.

Phoebe Palmer maintained that a sanctified person can be imperfect. She indicated imperfection in her own life when she noted: "I have lamented my shortcomings, and still feel my all is upon the altar." On the other hand, sinless perfection could be construed from these lines quoted by Palmer:

Let us, to perfect love restored, Thine image here retrieve,
And in the presence of our Lord The life of angels live.
But is it possible that I Should live and sin no more?
Lord, if on thee I dare rely, The *faith shall bring the power.*[64]

However, other comments by Palmer point to her emphasis on growth rather than sinless perfection. Sanctification placed the person at the beginning of the "highway of holiness," Palmer's terminology that indicated progression. Palmer spoke of advancement toward reaching the goal of holiness, which she understood as a process of maturity: "She could find no Scriptural reason, why each successive day might not witness the heavenly traveler at a higher point of elevation in his homeward course than the day previous." She sought to make "*daily* advances in the knowledge and love of God—'the way of holiness.'" Palmer testified: "My establishment in the blessing I have received has been more deep and thorough with the experience of each successive day."[65] While some subsequent theologians have faulted Palmer for her emphasis on the "shorter way," she definitely believed that holiness itself was a lifelong process.

A few women seemed to advocate the attainment of sinless perfection; however, even Abbie Mills qualified her position by contending that humans could not aspire to be like the angels. There was no consensus on the meaning of perfection. For the most part, women limited the scope of perfection. Hannah Whitall Smith, like most others, rejected the possibility of sinless perfection. She confessed that, in her own life, "temptations continued to arise, and sometimes failures befell."[66]

While Phoebe Palmer and Hannah Whitall Smith spoke generally of their failings, Sarah Cooke was the only American autobiographer to reveal specific shortcomings following sanctification. Mary Fletcher frequently listed faults that indicated the need for further growth in Christian holiness, but Cooke was the only American woman to follow her example. Cooke confessed to a "self-justifying spirit" that she sought to overcome with God's help. Speaking sharply to others and a lack of love were other traits she prayed to eliminate from her life. In a letter to a friend, she divulged that she had become calmer and more patient after pleading to God for these virtues. For Emma Ray, perfection resulted in a heart whose motives were pure even though its judgments could be imperfect. She still confessed to making mistakes and blunders. However, like Wesley, she maintained that sanctification made it "possible to live without actual transgression" even though it "was impossible to live without faults and failings."[67]

Several other autobiographers emphasized growth in holiness following their initial experience. Amanda Smith observed: "There is much of the human nature for us to battle with, even after we are wholly sanctified, so that we shall ever need the beautiful grace of patience." Being wholly sanctified did not mean that there was no room for growth. Lucy Drake Osborn made "more rapid growth in grace" after her sanctification. She was the only woman to use a technological metaphor to explain the difference: "My progress in the Christian life, before this baptism, might be compared to rowing up-stream in a row-boat; and after it, to being on a steamboat. The first was hard work and little progress, and a constant fear to stop for a moment the hard toiling lest I should drift down-stream; but when I stepped aboard the steamer my toiling ceased and I journeyed swiftly on by *steam-power.*" The Holy Spirit led Emma Ray "out into deeper depths. He didn't give us all the light at one time, but later, little by little, as we were able to receive it." Later, she spoke of "growing in grace." Lela McConnell spoke directly to her sanctified readers: "Go deeper, press on to know the Lord in all His preciousness. Exalt Him more and more until your heart is a garden where all the rich graces of the Spirit bloom; a temple filled with His beauty."[68] While the onset of sanctification was instantaneous, it signified for these women the beginning of a lifelong process of growth in holiness aided by the Holy Spirit.

When women used the word *perfect* to describe sanctification, they generally spoke of perfect love. Lela McConnell's emphasis paralleled John Wesley's position when she explained: "Our perfection lies only in loving God with all of our heart, soul, mind, and strength." Wesley frequently quoted this verse but also added "and your neighbor as yourself," which concluded the passage. Wesley defined love of God and love of neighbor as Christian perfection. In another location, however, McConnell recognized the relationship between love for God and love for others when she proclaimed, "He who loves God most, loves humanity most." What is perfect once an individual is sanctified is the relationship with God and neighbor, which is characterized by love. Emma Ray's succinct definition of sanctification included the emphasis on love for others: "Through the study of the Word of God and with the experience of my own heart I have become thoroughly convinced that the baptism of the Holy Ghost and fire, . . . purifies the heart by faith and causes it to overflow with the love of God to our fellow man."[69] Chapter 7 illustrates ways in which sanctified women exhibited "love toward others."

Lela McConnell blamed Satan for the misunderstanding surrounding the meaning of perfection: "The enemy of souls often uses deception by telling folk that those who have pure hearts claim absolute perfection, including freedom from error of judgment, infirmities, unpleasant dreams, wandering thoughts, and mistakes, etc. The enemy thus places the standard higher than the Bible does, and deludes folk into the belief that holiness is something more than 'perfect love from a pure heart.'" McConnell further contended that "perfection of maturity is impossible in this life. That would be a higher standard than in Eden." She also agreed with Abbie Mills that individuals could not aspire to be like the angels. Likewise, Julia Foote insisted: "I am not teaching absolute perfection, for that belongs to God alone. Nor do I mean a state of angelic or Adamic perfection, but Christian perfection—an extinction of every temper contrary to love."[70] *Perfection* did not mean perfect in the everyday understanding of the term. Instead, for most Wesleyan/Holiness women it signified a process of maturity characterized by love.

The Empowered Self

Sanctification resulted in personal inward and outward purity as well as the desire to grow in Christian maturity and love. Another consequence of sanctification was power, an equally important element of sanctification. It was the empowerment of the Holy Spirit that enabled Wesleyan/Holiness women to possess a self that successfully countered the weak, dependent self society sought to impose on them. Phoebe Palmer equated the doctrine of holiness and power by proclaiming: "Holiness is power!" For Palmer, "heart holiness and the gift of power should ever be regarded as identical." Perhaps Alma White was paraphrasing Palmer when she defined the theme of her ministry as "holiness of heart which brings the enduement of power." Gregory Schneider employed the term *empowered self* in reference to sanctified individuals. Schneider accurately claimed that "the self's quest for spiritual supernatural power was at the center of the holiness project." Holiness believers "sought a fully empowered self, untrammeled by the demands of wealth and status or by the functional boundaries of church organizations or of the larger social order."[71] While Schneider reported on male holiness adherents here, his conclusions also apply to sanctified women who likewise possessed empowered selves.

As women sought sanctification they assumed that the Holy Spirit's power would be forthcoming. The quest for sanctification included the expectation of power. Almira Losee anticipated "this endowment of power" while seeking sanctification. She was "waiting for the baptism of the Holy Ghost, with power." Lucy Drake Osborn also longed for the baptism of the Spirit as she sought sanctification. Prior to her sanctification, Anna Prosser reported: "I sighed for an unction and power in service, which as yet I did not possess." Following her sanctification, Prosser testified: "My anxiety as to the matter of power for service was now forever at an end. I saw that the Holy Ghost Himself, would be my power day by day, quite equal to any service to which He called me." Mary Still Adams also received the power of the Holy Ghost when she was sanctified.[72]

Linking sanctification with the baptism of the Holy Ghost provided a biblical basis for the association of sanctification and power. The use of Pentecostal language such as "baptism of the Holy Ghost" and the emphasis on Pentecost did not originate with John Wesley but with John Fletcher, Wesley's co-worker and the husband of Mary Bosanquet Fletcher. Hester Ann Rogers and Mary Fletcher popularized John Fletcher's equation of sanctification with the baptism of the Holy Spirit in their writings. Abbie Mills referred to her sanctification as a Pentecostal baptism and related her experience to that of Jesus' followers.[73] The baptism of the Holy Ghost occurred at Pentecost, an event described in Acts 1–2 of the New Testament. Jesus had told his followers before his crucifixion: "And behold, I send the promise of my Father upon you; but stay in the city, until you are clothed with power from on high" (Luke 24:49). Jesus' followers obeyed Jesus' instructions and approximately 120 people, women and men, remained in Jerusalem for the "baptism with the Holy Spirit" (Acts 1:5). Jesus had stated that power would accompany the baptism with the Holy Spirit, a power which would enable his followers to be "witnesses in Jerusalem and in all Judea and Samaria and to the end of the earth" (Acts 1:8). On the appointed day, "they were all filled with the Holy Spirit" (Acts 2:4), and people from many countries heard Jesus' followers recounting "the mighty works of God" (Acts 2:11) in their native tongues.

While such language today often is associated with the Pentecostal movement, Pentecostals actually appropriated it from Wesleyan/Holiness theology. Pentecostalism differed from the Wesleyan/Holiness movement in that Pentecostalism promoted speaking in tongues as evidence of the baptism of the Holy Spirit. Pentecost was a key event for Wesleyan/Holiness believers who, like Abbie Mills, spoke of Pentecostal power. Wesleyan/Holiness adherents contended this power was for ministry and did not refer to speaking in tongues. Palmer described her own experience in Pentecostal terms when she wrote of "waiting at Jerusalem for the promise of the Father" prior to her sanctification. The reliance on the experience of Pentecost as the model for the theology of sanctification provides a key illustration of primitivism, since Wesleyan/Holiness believers sought to model themselves after Christians in the New Testament church. Sarah Cooke clearly believed Pentecostal power was available almost two thousand years after the initial event:

"The power that came to the early disciples is the same that comes to us today, and comes in the same way." Abbie Mills made a similar observation: "The Holy Ghost shed abroad in hearts has much the same effect now as at Pentecost." Amanda Smith declared: "Oh, how we need the mighty Holy Ghost power that they had at Pentecost!"[74] Wesleyan/Holiness women claimed the precedent of Pentecostal power, which proceeded from the Holy Spirit to both men and women on the day of Pentecost and enabled these women to echo Palmer's assertion that "holiness is power."

Lela McConnell represents other women who quoted Scripture relating the Holy Spirit to power: "'Ye shall receive power, after that the Holy Ghost is come upon you,' Jesus said to His disciples." McConnell, likewise, claimed the promise of this verse was fulfilled not only at Pentecost but also in her own life. The Holy Spirit was the source of Christian power. Women explicitly acknowledged the power of the Holy Spirit. For instance, Jarena Lee "was filled with the power of the Holy Ghost." Emma Irick relied on "the indwelling of the Holy Ghost in His sanctifying power."[75]

Lizzie Miller relied on the model of Jesus as well as Pentecost: "It was after Christ had been anointed by the Holy Ghost that he entered the ministry, performed miracles and suffered on the cross for sinners." The apostles were additional examples: "The apostles did not have power to follow his [Jesus'] example until they received the Holy Ghost" at Pentecost. Miller experienced this power in her ministry. On one occasion, she reported: "I felt the power of the Holy Spirit filling my whole being and preached Christ as the crucified Redeemer for all mankind." Mary Lee Cagle preached once when she was recovering from an illness. She was so weak, she had to hold on to the pulpit initially to stand up. When she began preaching, "the power of the Spirit came upon her and she preached with as much strength as she ever did." Lela McConnell spoke "with the authority of God's word and the Holy Ghost" when the power of God came upon her as she addressed drunk boys who attended one of her services. These examples illustrate McConnell's contention that the Holy Spirit cannot operate alone but "works through human agency."[76] Women were willing co-workers assisted by the Holy Spirit.

The Empowered Self Obliterated Fear

In some cases, sanctification caused a personality change. Several women portrayed themselves initially as being shy. Sanctification destroyed their fear, which women sometimes identified as a characteristic of inbred sin. Alma White testified that sanctification enabled her to overcome her natural shyness and the paralyzing "man-fearing spirit" that had constrained her prior to sanctification. She learned that "the second work of grace destroys inbred sin and enables a person to overcome timidity and fear," explicitly relating purity and power. Julia Shellhamer also illustrated the close relationship between the two. Just as sanctification helped women overcome a man-fearing spirit, Shellhamer reported losing the "experience of heart purity" once when she yielded to a man-fearing spirit.[77]

Sarah Smith also used the term *man-fearing spirit* to define her timidity prior to sanctification. She reported that when God sanctified her, God "took all the shrink and fear of men and devils out of me." As was the case for other women, sanctification destroyed Smith's inbred sin and imparted power and confidence: "The body of sin was crucified and destroyed, then followed the glorious resurrection and I was filled with power and the Holy Ghost, and such boldness. All that man-fearing spirit was taken away, and my heart was overflowing with perfect love that was so unspeakable and full of glory." Smith explained the transformation that occurred in her life as a result of sanctification, a change that others noticed: "Everybody that knew me before I received this great blessing knew how fearful I was, and then when I came out with such boldness, everybody, preachers and all, that knew me before, were astonished and wondered how I came into such a blessed experience."[78]

Julia Foote and Amanda Smith alluded to the Bible verse that promises "perfect love casts out fear" (1 John 4:18). Foote claimed she "lost all fear" when "perfect love took possession" of her. Reading this verse inspired Smith to pray for the removal of her man-fearing spirit and her woman-fearing spirit.[79] She was the only autobiographer who spoke of a woman-fearing spirit as well as a man-fearing spirit. It is impossible to determine whether other women used the term *man-fearing spirit* in a generic sense or if they understood it as a sex-specific phrase. Since most of their opponents were men, one could assume that they feared males. However, it is possible that women also used the term in a general way to describe their initial hesitancy to preach.

Almira Losee described herself as "naturally timid" but claimed that sanctification had eliminated her "fear of man." Lucy Drake Osborn experienced "freedom from conscious fear of man" following her sanctification. Several women testified that sanctification transformed a timid self into a self characterized by holy boldness.[80] The eradication of the man-fearing spirit made possible a new construction of self distinguished by power instead of fear. The experience of sanctification and the resultant power of the Holy Spirit made this construction of self possible. Wesleyan/Holiness theology explicitly fostered the alternative construction of a confident self.

As an African American, Amanda Smith also experienced freedom from her fear of white people when she was sanctified. She recounted the transformation that occurred on the morning of her sanctification:

> Somehow I always had a fear of white people—that is, I was not afraid of them in the sense of doing me harm, or anything of that kind—but a kind of fear because they were white, and were there, and I was black and was here! But that morning on Green street [at a Methodist Episcopal Church], as I stood on my feet trembling, I heard these words distinctly. They seemed to come from the northeast corner of the church, slowly, but clearly: "There is neither Jew nor Greek, there is neither bond nor free, there is neither male nor female, for ye are all one in Christ Jesus" (Galatians 3:28). I never understood that text before. But now the Holy Ghost had made it clear to me. And as I looked at white people that I had always seemed to be afraid of, now they looked so small. The great mountain had become a mole-hill. "Therefore, if the Son shall make you free, then are you free, indeed." All praise to my victorious Christ![81]

The fears that women overcame as a result of sanctification ranged from a man-fearing spirit to fear of whites, in the case of Amanda Smith. The sanctified self was an empowered self, uninhibited by shyness and timidity. It was a self that had conquered these fears, thus making it possible for women to experience a freedom enabling them to rise above them.

Sanctification removed internal barriers to ministry when shyness no longer paralyzed women. Prophetic authority, recognized by Wesleyan/Holiness adherents, aided women in surmounting external barriers to ministry. The Holy Spirit directly authorized sanctified women to preach, regardless of any opposition they faced. Prophetic authority sanctioned women's actions as autonomous individuals answerable only to God. The sanctified self was responsible to God alone. Sanctified women did not seek approval or fear disapproval for their actions. Drawing on Acts 5:29, Mary Glaser asked pointedly: "Are we to obey man rather than God?" She answered her own question in the negative. Mary Cole likewise contended: "But if you are certain of the leadings of the Lord, even if God does not make it plain to others, you may do as God bids you with certainty of success."[82] Wesleyan/Holiness women exhibited holy boldness and asserted their autonomy as they pledged their allegiance to God rather than humans.

Kate Crawford Galea correctly credited sanctification for Phoebe Palmer's authority, which enabled her to engage in ministry: "Phoebe Palmer had a life-changing experience of suddenly discovering the Shorter Way and of feeling the assurance of God's sanction. She had always been a 'useful' Christian, leading classes and conducting the prayer meeting, but her breakthrough turned her into an energetic and public witness to God's gift. Her 'voice' came from her experience." Galea noted the parallel between Phoebe Palmer's religious authority and the authority of medieval women mystics who experienced a "mystical union with God that served as the source of these women's authority to speak." Galea acknowledged that sanctification was the event in Palmer's life that empowered her "to leave the safety of private life for public ministry."[83] Madame Guyon, of course, provides an example of a mystic who exemplified prophetic authority that paralleled the authority exerted by Palmer. Neither was ordained, yet they offered spiritual advice not only to other laypeople but to church leaders, irrespective of the ecclesiastical status they had attained by virtue of priestly authority. Although they lacked priestly authority, others recognized Guyon's and Palmer's prophetic authority.

The Empowered Self Defied Racism

Sanctification also fostered a woman's sense of her full humanity. Women possessing a sanctified self challenged the gendered conception of self promoted by their culture. While I will return to this topic in the following chapter, race presented an added burden that inhibited the development of a positive view of self among African American women who found their full humanity threatened on two counts—because they were women and because they were Black. Racist arguments that Blacks were not fully human or did not possess a soul sought to undermine the assertion of self by African American women. Black women declared a self with full awareness that there were those who attempted to deny them their selfhood. Donald Mathews claimed that sanctification played a role in promoting self-worth among Blacks because "the meaningful discipline was not white; the meaningful discipline was to answer to God for self, to act according to an inwardly developed sense of one's obligation and integrity."[84] Sanctification not only enabled women to challenge and overcome attacks on their full humanity based on sexist assumptions, but it facilitated their resistance to racist presuppositions as well.

Other analysts have recognized the significance of sanctification in the lives of African American women. "Radical spiritual mothers" is the term Rosetta Renae Haynes applied to African American women in the nineteenth century who wrote spiritual autobiographies. She maintained: "It is the experience of sanctification that is the defining event in the life of the 'radical spiritual mother'; it is a moment of transformed consciousness that enables her to see the world and her place within it in a new light. Through the sharpened vision that she acquires, she experiences a new sense of power." While the women themselves would have attributed power to the Holy Spirit rather than to a personal "sharpened vision," the result is the same. Haynes further accented the role of sanctification in the lives of radical spiritual mothers: "But through the experience of sanctification these women underwent a radicalization of consciousness that enabled them to view themselves as empowered agents of God and to posit a 'radical egalitarianism' against a cultural ethos that denied their full humanity. Sanctification allowed them to formulate theologies of liberation which provided them with a set of religious tools with which to name, analyze, critique, and transform oppression." Elizabeth Elkin Grammer analyzed the writings of four African American women who are also included in this study. She labeled them self-made women.[85] Again, these women would have rejected this assessment because it overlooks the spiritual component that was vital to their self-understanding.

Katherine Clay Bassard, in her analysis of the writings of African American women, acknowledged the role of the Holy Spirit in authenticating a self that asserted itself against both racist and sexist denials of self: "It is within the private encounters with Spirit that African American women often experienced a conferral of personhood denied by larger social constructions of African American and female subjectivity. For it is within this divine dialogue that black women's subjectivity is produced even as her agency is acknowledged and affirmed." Theorist Nellie McKay, likewise, recognized the intersection of race and sex as they influenced the development of self: "In the search for self, issues of gender are equally as important as those of race for the black female, a matter black men usually overlooked. Consequently, as male slave and spiritual narrators sought autonomy in a world dominated by racist white male views, black women writers demonstrated that sexism, inside and outside of the black community, was an equal threat to their quest for a positive identity."[86] While white women had to overcome barriers to a positive self-esteem that stemmed from sexism, African American women also had to transcend racist barriers.

Empowered by the Holy Spirit, African American women challenged sexism and racism, both of which threatened their assertion of self. Unintimidated by racist challenges to their selfhood, African American women narrators foregrounded their identity as Blacks. In four out of the five autobiographies authored by African American women included in this study, the book titles the women chose explicitly identified themselves as Blacks.

Jarena Lee described herself as "a coloured lady," while Amanda Smith labeled herself "the colored evangelist." Zilpha Elaw used the description "an American female of color," which sounds remarkably contemporary. Emma Ray referred more indirectly to her experience as a former slave when she titled her autobiography *Twice Sold, Twice Redeemed.*

Sanctification as the Crucial Event

Margaret Bendroth has observed: "The mounting literature on women's conversion experiences has shown the central importance of a dramatic spiritual event as a means of establishing personal authority and banishing fear of social disapproval." No doubt, conversion served as the crucial event for women from a Calvinist persuasion. However, for Wesleyan/Holiness women, the "dramatic spiritual event" was sanctification. Patricia Meyer Spacks affirmed that "spiritual autobiographies specifically declare meaning to inhere in the process of discovering and sustaining commitment to God. Their form and rhetoric characteristically speak of certainty, drawing energy and conviction from the affirmation of transcendent meaning."[87] This is particularly true for Wesleyan/Holiness women who placed the locus of their transformation in the experience of sanctification. They committed themselves to God through consecration and faith. In return, God empowered them to act in ways they had never imagined.

The doctrine of sanctification provides a framework for comprehending specifically the lives of Wesleyan/Holiness women who authored narratives explaining and justifying their assertion of self in the public arena. By examining the theological basis underlying their transformation of self, it is possible to identify selves that were empowered by the experience of sanctification. A. Gregory Schneider has rightfully contended that "with the self thus empowered, no outer circumstances could overcome it." Catherine Brekus's assessment of Zilpha Elaw holds true for other Wesleyan/Holiness women: "Paradoxically, her denial of self was also her greatest source of power."[88] Brekus recognized the paradox inherent in the doctrine of sanctification. The death of self made possible the empowered self.

Rather than sanctioning submission, sanctification empowered women to challenge those forces that attempted to prevent them from engaging in public ministries. The unsanctified self succumbed to pressures to remain in woman's circumscribed private sphere. It also acquiesced to the inferior view of self motivated by racism. In some cases, there was also a personality trait that constrained women. Timidity sometimes had prevented women from becoming involved in public ministry. In other cases, it was the lack of authority. At sanctification, the empowered self, capable of overcoming internal or external barriers to public ministry, replaced the fearful self.

Sanctification fostered self-reliance, or holy boldness. The Holy Spirit's power was consistently understood as a power enabling one to serve, whether by preaching or engaging in social holiness ventures to meet the physical needs of people. Subsequent chapters summarize the various ministries of sanctified women as they exerted holy boldness, or "holy energy," to use Jarena Lee's term for the empowerment women experienced when they engaged in public acts of ministry.[89]

CHAPTER FIVE

Affirmation and Opposition of Ministry

In her brief examination of three African American Wesleyan/Holiness women preachers (Jarena Lee, Zilpha Elaw, and Julia Foote), Liz Stanley stressed the importance of sanctification in legitimizing their "entirely deviant and unwomanly behavior: public preaching and thus taking on a role preserved for a male church hierarchy." Stanley recognized that "sanctification provided them with a route into public life and also an unanswerable legitimation straight from God for their conduct in doing so."[1] The close relationship between sanctification and ministry extended to white Wesleyan/Holiness women. The sanctified self undermined constructions of gender that society sought to impose on women, both African American and white. Several women related sanctification to their subsequent ability to preach. As demonstrated earlier, those who were shy or fearful credited sanctification for enabling them to overcome timidity and their man-fearing spirit. The empowerment of the Holy Spirit that accompanied sanctification enabled women to undertake the task of preaching despite their own initial misgivings and the vigorous opposition of others.

Mary Still Adams viewed sanctification as preparation for preaching. Equating the experience of Jesus' followers at Pentecost with sanctification, she quoted Acts 1:4: "And I did not want to go out without being wholly equipped for the warfare. Therefore I made up my mind to do as Christ had commanded his disciples to do, 'Tarry at Jerusalem untll [*sic*] endowed with power.'" She received "the joy and power of the Holy Ghost" when she was sanctified. Revealing her primitivism, Adams successfully sought to duplicate the experience of members of the early church documented in Acts. Other women credited the power of the Holy Spirit for equipping them to preach.[2] The Holy Spirit's power subverted the idea of keeping women in the home and out of the pulpit. Sanctified women resisted societal limitations and claimed the pulpit as woman's place.

Women relied on historical precedence by incorporating the experience of women before them to advance their argument for women preachers. Sarah Cooke concluded her defense of women preachers by listing Elizabeth Fry, Catherine Booth, and others whom God had endorsed by putting God's seal on their work "by saving multitudes of souls." Julia Shellhamer lifted up Susanna Wesley as an example of a woman who refused to be limited by the view that women should not speak in public. She was the mother of John Wesley and eighteen other children. Initially, she invited her neighbors to join in family prayers. This mushroomed into a religious meeting with a packed house. As Shellhamer told it, "her husband, a clergyman, hearing of it, became excited indeed and wrote back insisting that she must *stop such work as she was a woman!* She held her own, however, stating that she had not intended to conduct a public service but was only holding family worship; and since her neighbors were getting to God she did not feel clear to prohibit their coming to her home. He became reconciled and said no more against it." Susanna Wesley defied her husband's authority and continued holding the meetings. Lest her readers overlook Susanna Wesley as a possible role model, Shellhamer concluded the discussion: "There are many women all over the land who could hold cottage meetings, do personal work everywhere, and visit the jails, hospitals, lumber camps and asylums, if they would but take courage and try."[3]

Zilpha Elaw explicitly called on biblical precedent when she compared herself to Phoebe (Rom. 16:1–2): "It was revealed to me by the Holy Spirit, that like another Phoebe, or the matrons of the apostolic societies, I must employ myself in visiting families, and in speaking personally to the members thereof, of the salvation and eternal interest of their souls, visit the sick, and attend upon other of the errands and services of the Lord."[4] Elaw modeled her call to ministry after a biblical example.

God's Call to Ministry

In some cases, sanctification in itself initiated a woman's call. Mary Lee Cagle's process of consecration prior to sanctification included the willingness to preach. She had felt called to preach as a young girl, but with sanctification the call "was stronger than ever before." Alma White believed she was called to preach within a week of her conversion, but she assumed her ministry would take place on the mission field.[5] It was not until after her sanctification that she inaugurated her public preaching ministry.

Churches in the Wesleyan/Holiness movement are among those that value a divine call to ministry, whether the person called is a woman or a man. God calls individuals to preach. Often the call comes in the form of the specific command such as, "Go preach my gospel." For several women, a specific Bible verse inspired them. God called Sarah Cooke to the ministry as she was walking across the Madison Street bridge one evening in Chicago: "The Lord in His tender compassion spoke to me in these never-forgotten words: '*Lift up your voice like a trumpet, lift it up and be not afraid. Say unto the people, behold your God.*' No doubt, from that hour, has ever rested on me about woman's speaking in the churches; no doubt about my own call from His own Spirit to go forth in His name and preach the gospel." For Julia Shellhamer, the inspirational verses were Jer. 1:4, 9. Just as God spoke to Jeremiah, "*Behold, I have put my words in thy mouth,*" Shellhamer believed God repeated those words to her. While Jennie Smith was lamenting her weakness and ignorance she testified, "the words seemed to be spoken directly to me: 'For I will give you a mouth and wisdom which all your adversaries shall not be able to gainsay or resist.'"[6]

Sometimes the call came in a vision. A voice spoke to Zilpha Elaw: "Thou must preach the gospel; and thou must travel far and wide." Her call did not come from "mortal man, but from the voice of an invisible and heavenly personage sent from God." She recognized the voice from an earlier apparition at her bedside. Julia Foote received her call from an angel who carried a scroll with these words: "Thee have I chosen to preach my Gospel without delay."[7]

Celia Bradshaw Winkle also reported a visionary experience that confirmed her call at age eleven: "I was lifted up in the spirit and out of this world. I did not fall, to my knowledge, but I was completely lost to this world and my surroundings. God talked with me. He showed me a big, broad road and many, many people in it going down to hell. He spoke to me and said, 'Will you help to rescue these people?' I said, 'Yes, Lord, I will.' I surely did not comprehend, in my young mind, what all was implied in it. But finally I came back to myself and was conscious again." Others actually dreamed they were preaching. In her dream, Jarena Lee preached before a large crowd and woke herself with her violent exertions and loud exclamations. Jennie Smith dreamed all night that she was working as an evangelist. Lucy Drake Osborn dreamed of addressing "hosts of people . . . to win them from eternal death." She wrote that the dreams functioned to "prepare me to take naturally the work when it fell into my hands." Lizzie Miller's dream was allegorical: "I dreamed of seeing a wonderfully large field which I was expected to plow, harrow, and roll for wheat. In a very short time my work was done, leaving the ground smooth and beautiful. I sowed the seed throwing it broad cast with my hand upon the prepared earth, and wherever the grain fell it sprang up immediately, the green blades coming up as quickly as sown until the great field was covered thickly with the young grain. Beholding the beautiful green with much delight I found the wheat to be one foot high." Miller realized the meaning of this dream when the Lord said, "Preach the gospel."[8]

Susan Fitkin also heard her call to preach in connection with a dream. In her case, the dream was about Christ's Second Coming. While she responded in ecstasy to Christ's appearance, others cried out in fear. When she woke from the dream, she was aware of God's divine presence, which she described as being "like a person standing beside my bed." She heard an audible voice saying "Go ye into all the world, and preach the Gospel to every creature!" Fitkin never doubted this "clear, definite call."[9]

Emma Ray found herself in the awkward position of having already preached before receiving her call. While others referred to her activity as preaching, she could not bring herself to use the term but instead said she was giving a talk because "it seemed too big a mouthful to say 'preach.'" She was uncomfortable using the term because she had not been called. Prior to preaching before a large audience at a camp meeting, Ray prayed: "'If you have called me to preach, I should know definitely. As I have never gotten any definite witness to my calling, make it plain to me this afternoon, so then I can tell the people not to call me a preacher, but just a worker for the Lord.' . . . the Spirit of the Lord fell upon me and I said, 'Surely God is in this place.' I began to tremble and fell on my knees with my eyes closed and with my head bowed. There came a vision before me of a bright, blazing, fiery brand, and the glory of the Lord fell upon me. I did not hear the word 'preach,' but I felt it through my very being. I never doubted from that day as to my calling to preach the gospel."[10]

For several women, the call to preach related to illness. Mary Glaser's preaching focused on her testimony of personal healing. She reported that her healing occurred on 22 August 1883 after sixteen months of illness. On "that memorable night" God spoke to her: "Yes, you are healed, you are to obey my voice in all things; you are to go where I command you, and speak what I give you to speak." She believed God caused her sickness as the means of "crucifying me to become conformed to His own will." Glaser reported: "But if I would shrink from duty, I soon began to lose strength of body."[11] She was convinced her continued good health depended on her willingness to tell others about her healing. This was the essence of her ministry.

Mary Lee Cagle's and Alma White's calls to preach related to the sickness of family members. Cagle had married Robert L. Harris, an evangelist, and traveled with him. When her husband was on his deathbed, she bargained with God, offering to preach if God healed him. "God seemed to speak back to her in thunderous tones, 'Whether I heal your husband or not, will you do what I want you to do?'" The battle "raged hot and long" before she finally answered yes. Her husband subsequently died, and she became co-pastor of the church he had founded in Milan, Tennessee, before initiating her evangelistic ministry and founding numerous other churches. White believed her son's healing depended on her positive response to God's call to preach. She answered the call because she was convinced that God would spare her son's life if she preached.[12]

Sometimes women had to overcome their own hesitations and doubts before they could answer the call to preach. Mary Still Adams and Maggie Newton Van Cott tested their calls. If the call was valid, Adams asked God that one person respond to one of her sermons. Six people came to the altar for salvation following Adams's message, settling the matter for her. Van Cott also put God to the test. She prayed: "And now, dear Father, if thy servant is doing thy will in thine own appointed way, and hast not committed an offense in thy sight, show her, by converting Mr. Bloodgood this very night." God granted her petition and Van Cott knew "she stood on safe ground" when she preached from the pulpit.[13]

Mary Cole responded to God's call to preach with excuses: "Lord, I am not talented; my education is so meagre; there is no one to go with me; and, besides, I have a stammering tongue." God cut short her excuses by responding: "Who made man's mouth? I gave Moses Aaron as his spokesman; but I will do a better part by you, I will go with you myself."[14] In retrospect, Cole reported that God's promise had been fulfilled throughout her years of ministry.

Women sometimes credited the Devil for the doubts they harbored relating to their call. Just as their conversion and sanctification sometimes involved mental dialogue with the Devil, women reported conversations where the Devil raised doubts about their call. For Cole, it was a practical argument when the Devil suggested she had no means of transportation. In response, the Lord brought to her mind the verse, "Yea, the Almighty shall be thy defense, and thou shalt have plenty of silver."[15]

Reaction from others to a woman's call to preach were mixed. When Mary Lee Cagle informed her husband of her call to preach, he responded: "I have known that for some time." Her husband's positive affirmation inspired her. At the same time, her family, with the exception of one brother, offered no support and informed her that she was going to disgrace them. Her brother-in-law threatened that his children "should never call her Aunt again" if she persisted in her call to preach. Mary Still Adams's father, a Methodist minister, had looked to each of her five brothers to follow in his footsteps. When it became clear that none of them had received God's call to ministry, he pinned his hopes on her. While preaching at a camp meeting, he pronounced: "It is my desire at death, that if Elijah's spirit was permitted to fall on Elisha, to make him more useful or powerful for God, mine, or a portion of it, may fall upon my daughter Mary." The congregation, approving her father's endorsement, responded with "Amen."[16]

In several cases, women had to conquer their own negative stance toward women preachers in general. Julia Foote acknowledged she "had always been opposed to the preaching of women, and had spoken against it."

She had to come to terms with her former antipathy to women preachers before she could answer her calling. Lizzie Miller and Lucy Drake Osborn also had to overcome their prior hostility to women preachers when God called them to preach.[17]

Zilpha Elaw received support from another woman in ministry who affirmed her call even when she doubted her own ability to preach. Well aware of prejudice against women preachers, Lela McConnell initially resisted her call. Encouragement came from people at Asbury College when she testified that God had called her to devote her life to ministry in eastern Kentucky. Jarena Lee informed her pastor Richard Allen, founder of the African Methodist Episcopal Church, of her call only to be told that her church's Discipline did not recognize women preachers. On a subsequent occasion, Lee was tempted to voluntarily withdraw from her denomination due to opposition. She described her physical reaction to resistance to her call: "At times I was pressed down like a cart beneath its shafts—my life seemed as at the point of the sword—my heart was sore and pained me in my body."[18] Despite the opposition and the discomfort it caused, she stayed with her church. Later, Bishop Allen endorsed her preaching.

The most common characteristic of a woman's call to preach was the conviction that God directly addressed her. It is impossible to claim this as a universal experience, however, because Hannah Whitall Smith became a preacher even though she never received a call. She had believed a call was necessary for ministry but ultimately proceeded without one. While some women questioned God or offered excuses, Emma Irick bluntly replied to God's call: "I don't want to!" Others, such as Sarah Cooke, Mary Lee Cagle, and Mary Glaser, never questioned their call to ministry.[19]

The call came at various ages. Several besides Celia Bradshaw Winkle were girls when they first heard God's call to preach. Others were in their teens. The majority were adults, but it is impossible to state their ages because disappointingly this information is missing from their accounts. Mary Cole and Sarah Smith are among the few who provided their ages. Cole experienced a "definite call to the ministry" when she was about twenty-two. At age sixty-one, Smith probably was the oldest woman in this study to respond to God's call. She feared telling her husband, but he responded to her announcement by offering to arrange for money for her expenses. Ten days later, she joined an evangelistic company that traveled together for more than four years.[20]

In the late 1800s, most women outside the Wesleyan/Holiness movement, other than Quakers, who were called to preach had to settle for missionary service. Preaching in the United States was not an option for the majority of women.[21] Since she did not expect an opportunity to preach in the states, Alma White initially trained as a teacher, hoping to be sent to the foreign mission field. Mary Lee Cagle professed that when God had called her to ministry, she originally expected, like White, that she would serve as a missionary since this was the only outlet for women's ministry in her church. Both women were Methodists. As a young adult, Cagle recommitted her life to Christ, and at that time "the call came clear and plain," but it was a call to preach in the United States rather than a call to the foreign mission field. She would have preferred the missions option: "To go as a missionary would have been a summer vacation, compared to preaching the gospel at home, for all the people opposed it then."[22]

Emma Irick and Julia Shellhamer were the only women who mentioned giving up other career aspirations to become preachers. Irick's call to preach conflicted with her earlier desire to become a medical doctor, while Shellhamer had hoped to be a music teacher.[23]

The sanctified self, fortified by God's call to preach, confronted the notion of a gendered self characterized by the conviction that a woman's place was in the home, not in the pulpit. While many believed the pulpit was the locus of male religious power, sanctified women proclaimed that the pulpit also was woman's place. When Wesleyan/Holiness women encountered gendered constructions of self, they abruptly dismissed them by asserting their spiritual authority. Women overthrew the restrictions of a gendered self by drawing on their experience as sanctified Christians and by claiming the power of the Holy Spirit in a religious atmosphere whose polity was characterized by egalitarian primitivism.

Licensing and Ordination

For the most part, Wesleyan/Holiness denominations issued licenses and ordination papers regardless of sex. They validated a woman's divine call to ministry by licensing women to preach or ordaining them, thus furnishing official sanction for women's rejection of the gendered self. They were among the few churches that ordained women in the nineteenth century, but their numbers far surpassed all other women clergy combined. Research in 1892 indicated there were fewer than seventy ordained women. This did not include Quakers, and obviously Wesleyan/Holiness women were not counted. To further illustrate the contrast, a magazine article in 1920 provided the following statistics. There were 180 ordained women altogether in ten non–Wesleyan/Holiness denominations. The author also listed 350 ordained women in just one Wesleyan/Holiness group, the Church of the Nazarene. She did not incorporate statistics from any other Wesleyan/Holiness denominations in her report.[24] Even though this would have swelled the number considerably, women still constituted a small percentage of clergy in the United States.

Without mentioning her initial church affiliation, Anna Prosser switched her membership to the Methodist church, where she "obtained some advantages which women are not afforded in some denominations, i.e., liberty to speak or pray as led by the Spirit." During a brief period of time from 1868 to 1880, the Methodist Episcopal Church issued preaching licenses to women. In 1868 Maggie Newton Van Cott became the first woman to receive an exhorter's license, which authorized her to conduct meetings for prayer and exhortation on the Windham, New York, circuit. Like several other women, she had presided over such meetings prior to her licensing. By unanimous vote, Abbie Mills received a local preacher's license from her quarterly conference in 1875. Almira Losee, another Methodist preacher, held an exhorter's license. In 1876, Methodist Episcopal clergy identified her as a local preacher commissioning her to work among Mormons in Utah. The denomination revoked all women's licenses in 1880 when two women (Anna Oliver and Anna Howard Shaw) sought ordination. When Alma White, who grew up a Methodist, began preaching during the 1890s, the Methodist Episcopal Church no longer granted licenses. Lela McConnell was the only woman in the present study ordained by the Methodist Episcopal Church. Initially licensed a local preacher, she was ordained a deacon in 1924, the first year Methodists began ordaining women as local deacons and local elders. McConnell received elder's papers in 1926.[25] Women did not receive full membership in Methodist annual conferences until 1956.

Julia Shellhamer recorded the conversation that took place when her licensing came before the Free Methodist Board. Age, as well as sex, figured in the case against licensing her. Shellhamer was eighteen at the time. One preacher who also opposed women preachers argued that she was too young. Shellhamer, who was present during the debate, recorded that the speaker did not spare her feelings. A supporter contended that the refusal of a license might discourage Shellhamer. He argued: "Brethren, since most young women are far away from such an ambition, let us encourage the one in our midst who is willing to take the cross and go and rescue the fallen." Ultimately, her opponents won the day. Shellhamer "felt the slight keenly," conveying an enormous amount of emotion in a few words. After the meeting, Shellhamer remembered she had been given an evangelist's license earlier by the Evansville district of the Wisconsin conference of the Free Methodist Church while she was in school there. The license had expired, but Shellhamer's brother-in-law, a prominent pastor, was so upset over the matter that he took the license to the district quarterly conference, where it was quickly renewed. Shellhamer concluded, "When we refuse to fight our own battles some one else does it for us!" Reflecting on this early experience in her ministry, Shellhamer observed: "There have been a very few times in my life when we have met men who openly and strenuously opposed the idea of a woman preaching the gospel. This once greatly troubled my reticent spirit but I have learned to go right on as though there was no opposition. Time is too short and God's work too important to stop and parley with opposers." Again, she did not elaborate on the extent of her suffering. Attributing opposition to jealousy, she declared: "It is not my business to offer an apology to such men for the commission given me by the King. The fact that He has given it is sufficient proof that it is right to carry it out."[26]

Even though Shellhamer met the conditions for ordination, including the Theological Course of Study, she became ineligible for ordination when she married an ordained minister. This was a standard rule at the time within the Free Methodist Church. Shellhamer discussed her status with the following preface: "I have never said much about the ordination of women and have never fought for women's rights, but have felt that the best way to do this was to keep my mouth shut and let someone else do the talking." While this may have been her stated policy, when it came to recording her ministry in her autobiography, she wrote passionately. While the rule against ordaining wives of clergy was universal within the denomination, Shellhamer took it personally, wondering if others thought she did not have the ability to pastor. Even though this was speculation, and probably inaccurate speculation at that, she was humiliated. She allowed two sentences to summarize her feelings on the matter. She followed this with an experience she had at a camp meeting where she was assisting. "I was kneeling in the straw by the altar when, like a thunderbolt out of a clear sky (for I had not been giving the matter the least thought), the Lord appeared to me saying he had come to ordain me. Then the blessed hands of the triune God were laid upon my poor unworthy head and such a blessing bestowed by the sovereign grace of God the Father, God the Son, and God the Holy Ghost, as I had never received before. This was such a sweet experience I have never told it to anyone until this moment." God's ordination compensated for the lack of human recognition of her calling. However, it is hard to take at face value her assertion that she had not given the matter any thought, since she had already spoken of personal humiliation and pondered the possibility that she did not measure up to human expectations for ordination. Another comment, interesting more for what is not said than what is revealed, appeared within a page of the account quoted above. She reported she was sent to a circuit "which was so run down, they decided it was not fit for a man and would have to be given to a woman." No commentary accompanied her acknowledgment of sexism in job placement, other than the confession that "the work was so discouraging" and she "did not try very hard to do much" other than lead the regular services. Despite her lack of enthusiasm, several people were converted, including one young man who wished to be baptized. She had to tell him that, without ordination, she could not baptize him but that her husband could perform the baptism when he returned from his evangelistic work. No one else was available and since the man wanted to be baptized soon, Shellhamer asked a Methodist Episcopal pastor in town to conduct the baptism. He obliged and proceeded to successfully woo the man to his church. Ultimately, the young man turned away from the church, rejecting his Christian experience. Shellhamer concluded her account: "I confess I felt it keenly—but, am I responsible?"[27] Without explicitly calling names, she placed the blame for losing this young man on those who refused to ordain her, thus making it impossible for her to perform the rite of baptism and nurture the young man in his growth as a Christian.

Emma Irick was licensed by the Texas Holiness Association in 1907, having already preached for two years. Many from this group joined together with other holiness churches to form the Pentecostal Church of the Nazarene the following year. Dr. Phineas Bresee, a primary founder of the denomination, officiated at her ordination in 1911. Susan Fitkin was a recorded minister with the Society of Friends before affiliating with the Pentecostal Church of the Nazarene. Bresee also officiated at the service where Fitkin and her husband were ordained as elders. She reminded her readers that the service "was only the human sanction to God's work," quoting the Bible verse "Ye have not chosen me, but I [God] have chosen you, and ordained you, that ye should go and bring forth fruit."[28]

Lucy Drake Osborn reported receiving ordination papers before leaving for India to serve as a missionary in the fall of 1875. They were necessary in order for her to be able to administer the sacraments in an area where no other missionaries would be working. However, she neglected to note that her ordination was highly irregular. Six men, either pastors or presbyters representing five different denominations, signed the certificate. Generally, one denomination ordains a person for ministry. It is unlikely that any denomination, much less the denominations represented by the signers, would have recognized the certificate as valid. The content of the certificate likewise failed to note that this was extremely unusual. It stated: "We, the undersigned, in the name of our Lord Jesus Christ, and as far as He has given us power and authority, in accordance with His blessed will, give you commission to go forth as His messenger and minister, for the instruction of the ignorant, the recovery of the lost, the comfort and building up of His

Emma Irick, author of *The King's Daughter*
(Kansas City, Mo.: Pedestal Press, 1973).

people. This may be your certificate that we have ordained you to the Gospel ministry. In the name of the Father, and of the Son, and of the Holy Ghost. Amen."[29] While the certificate indicated support from clergy, the signers did not actually have ecclesiastical authorization to ordain people.

In several other cases, letters of recommendation served in lieu of licensing or ordination. Prior to being licensed a local preacher, Maggie Newton Van Cott received a letter signed by two pastors when she initiated full-time evangelistic work. Addressed "To All Whom It May Concern," it noted the number of conversions at two of her revivals, each lasting six weeks. The letter concluded: "*Whereas,* we are convinced that God has *called her to the work of an evangelist in his Church;* we, therefore, heartily, and prayerfully, recommend her to, and bespeak for her a cordial welcome, and the unhesitating and earnest co-operation of the Churches wherever she may choose to labor, believing that God will make her very useful in building up the Redeemer's Kingdom." Another testimonial, signed by seven pastors and laymen from three denominations (Methodist, Presbyterian, and Baptist), elaborated on her ministry. Twenty-two of her converts signed yet another letter.[30]

Elizabeth Wheaton relied on a letter endorsing her ministry from Gov. David R. Frances, dated 24 October 1891, to convince one prison chaplain to allow her to hold services for the inmates. Initially, the chaplain refused, in no uncertain terms: "I will never permit any women to take my pulpit." Upon being shown the letter, he backpedaled: "I never did allow a woman to speak in my meetings. But seeing the governor's request and your years of experience, I will allow you to come in the morning and conduct the women's meetings." Wheaton carried this letter and various other letters of recommendation in her purse.[31] Governor Frances, as the highest civil authority in the state (which Wheaton did not identify), and other political leaders affirmed Wheaton's public ministry.

Because a woman did not mention licensing or ordination did not necessarily mean she did not hold a license or ordination papers. Mary Lee Cagle never broached the issue in her autobiography, but she was ordained. The author of the introduction to her narrative referred to her as "Rev.," offering the only hint that she was, in fact, ordained.[32] Perhaps there were others whose silence regarding ordination did not necessarily mean they were unordained. It is extremely frustrating that autobiographers often did not report important information such as this.

Alma White left Methodism and established her own church in order to receive ordination. She founded the Pentecostal Union (soon known as the Pillar of Fire) in December 1901, which held its first ordination service in March 1902. Along with White, another woman and three men were ordained.

Lack of official credentials from a denomination did not prevent women from preaching. Maggie Newton Van Cott documented that she had spoken hundreds of times from texts of Scriptures for two years prior to her licensing. When someone questioned whether her first license allowed her to preach, Van Cott responded: "Don't it? Well, God allows it. I received my commission from him, brother . . . and God has honored the work in the salvation of hundreds of souls. I think what God owns and blesses, man has no right to condemn." Following this conversation, she received a preaching license from the quarterly conference of Stone Ridge, in Ellensville district in 1869.[33] While Van Cott claimed not to value her license, she noted in her autobiography that she could now refer to her discourses as sermons.

Gender-Based Opposition to Women Preachers

Women preachers faced opposition based solely on the fact that they were women. There is no escaping the fact that a woman's self is gendered. It is filtered through biased lenses that attribute stereotypical characteristics and roles based on sex. Simone de Beauvoir's *The Second Sex,* written in 1949, was revolutionary because it documented the gendered self. Without the benefit of Beauvoir's work, women preachers were cognizant of this reality. Their opponents, first and foremost, saw women through the lens of gender. Lest women preachers forget that others sought to use constructions of gender to mold their self identities, the primary argument of their adversaries was simply that preaching was unwomanly. Julia Shellhamer reflected this essentialist thinking when she described "a masculine woman" who tried to be "mannish" by being too "forward and brassy." She admitted, however, that while she criticized women preachers who were like this, she went to the other extreme and lacked sufficient boldness.[34] Opponents of women preachers constantly reminded women they were not fulfilling the gender expectations society outlined for them. The ideology of woman's sphere with its emphasis on domesticity embodied these expectations.

Overcoming a restrictive view of self occasionally was difficult because women had internalized a gendered self promulgated by their culture. As one scholar has observed: "It is hard to fight an enemy who has outposts in your head." Women were susceptible to criticism. Lucy Drake Osborn confessed: "My sensitive nature suffered keenly from the bands of public opinion, but the Lion of Judah broke the fetters, so that my soul was free."[35] "Lion of Judah" is an allusion to Christ found in Rev. 5:5, which identifies Christ as conqueror. Osborn drew upon theological language, but the meaning is clear. Rather than allowing herself to be enslaved by society's perception of her and the limits it sought to impose, she found freedom from the confinement of woman's sphere. She asserted a sanctified self independent of the restrictions society attempted to foist on her. The sanctified self ran counter to the constructions of gender shaped by the surrounding culture. The intensity of the struggle reflected the serious challenge a sanctified self posed to society's construction of woman's sphere that sought to prohibit women from participating in the public arena.

Phoebe Palmer, the role model for many women preachers, appeared to endorse woman's sphere and essentialism, which served as its foundation when she wrote, "Woman has her legitimate sphere of action which differs in most cases materially from that of man." However, the words "in most cases" undermine her case. Once exceptions are made, the argument for essentialism starts unraveling. Palmer specifically allowed that women may "occasionally be brought out of the ordinary sphere of action and occupy in either church or state positions of high responsibility." These words from the same paragraph as the first quotation further weaken her position. Palmer's extensive career as a preacher additionally subverts her essentialism. Wesleyan/Holiness women preachers followed Palmer's example rather than adopting her essentialist statements, which could be construed to limit women.

Women were well aware that their preaching defied the prevailing essentialist attitude that woman's proper place or sphere was in the home. They self-consciously rejected a limited construction of the self promoted by the ideology of woman's sphere. Wesleyan/Holiness women challenged essentialism by stepping outside woman's sphere to preach. Their activities did not go unnoticed. Opponents quickly offered specific suggestions for women preachers with respect to their responsibilities in the home. Jennie Smith overheard one detractor exclaim: "I don't believe in these women; they had better be at home washing dishes." She reported that many claimed preaching "is not women's place or work." Smith provided an example from her early ministry when she herself had accepted this argument. When asked to lead a Sunday morning service at a camp meeting in Summit Grove, Maryland, in 1880 where many ministers were present, she demurred, "that is not my place." The man responded, "but we consider it is your place," and Smith proceeded to fulfill the request to preach.[36] With this encouragement, she overcame her hesitancy to challenge the ideology of woman's sphere, which she had internalized.

In the mid nineteenth century, suffragists began seeking to stretch the boundaries in the political realm while women preachers tackled restrictions in the religious realm. Sometimes, the two agendas overlapped. The first woman's rights convention, held at a Wesleyan chapel in Seneca Falls, New York, in 1848, adopted a Declaration of Sentiments modeled after the Declaration of Independence. Included in a list of facts documenting the "repeated injuries and usurpations on the part of man toward woman" was this reference to woman's sphere: "He [man] has usurped the prerogative of Jehovah himself, claiming it as his right to assign for her a sphere of action, when that belongs to her conscience and to her God." The group passed the following resolution redefining and expanding woman's sphere: "That woman has too long rested satisfied in the circumscribed limits which corrupt customs and a perverted application of the Scriptures have marked out for her, and that it is time she should move in the enlarged sphere which her great Creator has assigned her."[37]

Proponents of woman's sphere insisted that women conform to the restrictions this ideology sought to impose on women. Women such as Alma White, though, were undaunted by fierce opposition to her public ministry because, as she reported: "The Lord had promised that I was to be the medium through which He would work." White knew her accomplishments as an evangelist bothered male pastors, not simply because she was a more successful evangelist but because she was a more successful *woman* evangelist. Alluding to her Methodist colleagues before she left Methodism, she speculated: "It was most humiliating to churchmen to have a woman wield the sword of truth, when no recognition had been given her by ecclesiastical authorities, and she was supposed to have no place except that of servant." White, along with other women, rejected society's attempt to force a narrowly gendered identity on them. With respect to the stereotype that women were too soft-spoken to speak publicly, White argued: "Woman has had but little opportunity to develop a voice necessary for public speaking. She has been made to believe that a voice with volume and power would make her appear masculine, and out of harmony with cultured femininity. And so the world continues its opposition to her liberation in social, civic, and religious circles, determined to perpetuate her chains."[38] White clearly associated rigid constructions of gender with the invisible chains that impeded women's equal involvement in the public arena. She and other Wesleyan/Holiness women were not fooled by the rhetoric of woman's sphere.

As indicated above, women in some cases had to overcome their personal aversion to the idea of women preaching before initiating their ministries. They needed to resolve the tension between their sanctified selves and the cultural construction of a female self that precluded preaching. In order to preach, they had to reject their prior conformity to the gendered self that society had imposed on them. Lizzie Miller had been taught as a child that women should not preach. Her lifelong training was overturned "in a moment" when she was called to preach.[39]

For other women, the struggle to come to terms with their own negative stance toward preaching was more prolonged. But once they settled the matter, it was determined once and for all. It was not an ongoing battle, resurrected whenever someone challenged their right to preach. When first asked to pray in public, Emma Ray responded with a definite "no."[40] Others, including Maggie Newton Van Cott, Mary Cole, Almira Losee, and Lucy Drake Osborn, also had to overcome an internalized view of self that precluded preaching from their repertoire of acceptable activities.

Like Ray, Van Cott had similarly refused to conduct a class meeting because she "did not think it looked well to see a lady speak in public." She shared this hesitancy later in a sermon, concluding: "But you see I have got bravely over it." The congregation laughed at the contrast she painted between her early behavior and her subsequent evangelistic career. Van Cott recalled her initial hostility toward preaching by reconstructing a conversation she had with a pastor who was encouraging her to preach. Reverend Battersby handed her a Bible, saying: "Look out a subject, and preach for us at the school-house to-night." Van Cott reacted with surprise, turned pale, and hesitated before responding: "Sir, I can not preach." Reverend Battersby replied that he had heard from his son that she preached several times a week at a mission. Van Cott defended her position: "I never attempted to preach; I do not understand the first rule. I do the best I can to *talk* for Jesus, and praise his name—he saves precious souls—but as to leading a meeting here, I can not do it." Refusing to take "no" for an answer, Reverend Battersby persisted until she cried. Even then, he consoled her with the promise that God would help her. Reflecting on the conversation, Van Cott recalled that "the word '*preach,*' as applied to her efforts, was always harsh, and undesirable." She also remembered a dream where she was commanded to preach despite her avowal that she did not know how. In the dream, she obeyed the command when it was repeated and addressed a large congregation. She dismissed the value of the dream but yielded to Reverend Battersby's entreaties to preach. A practical reality forced her to preach from the pulpit, an act which she had assiduously avoided up to this point. She found the sanctuary was too dark in front of the pulpit so she had to stand in the pulpit to see. Stepping into the pulpit "nearly overwhelmed her." She prayed that seekers would come to the altar after her sermon to indicate God's approval of her action. Her prayer was answered. Initially, Van Cott, like Emma Ray, abstained from using the word *preaching* to designate her activity even though she was in fact preaching.[41] She overcame this hesitancy by the time she was granted a local preacher's license within several months of the conversation with Reverend Battersby and her subsequent decision to preach.

Mary Lee Cagle, likewise, struggled to come to terms with the nomenclature of preaching. The first time a pastor announced that she would be preaching, she implored him to merely say that she was leading the service. Despite her request, the pastor insisted on saying she would preach. This upset her to the extent that she was unable to sleep or eat. Once in the pulpit, however, God "broke every fetter." She described the scene: "It was the first time in her life that she could turn the pulpit loose—she ran from one end of the large platform to the other and shouted and praised God, and preached with the Holy Ghost sent down from above." Her behavior was a far cry from her usual "shrinking, backward disposition." From that day, she experienced freedom in the pulpit.[42] Cagle's sanctified self prevailed over the former self that refused to even contemplate preaching.

At first, Almira Losee also denied that she preached even though the press and others recognized her as a preacher. While at a Merrick camp meeting, a woman asked Losee to preach in her church tent the following Sunday. Losee recorded the conversation: "'I am not a preacher, madam.' 'I hear that you preach,' said she, 'having seen an account of it in a newspaper.' 'No, ma'am, I have never tried to preach, but I sometimes *talk* in the meetings.' 'Then I engage you to come in two weeks to "*talk*" in my tent if you will.'" Losee agreed to go, taking as her text the Beatitudes in the gospel of Matthew. While Losee claimed to be just talking, it was obvious to others that she was preaching since she took a text and publicly commented on it during Sunday morning worship. Eventually, Losee must have come to terms with her preaching since Methodist Episcopal clergy later recognized her as a local preacher.[43]

The women discussed above indicated a change of heart in their autobiographies by briefly mentioning their initial convictions against the preaching of women. Lucy Drake Osborn, however, authored a chapter entitled "Sphere for Women" in her autobiography to describe the process by which she moved from opposition to acceptance. She had been taught that the Bible "gave explicit directions that this public witnessing by women should never be practiced." She, too, harbored a "prejudice against that word 'preach' as connected with a woman." Quoting from her diary, she professed, "I want to understand more about women speaking in meeting." In a subsequent entry, she wrote: "After receiving the baptism of the Spirit I became much more interested regarding the work of woman and her sphere in the Church. Especially was I concerned to know whether it was God's will she should testify of salvation in the social means of grace." Osborn believed the Holy Spirit was guiding her to speak publicly, but that contradicted the interpretation of the Bible that she had been taught. Osborn wrestled for six months, dreading the ultimate decision because, either way, she would offend others. She would alienate her family and friends by changing her mind and disappoint her Methodist friends if she maintained her current position. A Methodist pastor, hearing of her dilemma, advised her not to expect a revelation but to gather all the Bible references dealing with the work of women and ask for God's wisdom in interpreting them. She followed the pastor's counsel and "the matter was settled to my perfect satisfaction: it was God's will that women should prophesy. To question it again has never come to my mind. God had decided it for me."[44] Osborn elaborated on her change of opinion leading her to reject the restrictive construction of self that society prescribed for women.

Opposition from family and friends often supplemented women's initial aversion to preaching. In some cases, spouses raised objections. Alma White's husband did not oppose the fact that she preached, but he did criticize the content of her sermons, contending that her biblical hermeneutic or interpretation was faulty. Approximately one year after she began preaching, White recollected: "As I labored on from day to day and the work enlarged on my hands he became more bold in his denunciations and criticisms, sometimes assuming the attitude of an anxious and affectionate husband who wished to keep me from going too near the precipice. It was more difficult to withstand him under this guise than when he was openly hostile." During one revival, she endured her husband's wrath while staying in the home of a church family. She feared the impact that their arguments might have on the congregation: "It was his custom to speak loudly. I felt quite sure the people in the house had heard him and I feared it would be told among the parishioners the next day." Sometimes, she closed revivals early, claiming she could not withstand her husband's verbal attacks and preach simultaneously. During one holiness meeting, he publicly disagreed with her concerning a theological matter.[45] A former Methodist pastor, he ultimately left her after an ongoing doctrinal dispute over glossolalia, or speaking in unknown tongues. He had embraced the doctrine and pressured his wife to adopt it as a part of the creed for her churches. Alma adamantly refused to allow him to take charge in church matters. After leaving Alma and their two sons, he affiliated with a Pentecostal church that affirmed speaking in tongues.

Without forewarning, Florence Roberts's husband issued an ultimatum; she had to choose between her rescue work and him. When asked if he meant it, he replied: "I certainly do." She agonized in prayer and then opened her Bible. She believed she found her answer in 1 Cor. 7:23: "Ye are bought with a price; be not ye the servants of men." Yet her pastor advised that she reconcile with her husband and limit her activities to local church work. She summarized the conflict in one sentence: "Circumstances, which it is neither pleasant nor profitable to relate here, soon necessitated the breaking up of my home." She received a letter from Sacramento asking her to fill in for the matron of a rescue home there. She obliged, leaving Redding, California, and her husband to begin her work in the Peniel Mission at Sacramento.[46] Using the Bible to subvert her husband's authority, she applied the verse quoted above from 1 Corinthians to justify her refusal to be a servant of her husband's demands.

Parents were another hindrance to ministry. The fathers of Lucy Drake Osborn and Anna Prosser both raised objections to their daughters' preaching. Osborn's father feared it would cause division within the church. When Prosser's father urged her to quit her mission work, she replied: "Father I know that my highest earthly duty is to you, but there is one still higher, and if those two duties conflict I must choose the higher."[47] Like Roberts, Prosser claimed heavenly authority superseded earthly authority.

Alma White's mother actively opposed her daughter's ministry. White spoke of her mother's strong personality and her belligerent attitude. Her mother ultimately joined a rival Wesleyan/Holiness group and did her utmost to subvert White's work.[48]

In Mary Glaser's case, it was her children who objected. Her husband had abandoned the family years before. When Glaser began leaving home to share the story of her healing, her six children, the youngest of whom was twelve, were left to fend for themselves. Glaser reasoned that God allowed her to stay with her children while they were young and that the older ones were now in a position to take care of Ellie, the youngest. She informed them: "That I was not my own now, but wholly the Lord's, that they must arrange the house-keeping to their own pleasure; that I must be at liberty to go and come at God's command." Several children then went to work on surrounding farms. Her children wondered if their mother still cared for them. They felt that if she was well enough to travel, she should stay at home and handle household duties. She responded: "'Wist ye not, that I must be about my Master's business?'" She further informed her children that she "would be with them as much as the Lord would permit" since they were as dear to her as ever, but "now that God had ordained me to go and teach this way of faith, I could not do it by remaining at home." Glaser believed her children "were resisting the ordinances of God" by encouraging her to stay home. While she was traveling, Glaser's oldest daughter wrote that Ellie missed her mother. Glaser's heart ached for her daughter, yet she wrote to her children, asking them to be reconciled to the will of God. She related: "I prayed that they might see and understand that it was the Lord's will to leave them, to give all the honor and praise to Him. He did not answer my prayer." The three older children who had initially stayed at home and kept house decided to break up housekeeping and live with their employers. About a year later, Glaser disclosed that her children were all well provided for and now had come to believe that it was their mother's duty to obey God.[49]

Glaser faced intense opposition on other fronts as well. Opponents, including former friends, attacked her for leaving her children. They explicitly admonished her to stay home and make her children happy and comfortable. Glaser addressed her antagonists: "O, dear friends, who have been persecuting me for thus leaving my family, be careful for you know not what you are doing." She contended: "God calls many mothers from time into eternity, and very often to leave a large family of quite small children." Comparing her situation to mothers who died and left children behind hardly seems appropriate but she also argued her case on pragmatic grounds. If her ministry was "of man it would come to naught, and if of God, it would prosper. Glory to God it has proven itself long ago, for the Lord has restored my health, and has blessed my labors so that others have been healed, and others established in the faith, and some sinners brought to Christ." Another argument Glaser employed related to her health. God showed displeasure, she believed, when she was home by making her too ill to do housework. She was only well when traveling and speaking. Skeptics suggested she was just lazy.[50]

Other than Glaser's account, summarized above, Alma White provided the most detailed reckoning of opposition to her ministry. Her husband and her mother were not the only ones who sought to obstruct her calling. White chronicled her negative experiences at the hands of the Colorado Holiness Association, which was under the auspices of Methodist clergy. White's husband served as secretary of this group at its inception. However, White saw herself as the "energizing force back of the organization." She scheduled the preachers at the association's first camp meeting at Pleasant View in 1894. The following summer, Fort Collins hosted the camp meeting where a Methodist pastor led a faction who opposed women preachers. Explicitly attributing opposition to carnality or sin, White observed: "The holiness organization had done more for woman's ministry than all of the denominations, but there were so many carnal-minded people in connection with it that the opposition was sometimes very great." By the time of the fourth annual camp meeting in 1897, White reported that "the spirit of opposition against me had grown until I could have no fellowship with some of the leaders."[51]

Although White had helped organize the previous camp meetings, the program committee in 1897 did not invite her to preach. White's opportunity came when her husband, who had been allotted five minutes along with several other ministers, yielded his time to her. She proceeded to preach for fifty minutes: "The floodgates of heaven were opened and the long altar bench across the front of the tent was filled with seekers crying for mercy." Despite the congregation's positive response to her preaching, some leaders were displeased that she had taken over the service without an invitation. The following year at Greeley the program committee again overlooked White even though she was a member of the executive council and the membership committee of the association. She recollected: "For five years I had endured this kind of treatment after I had gotten the first and each succeeding camp meeting on foot without the assistance of any of those who had so bitterly opposed me."[52] The leadership of the Colorado Holiness Association consistently plotted to keep White out of the camp meeting pulpit and to undermine her influence. Rather than continue fighting, she ultimately left Methodism, "her spiritual mother," and formed her own organization.

Mary Cole recounted opposition she faced within the Methodist Episcopal Church, South. The summer before she left this denomination, Cole had been invited to conduct meetings in conjunction with the quarterly conference. Disbarred from the conference itself because she was female, she and several other women sat in an adjoining room where they could listen. She began her meetings as scheduled, but a wealthy contributor to the church objected. Clergy met privately and acquiesced to the man's demands that she stop preaching. She received a note at the conclusion of the third evening of services instructing her to close the meeting. Her emotions spilled over into her text: "I could not keep from crying. I had called the Methodist Church my mother; and now to think that my mother was treating me in this way, made me feel very bad."[53] Cole soon left Methodism and affiliated with the Church of God (Anderson, Indiana).

Methodist women preachers earlier in the nineteenth century had no option to leave their denomination and join one more sympathetic to their call to preach since Wesleyan/Holiness churches had not yet split from Methodism. Zilpha Elaw faced opposition from the superintendent of the circuit, who initially showed "great contempt . . . but after hearing somewhat more of the matter, his sentiments became changed, he was introduced to me, and became one of my very kind friends." Julia Foote also reported an about-face. An African Methodist Episcopal Church trustee declared that a woman should not preach. Affirming that "the God we serve fights all our battles," Foote recorded that by the time she left the city, "that trustee was one of the most faithful at my meetings, and was very kind to assist me on my journey."[54]

Other adversaries sometimes changed their minds. Jennie Smith revealed that one minister preached against her but "soon changed his mind and gave me a reception at his home." Sarah Cooke spoke at a soup kitchen in Chicago on one occasion where a man heckled her during her sermon. Afterward, she passed him as she walked down from the platform. He spoke to her, judging her "a first-rate preacher."[55] Opponents occasionally became supporters.

Like Cooke, other women sometimes faced hostility during the actual church services where they preached. One Sunday morning, Mary Still Adams filled Reverend Marshall's pulpit at his request. Entering the sanctuary, she discovered the Bible and large hymnbook were on a small stand in front of the chancel instead of at their usual location on the pulpit. The church board had moved the books to indicate their displeasure at their pastor's choice of a woman preacher. Adams recorded her response to the incident: "However, I being ignorant of the animosity to our sex, gathered up the ponderous books, and took my place in the pulpit. It was not an hour until I had delivered them my message, and the Lord had so blessed us they did not mind if I was a woman. I will add, if God did cause Aaron's rod to bud and bloom in the hand of Moses, he used me on that day to the opening of the eyes of the blind."[56] One suspects that Adams was more aware of opposition than she claimed.

Opponents sometimes resorted to spreading false rumors in their attempt to discredit the ministry of women. In Mary Lee Cagle's case, the male ministers in one city spread "the blackest falsehoods ever told," seeking to terminate a revival she was leading. Cagle revealed her opinion of them by referring to them as "so-called ministers of the gospel." She claimed that "if one-hundredth part that was told on her had been true, she should have been in the penitentiary instead of preaching the gospel." In situations such as this one, she relied on the promise of Isa. 54:17: "No weapon that is formed against thee shall prosper; and every tongue that shall rise against thee in judgment thou shalt condemn. This is the heritage of the servants of the Lord." Rumors circulated in Anson, Texas, that she had robbed the United States mail, run a house of ill-fame, and given away her four children. Cagle reported that it would be impossible to give away her children since she was childless! A preacher perpetuated the house-of-ill-fame rumor until a Methodist official confronted him with the possibility of a libel suit. Opponents spread the rumor that Jarena Lee was a man in woman's clothing. Some who instigated rumors were more creative. One circulated the notion that Mary Cole was a member of the James Boys, the famous outlaws, disguised as a woman.[57]

One evening, members of the family hosting Maggie Newton Van Cott during a revival repeated rumors they had heard, that she was "some broken-down actress" and a "bad woman." Everyone laughed but Van Cott, whose "heart fluttered like a wounded bird." Later, in her room, Van Cott recollected that "the bruised and aching heart cried out in agony." This was the first time negative rumors had reached her ears and she was devastated: "The barbed arrow was too sharp and well driven for a slight wound." She actually prayed to die in order to be removed from those who spread the rumors. During her prayer, she heard a voice "sweetly whispering in her soul, 'My grace is sufficient;' and at once a quiet peace stole over the troubled heart. Again, 'That God whom thou serveth, to whom thou must render an account, knoweth the innocence of thy soul concerning the things whereof these accuse thee.'"[58] Her assurance that God was on her side enabled Van Cott to ignore the rumors and to speak again the next evening.

Mary Lee Cagle's antagonists had sought to discredit her ministry by contending she had given away her fictitious children. Sadly, many women minimized information on their private lives in their autobiographies, making it impossible to determine how many were married or actually had children. Several women, however, discussed juggling family responsibilities and professional activities, which highlighted the tension between the gendered self

Mary Lee Cagle, author of *Life and Work of Mary Lee Cagle: An Autobiography* (Kansas City, Mo.: Nazarene Publishing House, 1928).

that was expected to have primary care of children and the sanctified self that was called to preach.

The call to preach was a priority that required mothers to arrange for child care so that they could maintain their public ministry. God empowered mothers to withstand the temptation to acquiesce to the doctrine of woman's sphere and forsake their public ministry. Once Mary Still Adams left two of their children with her husband so she could fulfill a preaching assignment. When she worried about her children, she blamed the Devil for her concerns about their welfare: "The tempter came to me like a flood, saying, 'what a fool you are to keep preaching against all odds;' there was not an argument in all his devilish mind which he did not use. He spoke of our poverty and of my leaving my children without a mother's care, suggesting that in all probability they would be dead upon my return home. The more he tempted me the more I looked through faith to God, who then and there turned into a present help in time of need, and filled my soul with power."[59] By placing the conflict on a cosmic scale, and blaming the Devil for any unnecessary second thoughts about neglecting responsibilities at home, Adams left her worries in God's hands. Adams believed the power of God overwhelmed the power of evil that sought to keep Adams from fulfilling her ministerial responsibilities.

Mary Still Adams sprinkled her autobiography with several other references to combining child care with preaching. She experienced another role conflict at a camp meeting near Kansas City in 1868. Her baby Mattie had contracted cholera, but the preacher in charge of the meeting had previously announced that she would preach at the 10:30 A.M. service the next day. Adams prayed that God would give her an omen, and her prayers were answered when a doctor who was a children's specialist came to the campground to care for her baby. When the horn blew announcing the service, she went and preached before several thousand people. After preaching, she saw her husband "looking so glad and happy" as he held the baby. She left the pulpit and soon learned that the medicine prescribed by the doctor had worked, and her daughter was out of danger.[60]

Adams recalled that when her children were young, she never stopped to worry about who would take care of them when she was asked to preach: "Oh! no, but I answered at once, 'here Lord I am, send me.'" If she could not secure a babysitter, she took her children with her. She recollected: "In scores of instances I have gone forth in this way to meet and stand before the people to tell them of Christ, who is able to save to the uttermost, and God has ever had some one in reserve to take and care for my children, one of these who perhaps would only be three or four months old, and as a reward of obedience and faith in God, my babe slept or played during the whole of the service, nor did my children ever disturb anyone while I preached." She mentioned one preaching tour where she took two children, Alvah, age six, and Mattie, five months.[61] Adams recorded that her seven children never prevented her from preaching.

Several other women briefly mentioned managing child care and preaching. Jarena Lee, writing in 1849, left her sickly son at home while she conducted a one-week revival thirty miles away. She reported gratefully: "During the whole time, not a thought of my little son came into my mind; it was hid from me, lest I should have been diverted from the work I had to do, to look after my son." Joycelyn Moody has noted: "Boldly, Lee contends that not she but God privileges her ministry over her submission to patriarchal standards of maternal duty." A couple of generations later, Emma

Irick remembered: "While in Alabama, both the flu and World War I were raging. Brother Irick and our baby, Ruth, came down with the flu, so I had to be nurse as well as evangelist." In this instance, Irick combined child care and preaching. When her family increased by two additional children, her mother and sister watched them when they were young. Once they were in school, the Iricks hired a housekeeper to care for the children. During the summers, the children traveled with their parents and provided music for the revival services. Maggie Newton Van Cott remembered one time her daughter became lonely when left behind while she traveled as an evangelist. She insisted that her daughter stay in a good home with kind friends. Her decision was difficult and caused a severe headache. After seven weeks, Van Cott took advantage of a two-day lull between engagements and went to get her daughter, unable to endure the separation herself any longer.[62]

Lucy Drake Osborn performed professional and familial duties simultaneously. She talked extensively about raising her children as Christians. With respect to her ministry and her children, she wrote: "Believing that no more important work can be delegated to a woman than to be a wife and mother, I suffered much in the fear that I might not properly fulfill these obligations, with the care of the school resting upon me."[63] Despite her misgivings, she continued managing a missionary training school she had established. Rather than accepting the responsibility for shortchanging one obligation while fulfilling the other one, she left it up to God by praying that "if it was against His will for me to continue the school, not to let the necessaries for its continuance be sent; but every time, and immediately, there would come much larger supplies than usual." With this positive response to her prayers, she felt that it was God's will for her to maintain the school while raising her children.

Alma White traveled extensively, conducting revivals and attending camp meetings. She generally secured child care for her two sons when they were young, but sometimes took them with her. White's longest evangelistic campaign without her children lasted fifteen weeks. On her return, she found that the boys were both well and had kept their salvation. White interpreted this to be "God's seal on my labors." When they reached their teens, her sons began to assist her with the preaching.[64]

Like Adams and White, Julia Shellhamer spoke several times of taking her children with her when she preached. She revealed her hesitancy about the enterprise: "It was better, thought I, to try and to fail than not to try at all." But things always worked out fine; her daughter helped sing and her son "was not much trouble." On another occasion, someone held her baby while she preached at one location and her husband preached elsewhere. In one pastorate, "a dear elderly sister" helped with household duties. With three small children, Shellhamer found she could not accomplish as much work in the church as she desired since she claimed to give priority to her children. It is important to note, however, that she pastored a church as a young mother. At pastoral appointments in Atlanta and Blairsville, she either had assistance with child care or help with housework. When she traveled to a five-day revival without any children, her empty hands echoed her loneliness. After the last service, she caught a midnight train home "anxious to see if the children were all well. When I arrived the house was still standing just where I had left it."[65] It appears she had fewer concerns when she traveled with her children than when she was alone.

One condition of Shellhamer's pastoral placement at Leechburg, Pennsylvania, was that she be granted permission to preach at camp meetings during the summer. She took her two daughters while her husband took their son, and they traveled to different locations to preach. One summer, she reported preaching at revivals and at a camp meeting before joining her husband and son at Aura, New Jersey, where they had both been invited to assist. Following this revival, husband and wife went their separate ways again, reuniting at Dayton, Ohio, where they once more had been invited to jointly assist at a camp meeting.[66]

Julia Shellhamer did more than offer herself as an example of a woman who successfully combined motherhood and preaching. She utilized her autobiography as a platform to admonish other women to follow her example. She bemoaned the fact that when women evangelists married, they often left the preaching to their husbands. "I felt that while a woman's place must be filled as wife, mother and housekeeper, yet if she is called of God, these duties do not excuse her from the work so near her heart and that if the time given by most women to idle chit-chat, fancy work and unnecessary things were properly used, a woman could find some time to work for the salvation of souls." If there was no time, Shellhamer advised that a woman hire someone to help with her housework while she did God's work, a radical suggestion for 1923. Shellhamer followed her own advice by hiring someone to assist with the housework while she pastored at Blairsville, Pennsylvania.[67]

Perhaps fearing her example and admonitions were not enough, Shellhamer incorporated an article entitled "How Women May Win Souls" into her text. She addressed the article to mothers with small children. After praising motherhood, she regretted that women who previously had been called to God's service abandoned this calling when they became mothers. Shellhamer outlined ten practical suggestions for ministry. Her advice has a contemporary ring. For instance, she encouraged mothers to get outside a little every day for their health. Of course, while outside they could recruit friends to join them in visiting jails, hospitals, or the almshouse. Other proposals included renting a cheap hall to hold services, distributing religious literature, or even loaning books to others or writing letters. She concluded: "If a woman is *conscientious* and *systematic* regarding the use of her time, something like the foregoing plan may be carried out without neglecting either her home or family."[68]

Rather than accepting the argument that motherhood precluded the possibility of preaching, women accepted their responsibilities as mothers but contended that the sanctified self gave priority to God's work. By doing so, they insisted that God rewarded their faithfulness by seeing that their children received the care they required. Theorist Mary G. Mason identified a double voice within American women's autobiographies by which women wrestle with both a private voice and a public voice that reflect a double identity.[69] Wesleyan/Holiness women counted the cost but did not appear to experience the extended conflict Mason described. Wesleyan/Holiness women accepted their private responsibilities, but their public identities predominated. More than likely, this was due to their conviction that God had authorized their public work and they did not have to accept the onus others attempted to place on them for not devoting their lives solely to their children.

Lizzie Miller used a children's sermon to inspire the next generation of women to Christian service: "Do not think, little girls, that your work will not be noticed. Anything you can do, no matter how small, will be acceptable with God. Look at the child Mariam, [*sic*] how she aided Israel, as a nation, in its darkest hours. She watched the infant Moses as he lay in a basket of papyrus on the river Nile until rescued. Though a very little girl she preserved the life of her brother Moses, who became the great leader of Israel. When she grew up to be a woman she did not fear the people or become slothful in duty, but worked for God and became a great prophetess and singer in Israel. She aided her brothers, Aaron and Moses, in Jehovah's work leading a nation from bondage to freedom."[70] As far as Miller was concerned, it was never too early to urge girls to consider a calling to ministry. Miller planted the seed by providing a biblical model for girls to follow, an example that would take them beyond woman's sphere. Her children's sermon called girls to reject a construction of self that would inhibit them. Instead, she challenged them to become leaders.

Besides defining motherhood as the only legitimate role for women, the ideology of true womanhood also advocated the tenet of submissiveness for women within the marriage relationship. Opinions with regard to male headship within marriage varied among Wesleyan/Holiness women. Some rejected the notion of male supremacy outright and others limited it to the home while claiming autonomy in the spiritual arena.

Hannah Whitall Smith and Maggie Newton Van Cott eschewed male headship. Smith did not "approve of letting husbands decide things for their wives." Van Cott's objections to headship were apparent during her wedding ceremony when the pastor asked her if she would obey her husband. She had determined ahead of time that she would omit that word from her vows. However, her mother had consulted with the pastor, who acquiesced to the mother's request that the word *obey* remain in the vows. The minister had to ask the question three times before Van Cott reluctantly responded affirmatively in a soft voice.[71]

Sarah Cooke revealed her opinion of headship by affirming the example of Mary and John Fletcher. At their wedding, John Fletcher read the passage from Ephesians 5—"Wives, submit yourselves to your husbands"—which Mary Fletcher quickly followed with "in the Lord." Her husband-to-be responded with hearty agreement and added: "if I ever wish you to do anything contrary to the Lord's will, resist me with all your might." While Cooke clearly rejected headship within the marriage relationship, her perspective on the role of men and women in ministerial leadership was conspicuously ambivalent. Apparently unaware of God's command at creation that men and women share joint dominion over the earth (Gen. 1:26–28), Cooke granted man supremacy "that God from the creation has given him." However, she severely diminished that supremacy when she continued her argument: "But in the glorious privilege of being co-workers in bringing back a lost world to Himself, women surely share. If woman may prophesy, surely she may preach." Before concluding her case, Cooke listed Priscilla and Aquila, co-workers in ministry during the New Testament era. Then, she finished with another defense of male supremacy: "When she tries to rule, ruin is almost sure to follow; but as the help-meet, the adviser—yea, the Aaron and the Hur to hold up the hands of those to whom God has delegated the government—she is a true help for him."[72] Cooke offered no attempt to resolve the noticeable contradiction in her statements.

Mary Lee Cagle gave lip service to headship when she claimed 1 Tim. 2:11–12—"Let the woman learn in silence with all subjection. But I suffer not a woman to teach, nor to usurp authority over the man, but to be in silence"—referred to "the home relations or relation of husband and wife. God is saying to woman that the man is the head of the household; and woman should be glad for him to remain there and not try to usurp his place." She continued by attributing the following words to God, which are not in the Bible: "I have put the man at the head, and you let him stay there, and you fill the place I have reserved for you." She demolished her case for male supremacy, though, when she added: "God made man and woman, not to be bosses one of the other, but to be helpmeets one for the other." Then, she described Eve, who was created to "stand right up by [Adam's] side on an equal footing with him."[73] Contrary to patriarchal interpretations of Genesis 1 and 2, Cagle's understanding supported equality between the sexes based on these passages.

Sometimes, actions spoke louder than words. Zilpha Elaw argued the strongest case for headship when she declared the wife "is subject to the authority of her husband" and identified headship as a regulation of Scripture and a dictate of nature. Despite her strong assertion of headship, Elaw refused to heed her husband's command that she refrain from public speaking.[74] As indicated earlier, Florence Roberts responded to her husband's ultimatum to choose between her rescue work and him by selecting the former. She was the only woman to discuss the fact that she separated from her husband to fulfill her ministry.

Wesleyan/Holiness women's views of headship ranged across a spectrum of opinion. Some rejected it outright. Others appeared to accept the position of male supremacy but confined it to the marriage relationship. Even then, their statements or actions often were contradictory. All of them, however, renounced the position that headship or female submission, a humanly constructed notion, mandated that they refrain from preaching. The sanctified self repudiated the gendered submissive self when it came to engaging in public ministries

Theological Responses to Opposition

Rather than avoiding the issue, most women responded theologically to the gender-based opposition of their preaching. Mary Lee Cagle reported, on one undated occasion, that, "as usual, she had to preach on 'Women's Right to Preach.'" The phrase "as usual" reveals that this was a common sermon topic for her. She and other women did not shy away from opposition but defended themselves from the pulpit. Once, Cagle related that the response to this sermon was overwhelmingly positive. A woman in the congregation began shouting encouragement about half way through the sermon. Others took up the cry and it was ten minutes before Cagle could proceed. Mary Cole responded to disapproval of her preaching, particularly in the early years of her evangelistic work: "At nearly every meeting I had to explain the Scriptural teaching on this subject." With God's help, she was able to "successfully drive these opposers out of their false positions and to show them that they were misusing the Scriptures." Alma White also spoke frequently on women in ministry, with sermon titles such as "The Door of Opportunity Opening for Women" and "Inequality of the Sexes in Church and State."[75]

Women employed various strategies to persuade others of their right to preach. While Cagle, Cole, and White faced the issue head-on and included a defense of women preachers in their sermon repertoire, others refused to defend their right to preach. Mary Glaser found prejudice everywhere. Her strategy was to "leave it all with the Lord as there is a day coming when these things will be made right." Amanda Smith refused to be drawn into arguments, "For it is like bodily exercise which profiteth little." When Emma Irick was asked to preach a sermon defending women's right to preach, she replied, "No, I don't have to. The proof of the pudding is in the eating."[76]

The Personal Narratives Group observed in 1989: "For a woman, claiming the truth of her life despite awareness of other versions of reality that contest this truth often produces both a heightened criticism of officially condoned untruths and a heightened sense of injustice." Rather than being intimidated, sanctified women generally judged their opponents harshly. Jarena Lee evaluated one antagonist who questioned her right to preach: "I found it was prejudice in his mind. He talked as if he had not known what the operation of the Spirit of God was. We may say, with propriety, he had not tarried at Jerusalem long enough." According to Lee, if he was truly sanctified and filled with the Holy Spirit, his prejudice against women's right to preach would evaporate. Instead of taking opposition personally, Lizzie Miller charged that her opponents "objected to God and His work of righteousness."[77] They had to answer to God, instead of to her, for their behavior.

Women such as Miller declared that the conflict over women preachers was a cosmic battle between God and the Devil. Those who opposed women preachers were on the side of the Devil. Other women credited the Devil for promoting the doctrine of woman's sphere. Alma White refused to mince words when she declared that the Enemy, referring to the Devil, enlisted pastors to promote a restrictive role for women: "Meanwhile the enemy kept busy in the churches. The pastors said it was a woman's place to stay at home and look after her husband and children." According to White, opposition was the work of the Devil: "The powers of darkness have reaped an awful harvest as the result of the opposition to woman's ministry." Those who sought to limit women's ministries by resorting to a circumscribed ideology of women's role were, by implication, aligning themselves with the Devil. This is the equivalent to today's judgment that sexism is sin. Women also blamed the Devil for tempting them to succumb to the dictates of woman's sphere and remain silent. Shortly before receiving her call, Sarah Cooke was moved to speak by the Spirit, but she allowed the Tempter or Devil to dissuade her.[78]

The Tempter once accosted Almira Losee and discouraged her from testifying about her sanctification. She succumbed to the temptation to keep quiet after the Devil reminded her to fulfill the expectation that a young woman be humble and modest. She curbed her zeal by "avoid[ing] all expressions that would attract attention." Then, after following this course of action, she felt the Devil chide her for not testifying to her family members that she was sanctified. Another time, Losee allowed herself to feel she had overstepped her bounds by speaking uninvited in a church service. She traced these feelings to Satan: "Satan had taunted me with having transcended the 'bounds of *female propriety,*' and of intruding myself upon the occasion, until my face tingled with shame."[79] The ideology of woman's sphere was so powerful that crossing its invisible boundaries created shame even though Losee believed it was God who had nudged her to speak and who had offered to help her. Despite Losee's initial apprehension, the person in charge of the service commended her comments on missions, placing himself on God's side rather than on the Devil's. Also, she received several invitations to speak at upcoming missionary gatherings, offering further encouragement to step outside woman's sphere and engage in public ministry.

Mary Cole wrote likewise of the Devil's unsuccessful efforts "to defeat the Lord's plan in regard to me." She described resistance which occurred shortly after her call to ministry. While sharing her call publicly, "it stirred up a spirit of jealousy in some and before night the devil tried to carry out his design to defeat the Lord's plan in regard to me. The devil began by starting a wicked falsehood against me and thus, almost crushing the life out of me. I did not understand the devil's cunning way and did not know how to lean on God, it was a dark hour for me. I remembered how the enemies of Moses tried to slay him when he was a child. God proved himself and protected me; he lifted me above all my persecutions and made me more than a conqueror."[80]

Likewise, Jarena Lee found that "the word of the Lord was verified" when she faced opposition: "When the Tempter raises a flood against you, I [God] will set up a standard against him."[81] Women blamed the Devil for antagonism they faced. Opponents had to answer to God for their role in attempting to thwart the advancement of God's work through the women God had called to preach. Convinced that God was on their side, women ultimately pursued their calling undaunted by any hostility they faced.

Being obedient to God's call to ministry overrode the restrictive humanly constructed notion of woman's sphere. Women rejected the notion of woman's sphere by associating it with the Devil, thus making it heretical. Identifying the Devil with the serpent in Genesis 3, Alma White affirmed that Christ's power over the serpent was complete: "But Christ, the seed of the woman, was promised, who would bruise the serpent's head and restore her to the place accorded her by the Creator as the helper and co-administrator with man."[82] By applying a spiritual interpretation to counteract the ideology of woman's sphere in this way, White and others appropriated Christ's authority to curtail any power that conventional role expectations might have had over them.

Women also dismissed male authority when it came to validation of their call to preach. God's authority superceded any dictates that men might utilize in their attempt to prevent women from preaching. They had no doubt that God chose women as well as men to preach. Elizabeth Elkin Grammer concluded from her recent study of seven women evangelists, including several African American sanctified women, that "the authority of God outweighs that of their parents, husbands, and friends, even that of their own consciences, which in many cases seem to assert quite forcefully their culture's prescriptive definitions of womanhood." Her observation holds true for white Wesleyan/Holiness women as well. All human authority lost its power under the weight of God's authority. Alma White insisted that preaching was one of women's "God-given rights."[83]

In light of this conviction, human recognition of their calling in terms of ordination had no appeal for some women. Mary Glaser began her ministry when God ordained her. Even though other women had been ordained, Amanda Smith remained satisfied with the Lord's ordination. She reported that ordination had never entered her mind: "For I had received my ordination from Him, Who said, 'Ye have not chosen Me but I have chosen you, and ordained you, that you might go and bring forth fruit, and that your fruit might remain.'" Others quoted this verse to signify where their priorities lay. Elizabeth Wheaton never spoke of ordination or licensing but did claim that God anointed her "for street preaching and for work in slums, dives and saloons."[84] Sanctified women often did not seek ordination from humans because they believed they had already been called and ordained by God.

Almira Losee initiated her preaching before being granted a preaching license. She reflected: "Many a time in years past our preachers had said to me, 'Surely we shall have to give you a license if thus you work in the vineyard.' I ever replied, 'Ah! my brethren, I shall not wait for a license to call a poor blind sinner, stumbling or rushing down to deep, dark despair; he may fall in while I am waiting for it. Do you think if I saw a house on fire, and people ready to perish in it, that I would wait until I got Church authority or license before I called out 'fire?'"[85] God's endorsement meant more to these women than human recognition.

When Bishop Richard Allen informed Julia Foote that the Discipline of the African Methodist Episcopal Church forbade women preachers and asked if she would comply with the rules of the Discipline, she answered, "Not if the discipline prohibits me from doing what God has bidden me to do; I fear God more than man." Lest there be any doubt about her position, she continued: "Man's opinion weighed nothing with me, for my commission was from heaven, and my reward was with the Most High." The African Methodist Episcopal Church ultimately revoked her membership. She fought back: "At that time, I thought it my duty as well as privilege to address a letter to the Conference, which I took to them in person, stating all the facts. My letter was slightingly noticed, and then thrown under the table. Why should they notice it? It was only the grievance of a woman, and there was no justice meted out to women in those days. Even ministers of Christ did not feel that women had any rights which they were bound to respect." Foote made no effort to excuse the sexist behavior of her church's leaders. She joined the African Methodist Episcopal Zion Church, where she became the first woman ordained a deacon and the second woman to receive full ordination as an elder.[86]

Dora Dudley rejected human opposition based on pragmatic grounds. She testified that God had honored her labors "so that I could not doubt my calling and acceptance in this work, and the approval of my Lord, though the whole world and church should combine against me." Jarena Lee likewise based her case on practical results: "As for me, I am fully persuaded that the Lord called me to labor according to what I have received, in his vineyard. If he has not, how could he consistently bear testimony in favor of my poor labors, in awakening and converting sinners?" Lucy Drake Osborn's father, who previously had opposed his daughter's activities decided that "the church must have been mistaken in its interpretation of Paul's words about women's speaking; for certainly God would not convert so many souls through them if they were working contrary to His will." Another detractor, this time of Jennie Smith, changed his mind after observing that people were experiencing conversion under her preaching.[87] God had blessed their work; therefore, women did not have to submit to human opposition.

The Biblical Basis for Affirming Women Preachers

Foes of women preachers turned to the Bible to authorize their attempt to maintain that women possessed a gendered self that prevented them from preaching. To them, the Bible fostered the essentialist agenda that claimed only men could preach. The Bible was their primary tool in constructing a gendered self. Rejecting such a patriarchal interpretation, women preachers brazenly appropriated the same authority and quoted liberating texts from the Bible to refute the opposition. Opponents hurled a few verses from the Bible their way, trusting they would silence women. Unintimidated, women methodically surveyed the Bible, discovering numerous precedents for women preachers. Wresting the power of Scripture from the hands of their opponents, they refused to allow the Bible to be used against them. "The right of women to preach in the Church has been, and is still, a question of much controversy." Thus began Maggie Newton Van Cott's chapter entitled "Shall Women Preach?" She continued: "There have been a great many learned authorities quoted on both sides; but, after a careful investigation, we unhesitatingly give it as our opinion, that tradition, the Scriptures, and the weight of learned authorities, are on the affirmative side of this question."[88]

Despite her opinion "that what we have been accustomed to all of our lives has more to do with our opinions than what the dear old Bible says," Mary Lee Cagle joined Van Cott and others in appropriating biblical arguments to vindicate her preaching. Alma White claimed: "There are no scriptural grounds for prohibiting women from preaching the Gospel or from leadership in the Church . . . There is nothing more unscriptural and more opposed to the principles of the New Testament than discrimination between the sexes in both Church and State." Some briefly mentioned verses that supported the case for women clergy. These include Jarena Lee, Mary Glaser, Zilpha Elaw, Amanda Smith, Lucy Drake Osborn, and Dora Dudley. Sarah Cooke, Alma White, Julia Foote, and Mary Cole offered abbreviated versions. Mary Lee Cagle appended her standard sermon on the topic to her autobiography. Maggie Newton Van Cott devoted a chapter to the subject, a portion of which was quoted above, while Julia Shellhamer and Sarah Cooke incorporated articles they had written on the topic into their autobiographies. Alma White published a tract entitled *Woman's Ministry,* much of which she repeated in her autobiography. Phoebe Palmer authored *The Promise of the Father,* a book-length defense of women preachers. Mary Still Adams was the only woman in the study who failed to provide a biblical defense for women preachers.[89]

The Wesleyan/Holiness movement documented a biblical precedent for women preachers. Women, and their male supporters, encouraged the movement to follow its primitivist impulses and model its leadership after the pattern established in the Bible. Mary Lee Cagle exhibited egalitarian primitivism when she contended: "I am persuaded that what [women] were allowed to do when the New Testament was written will be all right for them to do now." Dora Dudley agreed: "[God] chooses and sends out the willing and obedient ones to-day as well as then. I praise our dear Lord that he honors the labors of consecrated women as well as men; and He pours out His spirit upon them and calls them the 'daughters of the Almighty.'" Lucy Drake Osborn's observation that testifying by women was consistent with Bible truth reflected a general consensus.[90] No standard formula or outline emerged from a comparison of the Scriptural defenses. No one verse predominated. Women appeared to pick and choose from among the relevant passages. The following biblical basis for women preachers is a composite, drawing on the autobiographies as a whole.

Not content to limit themselves to the New Testament, women highlighted women prophets recorded in the Old Testament such as Miriam, Deborah, and Huldah. Maggie Newton Van Cott quoted Adam Clarke's commentary to corroborate Huldah's importance. Julia Shellhamer cited Jael as a warrior celebrated in song because she killed the commander of an opposing army by pounding a tent peg through his head. Esther, who saved her people, also joined the list of Old Testament women leaders. Along with the litany of specific women, Ps. 68:11—"The women who published the tidings were a great host"—afforded support for the cause. Sarah Cooke quoted the literal translation for this verse provided by Hebrew scholars, "of the woman preachers there was a great host."[91]

Jarena Lee confronted an opponent with the story of Balaam's ass, an unlikely example for promoting women preachers. "And here let me tell that elder, if he has not gone to heaven, that I have heard that as far back as Adam Clarke's time, his objections to female preaching were met by the answer—'if an ass reproved Balaam, and a barn-door fowl reproved Peter, why should not a woman reprove sin.' I do not introduce this for its complimentary classification of women with donkeys and fowls, but to give the reply of a poor woman, who had once been a slave. To the first companion she said 'maybe a speaking woman is like an ass but I can tell you one thing, the ass seen the angel when Balaam didn't.'"[92]

Turning to the New Testament, Wesleyan/Holiness women noted Anna, who "prophesied or preached at the presentation of the baby Jesus in the temple." Mary Lee Cagle described the scene: "Anna, the old prophetess came in, and as Simeon had done, she took the infant Christ in her arms and not only blessed the Lord but spake of Him, 'unto all them that looked for redemption in Jerusalem.' You see now, that the first one to preach Jesus after the angels announced His birth, was an old woman."[93]

It was enough for Dora Dudley that Jesus and his apostles worked with women. Others elaborated. Julia Shellhamer pointed out the women who traveled with Jesus (Luke 8:2–3). The Samaritan woman illustrated Jesus' approval of women evangelists. Alma White contended that her encounter with Jesus "shows God's seal on woman's ministry." Almira Losee pointed out that the woman told everyone in the city to "come and see" Jesus. They followed her advice and were converted. Jesus called Mary Magdalene to announce his resurrection. Jarena Lee claimed Mary Magdalene preached a sermon because the doctrine of the resurrection was "the very climax of Christianity." Julia Shellhamer labeled her the "first gospel evangelist." In choosing Mary Magdalene, Jesus "introduced woman to the world as a messenger of his truth" that he had "ushered into the world a new regime, wherein all the human race should be included in the great commission,

'Go ye and teach all nations.'" Mary Lee Cagle contended: "The first sermon that was ever preached on the resurrection was preached by a woman and she got her call, her commission and her message from Jesus himself."[94]

Wesleyan/Holiness women frequently listed Pentecost as the precedent for women's ministry. Pentecost functioned to initiate women's ministry in the early church just as the baptism of the Holy Spirit at Pentecost provided the example of empowerment for Jesus' followers. Acts 1:14 documented that women were present at Pentecost. Mary Lee Cagle noted that Mary, Jesus' mother, was there: "I don't believe that she would have been there if it was wrong." Women fulfilled the prophesy of Joel quoted by Peter and recorded in Acts 2:16–18: "But this is that which is spoken by the Prophet Joel; And it shall come to pass in the last days, saith God, I will pour out of my Spirit upon all flesh: and your sons and daughters shall prophesy, and your young men shall see visions and your old men shall dream dreams. And on my servants and on my handmaidens I will pour out in those days of my Spirit; and they shall prophesy." Women as well as men preached at Pentecost as a result of receiving the empowerment of the Holy Spirit.[95]

Almira Losee and Lela McConnell revealed the continuing fulfillment of Joel's prophecy by designating themselves God's handmaidens. In a more dramatic gesture, Sarah Cooke titled her autobiography *The Handmaiden of the Lord.* Amanda Smith prayed that Joel's prophesy might continue to be realized in her day: "Oh, that the Holy Ghost may be poured out mightily! Then shall the prophecy of Joel be fulfilled. For are we not living in the last days of this wonderful dispensation of the Holy Ghost?"[96] Pentecost was a cornerstone for the defense of women preachers.

Romans 16 provided a gold mine of women church leaders. Verses 1 and 2 mentioned Phoebe, a deacon in the early church. Maggie Newton Van Cott, quoting a Dr. Whedon, faulted translators who "have hardly done Phoebe justice in translating *diakonos, servant* and *prostatis, succorer;* for the former is the term for *deaconess or ministra, and the latter is patroness,* being radically the same word as is rendered '*he that ruleth,*' in chapter xi, 8. The ability and eminence of Phoebe appears from the apostle's earnest commendation, from these her titles." She was not a servant doing menial work but instead represented "the apostolic origin of a female *deaconship.*" Julia Foote pointed out that the word translated as *servant* when referring to Phoebe was translated as *minister* in Eph. 6:21 when referring to a man. Mary Lee Cagle expanded the comparison, noting that *diakonos* occurs twenty times in Paul's writings: "sixteen times it is translated 'minister,' three times 'deacon,' and only once 'servant'" in Rom. 16:1, when it referred to the woman Phoebe. Mary Cole challenged interpreters who claimed that Phoebe's role was one of a servant who performed domestic work only. She argued that if this was the case, "the preachers are not doing their duty, because in the second verse the Lord commanded the other ministers to assist Phoebe. If then the women's only service be to cook for the ministers, the ministers, if they would obey this scripture, should certainly help the women cook." Priscilla, another woman listed in Romans 16, also appears in other New Testament books (Rom. 15:3; 2 Cor. 8:23; Phil. 2:5; 1 Thess. 3:2.) She planted churches with her husband, Aquilla, and, at one point, the two had to take a prominent speaker, Apollos, aside and educate him. Tryphena, Tryphosa, Junia, the sister of Nereus, and Rufus's mother were among other names in Romans 16 that Wesleyan/Holiness women mentioned.[97]

Phillip's four daughters (Acts 21:8–9) who prophesied or preached also served as New Testament models for ministry.[98] Modern Bible scholars dispute whether 2 John was written to a woman church leader, but Alma White made that assumption. The fact that the letter was addressed to

> "the elect lady and her children," shows clearly that this woman had the oversight of a church, and her "children" were not the progeny of the marriage relationship, but were those whom she had begotten in the Lord. He says "Grace be with you, mercy, and peace, from God the Father, and from the Lord Jesus Christ, the Son of the Father, in truth and love" (2 John 3). Then he tells her how he rejoices to find her children walking in the truth. There is no mention made of this elect woman's husband. The apostle warns her and her spiritual children against the many deceivers that had gone out into the world, and also of the antichrist. In the tenth verse he says, "If there come any unto you, and bring not this doctrine, receive him not into your house [church], neither bid him Godspeed." The Beloved Disciple closes his epistle with the statement: "The children of thy elect sister greet thee." This "elect sister" was no doubt pastor of a church in another locality that the apostle had visited.[99]

Phil. 4:3, quoted by Julia Foote, documented the work of Euodia and Syntyche. According to Foote, "when Paul said, 'Help those women who labor with me in the Gospel,' he certainly meant that they did more than to pour out tea." Mary Lee Cagle used this verse once when a person in the congregation spoke out contending: "[women] cooked and washed for Paul." Cagle informed the harasser "that the Book did not say that they labored in the kitchen, and over the wash tub, but in the gospel; whatever Paul was doing they were doing."[100] Here Cagle challenged a stereotypical gender role imposed inappropriately on two women in the Bible.

Women employed Paul's declaration in Gal. 3:28 to counteract other Pauline statements used to prohibit women from preaching. Paul wrote,

"There is neither Jew nor Greek; there is neither slave nor free; there is neither male nor female, for ye are all one in Christ Jesus." Julia Foote claimed this verse "puts an end to this strife" over women's right to preach.[101] The argument from Gal. 3:28 is based on the affirmation that men and women are one in Christ. The emphasis is on sameness rather than on difference between the sexes. Those who utilized this verse to make a case for women preachers were not essentialists.

Women tackled 1 Cor. 14:34, the verse most often quoted by opponents in their attempt to keep women from preaching. Maggie Newton Van Cott suggested: "As the apostle Paul is so frequently quoted as opposed to women's preaching, let us see if there is any just ground for such *supposed* opposition." Alma White interpreted this troublesome verse: "Where Paul says, in 1 Cor. 14:34: 'Let your women keep silence in the churches,' he was merely trying to preserve order in the meetings. Women were speaking to their husbands in undertones. This disturbed the speaker and the audience, and they were told to wait until they got home if they wished to ask questions. The command was given only to married women, as the original manuscripts of the Scriptures show." In another volume of her autobiography, White wrote: "the apostle was merely giving advice in regard to discipline." Mary Lee Cagle interpreted the admonition in the verse as a local command, instructing women to refrain from asking questions during worship.[102]

Zilpha Elaw was the only woman who interpreted 1 Cor. 14:34 so that it placed restrictions on women. She contended that ordinarily women should follow Paul's rule and refrain from speaking in church. But this general rule was precluded by "extraordinary directions of the Holy Ghost, in reference to female Evangelists." She contended, furthermore, that the rule was not "to be rigidly observed in peculiar circumstances."[103] She evidently considered herself an evangelist who stood outside Paul's rule. It is unclear whether she believed that there were only a few women evangelists who were exceptions to the rule, or if all women called by the Holy Spirit were excluded from Paul's prohibition. If the latter was the case, her view corresponded to that promoted by other Wesleyan/Holiness adherents.

Women placed 1 Cor. 14:34 in the broader context of 1 Corinthians and the New Testament. In 1 Cor. 11:5, Paul instructed women concerning how they should pray and prophesy. Mary Cole logically assumed that if women received specific directives, they had the right to prophesy. Cole cited Paul's definition of prophesying in 1 Cor. 14:3—"He that prophesieth speaketh unto men to edification, exhortation and comfort"—to illustrate that if Paul recognized women's right to prophesy, then "she is granted all the privileges that any minister enjoys." Alma White observed: "No preacher of the Gospel can do more than this. To edify, to exhort, and to comfort the people covers the whole ground, and women were doing this in the apostle's time." White contended that to prophesy "simply means to preach the Gospel." Mary Lee Cagle employed *Webster's Unabridged Dictionary,* which defined the word *prophesy* as the following: "Prophesy, in Scripture, to preach. To instruct in religious doctrines, to interpret or explain Scripture or religious subjects, to exhort." Maggie Newton Van Cott contended that if the gift of prophesy was not bestowed on women, "the prophecy of Joel could not have had its fulfillment." What others implied in developing their argument, Cagle made explicit. She summarized all the biblical examples she had listed and concluded: "Now if this Scripture [1 Cor. 14:34–35] forbids woman to work for God it goes crosswise with the whole Bible."[104]

The passage 1 Tim. 2:11–12, sometimes coupled with 1 Cor. 14:34 by opponents of women preachers, received scant attention despite the fact that, according to Mary Cole, nearly all opponents to women's preaching fortified themselves with these verses: "'It is a shame for the woman to speak in the church'; 'Suffer not a woman to teach or to usurp authority,' etc." Cole did not share how she counteracted these verses from 1 Timothy. Neither did Alma White, who listed a specific instance when a Methodist bishop in Colorado chose a passage from Timothy to use in a devotion criticizing women's ministry. More than likely, the passage was 1 Tim. 2:12. Sarah Cooke listed it along with 1 Cor. 14:34 but did not discuss it. Mary Lee Cagle dismissed the verses by claiming they did not relate to the church setting but to the marriage relationship. Julia Foote advised women: "Be not kept in bondage by those who say, 'We suffer not a woman to teach.'"[105]

Women were convinced that the Bible supported their calling to preach. Extending the argument to the last book of the Bible, a few women quoted Rev. 3:8: "Behold I set before you an open door, and no man can shut it." Maggie Newton Van Cott had begun her chapter on women preachers by defending the ministry of women "unhesitantly" and ended it on an optimistic note: "We, therefore, readily conclude that WOMEN HAVE THE RIGHT TO PREACH." Alma White offered one of the most impassioned arguments: "Think of men so presumptuous as to assume that they should be the sole occupants of the pulpits, despite all that has been said in both the Old and New Testaments with regard to woman's ministry." Following a brief overview, White concluded: "These and other scriptures should be sufficient to silence every discordant voice." However, she realized this probably would not be the case. Blaming Satan again for any opposition, she wrote: "But while Satan is the prince and power of this world, the old hackneyed arguments will be used against woman's ministry . . . Let them [women] take up the Bible and attempt to preach the Gospel and the imps of perdition will be set in battle array." White bemoaned misinterpretations of Scripture that resulted in discrimination against women: "Why have not the modern ecclesiasticisms been just in their interpretation of the Word of God? Their failure has resulted in the discrimination between the sexes in the preaching of the Gospel, that has blocked the wheels of progress, and given the enemy of souls an advantage which he never could have gained had woman been accorded her rights in the Church."[106]

Opposition failed to silence preaching women. Undeterred by prohibitions from numerous quarters, whether cultural restrictions, family members, church officials, or strangers, women fulfilled their calling to preach. They found support in a theological environment that, for the most part, encouraged their activity. They read the Bible through the lenses of their religious context. The biblically based egalitarian primitivism of the Wesleyan/Holiness movement provided a theology that condoned the sanctified self, thus endorsing an alternate to the gendered self. The sanctified self successfully rejected a construction of self that sought to deny women the right to speak in public. Women refused to be silenced by arguments stemming from a gendered construction of self. Women responded with evidence based on experience and Scripture, which were the primary sources of their theology.

CHAPTER SIX

Evangelistic Ministries

The endpoints of a spectrum of opinion regarding interpretation of the self have been identified by feminist autobiographical theorist Leigh Gilmore: "At one end of the spectrum of interpretation, a poststructuralist position developed through deconstruction reads autobiography topologically and construes the self as an effect of language, a textual construction, the figuration of what we call identity. At the other, a feminist position grounds autobiographical form and meaning in the experiences of the women who write autobiography and looks to women's lives for the framework to understand self-representational texts."[1] This study of the sanctified self belongs at the end of the spectrum defined as the feminist position. It focuses on the lives of women in order to understand the sanctified self.

The next two chapters review the public undertakings of Wesleyan/Holiness women preachers. They document their experiences in ministry and comprise the historical *bio,* or biographical component, of autobiography. Exploring the ministries that Wesleyan/Holiness women detailed in their autobiographies reveals that sanctified women empowered by the Holy Spirit overcame the artificial restrictions that societal constructions of the gendered self sought to impose upon them. Unintimidated by this gendered self, they recounted their experiences outside the invisible but very real cultural boundaries of woman's sphere. Wesleyan/Holiness women preachers became public figures, founded and led churches and schools, and were recognized as leaders revealing the assurance and courage that exemplified the sanctified self.

Wesleyan/Holiness women's autobiographies offer evidence of the sanctified self that performed numerous public ministries, unfettered by gendered restraints. Again, because the women engaged in minimal introspection in their narratives, the focus is on the public rather than on the private self. Women experienced no hesitancy or misgivings about chronicling their public labors or recording positive assessments of their work by others. In many cases, women's accounts resembled a modern day-planner without the dates. They are simply a schedule of the cities where women preached, without the states and the dates. This is particularly disappointing from a historical point of view. The following pages include pertinent information when the women provided it. Information on women's families also was sketchy at best. Rather than defining themselves first and foremost as wives or mothers, women characterized the sanctified self by offering an account of their ministries. Their narratives then consisted primarily of information about their ministries instead of biographies recounting their life stories. Also, rather than developing a formal theology, women documented public ministries in their narratives, which illustrated their theology in action.

Emma Irick, like many Wesleyan/Holiness women, defies easy categorization. Women's careers often were fluid, encompassing various aspects of ministry. She reviewed her evangelistic career in one paragraph: "In these many years of ministry, I have travelled over a million miles, preached in nearly every state in the Union, in Hawaii and Panama. I was in Hawaii during the month of April, 1957, visiting every church there and holding services every night for a month. I have seen over 75,000 converts, and many hundreds of people adding their names to the membership of the church, with scores of young people being called into special services of the Lord's work." When asked to serve as the district evangelist for the Nazarenes in the Hamlin District in Texas, she had to cancel three years (1920–22) of evangelistic commitments to take the position.[2] She neglected in this summary to mention her joint work in church planting and her years as a pastor, which are discussed below.

This chapter highlights women's evangelistic efforts in such diverse areas as camp meetings, prisons, evangelizing on railroad lines, street meetings, general revival work, pastoring, church planting, founding independent Christian organizations, and establishing Christian schools and colleges. Their emphasis on ministries demonstrates that Wesleyan/Holiness women focused on the public rather than the private aspect of their lives in their narratives. Possessing sanctified selves, they were empowered to successfully challenge the narrow impositions of woman's sphere.

Preaching at Camp Meetings

Wesleyan/Holiness women often preached at camp meetings for the promotion of holiness, which were popular gatherings in the nineteenth and early twentieth centuries. Initially held at secluded areas where people came for one to two weeks and camped, some camp meetings evolved into areas where people built summer cottages. Camp meetings clearly recognized prophetic ministry and readily accepted women as preachers and workers. While aspects of egalitarian primitivism were present, camp meetings fell short of the ideal. For the most part, male Methodist clergy organized earlier camp meetings and provided leadership. Camp meetings that eventually came under the control of Wesleyan/Holiness groups, either sponsored by a denomination or multidenominational, continued the pattern of male leadership. However, the acceptance of prophetic authority at camp meetings guaranteed that their leaders acknowledged women's spiritual gifts bestowed by the Holy Spirit and utilized them to a degree unparalleled in most Christian groups. Women did not experience a stained glass ceiling at camp meetings but instead encountered a pliable tent that accommodated women's prophetic authority.

Along with preaching, women performed many tasks at camp meetings. They led children's meetings, counseled seekers at the altar, prayed, and did other personal evangelistic work. The following discussion focuses on public testimonies and preaching at camp meetings, activities that were clearly public in nature and outside the normal expectations for women.

The language women used to describe their ministries complicates the attempt to determine the extent of their public ministries. It has been impossible to determine precisely the degree of involvement some women exercised in camp meetings. Lucy Drake Osborn participated in nearly fifty meetings at Round Lake, New York, but gave no indication of the nature of her contribution. At Dresden, Maine, in 1871, she "spoke," and at Trenton, New York, she "addressed a large meeting." Did she preach or testify, or both? It is unclear from her own account. Others, such as Lizzie Miller, left no doubt about their role. For instance, Miller recorded that she "preached from the pulpit" at Taborsville, Missouri, in August 1882.[3]

According to the narratives, Abbie Mills attended more camp meetings than any other Wesleyan/Holiness woman. In at least one instance, she covered her expenses by selling her paintings of landscapes. In 1890, she traveled from camp meeting to camp meeting between May and the end of September. A year later, she bemoaned the fact that she had only attended six camp meetings that summer. However, it is difficult to ascertain the level of her involvement at the meetings. She mentioned that she "assisted" at Ocean Grove, New Jersey, on two occasions, one of them being in 1884. This ambiguous verb seemed to encompass all aspects of ministry, from preaching and testifying to altar work and prayer. Generally, she was vague, as illustrated by a comment she made regarding her ministry as Des Plaines, Illinois, in 1885: "[I] was delighted to find work to do for God." She responded to a request "to speak" at Warsaw. This may have been in Indiana, but as was so often the case for Wesleyan/Holiness women, she did not indicate the state. She gave testimonies, but it is impossible to document if she preached, based on her descriptions. On one occasion, she did exhort, but this activity usually followed the sermon, when the exhorter encouraged the congregation to respond to the preacher's words.[4]

Mills and other women testified at camp meetings, documenting specific instances in their autobiographies. While attending her sixth camp meeting of the summer at Bloomington, Mills received a request from a Brother Smith to testify, and she responded with a shout of "Glory!" through her ear tube, a nineteenth-century version of a hearing aid. Mattie Perry claimed that testimony "bubble[d] over on our lips in humble praise and thanksgiving" while attending Twelve Mile Campground at Pickens, South Carolina, in October 1887. Almira Losee testified during a camp meeting at Sing Sing, New York: "There I declared how great things the Lord had done for me."[5]

Also at a Sing Sing camp meeting, Amanda Smith provided an impromptu testimony, addressing a crowd that gathered around her. She climbed onto a stump so everyone could hear. Brother Smith had prodded, "suppose you tell the people your experience; how the Lord converted you." Amanda Smith responded: "And I asked the Lord to help me if it was His will that I should honor Him in acknowledging what He had done for me. And I felt He would help me, so I trusted in Him and ventured to speak. As I went on my heart grew warm, and the power of the Spirit rested upon me, and many of the people wept, and seemed deeply moved and interested, as they had

Amanda Smith, author of *An Autobiography: The Story of the Lord's Dealings with Mrs. Amanda Smith, The Colored Evangelist* (Chicago: Meyer & Brother, Publishers, 1893).

never been before. And God, I believe, blessed that meeting at that big stump on the old Sing Sing Camp Ground."[6]

While the prior episode occurred outside the tent, Amanda Smith also testified at the national Holiness Camp Meeting in Oakington, Maryland, in 1870. She spoke at the Sunday morning love feast, generally the camp meeting service with the highest attendance: "The Lord laid it on me to give my experience of how I found the great salvation, and as I spoke He blest me greatly and the people as well." On another occasion, she reported speaking at a Love Feast in Knoxville, Tennessee: "Brother Little was lead [*sic*] the Love Feast service. I was very glad Brother Little had charge of that meeting, as I knew he would not hinder me from speaking as the Lord might lead." It appears from this comment that perhaps Brother Little was more accepting of her prophetic authority than other leaders. Smith relied on the prophetic authority granted by the Holy Spirit: "Finally, the time came when the Spirit bade me speak . . . as I related how the Lord had led me, and my struggles and difficulties, the Lord blessed me and gave me great liberty in speaking. My! how my soul triumphed. The Spirit of God seemed to fall on the people . . . I suppose I talked about fifteen minutes."[7]

All was not easy for Amanda Smith at camp meetings. She also reported experiencing prejudice there:

> At [Kennebunk] the Lord cured a good old brother, Jacob C., of prejudice. He was a well-to-do man, and had lived in Maine all his life. He said he had never seen many colored persons, and never cared to have anything to do with them when he could help it. If he had any business to do with them, he would always do it as quickly as possible and get away. So now, when he saw me about in the meetings he was much disturbed. But still he felt that he needed the blessing [of holiness], and had come to camp meeting for that purpose. Whenever the invitation was given for those who wanted a clean heart, he would go forward and kneel down. But then the black woman would be in every meeting; would sing, or pray, or testify. He could not get on. One morning under a powerful sermon, . . . he was led to make a full surrender of himself. When Brother Pomeroy invited them forward, this man went. He had got the victory while praying in the woods, over his prejudice against me an hour or two before. It was a wonderful meeting that afternoon. The first thing he saw when he got up and stood on his feet, he said, was the colored woman standing on a bench with both hands up, singing "All I want is a little more faith in Jesus."

And he said every bit of prejudice was gone, and the love of God was in his heart, and he thought I was just beautiful![8]

When Amanda Smith considered attending a national camp meeting in Knoxville in 1872, a friend informed her that the leaders were afraid her presence would "hurt their meeting." While some women insisted that she go and offered to cover her expenses, another good friend discouraged her from traveling to Knoxville since there was the chance she might not be treated properly because of her race. As she pondered whether she should go, the thought of Ku Klux Klan activities in the South crossed her mind. She prayed about it and decided that if she received fifty dollars for expenses, she would interpret this as God's sign that she should go. She acquired the money, unsolicited on her part, and traveled to Knoxville, where one of her testimonies had a major impact on the audience, especially one man who had been a bitter opponent of the doctrine of holiness. The camp meeting leader concluded: "The Lord has been with us: and, after all, I was mistaken in not wanting Sister Smith to come." Smith understood that his hesitancy in inviting her to attend this camp meeting in the first place had stemmed from concerns for her safety. Reflecting prejudicial attitudes in Tennessee, the seating arrangement at the camp meeting was segregated, but it is noteworthy that the congregation did consist of both Blacks and whites.[9]

When observers commented that she was treated so well, Amanda Smith responded: "But if you want to know and understand properly what Amanda Smith has to contend with, just turn black and go about as I do, and you will come to a different conclusion."[10] She refused to let others live with the illusion that because she was well-known, she was immune from hurtful behavior stemming from racism.

Amanda Smith surely confronted racism at a camp meeting sponsored by the Colorado Holiness Association in 1897. In an instance of overlapping ministries, Alma White who was significantly involved in this camp meeting questioned Smith's appearance because it "would introduce the race question." She did not elaborate but did note that Rebecca Grant, who also was African American, was at the same camp meeting and "knew how to keep humble and in her place." White did not explain how Smith's presence would raise the issue of race while Grant's did not. Perhaps it was the fact that Smith played a larger role in the camp meeting as a preacher while Grant functioned in a supportive capacity. Another possible explanation for White's attitude is jealousy. She noted that Amanda Smith had been invited against her wishes. After acknowledging that Smith was a "well known colored evangelist," White also observed: "[Smith] was petted and flattered by many of the adherents of old Methodism in the northern states."[11] Since White's experience with Methodism had been negative, perhaps she envied Smith's popular status within her former denomination.

To those who were blind to mistreatment based on race, Amanda Smith counseled: "And I think some people would understand the quintessence of sanctifying grace if they could be black about twenty-four hours."[12] Sanctification empowered Smith to endure racist stereotypes and to speak out against racism when she faced it in her ministry. Smith relied on sanctifying grace to endure the racism she incessantly faced. Her sanctified self refused to succumb to racist accusations of inferiority.

Camp meetings were one of the few places in American society where whites and Blacks met together publicly. In some cases, such as the Knoxville camp meeting attended by Amanda Smith, Blacks and whites worshiped in the same place, but the seating itself was segregated. As a girl, Emma Ray served as a nursemaid to a couple who attended Methodist camp meetings in Missouri. She sat in the back or in the gallery and cared for the baby. She did not inform her readers if other Blacks sat with her. Perhaps, as in other cases, the seating was segregated to comply with local regulations and other Blacks joined her in designated seating. At other camp meetings, participants noted the presence of both races and the participation by African Americans but did not disclose whether or not the seating was integrated. For instance, Sarah Cooke recorded that Sister Brewington, "one of Africa's sable daughters," preached at a Vermont, Illinois, camp meeting in 1889. Much earlier in the century, Jarena Lee attended a camp meeting in 1824 sponsored by the African Methodist Episcopal Church in Delaware, where people came "without distinction of sex, size, or color." She further observed that "there appeared to be a great union with the white friends" but did not report on the seating arrangement.[13]

Emma Ray took advantage of an opportunity at an integrated meeting to educate a little girl who wondered why Ray was Black. She explained that she was not offended but realized the girl was merely curious. Ray recounted her conversation with the girl:

> She looked me right in the face as I told her the story of Jesus. Then I told her about the creation and how God made everything of its own kind, and that He loved variety. I told her of the different kinds of animals, birds, and flowers, and that He also made different colored people—some white, some black, some red, and some yellow, and that He loved them all, and that it was His choice to make me black and her white. She seemed perfectly satisfied

> with the explanation. I wish every one was as simple and childlike. I was glad to explain to her what I believe is the reason for my color, and if He has another purpose I can gladly say, "Good is the will of the Lord." I am perfectly satisfied with my color, and I would be almost frightened to death if I should turn white.[14]

Ray's words are remarkably similar to those of African American theologians who adopted the "black is beautiful" credo of the Black Power movement in the 1960s.[15]

Amanda Smith confessed her apprehensions when she first began working in integrated services: "I had not been accustomed to take part in the meetings, especially when white people were present, and there was a timidity and shyness that much embarrassed me; but whenever called upon, I would ask the Lord to help me, and take the timidity out of me; and He did help me every time."[16] In this case, it was not so much a generic man-fearing spirit Smith fought against but a fear of whites in particular.

Just as women did not always testify from the platform, women did not always preach from the platform. Lizzie Miller reported that at one camp meeting service in Jefferson County, Ohio, in 1874, she and other women were sent to the perimeters of the campgrounds "to speak to the indifferent who would not attend the public service."[17] Their congregation consisted of the hard-core sinners who refused to enter the tent.

One summer, Mary Lee Cagle traveled to Beebe, Arkansas, "only to enjoy the meeting," with no anticipation of taking any responsibility for the services. The person scheduled to preach was ill: "The leader continued asking her to preach until finally at least one-half of the preaching fell to her." She held camp meetings in her own right for three consecutive summers at Glen Cove. A widow, she married her second husband, Rev. H. C. Cagle, before one thousand people at a camp meeting in 1900.[18]

Not all camp meetings had a designated person in charge of the services. All the ministers, female and male, sat on the platform at meetings sponsored by the Church of God (Anderson, Indiana). The one who felt led to preach stood at the appointed time, proceeded to the pulpit, and preached. This understanding and practice of leadership illustrates the practice of prophetic authority where the Holy Spirit directly authorizes an individual to preach. Mary Cole provided several examples from her own ministry when she sat on the platform, believing God had given her the message for the service while it was obvious that another pastor on the platform felt he should preach. Chapter 1 above includes one situation Cole experienced. Cole described another instance at a camp meeting in Indiana: "If I should take the pulpit, it would look as if I wanted to be too forward, thus hindering one who might have the message." But she persevered and stood up just as the other minister began to rise to his feet. "'Oh, pardon me,' said I. 'No, you pardon me; go ahead,' he replied. 'No, you go ahead.' 'Oh, my message won't spoil.' 'Mine won't either,' I replied. Then he again insisted upon my going ahead; and as I knew God was ordering it, I delivered the message and God wonderfully blessed my soul."[19]

On another occasion, this time in Michigan, Cole reported: "I submitted the matter to the Lord, telling him that if he still wanted me to deliver the message, to hold the brother back until it would not appear that I was trying to get ahead of him."[20] She beat him to the pulpit. In this case, the opportunity to preach resulted as much from athletic as from prophetic impulses.

Cole cited her presence at numerous other camp meetings in Nebraska, Illinois, West Virginia, Oklahoma, North Dakota, and Louisiana. She reported one incident in Mole Hill, West Virginia, where a mob sought to disrupt the services: "The mob said that they had come on purpose to tear the tent down, but those who were defending us said that they should not, and that if they undertook to carry out their threat they would be 'laid low,' meaning that they would kill them. A number of shots were exchanged between the two parties, some of which came very close to me. You may think it very foolish, but I found myself dodging behind the [tent] canvas for protection. Afterwards I was amused at myself, but at such a time the weakness of humanity is on exhibition."[21] Threats and actual danger did not prevent Cole from continuing to fulfill her calling to preach.

Almira Losee once preached at a Merrick camp meeting during a thunderstorm that escalated into a hurricane. She was telling the congregation that Christ "could give rest from anxiety, care and fear" when the wind broke the ridgepole holding up the tent. The tent began to sway and cave in as men frantically attempted to hold the pole up while everyone escaped.[22] Losee exemplified the fearlessness of the sanctified self by calmly seeking an exit. After stepping around overturned seats and avoiding lanterns that had fallen, someone finally assisted her in finding a way out of the collapsing tent.

In her autobiography, Jarena Lee provided an extensive list of places where she preached, often including the biblical texts of her sermons. For instance, in 1824 she preached at an African Methodist Episcopal camp meeting in Lewistown, Delaware, taking as her text Eccles. 11:9, 10. She related her experience: "After I took my text, it appeared to me as if I had nothing to do but open my mouth, and the Lord filled it." Lee listed several other camp meeting engagements without providing specific locations.[23] Preaching sites she did include in her narrative are listed in the appendix.

Preaching at camp meetings provided sanctified women public platforms for their ministries and also offered opportunities for invitations to conduct revivals. At a camp meeting near Baltimore in 1836, Jarena Lee received two future appointments on her arrival and more came later. Emma Irick held her first camp meeting at Olive Hill, Kentucky, in 1908. Her exposure there resulted in other calls to preach. Likewise, at Yarmouth in 1868, Lucy Drake Osborn informed her readers: "I sank into God, and as I stood in His presence, ready to obey, He guided me into three tents within an hour to testify. As a result, I was invited to labor for the salvation of souls in the three towns which these tents represented." In this case, a mystical experience resulted in invitations to hold revivals. Lizzie Miller "received many new calls" while preaching at a camp meeting near Sedalia, Missouri, in 1881.[24]

Abbie Mills attended a service at Mountain Lake Park in 1887 conducted entirely by women: "Sister Lizzie Smith spoke a few moments, and then Sister Clara Boyd, with great earnestness told the vast multitude 'more about Jesus.' Sister Kenney followed, and invited seekers to the altar." Jennie Smith mentioned attending a Woman's National Camp Meeting in Denville, New Jersey.[25] On these occasions women dominated the platform and assumed total leadership of the camp meeting services. There were no limits on their spiritual authority; no men determined the program or who would be asked to preach. In this case, the sanctified selves of these women preachers were entirely unfettered from male control.

However, women-led camp meetings were the exception and not the rule. Alma White's negative experience at camp meetings illustrates the limits of egalitarian primitivism. She challenged the male-dominated leadership of the Wesleyan/Holiness camp meetings in Colorado. In many cases, nationally, women performed all the ministerial tasks that men did, with one exception: women generally were not in charge. White chaffed under the restrictions, but it appears that most other women accepted male leadership, given the opportunities for preaching at camp meetings that did come their way because of the recognition that both men and women possessed prophetic authority.

Prison Ministries

While many Wesleyan/Holiness women found an avenue for service at camp meetings around the country, others discovered more unusual audiences. Emma Ray and Florence Roberts understood prison ministry as an important part of evangelistic work. Ray spoke of visiting jails and sharing the testimony of her husband's victory over alcohol. The Colored Woman's Christian Temperance Union in Seattle appointed her county superintendent of jail and prison work. She noted that a few whites worked with her and her husband in the jails. Roberts addressed more than one thousand prisoners at

San Quentin in 1904. She also had an opportunity for individual heart-to-heart talks with many prisoners.[26]

While prison ministry was only one component of the broader ministries of Ray and Roberts, prisons were Elizabeth Wheaton's primary field of labor. Her first engagement was to lead a Sunday worship service at Fort Madison, Iowa, but she doubted herself and fled without fulfilling her obligation. After this inauspicious beginning, the sanctified self prevailed and she "got boldness," enabling her to travel throughout the United States, preaching in jail corridors, in prison yards, and on death row.[27]

Wheaton described her first service in a prison mining camp. Her congregation consisted of hundreds of men in rags with faces and hands black and grimy from the coal dust. Here, as in other jails, she preached a message of love. She visualized her listeners as small children who had once sat at a mother's knee hearing her pray. She also thought of the prisoners as her own children and she talked to them "as a mother." Prisoners perceived her love and concern and responded positively to her services. Wheaton also preached in churches, prisons, hospitals, alms houses, brothels, saloons, and on the street.[28] However, as *Prisons and Prayers,* the title of her autobiography, suggests, Wheaton's focus was on prison evangelism, and her narrative chronicled twenty-two years of labor in this field. Wheaton, Ray, and Roberts possessed empowered selves enabling them to pursue ministry in prisons where many male clergy feared to go.

Railroad Evangelism

Jennie Smith, an invalid for many years, began her ministry from a cot. People were converted even though she preached from her cot instead of a pulpit. After her healing, she conducted her ministry primarily among railroad workers. The state president of the Woman's Christian Temperance Union (W.C.T.U.) in Ohio appointed Jennie Smith as railroad evangelist. Ultimately, she became the National Superintendent of the Railroad Department for the W.C.T.U.[29]

Jennie Smith explained how she became involved in railroad evangelism: "My interest was awakened in railroad men when I was a helpless invalid, carried from one place to another for treatment. I traveled in the baggage cars. Wherever my couch was set down they would look for one of the police officers, who were *care-takers.* So I learned what noble hearts they and the railroad men had. Also, I had great opportunity to see with what they had to contend and how they were neglected spiritually." Smith inaugurated her work in 1881 with a noon meeting in Baltimore in an old car in the freight yard of the Baltimore and Ohio Railroad with a modest

Jennie Smith, author of *Valley of Baca: A Record of Suffering and Triumph* (Cincinnati: Press of Jennings and Pye, 1876) and four other autobiographical volumes.

audience of four men. She revealed her sincere appreciation and concern for railroad workers in a typical conversation she recorded after some men had hesitated to shake her hand. The men said: "Oh, my hands are too black and dirty to shake hands with a lady." She responded: "No, indeed; there is plenty of soap and water. I am only too glad to grasp these black hands, for I appreciate the fact that life is dependent upon the *faithfulness* of *their work*." Smith distributed tracts and "a kind word" along with the hand shakes, reporting, "it was evident that the hardest heart was touched with a feeling of interest."[30]

Smith preached in depots, baggage cars, roundhouses, freight yards, and shops where engines and railroad cars were repaired. Most often, she spoke in the repair shops over lunch hour. She described one evening meeting in a shop in Parkersburg, West Virginia, where a platform for forty singers and speakers had been set up, along with one thousand seats for the congregation. Local churches provided the singers for the choir. Some services were conducted in cooperation with the railroad-affiliated YMCAs as in Camden, New Jersey; Mount Vernon, Illinois; and Newark, Ohio. At several locations, women who probably were members of the W.C.T.U. organized the meetings. Smith conducted one meeting at the Music Hall in Cincinnati. In this case, uniformed men, police officers, and railroad men sat in the front seats, with more than two thousand in attendance.[31]

In terms of statistics, Jennie Smith reported 1,276 conversions during 1882 along the rails of the Baltimore and Ohio Railroad, primarily in West Virginia. Of this group, fourteen became ministers. She did not supply statistics for other years but did indicate the number of conversions at specific locations. For instance at Fairmont, West Virginia, more than one hundred were converted.[32] A Miss Sherman assisted her at these services.

During services, Smith's policy was to stop speaking whenever a train came and begin singing an old-fashioned hymn guaranteed to "stir hearts and bring up old memories." When freight trains passed, she would give her signal, which was an uplifted hand indicating "God bless you." She never shared the contents of her sermons in her multivolume autobiography, except for one illustration when she preached standing on the back end of an old railroad car in Elkins, West Virginia: "Just think, in a short time how changed this old car will be—all made over new so one would hardly recognize it as the same car. I wonder how many of you men have been in for repairs."[33]

A reunion of Jennie Smith's converts first took place in 1882 at Harpers Ferry, West Virginia. She noted, thirty-seven years later, that the gathering had been held annually since that time. Smith called the meeting "a picnic where souls were saved."[34] She combined the reunion with evangelistic services coordinated by the YMCA. The Baltimore and Ohio Railroad ran excursion trains to accommodate the crowd, which ranged from one thousand to eight thousand.

At some point in her ministry, Jennie Smith began combining railroad evangelism with revivals in nearby churches. For instance, she conducted a week's meeting in Parkersburg, West Virginia, while holding noon meetings at the railroad shops. While in Newark, Ohio, she held meetings at a Methodist Episcopal Church. She held services in Oswego, New York, and spoke in a United Brethren church in Pittsburgh (1917) in addition to her railroad work in these cities.[35] The Baltimore and Ohio Railroad recognized and authorized Smith's public ministry by furnishing space for her services and providing transportation to her annual reunions, which resembled revivals. In this case a corporate entity enabled Smith to fulfill her calling to preach.

Street Meetings

Many women followed the example of the Salvation Army and conducted religious meetings on street corners to entice people to attend their indoor services. Not content to preach from the pulpit in the sanctuary, they occupied public space outside the church building, which further demonstrated their refusal to remain confined by the dictates of the ideology of woman's sphere. The sanctified self engaged actively in the public sphere, disregarding any antagonism. Maude Kahl, Florence Roberts, and Sarah Cooke were among Wesleyan/Holiness women who conducted street or outdoor meetings. Emma Ray, another street preacher, described her schedule for street meetings in Kansas City. She and other workers would meet at a mission and march to a nearby corner singing. Once at the corner, they formed a ring, standing between two saloons, and began to pray. A crowd gradually gathered. After an hour, everyone marched back to the mission for an indoor service. When she returned to Seattle, Ray conducted street meetings from 10:00 P.M. to 11:00 P.M. on Tuesday nights.[36]

Alma White and Julia Shellhamer reported encounters with police as they engaged in street parades and meetings. White's followers participated in street parades, hoping to assemble a crowd that, like Emma Ray's, would then be led to indoor services. On two occasions in 1903, Denver police disrupted the parades and arrested White's workers. As a girl, Shellhamer, along with her mother and sisters, conducted street meetings. The outdoor services were held in front of a saloon, just as Ray's were. Shellhamer preached her first sermon at a street meeting when she was fourteen. One wishes she had given her birth date or the year of her initial sermon. As an adult, she and her husband held a street meeting in Lakeland, Florida. Informed that they needed a permit, they requested one but were denied. They decided to proceed without one. Subsequently, Shellhamer's husband was arrested. As he was taken away to jail, he encouraged his wife to continue the meeting. The police officer responded with an emphatic "No, she won't." Undeterred, Shellhamer stepped into the ring and began preaching. The audience, impressed by her audacity, created an atmosphere that "was electric. Men cheered and cheered until my voice was drowned. Then I continued and others followed and the meeting closed with a fine spirit." Her husband was jailed two more times, but ultimately his case was thrown out. Five evangelists, four men and one woman, were jailed in subsequent street meetings. In this case, opposition extended to men as well as women street preachers.[37]

Mary Lee Cagle also experienced a negative response to a street meeting. In Fort Worth, the group sang and played instruments as they marched, two by two, in the slums. As they assembled in front of a theatre and a saloon, "it was rather rocky." As one person preached standing on a barrel, the saloon owner came out and overturned it. The preacher continued his message from the sidewalk. After he finished, Cagle took over.[38] In her narrative, she did not allude to any apprehension she may have felt as she preached.

Elizabeth Wheaton and a female colleague arrived at a town in Mississippi, dropped off their luggage at a hotel, and proceeded to hold a street meeting. Their singing attracted a crowd, including "a number of colored people." Asked to preach again, she promised to return that evening. On the way back to the hotel, an African American asked them if they intended to hold another street meeting. In reply to their positive response, he advised: "You have shaken hands with the colored people and the white people are angry, and they will mob you. I came along here for the purpose of warning you. If they saw me talking with you my life would be in danger." Wheaton thanked him, assuring him she was not afraid. Back at the hotel, the landlord asked if they were planning to hold an evening meeting. Wheaton responded again in the affirmative, so he informed her that the townspeople had forbidden the service and also that Wheaton and her co-worker needed to leave his hotel because they shook hands with African Americans. He sought his wife's support, but she refused to back him up. Out on the street again, Wheaton heard the mob and decided to step into a "colored people's church where God's presence was revealed in mighty power and souls were convicted and converted." The next morning, two Black women came to caution them about the further potential for harm and to escort them to the train. The husband of one of the women was the person who had initially warned Wheaton of the danger. The woman had had a dream about a woman preaching on the street, and sent her husband four miles to investigate. A second dream convinced her to travel the four miles herself and tell Wheaton that her life was still at risk. Wheaton took her advice and left.[39] More than likely, she feared the potential of racial violence.

In this case, Wheaton heeded the warning to cancel a street meeting. On another occasion in Bellville, Illinois, Wheaton refused to be silent, even after the mayor rejected her request to hold open-air meetings. Instead, she sang at the door of the mission on Christmas Eve 1899. That was enough for two police to grab her and carry her off to jail. Friends provided bail before she was placed in a cell.[40]

Women engaged in street preaching despite the threat and sometimes the actuality of being arrested. Opposition to street preachers was not restricted to women; male preachers faced resistance as well. Even though preaching outdoors made women more vulnerable to hecklers and other opponents, including police officers, women persisted and publicly flaunted their call to preach, again demonstrating the spiritual authority of the sanctified self.

Revivals

Churches sponsored revival meetings with the explicit intention of seeking converts to Christianity. Revival sermons in Wesleyan/Holiness churches also incorporated pleas for Christians to seek sanctification. Speaking at revivals enabled women to gain experience and to occupy pulpits, the public space that signified spiritual authority and that, in most other churches, was reserved for men. Revival services differed from camp meetings in that they were generally sponsored by a local church.

Evangelists depended on offerings taken during the services to cover their expenses. Sometimes they did not break even. Following one revival in Iowa in November 1875, Abbie Mills ended up several dollars short. After a six-week engagement in Leeds, New York, Maggie Newton Van Cott paid all her bills, with ten cents left over. Dora Dudley frequently walked miles because she lacked five cents for her fare. She reported: "I have no collections and no price for my services. I believe that all should be 'free will offerings' as unto the Lord." Yet, just a few pages later in her narrative, she requested that people "send money for expenses" if they wanted her to come to their town to hold a meeting. She did not explain her equivocation. While other women also may have solicited money to cover expenses prior to a meeting, she was the only one to mention this in her autobiography.[41]

Generally, pastors invited an evangelist or a team of evangelists to take charge of the meetings, which could last up to seven weeks, with services every evening and two to three services on Sunday. Sometimes multiple services were held during the week. For instance, Mary Cole preached twice a day during one week, and Mattie Perry led up to three services a day. Abbie Mills and Lucy Drake Osborn described their daytime activities during a revival. Mills went door to door in Osage, Iowa, with a holiness book and talked to residents about holiness. In January 1871 at Ilion, New York, Osborn visited homes in the morning without indicating whether the inhabitants were church members or not and held informal women's meetings in the afternoon.[42] Clergy who invited women to preach revivals gave public endorsement to the efficacy of their preaching in bringing people to conversion and sanctification. By doing so, clergy also called into question the limitations of woman's sphere by sanctioning women's public activity outside the home.

Florence Roberts did not always wait for an invitation to hold a revival. She described her plan of action when she arrived in a new town: "[I] walk around in order to get my bearings and familiarize myself with the town, the churches, the press, the pastors, etc. As soon as possible I call upon the pastors and make engagements to fill pulpits."[43] In Roberts's case, she solicited opportunities for preaching. The ministers who obliged her requests likewise facilitated Roberts's escape from the narrow confines of woman's sphere.

In many cases, a revival was a testing ground for a woman who preached her very first sermon before a revival crowd.[44] The criterion was pragmatic. If her efforts resulted in converts, she was encouraged to continue. Some women became full-time evangelists, while others combined pastoring and revival work.

A few women kept records sporadically, listing locations, conversions, and miles traveled, while others provided general statements summarizing

Mattie E. Perry, author of *Christ and Answered Prayer; Autobiography of Mattie E. Perry* Cincinnati: By the author, 1939).

their work. Maggie Newton Van Cott and Jarena Lee provided some statistics of their activities. In her first year as an itinerant evangelist beginning in 1868 and extending into 1869, Van Cott preached 335 sermons averaging one hour in length, traveled 3,000 miles, and received $735.35 for her work. In terms of results, she listed that 500 probationers were added to her denomination, the Methodist Episcopal Church. Lee traveled 2,325 miles and preached 178 sermons during 1827.[45]

Mattie Perry summarized her revival locations by city and/or state in a paragraph: "I would be happy to mention by name and tell you the places where we have had such glorious results in his service, in Brooklyn, Nyack, White Plains, New York and in New York City; also in many places in this country during these years of constant going and serving from the Atlantic to the Pacific Oceans, and especially in North Carolina, South Carolina, Georgia, Alabama, Tennessee, Kentucky, Pennsylvania, Ohio, Texas, but time and space forbid it." One year, she traveled twelve thousand miles. Overall, she averaged eleven thousand miles a year until retiring from evangelist work in 1937.[46] Other women listed specific locations, providing a geographic record of their ministry. See the appendix for a list of revival sites provided by Mary Lee Cagle and Jarena Lee, which are representative of the extent of the travels of Wesleyan/Holiness women evangelists.

As was the case with camp meetings, women sometimes used vague language when referring to their revival work. They "assisted" or "helped." However, given a closer reading, in the case of revivals, women were assisting pastors of churches by coming to hold revivals themselves rather than assisting other evangelists. For the most part, the pastors were male, with an exception noted by Emma Ray in 1902 when Hattie Teegarden, who pastored the Free Methodist Church in Pleasant Valley, Washington, invited her and her husband to help at a meeting.[47] Sometimes women "spoke" instead of preaching. However, in the case of revivals, "speaking," like "assisting," appeared to imply preaching. Women such as Lizzie Miller, Abbie Mills, and Mattie Perry who assisted or helped also preached. While testifying was an important component of camp meetings, it was rarely mentioned in conjunction with revivals.

Revivals took place generally in churches or in large tents. Emma Irick and Julia Shellhamer vie for the most unusual preaching location. Irick preached in a mine in Alabama that was one and one-half miles below the surface and one mile back. Her transportation was a cart pulled by a burro, and her pulpit was a pile of rocks in ankle-deep mud. Allotted two minutes during an intermission at a boxing match in San Diego, Shellhamer stood on blood stains in the middle of the ring and quickly told the story of the Prodigal Son.[48]

Mary Lee Cagle and Julia Shellhamer observed that their sex contributed positively to the size of their congregations. In Lubbock, Texas, Cagle recognized that "the excitement began to run high" because "a woman preacher had never been heard of." Shellhamer acknowledged that some in the congregation at Ashville, North Carolina, had come to the service out of curiosity since "it was new to these people to hear a woman."[49]

Over half of the women evangelists spoke explicitly of their success in the pulpit. This confirmed the contention that God had authorized their preaching. Women with an empowered self preached effectively. Rather than seeking to minimize their accomplishments outside woman's sphere, women drew attention to them. The sanctified self was not humble. Some were general in their assessment. Sarah Smith remembered that God "wonderfully used me in revival meetings." Others were more specific. Lizzie Miller described a crowded mourner's bench after one sermon with many converts. Lucy Drake Osborn noted that there were converts at a revival she conducted in Mohawk, New York. Elizabeth Wheaton described one meeting where "souls were saved, Christians quickened into new spiritual life and power, and sinners awakened." Mary Cole claimed "God blessed and owned" a five-week revival she led in Summitville, Indiana. Julia Foote worked in Rochester, where she recounted that God "rewarded me in the salvation of souls." Mary Lee Cagle estimated between 75 and 100 converts at a three-week revival in Roby, Texas. After preaching in Oregon one evening, Emma Ray described the results: "Souls were at the altar and we closed with victory." Other women provided specific numbers. During the summer of 1925, Lela McConnell and Mrs. R. L. Swauger held meetings in Vancleve, Kentucky, where there were nine converts and three sanctifications, and in Hampton, Kentucky, where there were twenty-three seekers and eight sanctifications. In this case, McConnell even counted those who came forward to seek conversion. Abbie Mills reported about fifty converts as a result of her preaching in Coldwater in 1891.[50]

Women rarely recounted the travel conditions they faced. Abbie Mills offered a rare complaint when she described one trip as uncomfortable. Even so, she did not elaborate. Julia Shellhamer rejoiced when she was housed in private rooms while in Centralia, Washington, during a revival. She contrasted this with the usual arrangements: "Oh, how we did enjoy this, after suffering from various inconveniences which come from living a public life and staying in different kinds of homes. Indeed, we do not feel free to spend time in prayer or urgent writing while the hostess is laboring in the kitchen for us. This living under a constant strain is really much harder on us than the revival itself, for it is the inconvenience added to the work of soul saving that wears an evangelist out so soon. Many, many times when suffering from complete exhaustion from living in private families during a revival I have prayed, 'O merciful Jesus, hast thou not money enough to let thy suffering servants board at hotels (or somewhere as convenient) while we are giving our very lives for others?'"[51] This isolated comment affords uncommon insight into the conditions women faced on their evangelistic trips. While men undoubtedly encountered similar hardships, one suspects that they never experienced the guilt of not assisting their host in the kitchen.

African American women recounted the racial prejudice they experienced when traveling to preaching engagements. A steamer captain prohibited Zilpha Elaw from boarding his boat to travel from Utica to New York City. He claimed the boat was full, but Elaw reasoned: "My complexion appeared to be the chief reason for his refusal."[52] Amanda Smith offered one example and then added a broader critique:

> When on my way to California last January, a year ago, if I had been white I could have stopped at a hotel, but being black, though a lone woman, I was obliged to stay all night in the waiting room at Austin, Texas, though I arrived at ten P.M.; and many times when in Philadelphia, or New York, or Baltimore, or most anywhere else except in grand old historic Boston, I could not go in and have a cup of tea or a dinner at a hotel or restaurant. There may be places in these cities where colored people may be accommodated, but generally they are proscribed, and that sometimes makes it very inconvenient. I could pay the price—yes, that is all right; I know how to behave—yes, that is all right; I may have on my very best dress so that I look elegant—yes, that is all right; I am known as a Christian lady—yes, that is all right; I will occupy but one chair; I will touch no person's plate or fork—yes that is all right; but you are black! Now, to say that being black did not make it inconvenient for us often, would not be true; but belonging to royal stock, as we do, we propose braving this inconvenience for the present, and pass on into the great big future where all these little things will be lost because of their absolute smallness! May the Lord send the future to meet us! Amen.[53]

Smith's recitation reveals her frustration that there was nothing that she could do to exempt herself from the prejudice so prevalent in society. Her hope for a future without prejudice prevented her from succumbing to total despair, but it did not keep her from lamenting the racism she endured in the present.

Julia Foote also remembered several specific negative encounters motivated by racism that she endured when traveling. Once, on a canal boat in

New York, she sought a place to sleep: "That night, at a late hour, I made my way into the ladies' cabin, and, finding an empty berth, retired. In a short time a man came into the cabin, saying that the berths in the gentlemen's cabin were all occupied, and he was going to sleep in the ladies' cabin. Then he pointed to me and said: 'That nigger has no business here. My family are coming on board the boat at Utica, and they shall not come where a nigger is.' They called the captain, and he ordered me to get up; but I did not stir, thinking it best not to leave the bed except by force. Finally they left me, and the man found lodging among the seamen, swearing vengeance on the 'niggers.'"[54] Foote's nonviolent resistance foreshadowed Martin Luther King Jr.'s strategy for dealing with societal racism during the Civil Rights movement of the mid twentieth century. Foote remained silent regarding the emotional price she paid for holding her ground. Likewise, she did not share the personal trauma she must have experienced when confronted by the abusive passenger and later the captain of the boat.

On another boat trip from New York to Boston in 1849, Foote caught a severe cold because she was prohibited from the cabin and had to remain on the deck all night. On a third occasion in 1851, this time on a stage coach, her departure from Columbus to Cleveland, Ohio, was delayed by four days due to the fact that white passengers each day refused to ride with her because she was Black. Blacks could only ride if whites already on the stage did not object.[55]

Whether suffering from lack of funds or experiencing racism en route to revival engagements, women rose above these conditions and persisted in their evangelistic work as revivalists. The sanctified self, empowered by God, participated in revivals despite the hardships.

Several women traveled with their husbands to revivals. Emma Irick and her husband worked together as evangelists for twenty-five years. She preached her first revival sermon during their wedding trip in Oklahoma in 1908. Susan Fitkin engaged in evangelistic work with a young man for six months. At the completion of their assignment, they decided to get married and then continued working together for several more years. Emma Ray always traveled with her husband. Julia Shellhamer sometimes worked with her husband and sometimes traveled alone. They had first met at an African American camp meeting where he was the evangelist. As indicated earlier, their summer schedules often included individual engagements interspersed with joint revivals. Once, she anxiously waited for her husband to return home. They had not shared a meal alone in two and one-half months. She anticipated her readers' sympathy: "'It is a hard life,' you say, 'to be separated so long.' Yes, it is but think of the souls that have been saved and encouraged toward heaven by this sacrifice."[56]

Mary Cole frequently held revivals with her brother George. She also worked as a member of a company of evangelists who traveled together. This was a frequent practice in the Church of God (Anderson, Indiana). Generally, companies consisted of men and women, although there are a few cases of all-women companies. A company consisting of Cole, two couples, her brother, and Lodema Kaser worked together for sixteen months in California. Cole also held a meeting with Father and Mother Bolds, who were spiritual parents rather than birth parents. Mattie Perry worked six years with J. A. Williams and H. H. Merritt. They were probably men, since she listed her sister Lillie as a companion. She did not mention if Lillie played a role in the services. At some point, her brother and her father joined the evangelistic team, which ministered mainly in the Carolinas and Georgia, but in all traveled to about twelve states.[57]

Along with the all-woman companies of the Church of God (Anderson, Indiana), other women also traveled with women. As pointed out earlier, Lela McConnell traveled the summer of 1925 with Mrs. R. L. Swauger. Mary Cole frequently worked with Lodema Kaser, but also ministered several months with Julia Meyers and accepted at least one engagement with Maude Smith. Maude Kahl and Sister Alvine served together as evangelists before assuming a joint pastorate in La Harpe, Kansas. They took turns preaching and sang together. In Lela McConnell's case, she did all the preaching while two women helped with singing. Celia Bradshaw Winkle and Helena Saneholtz were known as "two young lady preachers." Sarah Cooke worked with Mary Knecht in a six-week meeting in Michigan in 1887. While many others remained silent on the issue, Cooke provided an assessment of her co-worker: "She is wonderfully used of God. When the Spirit of the Lord is upon her, in preaching or exhortation, I have scarcely ever heard any one so impressive." Julia Foote organized an eleven-day revival in Philadelphia under the sole leadership of women. She reported that some attended the meeting "to receive good, others to criticise, sneer, and say hard things against us."[58] She did not indicate whether the negative reaction was due to the sex of the revivalists, their race, or both.

Thus far, the attention has been on the evangelists. The following briefly examines revival audiences, particularly focusing on the racial makeup of the congregations. While Blacks and whites attended camp meetings together, generally revivals sponsored by individual churches were not integrated. Several women held revivals in white churches and Black churches simultaneously. Elizabeth Wheaton remembered: "Often I would have services in the white people's church till 9 P.M., then hurry to the colored people's church and preach and sing and pray till 11 o'clock." In 1886, Wheaton was preaching in a Black church in Houston, Texas, where a woman was converted and "received a call to preach after vowing that women were never called to preach." Years later without providing the specific date, Wheaton met the woman in Oklahoma City and learned she had become an evangelist. Wheaton also preached in other Black churches. She expressed the conviction soon after her conversion that her ministry should extend "to the colored people and the Indians, and to the poor unfortunate ones of my own sex." During the early years of her ministry, she worked in the South and found it difficult. When she preached to Blacks, often she was not allowed to stay with white people: "THE RACE QUESTION ran high and the color line was very closely drawn." She could not understand this behavior because she believed the words of the Bible that "all nations were made of one blood and that God was the Father of us all."[59]

Other white women revivalists led services in Black congregations. In July 1879 Jennie Smith recorded holding a meeting for Blacks in Kentucky. Maggie Newton Van Cott accepted an invitation from a Black minister to hold a revival in his church. Despite the disapproval of her family, Mary Lee Cagle preached at a Black church at Landersville, Alabama, near her home. Mary Still Adams held ongoing meetings for African Americans in Kansas following the Civil War. In Lawrence, Kansas, she established a Sunday school with more than one hundred members at an African Methodist church. She reported: "My labors among the colored people in Lawrence were successful far beyond my most sanguine expectations." Twenty years later, she met two African American women at a church service in Los Angeles who remembered her ministry among Blacks in Lawrence. Moving to Atchison from Lawrence, Adams continued to preach at white and Black churches. Thousands of African Americans had come to Kansas after the Civil War hoping for a better life. The promises they followed to Kansas turned out to be empty. Adams and her children ministered to those who lived at a fairgrounds near Topeka. For months, they conducted services, spending all day Sunday at the fairgrounds.[60]

One Black man testified frequently in Kansas City that he was converted under the preaching of Lizzie Miller: "I am saved, Sister Miller, the Lord sent your message right home to my heart, and I must confess that my sins are all taken away." Miller reflected: "How I thank my blessed Savior that it is 'with the mouth confession is made unto salvation,' whether it is from a white or black brother." In one service at Rentcher, Illinois, conducted by Abbie Mills in 1885, a Black girl was the first to be converted, while at the end of another service, two Black men came forward to pray. While it is impossible to determine how many of Mills's revivals were attended by both whites and Blacks and how many were attended by only whites or only Blacks, she was clear on two occasions, in Evanston, Illinois, and Windsor, Florida, that she attended meetings sponsored by Blacks.[61]

Zilpha Elaw noted that white brothers and sisters flocked to hear her sermons. She also referenced one meeting attended by Blacks and whites in Maryland, where the seating was segregated. Julia Foote and Jarena Lee addressed integrated audiences as well. In Zanesville, Ohio, Blacks were admitted to the white Methodist church for the first time during a revival conducted by Foote in 1851. Hundreds were turned away while "perfect order prevailed" inside the church. Lee's congregation of whites and Blacks likewise was well behaved. In both cases, the language affirming proper behavior indicates that there must have been some apprehension about holding services for both whites and Blacks, but that the fears proved to be unfounded. Just as white women evangelists spoke of Black converts, so, too, African American women evangelists recorded white converts. Lee spoke of a white woman who had become a Christian under her preaching. In another service in Smyrna, Delaware, "seven individuals, white and colored" responded to her appeal to become Christians. Lee listed several of her congregations that were integrated, including Dutch Hill, Long Island, on 28 July 1823 and Stanton Mills in 1824. At Snow Hill, she preached to an "immense" Methodist congregation of slaves and slaveholders.[62]

Mattie Perry described segregated seating at revival services: "At many places certain seats were given to the colored people until they were crowded out by the large congregations, when they gave way for the white people." The seating arrangement parallels the policy that was in place on buses in the South until the boycotts of the 1950s. While this practice is deplorable, it still must be noted that it was highly unusual for the two groups to be meeting together even with these restrictions in place. Perry further explained that during one service of each revival, Blacks led the singing and prayer. Perry, who must have been working with others at the time, reported that she generally preached at this service.[63]

Maude Kahl recounted an incident where a leader uttered a racial slur at a tent revival meeting in Indianapolis, where "quite a number of colored people" were in attendance. From her language, it is impossible to tell if whites were there as well, other than her group and the organizer. The leader had worked hard setting up the tent and arranging all the details. He stood before the crowd and said, "I've been working like a 'nigger' all day." Immediately, he realized his error. Kahl speculated: "I guess he wished the floor would open up and swallow him." He tried to compensate by "brag[ging] on the colored folk and commend[ing] them on their good behavior in the meetings, etc." Kahl "felt sorry for him and wanted to laugh, all at the same time. He was in such a ridiculous position. If he had not been in the habit of calling them by that name, he would not have been caught off his guard. Moral: Let us all be careful of that unruly member, the tongue."[64]

The surprising thing is not that the incident occurred, but that the man was embarrassed by his language and that Kahl judged him harshly for his use of the derogatory term.

In an era that included institutional slavery, Jim Crow laws, and extreme racial tension, these sanctified women preachers, Black and white, crossed invisible racial lines constructed by a prejudicial society. They preached to multiracial audiences or to audiences composed of a race other than their own. They challenged the separatist patterns established by American culture and the church. They not only defied the boundaries of woman's sphere by taking up preaching as a calling but they also sought to overcome barriers to racial unity, particularly in the church.

Church Planting

New churches occasionally emerged from successful independent revivals that were not sponsored by a local congregation. Several Wesleyan/Holiness women played key roles in establishing and pastoring church plants. Maude Kahl and Myrtle Antrim began a church in McEwen, Tennessee. Later, Kahl traveled to Vevay, Indiana, and stayed there three years establishing another new church.[65]

In August 1882, at the request of a man who was not a church member, Lizzie Miller canvassed the town of Taborsville, Missouri, where she had just preached at a camp meeting. Overwhelmingly, the townspeople supported her plan to establish a church. She founded a Methodist congregation, since a Methodist conference had donated the land for the church.[66]

Julia Shellhamer and her husband held a tent meeting in Harrisburg, Pennsylvania, for several weeks before renting a store building for a Free Methodist mission hall. A church emerged from these meetings. From there, the couple traveled to Altoona, Pennsylvania. After holding services, they secured an unused church and began regular worship services. She remained in charge of the congregation while her husband held evangelistic services elsewhere.[67]

Emma Irick and her husband worked together as evangelists for the Church of the Nazarene. In the first twenty-five years of their joint ministry, they organized several churches. She mentioned congregations in Ashland (founded in 1915) and Olive Hill, both in Kentucky, a church in Morrilton, Arkansas, plus one near Miami, Florida.[68] She and her husband pastored the Ashland church during its first year of existence.

Planting a church required more effort than conducting a revival. A woman's prophetic authority had to extend beyond a temporary engagement at a church. The significance of church planting for women is that it also required the recognition of priestly authority in granting women institutional leadership required to inaugurate and grow a church. In order to begin a church, the minister had to earn the respect of Christians and non-Christians alike, whom she sought to gain as church members. It is estimated that the women mentioned here are only the tip of the iceberg in terms of Wesleyan/Holiness women church planters, especially in urban areas. Unfortunately, in most cases church records are incomplete and it would be impossible to calculate the number of female church planters without an extensive amount of local research. Even then, the story would probably be sketchy.

Pastoring

Several women pastored churches they had founded while others pastored established congregations. A few, such as Maude Kahl and Julia Shellhamer, did both. Kahl, who was single, pastored a church in Bellaire, Michigan. She also served as a co-pastor with Sister Alvine in La Harpe, Kansas, and Gas City, where they took turns preaching in each location. They also pastored at Pittsburg, Kansas, from 1947 to 1957. The congregation at Pittsburg had ceased functioning by the time they arrived, so they started over with one remaining member. While at Pittsburg, they supervised the construction of a church building and parsonage. Kahl drew the plans for the parsonage and provided helpful guidance to the contractor. At one point during construction, water was gathering on the roof of the basement. She suggested to the contractor that the water be run off through a down spout and directed through a tiled ditch to the curb. He responded that her plan would never work. Then, the contractor walked across the yard and shared his solution to the problem with Kahl's co-pastor, Sister Alvine. His answer to the dilemma just happened to be Kahl's recommendation. Kahl observed: "He did not like to take advice or directions from a woman."[69] She said nothing more about the frustration this must have caused.

The co-pastors believed in a hands-on approach to dealing with the building project. Twice, they got up on the roof and broke up six inches of ice that began leaking through the roof as it melted. When the two women left the church, it was debt free. They appointed a clergyman to take their place. Kahl reported this action was taken because the "church might build up faster under a man." It appears in this case that she conceded to society's definition that successful leadership was a male prerogative. Then she and Sister Alvine moved on to Wichita. After three years, Kahl resigned to care for her ailing sister. After her sister died, Kahl returned to Pittsburg to pastor the same church again with Sister Alvine. Two male pastors had served in the meantime.[70] Kahl did not mention if they had been successful in growing the church during their tenure. Kahl's book dedication revealed that she and Mamie Alvine had worked together for more than thirty years.

Julia Shellhamer neglected to tell the whole story when she titled her autobiography *Trials and Triumphs of a Minister's Wife.* It is true that she was a minister's wife, but she was also a Free Methodist minister in her own right. At times, she was solo pastor of a church while her husband served as an evangelist. This was the case in Lakeland, Florida, and Blairsville, Pennsylvania. At McKeesport, Pennsylvania, her husband served as senior pastor while she was assistant pastor. It was understood that he would continue holding revivals in other locations while she would fulfill all the pastoral duties in his absence. She recorded her initial response when asked if she would serve as solo pastor in Atlanta: "I was shocked for [this] was the largest church in the conference and as I was a woman I feared that it would not be satisfactory." She demurred but her husband advised her to take the position. While she was tempted to succumb to society's expectations for women, it appears that her husband had fewer problems with a woman serving in this capacity than did his wife. She rose above her apprehensions, and "the church began to take on new life and energy . . . and the congregation increased." She was reappointed to the church for a second term. Her husband and her growing congregation affirmed her leadership. From Atlanta, the Free Methodist conference sent her to Leechburg, Pennsylvania, to pastor.[71]

Emma Irick and her husband, while in the Church of the Nazarene, followed a pattern similar to the Shellhamers. In both cases, husband and wife were evangelists and the wife held pastorates on her own. Irick pastored the Lufkin, Texas, congregation from 1933 to 1959 while her husband engaged in evangelistic work. Attendance increased from 31 to 442 under her leadership.[72] She left Lufkin to become an evangelist again. Irick and other women held pastorates where parishioners recognized their spiritual authority on a formalized basis. While an evangelist or a camp meeting preacher received endorsement for the duration of a revival or camp meeting, congregations selected women pastors validating them as their leaders throughout their pastorates. Pastors like church planters warranted priestly authority because their work required institutional recognition beyond the prophetic authority exercised in revivals and camp meetings.

Organizational Founders

Several women established religious organizations. Mary Lee Cagle preached at revivals, planted churches, and then organized them into a loose coalition. On the other hand, Alma White and Lela McConnell established religious organizations where they held total control. White and McConnell created an autonomous space where they could fulfill their callings unfettered by any outside constraints. Along with churches, White and McConnell established schools and colleges and purchased radio stations to expand their ministries.

Cagle and Her "Holiness Organization"

Mary Lee Cagle began her ministry and her first marriage by accompanying her husband, R. L. Harris, on an evangelistic tour in the Southern Methodist Church. She knew she was called to preach and promised God she would begin preaching on this tour, but she found herself deferring to her husband because he was a good experienced preacher. Although she refrained from preaching at this time, she assisted by singing, praying, doing personal work, and holding prayer meetings. Frustrated with Methodism because of its opposition to holiness and evangelists, her husband organized several independent churches that resulted from their revivals.[73]

After her husband's death, Cagle began traveling with other evangelists to cities in Arkansas, Texas, Alabama, and Tennessee. Among her co-workers was Fannie Hunter, a "splendid singer and quite a good preacher." Another partner was Sister Mitchum, who did not preach but was gifted in individual counseling with seekers and working at the altar with those who had come forward to become Christians. She also worked with Miss Trena Platt, another excellent musician, for four years. She compared their relationship to that of David and Jonathan in the Old Testament, who were devoted to each other. On one occasion, she traveled with Miss Annie Johnson, who had been called to ministry under her preaching. Speaking in the third person, she reminisced: "She has had many, many girls with her in her long years of work, but none that she ever loved more dearly than this, her first one."[74]

Many of Cagle's revivals resulted in church plants. She organized the congregation in Swedonia, Texas, with thirty-one charter members after preaching on God's plan for a church and laying out God's rules and regulations for a church. Sometimes she traveled to an area where individuals had indicated an interest in establishing a "holiness church." She planted churches in Dora, Buffalo Gap, and Oak Cliff, neglecting to mention the state where these cities were located. She made her home in Buffalo Gap and pastored the church there for eight years. She and her second husband, H. C. Cagle, pastored the church plant in Lubbock. Sometimes a church began with a Sunday school, as in Roby, Texas, and Alma, New Mexico. In Roby, she appointed a Brother Juhlin to be in charge. Still another church in Abilene started as a city mission.[75]

The churches she and other workers planted were congregational in polity, maintaining their independence with no connection between them.

When they decided they wanted to be more closely aligned, Cagle called an organizational meeting and invited each church to send at least two representatives. She did not give the date. Approximately ten churches participated. Cagle served as "chairman pro tem" until J. S. Logsdon was "duly elected." Cagle is silent as to why a man was elected instead of her.[76] Other than a brief reference to traveling to a council of the Church of Christ, "afterward the Church of the Nazarene," her autobiography contains no information on subsequent mergers that ultimately resulted in the Church of the Nazarene. After aligning her churches with other churches to form the Church of the Nazarene, she continued to found churches in Arizona, Albuquerque, and Cheyenne. Even though her second husband was one of her converts, it is worth noting that he became the district superintendent while she assumed the position of district evangelist in the New Mexico district. Likewise, the Iricks assumed these same two responsibilities, with the husband holding the administrative role. The district superintendent exercises priestly authority authorized by the denominational leadership, while an evangelist primarily relies on prophetic authority. It is impossible to ascertain if this arrangement was their preference or an indication that the church was more comfortable with men in denominational leadership. While this may serve as an example of not living up to Wesleyan/Holiness egalitarian ideals, it is still remarkable that the Church of the Nazarene recognized both women as district evangelists, conferring an ecclesiastical seal of approval on their work. Statistics are scarce, but Cagle did report that as district evangelist during one year, again without providing the date, she conducted thirteen revivals, preached 175 times, had 216 conversions and 118 sanctifications, and traveled ten thousand miles during one year throughout the Hamlin District in Texas, where she had been appointed district evangelist following her work in New Mexico.[77] The Cagles also co-pastored the church in Peoria, Arizona, until he was elected district superintendent there. She served as sole pastor during his two terms of service.

Alma White and the Pillar of Fire

Alma White began preaching in 1893 and conducted more than three thousand revival services between then and 1900. Sometimes she traveled alone, and at other times she traveled with her husband, her brother, or her two sons. During this period, she established and supervised five missions in Colorado and Wyoming. White founded the Pentecostal Union in Denver in 1901. She and her church members did not speak in tongues, which is a practice that today is associated with the term *Pentecostal*. Instead, she chose the name to highlight the primitivism of her group by drawing a parallel with

Pentecost (Acts 1–2). She was explicit about her rationale for leaving the Methodist Episcopal Church, where she had been raised and where her husband was an ordained pastor: "Seventeen years before [in 1887], I was wrapped in the old ecclesiastical mantle and ready to lay my life down in sacrifice on the altar of the Methodist Church; but she made no provision for me to preach the Gospel and therefore it was in the mind of God to establish a new, soul-saving institution where equal opportunities should be given to both men and women to enter the ministry." Followers left their jobs and worked full time for the Pillar of Fire, the name her group soon adopted. Members did not receive a salary but lived in branches throughout the United States and London. They raised money by selling Pillar of Fire literature, including White's autobiographies, door to door. They had sold 250,000 books by 1918.[78] White ministered through the medium of the printed word by authoring more than thirty-five books and editing seven magazines. The church provided for all their members' material needs. White closely supervised every aspect of her members' lives; there was no second in command.

In 1908 White transferred her headquarters from Denver to Zarephath, New Jersey. Education was another important component of her ministries, with colleges established in Denver, London, and Zarephath, along with a seminary in Denver. Branches sponsored Christian schools throughout the country.[79]

White was consecrated bishop in 1918. She holds the distinction of being the first woman bishop in the United States. She wielded priestly authority from the initiation of her first mission to her dying day. To do so, she had to found a denomination. A reporter aptly characterized her as a Cromwell in skirts.[80] The reporter identified her empowered self even though he probably would not have understood this designation, much less the theology that supported it.

Lela McConnell and the Kentucky Mountain Holiness Association

Lela McConnell was founder and president of the Kentucky Mountain Holiness Association (KMHA). Prior to settling in Kentucky, she founded a Bible school in Edmonton, Alberta, and served as principal. She also served as an assistant pastor for a few years and then worked as an evangelist. She initiated her ministry in Kentucky by establishing a high school in 1924 in a remote area located in Breathitt County in the eastern part of the state. By 1926, thirty-nine workers from nineteen states joined her in evangelistic work. She oversaw twelve preaching stations in 1925 that initially operated only in the summer. Within two years, nine stations remained open year

Lela G. McConnell, author of *The Pauline Ministry in the Kentucky Mountains, or A Brief Account of the Kentucky Mountain Holiness Association* (Louisville, Ky.: Pentecostal Publishing, [1942]) and four other autobiographical volumes.

round. Communities requested a station by petitioning McConnell, who determined where stations would be located. Women and men pastored the stations. McConnell did not always provide statistics on her clergy, but in 1942 she oversaw twenty-six pastors, nineteen of whom were women. These stations eventually became churches.[81]

A Methodist bishop sought to place her work under his jurisdiction, but McConnell refused his offer to pay the groups' debts and provide a salary. Remaining independent, she incorporated her association in 1931. The only institutional support her group received was from Asbury College, a Wesleyan/Holiness school in central Kentucky that she had attended. The college took up an offering once a year and provided teachers for her school. All KMHA workers operated on the "faith line" rather than receiving salaries. They believed that God would supply their material needs. They never asked for money, depending solely on unsolicited donations to support themselves. McConnell explained: "The Association builds the churches and parsonages (homes) and furnishes them and takes care of the upkeep, but the workers themselves are living entirely by faith."[82]

McConnell founded three other schools and numerous stations. Two were boarding schools housing three hundred students in 1962. The third was the Kentucky Mountain Bible Institute, a Bible training school begun in 1930–31 that offered a three-year religious program that prepared students for a life of ministerial service. By 1962 she had established twenty-nine churches and supervised 129 workers who pastored churches or worked in the schools. Her association owned eighty-two buildings.[83] Besides holding revivals and camp meetings for evangelistic purposes, KMHA purchased a one-thousand-watt radio station in 1948, providing another venue for McConnell's preaching.

McConnell's references to leadership are minimal, especially surprising in light of the fact that she authored five volumes describing her life and work. She insisted there was no division among her workers, who were committed to lifelong ministry under her leadership. She noted that after twenty-eight years of her organization's existence there had been no splits. She did lament: "Many times I have found the price of leadership is a lonely way."[84] Unfortunately, she did not explain this comment or give examples of this or of any other facet of leadership.

Mary Lee Cagle, Alma White, and Lela McConnell founded religious organizations where they exerted authority far beyond most women of their time. Wesleyan/Holiness women preachers such as these broke free from the shackled self that society attempted to impose upon them. Instead of accepting the restraints promoted by the advocates of woman's sphere, they threw them aside for public ministries. Rather than adopting a humble demeanor and abbreviating their public work, women used their narratives primarily to document their activities that transcended the boundaries of woman's sphere. Sanctified women preached at camp meetings, revivals, and even at railroad yards and prisons. They defined the sanctified self by their actions. Such a sanctified self was not a passive self, withdrawn from the world. The language of the crucified self that Wesleyan/Holiness women sometimes used to characterize the sanctified self may appear to depict inaction. However, actions drown out their words. The sanctified self was empowered to do God's work in the world.

CHAPTER SEVEN

Social Holiness Ministries

Calling herself a city missionary, Mattie Perry in 1891 visited door to door in Spartanburg, South Carolina, prayed with people, sought to point them to Christ, and also nursed the sick and ministered to the poor. On one visit, Perry brought wild flowers along with food, clothing, and bathing supplies for some children who lacked care. Like John Wesley, Perry and other Wesleyan/Holiness women combined evangelism and social ministry. While considered separately here for the purpose of organization, evangelism and social outreach cannot be disengaged. Mary Alice Tenney's study of John Wesley confirmed that ministry was never an either/or proposition for him: "Social amelioration in the early years of the [Wesleyan] Revival held a place of equal emphasis with religious experience. Wesley could not have conceived of divorcing the two. Evangelism was not placed in one compartment and social work in another."[1] Wesley and his Wesleyan/Holiness heirs believed that meeting people's material needs went hand in hand with sharing the gospel.

While Wesley and many others practiced social Christianity, the term itself was not coined until the late nineteenth century to describe efforts to address problems in society from a Christian perspective. Individuals who embraced social Christianity sought to transform society, so that it more closely resembled their understanding of God's design for redeemed humanity. Social Christianity is often mistakenly equated with the social gospel, yet the social gospel is only one segment of the broader spectrum of social Christianity. Another expression of social Christianity is social holiness, which encompasses the social impulses of Wesley and his followers in the Wesleyan/Holiness movement.[2]

The social gospel and social holiness were similar in their goals. Theologically, however, the social gospel emphasized the motif of the kingdom of God. Walter Rauschenbusch, the primary theologian of the social gospel, contended that the kingdom of God embraced the whole of human life and that "the doctrine is itself the social gospel." In contrast, social holiness traces its theological roots to John Wesley, drawing on his emphasis on love as the motivation for social holiness. In this understanding, social ethics based on holiness is an ethics of love.[3] Love characterizes the sanctified self that is becoming more Christlike as it manifests greater love to God and to one's neighbor. Wesley frequently paraphrased Luke 10:27 as the mandate for social holiness: Love the Lord your God with all your heart, soul, mind and strength, and your neighbor as yourself.

While the social gospelers developed a comprehensive theology to justify their beliefs, Wesleyan/Holiness women did not undertake this task. A few provided Bible verses to support social holiness, but most implicitly lived their convictions rather than explicitly articulating them. Holy living did not necessitate a highly developed theology. Sanctified women saw no need to formulate a theology to legitimate their ministry; following the biblical mandate was enough. For the most part, Wesleyan/Holiness believers did not express a theological rationale to justify their social holiness efforts. They merely contended that Jesus called them to love their neighbors and then acted on that belief.

For Wesleyan/Holiness advocates, sanctification resulted in social holiness. From her study of the Bible and her own experience, Emma Ray confirmed that "the baptism of the Holy Ghost and fire . . . purifies the heart by faith and causes it to overflow with the love of God to our fellow man." Her emphasis echoed Wesley's repeated use of Luke 10:27, which she paraphrased: "God is love and He has set forth the command that we should love Him with all our heart, soul, and mind; also that we should love our neighbors as ourselves." Phoebe Palmer was convinced that God required Christians to be useful to others and contended that holiness enabled one to live a useful life.[4] The sanctified self possessed a confidence that expressions of God's love through acts of usefulness could make a difference in people's lives and in the world.

Jane Dunning stated her conviction bluntly, concluding with several verses to support her position: "Those who do not feel a tender pity for the poor, and a desire to do all that is in their power to relieve them are not true disciples of Christ. 'Whoso hath this world's goods and seeth his brother have need and shutteth up his bowels of compassion from him, how dwelleth the love of God in him?' (I John iii., 17.) 'Pure religion and undefiled before God and the Father is this, to visit the fatherless and widows in their affliction.' (James i., 27.) The destitute widows and orphans are here meant, as is shown by our Saviour's words, 'Inasmuch as ye have done it unto one of the least of these my brethren, ye have done it unto me.' (Matt. xxv., 40.)."[5]

Jesus told a parable, recorded in Matt. 25:31–46, where God commended those who met the physical needs of others and condemned those who did not. Jesus specifically mentioned the needs of those who were hungry and thirsty, those who were strangers, those who needed clothing or to be taken care of because they were sick, or those who needed to be visited in prison. Emma Ray offered a rationale for her work at the Olive Branch mission in Seattle based on this parable: "It was all done not unto tramps, or hoboes, or drunks, but unto the Lord. 'Inasmuch as ye have done it unto these, ye have done it unto me.'" Ray went beyond Christ's admonition in these verses to visit those in prison when she and her husband took former prisoners into their home upon their release from the Seattle jail. Wesleyan/Holiness women showed their love to God by sharing love in tangible ways with others. They demonstrated Wesleyan/Holiness theologian Leon Hynson's thesis that "love sets the tone for action."[6]

Mary Still Adams used the parable in Matthew 25 extensively to justify her ministry of social holiness among African Americans in Kansas following the Civil War. She told a story of a man who ministered to someone in need and so discovered he had ministered to Christ, thus fulfilling his mandate to clothe the naked and feed the hungry. She admonished herself and her readers to follow Christ's command. Explicitly referencing Matthew 25 as her rationale for service, Adams fed a mother and her children, and took an old woman into her home who had no place to live. Once a young man dying of consumption requested that Adams visit him. Tempted to remain home, Jesus' words, "I was sick and ye visited me not," came to mind, and she hurried to his sick room. Again, she quoted from Matthew 25: "In as much as ye did it unto one of the least of these, ye did it unto Me," and continued, "the above has been one of the golden rules by which much of my life as been squared." Adams clearly identified those in need with Christ. When she ministered to others, she was serving Christ. Her actions bear out her words.[7]

Several women revealed through their book titles that social holiness was their primary ministry: Florence Roberts's *Fifteen Years with the Outcast*, Martha Lee's *Mother Lee's Experiences in Fifteen Years' Rescue Work*, and Jane Dunning's *Brands from the Burning: An Account of a Work among the Sick and Destitute in Connection with Providence Mission, New York City*. Roberts referred to herself as a rescue missionary. Other women also committed their lives to social holiness. Emma Whittemore concentrated her ministry in urban slums. Emma Ray summarized her years of ministry: "Over thirty years have been spent in slum work, with the exception of some occasional evangelistic work." She went into homes, cleaned them, and did anything else she could. Seattle was her primary location of ministry, but she also spent two years (1900–1902) with her husband at a mission they established in Kansas City. She preached while her husband held a secular job to cover expenses. Primarily ministering to other Blacks, Ray noted that one or two whites would sometimes join them, in one case a neighborhood butcher who became a Christian at their mission. After returning to Seattle, they worked at the Olive Branch Mission, established in 1903, with responsibility for the Sunday night services. When Mrs. Ruey Witteman assumed the superintendency, they continued to work under her leadership from 1905 to 1925.[8]

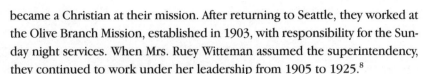

Meeting people's physical needs takes several forms. Ron Sider has contended: "Social action is that set of activities whose primary goal is improving the physical socio-economic and political well-being of people through relief, development and structural change."[9] He briefly described the three types of social action:

1. relief—providing for immediate needs
2. development—helping people to care for themselves
3. structural change—dealing with the cause; through politics, changing societal structures to create justice.[10]

Social holiness embraced all three aspects of social action.

Relief: Door-to-Door Work and Urban Missions

Some women ministered in pairs, going door to door, seeking out those living in substandard tenement houses who had spiritual or temporal needs. To minister spiritually, they handed out religious tracts, sang, read the Bible, and prayed. Along with other women mentioned below, Maude Kahl and Lucy Drake Osborn wrote of visiting door to door as part of their ministry in Indianapolis and in Boston, respectively. For Jane Dunning, meeting physical needs on behalf of the Providence Mission in New York City included paying one month's rent and/or providing clothing, bedding, medicine, heating fuel, and food. One man received an air pillow to alleviate his bed sores. Dunning took care of the material needs of people before presenting the gospel. Giving one woman as an example, she described her strategy: "We first obtained access to this woman's heart by relieving her temporal wants. It is the only way we can reach the hearts of those who are freezing and starving. The missionary who has only tracts and prayers to give, when the poor are suffering the want of all things, might as well stay at home." Addressing donors and potential donors, Dunning continued: "So our friends will see that the money and means they send to this mission is doing a two-fold work, as by relieving their temporal wants we get access to their souls. We have seen scores converted that we never could have reached in any other way." Emma Whittemore's equipment for ministry in New York City consisted of a tin pail filled with gruel, soup or tea, and a large package of old clothing done up in newspaper. More important than these necessities was

God's "love in our hearts." Her ministry included sweeping rooms, heating tea, and making beds.[11]

Not everyone received the women visitors kindly. Emma Whittemore summarized negative receptions: "In loud and indignant tones we would get something like this: 'Be off with you, you old paid machines: we want none of your religious nonsense around here. Bloodsuckers that the whole gang of you are! Get off with you as quick as you know how. Not another word out of you.' In angry fashion, the door would be slammed after us, or the inmate would stand in the doorway pouring out a perfect torrent of oaths and curses as we walked away."[12] Women did not dwell on antagonistic refusals to their offer of ministry. In fact, most women did not even mention hostility, which they must have inevitably encountered.

Emma Whittemore sought to avoid rejection by dressing in a manner that identified her with the occupants of the tenements she visited rather than flaunting her upper-class status. She and her co-worker dressed in a dark calico wrapper with patches and a brown and white gingham apron. They wore an old shawl on cold days and a "plain black straw hat, a bit out of style."[13]

Women described the conditions they found behind the doors that were opened to them. Anna Prosser offered a general assessment: "The sights and sounds and sickening smells which greeted us as we climbed rickety, creaking stairs day by day in this house-to-house visitation, often so weighed down my spirit and exhausted my body, that, but for a living faith in God, I should not have been able to either eat or sleep after reaching my home." Women also described specific situations they encountered. In one case, Jane Dunning discovered a dying Black woman in an attic chamber who was unattended: "She had so long been neglected, that the air of the room had become so impure, it made us quite sick to stay long enough to discharge our duty." Despite the smell, Dunning prepared food for the woman and attended to her needs. Emma Whittemore told of visiting a tenement apartment in New York City where two women lived. They were preparing to eat a lunch of bologna and bread. Bugs were crawling all over the food. One woman pushed them aside and took a bite. Placing her food back on the table, it was immediately covered again with bugs. The other woman scooped up a large number of insects and threw them on the floor near Whittemore. Whittemore cringed as the "whole regiment were having a race in my direction." She drew her feet closer and tried not to watch the insects' progress. At the conclusion of their visit, they knelt on the floor and prayed. Whittemore credited God's power for enabling her to minister in such circumstances without fear.[14]

Door-to-door work was often an outreach ministry of urban missions that also provided assistance on site. Generally, urban mission workers served a meal, held a worship service, and provided overnight lodging for those who attended the service. Several women preached in urban missions. Lizzie Miller preached at the Hudson Street Mission in New York and across the country in the Peniel Mission in Los Angeles. Abbie Mills also preached at this latter location. Elizabeth Wheaton preached at the Pacific Garden Mission in Chicago, where Sarah Cooke spent much of her ministry.[15] While sometimes impossible to verify, it is safe to assume that these women visited missions and delivered sermons when they were staying in cities holding revivals or, in Wheaton's case, when she also was conducting prison ministry.

Almira Losee ministered to various groups of people over her career. At one point she and another woman opened a mission for "the lowest class of boys and girls." In 1871, they established the Rutgers Place mission, which soon ministered to three hundred boys and fifty girls ages six to twenty. Later, she and her co-worker opened a home for "aged and friendless women."[16]

A physician founded the nondenominational Providence Bible Missionary Society in 1860 and hired home missionaries to "carry the Gospel into the highways and by-ways of the most destitute and neglected portions of our Lord's vineyard, especially to the poor and oppressed colored population." Jane Dunning had already been affiliated with this mission for more than ten years when she authored the account of her religious work. She described the recipients of her ministry as being "mainly among the sick and dying, the outcast and fallen, which calls the missionaries into the most unhealthy parts of this densely populated city." Working under the auspices of the Providence Mission, Dunning ministered among the "outdoor poor" in New York City and also rendered service at the Colored Home, which claimed to be the first home of its kind in the country devoted solely to meeting the needs of Blacks. The home consisted of "a hospital, home for the aged and indigent, nursery and lying-in department."[17] "Conversions at the Colored Home," a section of Dunning's book, consisted of sixty pages of firsthand accounts of her work at this home.

Jane Dunning attempted to undermine negative stereotypes about Blacks by reporting on her visits with the Green family, whose accommodations were "elegantly finished." Their children were well dressed. They illustrated Dunning's viewpoint that "many of the colored people of New York City are *beautiful, intelligent,* and *refined.*" Her door-to-door visits also brought her in touch with Black families and individuals who needed not only her words of spiritual guidance, but her acts of social holiness as well.[18]

Several women supervised missions. Anna Prosser established a mission at the former Canal Street mission, probably in Buffalo, and managed it for five years under the auspices of the Christian Alliance. Men primarily composed her congregation. Martha Lee and Rev. Lydia A. Newberry founded a rescue home in Omaha in 1891, incorporating their work less than one year later as the Rescue Home Association. The association consisted of a home with nine rooms for the homeless. From Omaha, Lee went to Wichita, where she organized and served as superintendent of the Home of Redeeming Love, modeling it after the facility in Omaha. The Wichita home was a spacious forty-room building. Lee also served as assistant superintendent of a mission in Kansas City, Missouri, in 1896, again working with Reverend Newberry. Mrs. E. M. Coffey assisted Lee in the mission Sunday school and as housekeeper and helper of the home, a position she also filled in Omaha. A caption under her picture in Lee's book identified Coffey as Lee's private secretary for fifteen years. Mother Lee's Waifs' Home was also established in Kansas City in 1896. The purpose of this home was "to care for and find homes for the friendless and homeless and to assist those that are willing but unable to support their little ones. Children left on doorsteps, in alleys, on river banks, in parks and depots were brought here to die or live as the case might be." She lasted less than one year in this ministry, reporting that this was the most unhappy period of her life. While not explicitly naming the reason, it appears that this work with children was too depressing for her to remain at it for very long. She returned to rescue work, concluding that God had called her to work with needy older individuals. Later, in 1902, Lee served as superintendent and treasurer of another Good Will Mission Home for "unfortunate girls" in Orleans, Nebraska. This work included a building "suitable for hospital purposes, eleven rooms with halls and stairs, two new cottages of two rooms each, a laundry and printing office, [and] two fine baths."[19]

Florence Roberts, Mary Cole, and Julia Shellhamer also supervised missions. Roberts was in charge of the Woodland undenominational gospel mission for three years. From there, she went to the Home of Peace in San Francisco, where she worked with Sister Elizabeth Kauffman, providing clothing and medical care for unwed mothers. Roberts had met Kauffman on an earlier occasion when transferring a woman to her home from another location. According to Roberts, Kauffman's "noble work . . . is known to the thousands." Roberts also served as field secretary of a nonsectarian industrial home for women in San Jose. Cole and her brother assisted in a missionary home in Chicago for one year and then managed the missionary home from 1899 to 1908. Shellhamer and her husband shared leadership of the Hebron Rescue Home in Cleveland, Ohio.[20]

Women who supervised missions exercised spiritual authority not only as preachers; they also bore the responsibility for their missions and the other mission workers. Their leadership exhibited the assurance of a sanctified self. Their authority in the public arena extended beyond the pulpit. Women performed social holiness ministries as they worked in urban missions, meeting both the spiritual and physical needs of people. They did not create a false distinction between the two but understood that their calling was to address both the spiritual and the temporal aspects of people's lives. Going door to door in urban slums gave women opportunities to witness firsthand the extreme poverty people endured. They provided relief such as food, clothing, medical assistance, and, in some cases, mission housing.

Development: Rescue Homes for Prostitutes

Before initiating developmental programs for prostitutes, Wesleyan/Holiness women had to come to grips with the repugnance they initially felt toward prostitutes. With God's love, they overcame their negative feelings, and with the help of the Holy Spirit they manifested God's love to the women they served. Sanctified women ministered to prostitutes by offering them an alternative occupation. They provided homes where women could be trained to earn a legitimate living rather than being dependent on prostitution for their income.

Emma Whittemore initially resisted working with prostitutes. She explained the transformation of her attitude: "Something innate, however, caused a shrinking from it all, for up to this time I had ever felt such a loathing for anything bordering upon impurity that I never could tolerate a wicked woman. Even when in the Mission, where they would sometimes come, I always gave plenty of opportunity to the other workers to labor amongst them rather than get into close contact with them myself. [God] caused me to realize that there was in my heart a serious lack of love for such a class, and in great gentleness He gave me distinctly to understand that though He does not hold one responsible for traits not naturally possessed, He does hold one responsible for not accepting His unchangeable love." Motivated by love, Whittemore became acquainted with some of the women and soon realized that gospel work was not enough: "It became evident that something more than an occasional visit or a kind word was required. If ultimate results in reclamation were to be attained, there must be a loving nurture and care that were impossible when contacts were only occasional." Comments relating to her early ministry among prostitutes revealed Whittemore's emphasis on love: "Sympathy and love combined with God-given tact gained an entrance for Christ into many a stubborn heart . . .

Emma M. Whittemore, author of *Mother Whittemore's Records of Modern Miracles* (Toronto: Missions of Biblical Education, 1931).

Endeavors were lovingly made to enter into their trials and griefs while conversing and praying with or amongst them." Whittemore shared her insights for successful ministry among prostitutes: "In dealing with such girls my experience has invariably been that a kind look, a warm pressure of the hand, and Christ-like compassion often recalled days of purity and home. Unless one can prove one's interest through actions as well as words, little comparatively, will ever be accomplished in rescuing these poor girls. Often they are far more sinned against in the beginning of their downfall than willingly entering a wild life of debauchery and shame. In the majority of cases, too, they are more cruelly censured than they deserve."[21] Whittemore knew that words alone would have little impact on women's lives.

Whittemore's plan of action involved founding a home for prostitutes. She contrasted her approach with popular attitudes toward prostitutes: "Loving consideration such as the Master Himself gave will be much more effective in helping poor sinners regain their womanhood than will the brutal publicity of self-righteous critics." She opened the first Door of Hope mission in 1890 in New York City. The name came from Hos. 2:15: "And I will give her her vineyards from thence and the Valley of Achor as a Door of Hope; and she shall sing there as in the days of her youth." Intended to minister to "fallen and outcast" women, the home provided three types of training: "instruction in housework, in dressmaking and fancy sewing, and in gardening and the raising of poultry." The women received 10 percent of the proceeds from their work, which was deposited in a bank account that was turned over to them when they left the home to begin their new careers. Whittemore explained how love influenced the operation of Door of Hope missions: "We never forcibly restrain such girls from leaving the Home; no bolts nor bars are ever upon the doors. Our only restraint is love; if that does not keep them with us, nothing else is likely to win them to Christ." Her approach was both nonjudgmental and nonpunitive. Near the end of her book, Whittemore reiterated the crucial role of love in her ministry: "We trust enough evidences have been given to prove without a question that those who are so often despised and shunned are capable of responding to higher things if only some one will seek to love them back. God grant that these incidents may spur many into holy activity in behalf of such broken human material that the Great Potter is able to gloriously remake."[22] Whittemore's emphasis on love illustrates the social holiness approach to ministering among those whom Christ had identified as "neighbors." The primary approach of social holiness workers was one of love rather than judgment. They believed their activities fulfilled Christ's injunction to love their neighbors.

Emma Whittemore advertised the Doors of Hope, along with her other ministries, at the St. Louis World's Fair in 1904: "Our exhibit had been carefully prepared over a period of many months and from time to time, crowds would gather to examine the contents of the revolving many-panelled cabinet, which contained a collection of fine photographs of some of the various Doors of Hope opened since the Mother Home was founded in New York. Besides these photographs, other phases of our wide ministry were also pictorially represented, namely Street Work, Monstrosity Work [among circus performers], Slum Work, Children's Work and the Door of Hope Mission. Then there were pictures and fancy articles made by the poor 'monstrosities' and a Tract Exhibit giving accounts of some of our converted girls."[23]

An editorial note in Whittemore's book reported that there were ninety-seven Doors of Hope established before her death. The homes were independent auxiliaries that formed a Door of Hope Union. By her own wish, Whittemore had no jurisdiction over the homes.[24]

Other sanctified women shared Whittemore's motivation for working with prostitutes. In the preface to her autobiography, Martha Lee spoke of her "labor of love in rescuing my fallen sisters from lives of sin and shame." Like Whittemore, Lee also expressed sympathy for prostitutes: "Do not think for a moment, dear readers, that these fallen ones have deliberately chosen a life of sinfulness and degradation." The Good Will Mission in Omaha, which Lee oversaw, offered meals to prostitutes. If women wanted to leave prostitution, they were transferred to a home to prepare for this transition. One young African American woman who sang in a brothel barely escaped arrest. Fleeing to Martha Lee and the other workers, she received suitable clothing enabling her to return home. Lee also told of a woman who showed up partially clothed at a rescue home late one evening. The matron of a brothel had learned she planned to escape and had hidden her clothes and arranged for her to be given alcohol laced with drugs. The woman managed to escape and came to the home where Martha Lee asked no questions and offered no words of reproof. Lee's philosophy of discipline was also similar to Whittemore's when working with prostitutes. She never resorted to compulsion.[25]

In 1881 Jennie Smith favorably cited a matron of a Magdalene Home for prostitutes in Philadelphia who asked rhetorically: "Is it right that we as Christians . . . should draw back, and think ourselves holier than these fallen sisters?" Smith also quoted Jesus, who said, "Neither do I condemn thee; go and sin no more," to illustrate how former prostitutes should be treated.[26] Smith, like Emma Whittemore, emphasized that love rather than judgment was the appropriate motivation for social holiness.

Florence Roberts, also like Whittemore, had to overcome negative feelings she harbored against prostitutes before she could initiate her ministry among these women. When the matron of a home in Sacramento asked her to accompany thirteen former prostitutes to church on Sunday morning, Roberts refused outright. She admitted she was worried about what her friends would think if they saw her with these women, but then she decided she would not encounter any of her friends on the way to church. Contrary to her wishes, she saw several friends as the group walked to church. She confessed: "Never did I so long for even a knot-hole into which to crawl, but no such place presented itself." God's love and wisdom forced her to come to grips with her prejudice. Roberts's ministry ultimately included visiting brothels in the "undesirable districts" of Eureka, California, and developing relationships with the women who worked there.[27] Roberts, like others, relied on God's love to conquer prejudice and enable her to treat prostitutes as potential sisters in Christ.

Roberts told of two encounters that revealed her change in attitude. Once, she was preparing to go out in public with a prostitute who went to change her clothes and came back heavily veiled. Roberts asked why she was wearing the veil, and the other woman replied: "I don't suppose you will want to be seen walking on the street with me, Mother Roberts." Roberts explained her nonverbal response: "With my own hands I removed the veil whilst the tears of tender, humble appreciation and love, gathered and flowed down her cheeks." On another occasion, Roberts obtained permission to have a woman stay with her who had just been released from jail. Lucy wondered where she was to sleep since there was only one bed. She was shocked to learn that Roberts expected them to share the bed: "Mother, do you mean it? Would you let me sleep with you?" Roberts replied: "Why not, dear? You're my honored guest. You're my spiritual daughter." Roberts was convinced that love was essential in working with prostitutes.[28] The love displayed by Wesleyan/Holiness women such as Roberts exemplified John Wesley's emphasis on love as the primary manifestation of holiness. This love inspired prostitutes to leave their former haunts and commit themselves to the developmental ministries offered by their Christian sisters.

Structural Change

Sanctified women did more than respond to social needs by engaging in ministries of relief and development. Martha Lee made a strong case for eliminating the conditions that resulted in the need for rescue work. Her insights sound amazingly contemporary:

> The wise mariner, seeing his fellow seamen wrecked upon hidden rocks and treacherous shoals, will endeavor to locate the causes of their calamity and steer clear of the dangers that, unavoided, brought them to grief.
>
> The philanthropist and the reformer who wish to accomplish the greatest amount of good possible will not only reach out the helping hand to the unfortunate and the erring, but by investigation will ascertain what are the things which make necessary their work of charity and reform; and by endeavoring to remove those circumstances and conditions will lessen the necessity for the work of philanthropy and reform in which they are engaged.
>
> The true rescue worker is as much, or more, interested in bringing about a condition, so far as possible, under which there will be less need of rescue work, as in rescuing those who have succumbed to temptation and gone into sin and shame.[29]

Wesleyan/Holiness women supported a variety of causes intended to transform society. Activities ranged from advocating a living wage to reducing prostitution and promoting suffrage and the Equal Rights Amendment. A personal commitment to eliminating racism motivated many women to minister with those of another race. The issue that received the most attention, however, was the need for abstinence from alcohol. Frequently aligning themselves with the Woman's Christian Temperance Union (W.C.T.U.), sanctified women worked in various capacities to address the abuse of alcohol and its effects of families and crime. While the W.C.T.U. fought for structural change in numerous areas, the women included in this study focused primarily on alcohol.

A Living Wage

Emma Whittemore's sympathetic understanding of the occupants at her Doors of Hope reflected an economic reality many women faced before choosing prostitution: "Many a poor girl has sold herself, thinking thereby to keep body and soul together, because every other avenue seemed closed. Perhaps a mother or child was also dependent upon her."[30] Whittemore advocated structural change by addressing the fact that most women could not make enough money in a legitimate occupation to support themselves, much less their families. She encouraged others to become involved in addressing the plight of prostitutes:

> Oh! if the women of our land would but band together and earnestly wait upon God to see what could be done regarding the starvation prices paid for the labor of so many of our dear young girls. They simply cannot live decently on what they receive. It is truly heart-rending to listen to the stories of how many a girl has been reduced to abject poverty and also robbed of the physical charm that might and should have been hers through the greed of wealthy men. They were willing to work hard, very hard, for an honest livelihood, but while their employers received the homage and compliments of individuals and organizations, these girls whose life-blood was sweated out to produce the wealth, were allowed to languish in conditions of wretchedness on a wage that would not supply a livelihood. Many in desperation have been driven into a life that is worse than death through this gateway of oppression.[31]

Florence Roberts also recognized the economic hardships that led to prostitution: "In visiting among the outcasts, I have learned from the lips of many that the primary cause of their downfall was the inadequacy of their wages as saleswomen, stenographers, etc., for their direct necessities; temptations became too great; the ultimate results were, alas! inevitable." Martha Lee agreed. She wrote in 1906 regarding "starvation wages": "Of the 290,000 girls and women, more or less, who work for a living, many of them receive wages entirely inadequate to meet their needs. This coupled with a desire on their part, or a demand on the part of their employers, to dress beyond their means, causes many women who would otherwise lead virtuous lives to resort to shame that they may secure the money needed to meet these demands."[32] Florence Roberts's, Emma Whittemore's, and Martha Lee's insights prefigured contemporary arguments for the necessity of a living wage. Following the example of John Wesley, Wesleyan/Holiness women believed that sanctification resulted in societal holiness as well as personal holiness. They promoted changes in the structure of society, such as a living wage for women, as a means of realizing the goal of a sanctified society.

Women's Rights

Of the women in this study, Hannah Whitall Smith and Alma White were the most outspoken Wesleyan/Holiness advocates of women's rights in society. While appreciating the fact that her religious tradition, the Friends, had never curbed women's liberty in religious leadership, Smith observed the contrast with "the injustices of the position of women in the outside world." She and White actively promoted woman's suffrage. White believed that woman's suffrage would be attained because "God is on the side of truth and justice." When the suffrage amendment became law with Tennessee's ratification in 1920, White editorialized in one of her magazines: "God and angels have fought in this battle and justice has at last taken the throne." She celebrated the passage of the woman's suffrage amendment, calling it "the triumph of the Cross in the liberation of women."[33]

White, by far, was the most active Wesleyan/Holiness woman in terms of promoting women's rights in society. She sought to expand women's opportunities into the political arena as well as in the church when she argued that women's "intended sphere" included the ministry *and* involvement in legislative bodies. She declared: "The political bondage of women was unspeakable tyranny."[34] White firmly grounded her feminist views in the theology of the Wesleyan/Holiness movement and zealously preached a feminist message advocating autonomy for women in every area of their lives.

The biblical texts utilized in the Wesleyan/Holiness movement to affirm preaching by women also endorsed women's equality in the political arena. White appropriated an egalitarian hermeneutic that was already available. She utilized Genesis 1–3, Jesus' relationships with women, and Gal. 3:28 to argue for the equality of women in the state. White frequently preached sermons on women's rights, such as "Woman's Triumph," "Emancipation of Woman," and "Woman's Equality in Church and State." To supplement her preaching, she also authored pamphlets on women's rights, explaining "that the Lord wanted me to enlighten the people, as part of the ministry to which I had been called." White identified the "religious and political equality of the sexes" as part of the Pillar of Fire creed. According to White, those who had argued against suffrage by claiming woman's sphere was in the home had to answer to a higher power.[35]

Not content with the vote, White joined National Woman's Party (NWP) members in promoting the Equal Rights Amendment (ERA) when they introduced it in 1923. She articulated her position forcefully: "After women obtained the franchise in England and the United States they continued in subordination to their ecclesiastical and political masters, unable to rise above the handicap acquired through six thousand years of inequality and oppression." The initial version of the amendment was as follows: "Men and women shall have equal rights throughout the United States and every place subject to its jurisdiction." Alice Paul, leader of the NWP, contended that the vote did not ensure women's equality: "it is incredible to me that any woman should consider the fight for full equality won. It has just begun." White concurred with Paul: "The world continues its opposition to [woman's] liberation in social, civic, and religious circles, determined to perpetuate her chains."[36] White and NWP members were among a small minority who recognized subordination did not end with suffrage.

The amendment initially was unpopular, even among most women's organizations, who refused to endorse it at its inception. Undeterred, White staunchly defended the necessity for the ERA. Her sermons incorporated information on laws that discriminated against women that had been compiled by the National Woman's Party in the early 1920s. For instance, she referenced laws in New York that gave fathers preference in guardianship of children and control over their wives' earnings and property. She also noted that women could not serve on juries.[37] Passage of the ERA would have nullified all such discriminatory laws.

White justified her advocacy by claiming, "Christ is the great emancipator of the female sex." On another occasion, she spoke of Christ's role in restoring woman "to the place accorded her by the Creator as the helper and co-administrator with man." She recognized that resistance was inevitable: "A narrow mind may fail to grasp this, and it may take other sledge-hammer blows to release the public mind from the old traditions against equality of the sexes." Not intimidated by the task, White asked, "Should not old traditions and customs be forgotten, and every effort put forth in this the dawning of a new era to place woman in her intended sphere, that she may help to start society on the upward grade?"[38]

In her autobiography, White included a report of a church service authored by one of her church members in 1924: "The laws that discriminate against women were commented on by Bishop Alma White. Her statements were a great revelation to the listeners, and no doubt will be productive of much good in the reform movement that is on foot to remedy this monstrous evil.

An Equal Rights bill is now before Congress and should have the support of every true American citizen."[39]

Having preached against the chains that kept women "from political and ecclesiastical bondage," it is not surprising that in 1924 White established *Woman's Chains,* a magazine to promote women's rights. Convinced that God was on the side of equality, her support for women's rights never wavered. By promoting the ERA, White advocated structural change that would ensure women's equality within the legal system. In White's case, the sanctified self asserted autonomy not only in the church but in the political arena as well. While today numerous states have adopted equal rights amendments, the amendment has yet to be added to the U.S. Constitution.

Alcoholism

Women also sought structural change by opposing the sale of alcohol. The temperance crusade that took place during the winter of 1873–74 resulted in the founding of the W.C.T.U. less than a year later. The significant role of holiness theology in the crusade has yet to be explored. Accounts of the crusade incorporated the language of holiness or sanctification. The report submitted from Alliance, Ohio, divulged the primitivism that inspired the women there: "Realizing fully that only from Jehovah sufficient strength could come, we remembered the command of the Master to earlier disciples: 'Tarry ye in the city of Jerusalem, until ye be endued with power from on high.' And we tarried long at the foot of the cross. Ten days we 'waited on the Lord' to renew our strength." Another firsthand account described the crusade's commencement in Fredonia, New York: "The Holy Spirit descended upon that audience, and its power, if not manifested in similar manner, was felt as sensibly as on the Pentecost. I there received a baptism that had kept me to the work all these years." Again, women waited for the power of the Holy Spirit just as Christians did at Pentecost before initiating their work. Applying holiness doctrine to temperance work, Mother Stewart, a key figure in the crusade and author of a comprehensive history, testified: "I received my full baptism into the work." Likewise, Almira Losee declared around 1875: "While renewedly consecrating myself, and to this work especially, I received what I call my temperance baptism." Other personal narratives specifically mentioned the baptism of the Holy Spirit.[40] The power of the Holy Spirit enabled women to leave the churches where they were praying and to walk to taverns where they confronted the owners and their customers. Singing and praying, they stormed the saloons, demanded that owners close their establishments, asked customers to sign the temperance pledge, and, in some cases, created a list of names of those patronizing the saloons.

Numerous Wesleyan/Holiness women preachers, like Losee, promoted the prohibition of alcohol prior to the organization of the W.C.T.U. in 1874. Julia Foote admonished Christian men to pray and to vote to abolish the legal traffic in alcohol. After encountering a drunk person in a revival service, Maggie Newton Van Cott experienced "a most fervent desire to battle the monster intemperance, and pour a withering flame of rebuke upon any who gave aid, countenance, influence, or votes in support of the nefarious traffic." She ultimately joined the Sons of Temperance in New York and encouraged others to follow her example. As a young woman, Mary Still Adams and three other women broke into a saloon at Centropolis, Kansas, smashed bottles, and emptied kegs. Following the Civil War, Adams associated with temperance workers in Kansas. Mattie Perry testified, "It was part of my work to try to bring about prohibition." She labored in a town of one thousand, which supported three bars and forty-six distilleries.[41]

After its establishment, some women worked independently for prohibition while others aligned themselves with the W.C.T.U. The extent of their involvement varied from membership in the group to serving as local and national W.C.T.U. officers to lecturing under the auspices of the W.C.T.U. Abbie Mills attended meetings in 1899 at Pasadena, California, and wore the white ribbon on her lapel indicating affiliation with the W.C.T.U. Anna Prosser preached her first sermon at a W.C.T.U. mission, where she also first heard a woman speak in public.[42] Almira Losee served as a delegate to a New York W.C.T.U. meeting in Poughkeepsie.

Emma Ray served as president of the W.C.T.U. for African American women in Seattle. While segregated chapters were more common in the South, the Seattle W.C.T.U. succumbed to separation as well. Upon moving to Kansas City, Ray discovered that there was only a W.C.T.U. for white women, and no organization for Black women. Despite the racism explicit within the organizational structure itself, the organization extended its support to Ray's ministry. Dora Dudley spoke of "entering into the W.C.T.U. work." In the midst of an account of a prison service, Elizabeth Wheaton mentioned that she had led temperance meetings, but she did not indicate where they were held. No other details were forthcoming.[43]

Temperance work was an important component of Jennie Smith's ministry. She participated in the temperance crusade, which occurred while she was still an invalid. Due to her infirmity, she did not march with the crusaders to the taverns, but remained at a courthouse where the organizational meetings were held. Smith led later temperance meetings and also spoke. Following one temperance speech at Berkeley Springs, West Virginia, several confessed: "You have won us; we will vote the temperance ticket." She organized temperance unions in various cities, including Martinsburg, West

Virginia, and Baltimore. Smith also directed a temperance convention at Mountain Lake Park, Maryland, in 1882. She accompanied Mother Stewart, acknowledged leader of the crusade, and other women to the national W.C.T.U. conference in 1879. During a period of thirty-seven years, Jennie Smith missed only three national gatherings.[44]

Lizzie Miller also participated in the temperance crusade and then affiliated with the W.C.T.U. She labored for several months under the auspices of the W.C.T.U. in Pittsburgh, Pennsylvania, in 1875. She reported her work to the group monthly. She understood her ministry as a "labor of love." Later, she spent many months working for the temperance cause in Missouri. Her book included a temperance sermon, in which she quoted verses from Proverbs, Leviticus, and Luke, to fortify her plea for total abstinence. She concentrated on the dreadful consequences of drinking.[45]

Women had witnessed the harmful results of drinking firsthand in their ministries of social holiness. In 1906 Martha Lee identified "*the 250,000 licensed saloons, beer gardens and wine rooms*" as "the natural ally of the brothel." Elizabeth Wheaton addressed her readers pointedly: "Sisters, brothers, are you and I clear? Are we doing our best to stop this horrible traffic in whisky and girls, for one of these places can scarcely exist without the other. How many girls and boys are sacrificed yearly to fill the saloonkeepers' coffers and fill up hell? Think of these things." Wheaton's ministry among prisoners offered her ample opportunities to observe the positive correlation between alcohol and crime. In one instance, she commented on three men sentenced to die. She placed the blame where it belonged, but also revealed her compassion for these men: "Poor boys! far away from home and friends, with few to care and many to cry out, 'They deserve to die'—never seeing the cause, the rum traffic." She concluded with a plea to her readers: "Why not stop that which sends our young men by the thousands to a drunkard's or a criminal's grave?"[46]

Florence Roberts, another W.C.T.U. speaker, blamed "the downfall of the masses . . . at the door of the licensed saloon." Like Martha Lee, she specifically attributed crime to alcohol: "The prison-ship was filled with young men serving short terms or awaiting trial for some serious offense. *In almost every instance liquor was responsible for their being in trouble. It was heartrending.*"[47] Roberts spread her message at speaking sites such as Portland and St. John's, Oregon, and in numerous cities in California.

Wesleyan/Holiness women worked in close association with those who suffered from the deleterious effects of alcohol and discerned the influence of drinking on home life. Jennie Smith asked rhetorically: "How many homes are robbed of comfort and happiness by the *wine-cup!*"[48] They knew that drinking ruined families and contributed to crime and poverty. Often mistakenly faulted for being naive, these women had experienced firsthand the harm caused by alcohol and attacked the problem at its source. Advocating structural change by eliminating alcohol throughout society, they hoped to reduce its negative ramifications and contribute toward the creation of a sanctified society.

Racism

In terms of structural change through the abolition of slavery, Jarena Lee, one of the few sanctified women preaching prior to the Civil War, attended a convention of the American Anti-Slavery Society in New York City in 1837 and decided to join the organization: "I heard some very eloquent speeches which pleased me very much, and my heart responded with this instruction: 'Do unto all men as you would they should do unto you;' and as we are all children of one parent, no one is justified in holding slaves. I felt that the spirit of God was in the work, and also felt it my duty to unite with this society. Doubtless the cause is good, and I pray God to forward on the work of abolition until it fills the world, and then the gospel will have free course to every nation, and in every clime."[49] Lee's involvement in the antislavery society represented a commitment to structural change on a broad level. The Christian principles that undergirded the American Anti-Slavery Society motivated Lee to join in its quest to abolish slavery.

Wesleyan/Holiness women other than Jarena Lee did not address racism in terms of the potential for changing society through structural means. One opportunity to do so would have been through support of the Fourteenth Amendment, which granted Black men the right to vote. No women, white or Black, mentioned the amendment. Perhaps because they were disenfranchised themselves, they realized they had little voice in the discussion. There were few other possibilities for advocating structural change until the Civil Rights movement of the 1950s, by which time most of the women had died.

Racism, however, was one area of injustice that African American women experienced firsthand. They did not ignore the history of racial oppression in the United States or in their own lives. Amanda Smith began her narrative with the fact that at her birth in 1827 in Long Green, Maryland, her parents were slaves. Like Amanda Smith, Emma Ray and Julia Foote recorded that they, too, were born of slave parents. Ray chose the title *Twice Sold, Twice Ransomed* for her autobiography. She succinctly explained its meaning, intertwining the experience of slavery and salvation: "I was born twice, bought twice, sold twice, and set free twice. Born of woman, born of God; sold in slavery, sold to the devil; freed by Lincoln, set free by God." Julia Foote also credited God for the elimination of slavery: "We were a despised and oppressed people; we had no refuge but God. He heard our cries, saw our tears, and wonderfully delivered us."[50] African American women faced the added burden of racism and were not reluctant about addressing the issue in their narratives.

Emma Ray sought to undermine prejudicial attitudes based on racism: "I want to say right here that many of the white people think that the colored people are all alike. Human nature is the same the world over. However, there are different classes of us people the same as in other nations, and some just as refined, considering opportunities. They have their societies, churches, doctrines and ideas just as other people." Lizzie Miller, who was white, challenged racial stereotypes in Pittsburgh in 1875 by describing Blacks she encountered when she visited door to door. She reported: "In thirty families I visited, not one needed assistance. Most of them were church members, enjoying the Bible and religious conversation. They were comfortably clothed, cleanly and their homes well kept." Other white women expressed awareness of racism in society. Due to prejudice, Jane Dunning was unable to find suitable housing for a Black woman who was near death.[51]

It is impossible to determine the prevalence of racism among the white women in this study. The ministries of those who worked with Blacks have been summarized in discussions of revivals and urban missions. Clearly, one can still harbor prejudicial attitudes even while working among Blacks, as witnessed by Alma White's comment, quoted earlier, that a Black camp meeting worker knew how to keep in her place. However, no other derogatory terms or racist characterizations of Blacks appeared in the autobiographies. The evidence available suggests that, for the most part, white women sought to overcome prejudice and rise above stereotyping.

Maggie Newton Van Cott provided a detailed account of confronting her own racism. Her story reveals one woman's struggle to come to terms with the sin of racism and the role she attributed to God in making that sin known to her. She had been asked to minister to a small group of people and gave her consent before being told that the congregation was Black. She was "quite indignant" and persuaded herself that this was not her duty. She confessed that the thought of leading the meeting "was perfectly revolting," that she feared involvement with this congregation would jeopardize her future ministry. She decided not to go but then discovered that her relationship with God had been affected by this decision. Writing in the third person, Van Cott remembered:

> She tried again and again until utterance and communion were both cut off. "O, well, I am too weary to-night to pray or ask a petition; I

> will go to bed and shall feel better in the morning." . . . when again the petitions were asked; still she was debarred intercourse with her Savior. Prayer seemed a mockery, and all light of heaven gone. In the bitterness of soul she tried to repeat the Lord's Prayer, but even in this utterance and memory failed. She could not repeat it, even if her life had been at stake. And there before the God of heaven, with a spiritual darkness indescribable, she waited in agony. At the breakfast table her kindred tried to comfort her as they saw the flood of tears. Finally, after a fearful mental struggle, she cried to God, "Give me my peace again or thrust me down to hell."
>
> In a moment the scene of the apostle Peter's vision [Acts 10:1–48] passed before her, and she heard the words of inspiration, "What God has cleansed, call not thou common or unclean."
>
> At this she cried out with a full heart, "I will go." From that hour the former prejudices of caste or color vanished, and she felt that all were one in Christ.[52]

Van Cott compared her experience to Peter in the Bible, who learned from God that his ministry should extend to non-Jews. In her case, God called her to enlarge her revival work to include African Americans. Van Cott willingly shared in her narrative that she wrestled with her personal racism toward African Americans and overcame it. Van Cott exposed her racism and credited God with making her both aware of her racism and discomforted with her prejudice. More than likely, she shared this experience to offer an example to other whites who harbored racism. Sanctification included the removal of racist attitudes and actions. In the pages following this confession, Van Cott summarized her evangelistic work among Blacks.

Racism rampant in society likewise permeated church walls. A Methodist Episcopal congregation once invited Julia Foote to preach with the stipulation that other Blacks could not attend. They were willing to integrate the pulpit but not the pews. Foote observed: "Prejudice had closed the door of their sanctuary against the colored people of the place, virtually saying: 'The Gospel shall not be free to all.' Our benign Master and Saviour said: 'Go, preach my gospel to all' [Mark 16:15]." She declined the preaching opportunity since it would incriminate her in the church's racist behavior.[53]

Amanda Smith attended a Free Methodist Church in New York City that initially welcomed her. She considered leaving the African Methodist Episcopal Church and joining this denomination, which had left the Methodist Episcopal Church in 1860, over several issues, including the belief that the mother church had become lax in its opposition to slavery. Members assured Smith that the congregation was free of prejudice and that "colored people were always treated well." When Smith returned with a friend, a church member snubbed them. Smith concluded: "Well, they say they have no prejudice. But she acts just like she had, anyhow. After all, perhaps I had better not join." Rather than departing in silence, she addressed the congregation during the period for testimonies: "I think you have the spirit of prejudice among you just like other people."[54]

Apparently, Smith's judgment did not extend to the entire congregation. After the service, a sister accompanied her out and spoke with her, acknowledging that Smith's assessment had been accurate. Since Smith identified her as "a good sister," it appeared there was at least one exception to her blanket pronouncement. Bluntly stating her reaction to the prejudice, Smith recorded: "So I never went back again."[55] In contrast, Emma Ray, an African American member of the Free Methodist Church, never mentioned racism within her denomination. While many women self-published their autobiographies, the Free Methodists published Ray's autobiography.

Amanda Smith also discovered prejudice at the venerated Tuesday Meeting for the Promotion of Holiness, over which Phoebe Palmer presided at her home in New York City. She recounted the incident: "A lady came in, and there was a very comfortable seat by me, and after looking about for some other place she finally decided to take the one by me; but I saw she was uncomfortable. She fanned and fidgeted and fussed and aired herself till I wished in my heart she had gone somewhere else. Before the meeting closed I arose and spoke; the Lord helped me and blessed the people. At the close of the meeting this lady turned to me so full of pleasant smiles, and said, 'Oh, I did not know I was sitting by Amanda Smith; I feel myself highly honored.' I looked at her and pitied her, but felt sick! I said in my heart, 'From all hollowness and sham, Good Lord deliver us!'"[56] Smith was not impressed by the woman's change in attitude, which obviously resulted only from a belated awareness of Smith's popularity.

Once, when traveling on a streetcar in Philadelphia, Robert Pearsall Smith, the husband of Hannah Whitall Smith, boarded and sat next to Amanda Smith. Observing that he "did not have any fear or embarrassment from my being a colored woman," she acknowledged, "how real, and kind, and true he was." He urged her to attend readings being conducted by his wife. His enthusiastic invitation induced Smith to overcome any hesitation she may have had about going to the meeting. She wrote: "I always tried to avoid anything like pushing myself, or going where I was not wanted. And then I knew how sensitive many white people are about a colored person, so I always kept back." On the way to the meeting, she encountered two other women who were also going to the meeting. They discouraged her from proceeding further with the caution that the readings were intended for upper-class women. Smith recorded her response: "I never said a word. I was dumbfounded." Instead of returning home, however, she continued walking to the meeting and stood just inside the door. Her action belied her earlier claim that she did not go where she was unwanted. Smith contrasted this encounter with her later ministry: "And now, the change is, instead of Amanda Smith, the colored washwoman's presence having a bad effect on a meeting where ladies of wealth and rank are gathered to pray and sing His blessing, they think a failure more possible if the same Amanda Smith, the colored woman, cannot be present."[57] Once she became well known, Smith's reputation granted her access to private meetings, overcoming momentarily the racism and classism that persisted around her. Wesleyan/Holiness African American women documented the racism they faced in church and society. They worked primarily in the church to overcome segregation. Some of their white sisters in Christ likewise joined this effort.

Just as they relied on the Holy Spirit to transform themselves, Wesleyan/Holiness women trusted that the Holy Spirit would aid them in transforming society as well. Motivated by love, sanctified women ventured beyond the church walls and revival tents to engage in social holiness. Sanctification produced a self that possessed confidence to address societal problems by offering relief, by supervising developmental programs where individuals could be trained to help themselves, and by advocating structural changes in society.

CHAPTER EIGHT

How and Why Wesleyan/ Holiness Women Wrote

The narratives of Wesleyan/Holiness women preachers confirm Domna C. Stanton's contention that "the *graphing* of the *auto* [self] was an act of self-assertion that denied and reversed woman's status." An examination of the *graph,* or the act of writing about the self in autobiographies, by sanctified women further supports my contention that the sanctified self was empowered to overcome narrow constructions of gender. Writing one's autobiography constituted a strong defense against those who condemned women preachers. Women documented their experience as preachers to demonstrate women's ability to preach. Their written words reinforced the spoken words they preached, thus supporting Sidonie Smith's argument: "Women who do not challenge those gender ideologies and the boundaries they place around woman's proper life script, textual inscription, and speaking voice do not write autobiography."[1]

The Wesleyan/Holiness movement offered a rival paradigm that condoned preaching by women rather than enslaving them within the narrow confines of woman's sphere. Empowered by the Holy Spirit, they moved beyond these boundaries. Autobiographies functioned as "counter-narratives—narrative elements in personal accounts which contrast self-image and experiences with dominant cultural models."[2] The sanctified self contrasted with the cultural view of woman's self.

Gender-Marked Writing

Autobiographical theory incorporates several topics within the category of gender-marked writing. This section will briefly touch on the issues of subversiveness, death of the author, silences, and male/female differences in writing autobiography as these subjects relate to the narratives by Wesleyan/Holiness women.

Feminist theorists define women who write autobiography as subversives who challenge the boundaries established by society to confine their activities. Women's autobiographical writing is an act of resistance to restrictions imposed by their culture. Wesleyan/Holiness women preachers had already breached invisible boundaries by preaching. Documenting their activities in their narratives reinforced their rejection of the status quo. Writing autobiography became a subversive act for a woman because, according to Leah D. Hewitt, "to write in the public eye is to 'make a spectacle of herself,' to transgress the boundaries that have historically confined women to traditional roles in the private sectors of home and family." The female autobiographer refused to remain on the fringes of society. The act of writing autobiography challenged the perspective that women belonged there. Instead, women's autobiographies placed their authors at the center of public discourse. According to Sidonie Smith, "in daring to write about herself for public consumption, the autobiographer already transgressed cultural boundaries, straying beyond the boundaries of a 'selfhood' situated at the very margins of cultural action, meaning, and discourse into another's territory at the center of culture."[3]

Wesleyan/Holiness women preachers were not defensive about writing their autobiographies, because women before them, such as Mary Fletcher and Hester Ann Rogers, served as precedents within their religious tradition. They were extending a trajectory that for them began with Madame Guyon. Perhaps more so than for other women, autobiography for Wesleyan/Holiness women was "a sanctioned discourse to challenge the social, political and religious conventions that defined them." Mary Still Adams, writing in 1893, appeared to be unaware of the subversive implications of her undertaking and made no attempt to justify it: "I have no apology to present for offering this sketch of my life-work to the people."[4] She was not defensive because she was merely following the example of others. Mary Lee Cagle, on the other hand, in 1928 magnified the subversive nature of her writing by adding her sermon "Woman's Right to Preach" at the end of her story.

Women preachers heralded their public ministries. Book titles boldly proclaimed the subversiveness of their contents. Titles such as *Mother Lee's Experiences in Fifteen Years' Rescue Work* and *The Preacher Girl* alerted prospective readers to the fact that their authors planned to emphasize their public ministries. Their textual self-representations counteracted the scripts that authors of prescriptive literature for women sought to impose on them. While prescriptive literature promoted the doctrine of woman's sphere by advising women to be content within the confines of domesticity, Wesleyan/Holiness women exemplified another option.

Despite, or maybe because of, the subversiveness of her writing, Mary Still Adams wrote: "I have also prayed that the sketches and incidents be so clothed with the power of the Holy Ghost that the writer may be lost sight of in the things written." She was the only sanctified woman who seemed to be advocating the death of the author, long before this phrase entered the vocabulary of literary criticism. Quoting Samuel Beckett, Michel Foucault asked: "What matter who's speaking?"[5] Foucault's question revealed disregard for the author.

While Foucault and others such as Adams argued for anonymity, in this study the author is of utmost importance and must be identified. The fact that the authors are female is crucial to an examination of women who challenged woman's sphere by preaching. I disagree with Foucault's assertion that "the task of criticism is not to reestablish the ties between an author and his work or to reconstitute an author's thought and experience through his works and, further, that criticism should concern itself with the structures of a work, its architectonic forms, which are studied for their intrinsic and internal relationships." Foucault further claimed, "We can easily imagine a culture where discourse would circulate without any need for an author." Although Foucault contended that such a culture is within the realm of a postmodern imagination, many feminist theorists renounce his declaration. While Foucault and Ronald Barthes, and others following their lead, promote the author's death and reject the notion of selfhood, Katherine R. Goodman is representative of feminist critics who refuse to kill the author. Goodman observed that the death of the author results in "the absence of any connection between the autobiographer and the life described . . . An autobiographer becomes a linguistic construct severed from authentic experience." She concluded: "Feminists, however, know that it makes a great deal of difference who is speaking." Liz Stanley offered a scathing critique of those who proclaim the author's death at the very time when authors are writing in favor of human rights, including women's rights. Domna C. Stanton, likewise, has declined to embrace the arguments supporting the case for the death of the author.[6]

Also opposing Foucault's endorsement of the death of the author, Hilary Hinds contended that the identity of the author is fundamental. In her critique of the work of Christian Englishwomen who wrote in the seventeenth century, she explored "who the authors were, how they lived and under what kinds of circumstances they came to write," and the gender relations of seventeenth-century England. Hinds summarized the necessity of the affirmation of the author from the perspective of feminist critics "whose work is more clearly rooted in specific political agendas": "The retention of the author-figure, and with it the concept of the social identity of an author . . . ensures that groups usually marginalised in literary studies can no longer be excluded. The 'self' may be acknowledged as an endlessly complicated and contradictory structure, but it is nonetheless assumed to connect to at least some kind of social and political identity."[7] The text has little value as a free-floating entity, separate from the author who wrote it and the context in which it was written. Rather, it is intimately related to the author and her social context. The sex of the author is critical. These autobiographies cannot stand alone as literary pieces. Their value emerges from their authors' interactions as women with their society.

Along with subversiveness and the death of the author, silences within autobiographies also are examined in an analysis of gender-marked writing. Wesleyan/Holiness women's narratives were silent with regard to any information that would undermine the successful self they sought to portray. Ann D. Gordon has observed: "Woman suffragists, like other leaders of women in the nineteenth century, approached the art of autobiography with their public identities well crafted and their public voices tuned closely to a particular pitch of the cultures they sought to influence."[8] Wesleyan/Holiness women preachers likewise projected a particular public identity. Their constructions of self heralded success. The public identities of Wesleyan/Holiness women did not allow for failure. They never wrote about revivals where no one responded to their offer of salvation. They rarely revealed discouragement in their work or doubts about their own sanctification.

Women autobiographers in general also consider the interpretation of their public identities by those who read their narratives. Sidonie Smith maintained: "Attuned to the ways women have been dressed up for public exposure, attuned also to the price women pay for public self-disclosure, the autobiographer reveals in her speaking posture and narrative structure her understanding of the possible readings she will receive from a public that has the power of her reputation in its hands." Alma White did not simply rely on "posture" or "narrative structure" to convey her concerns about a misreading of her views. Quoting from one of her own sermons, she anticipated a negative reaction to her feminist convictions: "I do not want you to get the impression that I am a man-hater by the attitude I take on the woman question." White sought explicitly to modify possible misinterpretations of her convictions. The memoirs of women clergy active between 1740 and 1845 also revealed a concern for audience response similar to that of White: "Whether they wanted to inspire, provoke, or justify, they used their narratives to influence public perceptions of them."[9] These women, as well as Wesleyan/Holiness women, exercised self-censorship in order to project a positive public identity.

Most Wesleyan/Holiness women disregarded their private lives in their narratives because they were focusing intentionally on their public ministries. Florence Roberts provided a rare example of an acknowledged omission when she noted the death of her husband, with the following information placed in parentheses: "Reader, I have refrained from stating in this book under what circumstances and at what time Mr. Roberts came back into my life, simply because that matter has no direct reference to the title of the book and also because it recalls too much pain and distress of a private nature. This I will say: With the other duties an added heavy cross was mine, owing to his mental and physical condition—a cross which, I regret to say, I did not always bear as patiently or as cheerfully as I might have borne it. It lasted from February, 1905, to November, 1909."[10] Roberts opened the curtain briefly to a distressing domestic situation but closed it again before answering any questions the glimpse raised. One yearns to know what distress she experienced and how she managed to continue her ministry in light of the "heavy cross" she bore. Was she too hard on herself or should she have been more patient? How many other women, without admitting the oversight, censored personal material that they deemed would tarnish their public identity? Unfortunately, these questions cannot be answered.

An analysis of gender-marked writing also includes an investigation of the differences between women and men in the writing of autobiography. In *The Tradition of Women's Autobiography,* Estelle Jelinek underscored her hypothesis that male and female stylistic differences exist in writing autobiography. Based on her research, she concluded that women's writing style is "episodic and anecdotal, nonchronological and disjunctive," while men write progressive and linear narratives.[11] Jelinek allowed for exceptions but maintained that the pattern she outlined is the norm. Alma White is the clearest challenge to Jelinek's model. White consulted her daily journal as she wrote and listed the year at the top of every page of her five-volume autobiography.

The writing style of most other sanctified women, though, matched Jelinek's description. In many cases, their narratives reflected a stream-of-consciousness writing style. However, when chronicling their ministries, many adopted a travelogue approach, simply listing where they preached. Rather than undermining Jelinek's assessment of women's writings, Wesleyan/Holiness women's autobiographies tend to fit her hypothesis. However, I suspect that an examination of Wesleyan/Holiness men who wrote autobiographies would reveal that their writing style is more similar to the one Jelinek ascribed to women. This was true for the autobiographies of clergy written between 1740 and 1845 that Brekus investigated: "Men's and women's narratives closely resemble one another in style as well as content. Fragmentary, rambling, and often shapeless, they tend to simply list the 'facts' without explaining or interpreting them. These memoirs overflow with the details of dates, names, and places, but with a few notable exceptions, they contain comparatively little personal reflection."[12] Brekus's research indicated that spiritual autobiographies written by men and women reflected the same writing style. A comparison of the writings of

Wesleyan/Holiness women and men in subsequent generations would probably yield the same conclusion.

In terms of content, Jelinek also believed men's and women's autobiographies differed. She maintained that women write about "family, close friends, domestic activities" and "emphasize the personal over the professional." Liz Stanley and Leigh Gilmore have questioned the universality of Jelinek's theoretical model in terms of content.[13] Wesleyan/Holiness autobiographies also challenge Jelinek's thesis. Sanctified women placed the emphasis on their public lives as ministers. Details about their personal lives were frequently missing. For instance, Susan Fitkin mentioned that she was married, but she never provided her husband's name. In her narrative, Fitkin's professional life overshadowed her personal life.

Wesleyan/Holiness women generally adopted the style of writing Jelinek described as distinctive of women's autobiographies. In terms of content, however, they departed from her blueprint and highlighted their professional lives while almost completely excluding information on their families, friends, and home life. An expansion of Jelinek's canon to include autobiographies by Wesleyan/Holiness women would require a reassessment of her initial conclusions in terms of the content of women's autobiographies.

Other theorists posit that men write autobiographies that stress individual development, while women's writings reflect an emphasis on relationships. When Wesleyan/Holiness women referred to other women, most often it was in reference to a professional relationship only. Lela McConnell referred to Amanda Smith as "a powerful preacher of the Word" who ministered at Ocean Grove. Jennie Smith also reported hearing Amanda Smith speak at Ocean Grove. She did not elaborate other than to note that Amanda Smith "drew an impressive lesson" from the fact that the lights went out while she was speaking." Abbie Mills acknowledged the ministries of Jennie Smith and Lucy Drake Osborn in one or two sentences and also mentioned Hannah Whitall Smith and Maggie Newton Van Cott. Abbie Mills recorded meeting with Sarah Cooke and Amanda Smith. In Chicago, Mills went with Sarah Cooke to a service at the Pacific Garden Mission. On a later visit to Chicago, she visited Amanda Smith in her home and found her completing her autobiography. In both cases she revealed no further information. This was also true for Osborn, who visited Jennie Smith. Obviously, women who spent time in each other's homes were friends, but they told their readers nothing about the nature of these friendships. Camp meetings also offered an opportunity for women to meet and share their spiritual progress and their frustrations. No autobiographies suggest gatherings of this nature, but they surely must have taken place because many women participated in the same camp meetings. While she did not discuss this in her autobiography,

Mary Lee Cagle and her female co-workers formed a close network of friends.[14] I had hoped to uncover numerous other examples of support systems among women preachers. While they may have been in place, the autobiographers were silent on the issue. Did women talk about opposition they faced? Did they cry on each others' shoulders? Did African American women help raise the consciousness of white women with respect to racial prejudice? Did they have heart-to-heart discussions? Unfortunately, autobiographers provided no clues regarding the answers to these questions.

Women rarely mentioned women friends whom they confided in or who encouraged them in ministry. Unlike Madame Guyon, they did not acknowledge mentors. Mary Cole is the exception. Cole was the only autobiographer who recorded mutual encouragement between women colleagues in ministry. On two occasions, older women comforted her. According to Cole, Sarah Smith "was quite helpful to me, as the enemy tried to depress and crush me; but the Lord brought me off more than conqueror." A Mrs. Bolds also supported her as well as assisted in revival meetings after Cole had been ill. Cole reciprocated with other women. Once, she traveled to Iowa "to be what help I could to a dear sister who was going through some deep trials." She remained there five weeks, helping the woman understand that she had "set her spiritual standard so high that she could not live up to her own ideal." Later, she went to Sioux Falls, South Dakota, spending six weeks counseling another woman.[15] Perhaps other women duplicated Cole's actions and concern for other female ministers but chose not to write about it.

Nellie Y. McKay concluded that, for women and minority narrators, the self in relation to a group is significant: "Community identity permits the rejection of historically diminishing images of self imposed by the dominant culture; it allows marginalized individuals to embrace alternative selves constructed from positive (and more authentic) images of their own creation."[16] For most sanctified women, it appears that community identity rested in their affiliation with the broader Wesleyan/Holiness movement rather than with other women in ministry.

Mary G. Mason proposed several paradigms that incorporated relationship as a means of formulating self-identity. She asserted that "the self-discovery of female identity seems to acknowledge the real presence and recognition of another consciousness, and the disclosure of female self is linked to the identification of some 'other.'" The paradigm that corresponded to Wesleyan/Holiness women was "relation to one single, transcendent other," which Mason illustrated by referring to the writings of Julian of Norwich.[17] Likewise, the sanctified self relied on God for its authority to undermine the shackled self constructed by society. The community comprised of Wesleyan/Holiness believers recognized that God's authority empowered the sanctified self. While most Christian denominations deemed their life stories unorthodox, sanctified women labored in a religious environment that fostered their subversive public religious activities.

Perhaps women placed more reliance on fellow church members for support and confirmation because it was the very notion of a sanctified self that propelled them out of the constraints of society's construction of self. With respect to the sanctified self, however, men as well as women relied on the religious community for self-definition and affirmation. Did women stress the benefits of an empowered self more than men? Did women and men equally depend on the Wesleyan/Holiness movement to attest to their identity as sanctified individuals? These are questions requiring further research. A comparison of male and female autobiographies is outside the scope of this study, but it offers potential for further exploration into the differences and similarities between their stories.

There are specific instances of gender-marked writing, however, in the autobiographies of sanctified women since they had to justify and defend their public ministries because they were women. No male Wesleyan/Holiness preacher ever had to wield his pen as a weapon to defend his public ministry. No man had to challenge a construction of self that sought to prevent him from assuming professional ministry. Men were not, and still are not, expected to conform to societal expectations that would confine them to the role of husband or father. While Wesleyan/Holiness women and men documented their quest for sanctification and its resultant impact on the self, women had to assert the sanctified self and place it against constructions of the female self that others sought to impose on them. Their autobiographies raised political and social issues that male autobiographers did not have to address. Sanctified women illustrate Lois and David Fowlers's contention: "In looking at women as autobiographers, we must remember that the selves they put forward are inevitably shaped, perhaps in ways of which they are unaware, by a circumstance of which they are very much aware: their need to conform to—or rebel against—a society largely defined by the values of a sex that is not their own. Men do not face that challenge."[18]

It will be impossible to ascertain other differences between autobiographies by Wesleyan/Holiness men and women until an examination of male writers has been undertaken. This is particularly true with respect to self-abnegation. Researchers have noted that Christian women usually engaged in self-deprecation in their narratives. Amy Oden has observed: "In much of the writing by women in almost all periods of Christian history, self-depreciating disclaimers and phrases were used. Often self-depreciation was a literary device that would no more be left out than good grammar."

Oden recognized self-depreciation as "a literary device" used by women writers. Rather than projecting an accurate self-portrayal, such language reflected the presumption that such language with respect to the female self was expected. Sanctified women rarely depicted themselves by using terms, either as a literary device or as descriptive language, that diminished their self-worth. Amanda Smith was the only woman in this study to refer to herself as a "worm," a popular disparaging Christian expression. Sarah Smith also engaged in self-abnegation when she insisted she was "nothing": "What I am God has made me, so all glory belongs to him."[19]

Self-deprecation among Christians also included using the term *instrument* to imply that a person's demeanor was passive while God worked through her. For the most part, sanctified women did not describe themselves as passive instruments fulfilling God's calling to write or minister. As Arminians who believed God grants humans free will, they portrayed themselves as active participants who chose to answer God's call to ministry. They were not pawns of God but played an active role with the assistance of the empowerment of the Holy Spirit. Zilpha Elaw and Jarena Lee were the only women in the study who described themselves as instruments. Elaw referred to herself as a "simple and weak" instrument, yet she was "sustained by the mighty power of God." Calling herself "a poor coloured woman" and an "instrument," "Lee subverted the cult of true womanhood: accentuating her femininity while simultaneously asserting both a personal autonomy *and* a spiritual deference, she inscribes herself freed from the cultural and social expectations of women, especially mothers, of her day."[20] In Lee's case, her actions overshadowed the language that implied she was a mere passive instrument in God's hands.

The sanctified self was not inferior. Self-confidence exuded from the narratives of sanctified women. They rejected the societal construction of a weak female self and posited, in its place, a strong sanctified self. This self, however, was not empowered by the act of writing autobiography, as Rosetta Renae Haynes suggested. She analyzed eight African American spiritual autobiographies by women, including four in this study (Zilpha Elaw, Julia Foote, Jarena Lee, and Amanda Smith). Haynes argued that these women "create[d] authentic selves in and through the genre of autobiography."[21] On the contrary, women credited the Holy Spirit for empowering them and described a sanctified self that was in existence prior to their writing. They did not intend to create a self through the act of writing.

Elizabeth Elkin Grammer concluded from her study of nineteenth-century traveling evangelists (including the four mentioned above): "Their quest for an identity remains, sadly I find, incomplete at the 'end' of their textual self-representations . . . I strongly suspect that they did feel that theirs was an almost impossible project, that no manner of shoring up the self with journalistic fragments would build them a 'new house.'"[22] On the contrary, Wesleyan/Holiness women saw no need to bolster the self with "journalistic fragments." In their estimation, the sanctified self was complete in itself. Likewise, they would decry Grammer's characterization of their self-understanding as a "fragile creation." There was nothing fragile about these women.

Why They Wrote

Clearly, Wesleyan/Holiness women authored their narratives to justify their ministries by chronicling their activities and providing biblical and theological justification for rejecting woman's sphere. Also, women were motivated to write for evangelistic and pastoral purposes as well as for economic necessity. Martha Lee was one of the few to admit self-motivation for writing: "For a number of years I have felt that a book ought to be published."[23] In most cases, women recorded that they wrote in response to the requests of others. They also believed it was God's will for them to take pen to paper and tell their stories.

Jennie Smith, Almira Losee, Mary Lee Cagle, and Celia Bradshaw Winkle were among those who wrote at the urging of friends. Mary Still Adams was motivated to write after her sister made the request from her deathbed. A Sister Powers had given Emma Irick five dollars to apply toward the expenses of her book. However, it was sixty-two years later before she undertook the task, even though her husband also had coaxed her to write. She commented: "Better late than never." In some cases, male clergy facilitated the process. Jennie Smith credited Rev. M. P. Gaddis for inspiring her to write what became the first volume of her autobiography. He read a partial draft and commented positively: "I am now more than ever convinced that it is your duty to persevere with the work, and get it done as soon as possible." Another male friend prompted Smith to make the project "a business and not a pastime." A Brother J. offered his support and read the manuscript of a subsequent volume of Smith's autobiography. Jarena Lee credited an unnamed pastor and a bishop for encouraging her to write. At the conclusion of her autobiography, she wrote: "It is certainly essential to life, as Mr. Wesley wisely observes." A Rev. L. B. Kent several times prevailed upon Sarah Cooke to write her autobiography. When she finally agreed, he helped her prepare her manuscript for publication and also wrote the introduction, commending not only the book but praising Cooke's life of ministry. Cooke also sensed a strong impulse "that it was the will of God that I should write a record of His lovingkindness and tender mercies." She further reported "the Lord's voice also was urging me."[24]

Some women waited specifically for God's leading before writing. Lizzie Miller wrote: "For several years I have been particularly requested by my spiritual children, co-workers and warm friends, to give a history of my life and how I was called to work for Jesus. But my shrinking nature recoils from saying so much about myself and the many revivals in which I have been engaged in the United States. It is for this reason I have declined and could not write until directed to do so by the Lord."[25] Miller was able to cast aside her "shrinking nature" and document her extensive ministry.

Initially, Alma White, too, lacked the confidence to write. Phoebe Palmer's articles in *Guide to Holiness* inspired her but she considered Palmer "better qualified to write than any ordinary person."[26] White reported that she had received "clear light from the Lord" to document her experience. Her belief that God called her to write compelled her to begin the project despite her qualms.

Emma Ray was doubtful even with the encouragement of friends and the belief that God wanted her to write, which was confirmed by the Bible verse "ye are my witnesses." Her doubts led her to prayer. She turned to Psalm 26 and read the verse "that I may publish with the voice of thanksgiving, and tell of all Thy wondrous works." This verse was enough to dispel her hesitation. Like Ray, Amanda Smith received confirmation to undertake the task from the Bible when she read: "Now, therefore, perform the doing of it, and as there was a readiness to will, so there may be a performance also out of that which ye have." Sanctified women were called to write just as they had been called to preach. When Smith became discouraged, she again prayed and received the promise, "fear thou, I will help thee."[27] Whether preaching or writing, women relied on God's power to accomplish the task.

The Holy Spirit also played a role in a woman's decision to compose her narrative. According to Lela McConnell, the Holy Spirit compelled her to write. Mary Still Adams invoked the imprimatur of the Holy Spirit when she claimed: "I have said and written all the Spirit hath revealed to my poor finite mind." Julia Shellhamer's impetus to write proceeded from a dramatic encounter with the Holy Spirit. She told of sitting in church "when the gentle Holy Spirit appeared and as sudden as a thunder clap out of a clear sky, dropped the idea of the book into my waiting mind just as distinctly as though someone had dropped a volume into my hands. At first I felt too unworthy to write any of my own brief experiences but the conviction of duty has grown with each successive chapter and I have felt the kiss of Divine approval with the penning of each page."[28] The belief that God or the Holy

Spirit initiated and inspired their writing served as authorization for the subversive activity of authoring autobiographies.

Several women wrote solely at God's command. Just as they would not think of preaching without God's call, women authored their autobiographies only at God's direction. Elizabeth Wheaton confessed: "I was made to feel that the Lord required me to write of the victories He had wrought and of the work yet waiting to be done." Likewise, Sarah Smith relied on God to bring to her mind topics that she should cover in her autobiography.[29]

Wesleyan/Holiness women autobiographers frequently addressed comments directly to their readers, prefacing them by "dear reader" or other phrases, thus drawing attention to the fact that they were explicitly engaging in a conversational style of writing. This was a common technique during the nineteenth and early twentieth centuries, but, no doubt, this approach also reflects the fact that preaching is a verbal act. When women preachers wrote, they mimicked the verbal style of communication they employed most frequently. More than likely, much of the counsel the authors included in their books echoed statements they had made from the pulpit.

Authors interspersed general admonitions and appeals to parents in their books that served as extensions of the oral advice in their sermons. Mary Still Adams admonished parents to create an inviting home for children and to give them "little loving surprises." At the same time, though, children should not be allowed to talk back when told to do something. Mary Cole told parents to set a good example for their children, while Jarena Lee admonished parents to pray for their children. Julia Foote asked pointedly, "Are you bringing your little ones to Jesus?" Foote also warned parents to keep alcohol away from their children, and Julia Shellhamer cautioned against worldly music. Women addressed several comments specifically to mothers. Mary Still Adams told mothers to train their daughters in housework and also to provide as much education for them as they could afford. Mattie Perry encouraged mothers to use their influence to guide their children to Christ.[30] All of these statements could easily have been voiced from the pulpit.

Other counsel directed to readers ranged across a broad spectrum. For instance, Julia Foote asked male readers to vote to make alcohol illegal and to oppose capital punishment. Florence Roberts sought recruits for rescue work among parents who grieved for their dead children: "Christian parents, you that through death or other means have been deprived of the companionship of your children, why not occasionally join some of the rescue workers in their efforts to save somebody's wandering boy or girl, instead of sitting in a rocking-chair, nursing your sorrows?" Roberts encouraged those who worked in the slums to learn from her mistakes and not be overly zealous, resulting in more harm than good in fostering the spiritual progress of those living there. Further, workers should eat with those to whom they are ministering. Roberts asked incisively: "Have you, my reader, helped 'grease the hill' that 'one of these little ones' was sliding down, so that she soon reached the bottom? or are you helping and cheering them on the upward way until they reach the goal?"[31] Women encouraged their readers to engage in social holiness just as they no doubt endorsed social holiness from the pulpit.

Wesleyan/Holiness women offered other miscellaneous advice on Christian living. Lela McConnell, who remained single, admonished young women: "It would be ten thousand times better to go alone and answer the call of God than to be unequally yoked together and fail to fulfill God's plan for your life." In McConnell's estimation, God's call to ministry sometimes superseded marriage, another direct challenge to society's emphasis on domesticity. Jennie Smith provided a general injunction: "Dear reader, we cannot be too careful of our words; we shall have to meet them at the final account. Let us remember to 'do unto others as we would wish to be done by,' ever ready to help raise up humanity instead of casting it down."[32]

Along with advice on numerous topics, evangelism also was an important motivation for writing. Jennie Smith shared: "If one soul is saved and hearts encouraged by this instrumentality, I can bear to be torn to pieces by critics and endure everything in selling the book." She maintained her goal of saving souls in subsequent volumes of her autobiography.[33] Addressing their readers directly, sanctified women urged them to become Christians. Writing was clearly an extension of their preaching. Frequently, their pleas sounded like verbatim transcripts from sermons. Abbie Mills called herself the "book evangelist," making her agenda for writing her autobiography explicit. Likewise, Mary Still Adams confessed: "If I can once get my readers to think, then they will begin to act, and the next step will be the salvation of their souls." Jarena Lee equated preaching and writing when she described the fact that she experienced the "holy influence of that fire now" both when she preached and when her pen "makes record of the same to a dying world." Maude Kahl shared her evangelistic purpose in the preface of her autobiography: "I know of no better way to witness to those outside my sphere of influence. I hope this book will travel far and wide and to many whom I shall never perhaps contact in this life. If some souls will be encouraged to a closer walk with God and have a greater hunger for the companionship and love of God, I shall feel well paid for anything that it has cost me to write this book." Almira Losee and Florence Roberts also regarded their autobiographies as evangelistic tools.[34]

The majority of direct spiritual entreaties to readers in the autobiographies of sanctified women resembled altar calls where the preacher appeals to listeners after the sermon to commit their lives to Christ and become Christians. Mary Still Adams admonished: "My dear readers, I have now come to one of the last chapters of my book. And I feel that I cannot do better, by way of closing, than to direct your attention to the Saviour of the world; . . . If you have never received Christ as your Savior, I beg of you, as sister, mother, friend, make no delay." Mary Glaser confronted her readers with numerous questions throughout her book: "Dear reader, are you in the narrow path that leads from earth to glory?" "O dear hungry souls, you who are longing for more of this fullness, will you not make ready your 'guest-chamber' and receive Him joyfully?" "Would you not think it desirable to be saved from sin in the fullest possible sense?" Others also questioned their readers. Julia Foote asked: "Reader, have you this salvation—an ever-flowing fountain—in your soul?" One can imagine hearing Mattie Perry making the following statement from the pulpit: "Jesus loves you and wants to save you now, if you will only yield yourself to Him and believe in His name." Jarena Lee's words also could have been uttered from the pulpit: "If you have not, I charge you to make your peace with God while time and opportunity is given, and be one of that number who shall take part and lot in the first resurrection." Likewise, Sarah Smith admonished: "Oh sinners, let me warn you in the name of Jesus, never reject the Spirit of God when it is knocking at the door of your heart."[35]

Most authors thus focused on conversion in direct pleas to their readers. More than likely, this reflects the belief that many of their readers would be unconverted. Lela McConnell was an exception in that she assumed readers were already Christians and thus focused on holiness or sanctification. She testified: "We praise the Lord for this added ministry through these books, of spreading scriptural holiness around the world." Perhaps she recognized that many of the books recounting her leadership of the Kentucky Mountain Holiness Association would be read by her supporters, who were already Christians. McConnell explained: "Dear friends, as to this dual experience, you will readily see that the Bible, church creeds, and individual experience of God's children of different denominations all unite in telling with one voice that conversion is not complete cleansing, but that all believers who have not yet received it still need the double cure. So if, my dear converted friends, you will follow the flutterings of your own longing hearts, you too will know the blessedness of full salvation and sing, 'With voices glad and hearts made pure, We'll magnify the double cure.'" McConnell ended another book with these words: "My final word is to tell you how to obtain this Bible experience of sanctification." Abbie Mills and Lizzie Miller were among the few other women who specifically admonished their readers to seek sanctification. Florence Roberts defined the term for her readers.[36] While most sanctified women may not have made direct appeals to their readers to become sanctified, their personal testimonies of sanctification in themselves offered an impetus for Christian readers to seek the same experience.

Those who authored multiple volumes of their autobiographies reported the success of their prior books in terms of evangelism. Lela McConnell reported:

> I have received thousands of letters telling me how my two books, THE PAULINE MINISTRY IN THE KENTUCKY MOUNTAINS and FAITH VICTORIOUS IN THE KENTUCKY MOUNTAINS, have been a blessing. I rejoice to know that many souls have been born into the Kingdom through this means and also that many have come to know Jesus in His sanctifying power by reading what the Lord has done in answer to prayer. Furthermore, to know that God's saints have been built up in the most holy faith and encouraged in the divine life repays me for all the hours of writing, and fills my soul with praise to God for ever counting me worthy of this ministry. Some folk say they have read the book many times. One man said he had read my first book seventeen times. Others say that they were so helped by them that they have loaned them to dozens of other people.[37]

Jennie Smith noted that several conversions had resulted from individuals reading her first book, *Valley of Baca.*[38]

Pragmatically, some women wrote in order to sell their narratives for profit. Alma White's members sold volumes of her autobiography door to door, not only enhancing the potential for evangelism but earning income for her church branches as well. Dora Dudley used the profits from her book sales entirely "in the work of the Lord." More than likely, she meant that the money supported her religious work. Almira Losee hoped the sale of her books would help defray her travel costs to Utah to work as a missionary among Mormons. Jennie Smith planned to pay for her home with the profits from her books: "Each one who buys or helps sell the books will aid me in this effort." Before earning profits, though, she had to raise the money to repay publishing costs. This amounted to several hundred dollars for *From Baca to Beulah.*[39]

Jarena Lee authored her autobiography in 1836. When she wrote an expanded version thirteen years later, she recounted her dilemma regarding the initial distribution of her book. She had hesitated to sell copies herself because that seemed too commercial. However, because she had self-published, she had the printer's bill to consider. This propelled her to take to the streets, where she could make sales. She also sold copies at camp meetings and other religious gatherings. Besides paying the printer, she used profits from the sale of her books to cover her preaching expenses. She sold one thousand copies and printed another one thousand.[40]

Women preachers also wrote to inspire others to become ministers or to encourage others already in ministerial work. Elizabeth Wheaton's recruitment plea was as follows: "One reason I have for writing, is to show the great need of Holy Ghost workers—those whose hearts God has touched to carry the gospel to those whose lives are darkened, blighted and blasted, and tell them of a mighty deliverance from the bondage of sin, and of freedom in Christ." Emma Irick prayed that her book would "inspire someone to be a worker for the Lord." Lucy Drake Osborn, too, was candid about one of her reasons for writing: "It is, therefore, to incite the young of all classes to seek divine equipment for their work that this narrative of the exceedingly rich and priceless gifts which God in His mercy has dropped into my life has been written."[41] Wheaton, Irick, and Osborn all hoped their autobiographies would result in readers considering God's call on their lives to become preachers.

Mary Cole addressed encouraging comments to young ministers and Christian workers throughout her book. Her address to the younger generation in the last chapter of her book was entitled "Exhortation to Workers and Ministers." It concluded with these words: "If this little volume points out any pitfalls that should be avoided or any pleasant paths that your feet may walk in with safety; if it encourages you to trust the Lord more fully for all things and inspire you to place yourself more fully in his hands for service, it will have accomplished the purpose of the author." She did not restrict her comments to the designated chapter, however. In another portion of the book, she wrote: "Dear young ministers and workers, God may call you to his work and send you forth at once into the field; but do not be impatient or discouraged if the Lord sees fit to have you tarry awhile after he has called you." She advised older workers to display tolerance toward their younger colleagues: "Dear brothers and sisters in the ministry, right here I would sound a note of warning. Let us be careful when a young worker comes among us. Even if he does not seem promising at first, let us have patience with him and give him a chance; let him prove himself."[42] While Cole's language made it appear she was directing her comments to males, more than likely she was including females as well since she addressed her colleagues in ministry inclusively.

Amanda Smith and Julia Foote explicitly urged other women to be open to God's call to ministry. Smith addressed women: "I pray . . . that the Spirit of the Lord may come upon some of the younger women who have talent, and who have had better opportunities than I have ever had, and so must do better work for the Master; so that when I have fallen in the battle, and can do no more, they may take up the standard and bear it on, with the inscription deeply engraved on heart and life. 'Without holiness, no man shall see the Lord.'" Foote also targeted women. In a chapter entitled "A Word to My Christian Sisters," she wrote: "Sisters, shall not you and I unite with the heavenly host in the grand chorus? If so, you will not let what man may say or do, keep you from doing the will of the Lord or using the gifts you have for the good of others . . . Be not kept in bondage by those who say, 'We suffer not a woman to teach,' thus quoting Paul's words but not rightly applying them."[43] Women's narratives were extensions of their public ministries. Their autobiographies were subversive texts that documented their lives. Amanda Smith and Julia Foote not only engaged in subversive activity as a result of their sanctified selves; they wrote about it and unabashedly exhorted other women to follow their example and step outside the sphere of domesticity.

Wesleyan/Holiness women preachers' autobiographies served as testimonies demonstrating the impact of sanctification on their lives and summarizing their subsequent ministries. Rather than the death of the author, which Foucault and others have advocated, Wesleyan/Holiness women experienced a death of the sinful self, which resulted in a sanctified self enabling women to overcome their "man-fearing spirit" and assume public ministries. Their narratives highlighted the self-confidence that they possessed as sanctified women. A worship leader prayed prior to a sermon at a Wesleyan/Holiness camp meeting in 1999: "Bless the preacher tonight. Take her out of herself that she may be filled and overflowing."[44] The individual's prayer illustrated the paradox of the death of the self and the sanctified self filled with the Holy Spirit and enabled to preach.

Wesleyan/Holiness women worshiped and ministered in a religious context that fostered and nurtured a sanctified self, which they believed was divinely constructed. Committed to egalitarian primitivism, the Wesleyan/Holiness movement emulated the early church by validating the prophetic authority of women. The proponents of woman's sphere contended that their construction of gender reflected the innate nature of women and was unalterable. Sanctified women ripped the foundations out from under this essentialist construction. Their public ministries nullified the claim that all women by their very nature were incapable of operating outside woman's sphere. Sanctification and the empowerment of the Holy Spirit made it possible for Wesleyan/Holiness women to overturn society's expectations of women. Sanctified women's narratives documented their lives as ministers, whether they engaged in evangelism or social holiness or both. Exhibiting holy boldness, Wesleyan/Holiness women demonstrated an alternative to society's script for women, which prescribed a narrow role limited to the home. For Wesleyan/Holiness women preachers, the ethic of empowerment displaced the ethic of domesticity.

APPENDIX

Preaching Locations as Reported by Mary Lee Cagle and Jarena Lee

Spellings used by the authors have been preserved. States are included when provided by the author.

Mary Lee Cagle

Miss.
Ky.
Memphis
Little Rock, Ark.
Beebe, Ark.
Searay, Ark.
Gadsden, Tenn.
Hillsboro, Tex.
Roby, Tex.
Swedonia, Tex.
Hickory Flat Springs
Sanderson's Chapel, Tenn.
Newberg, Tenn.
Hillsboro, Tenn.
Eskota, Tex.
Buffalo Island, Ark.
Lake City
Ala.
Milan, Tenn.
Neinda, Tex.
Hitson
Nubia, Mulberry Canyon
Anson
Truby
Abilene
Eula
Buffalo Gap
Potosi
Monett, Ark.
Hylton
Snyder
Red Bluff
Big Spring
Lamesa
Hollow Tank
Tahoka
Lubbock
Portales, N. Mex.
Gail, N. M.
Oak Cliff
Arlington
Dallas
Magdalene, N. Mex.
Kelly
Reserve
Alma
West Nashville
Sparta Dalhart
Stratford
Tularosa, N. Mex.
Cucumonga, Calif.
Upland
Roswell
Peoria, Ariz.
Rally Hill, Tenn.
El Paso, Tex.
Stanton, Tex.
Trinidad, Colo.

Loveland, Colo.
Holyoke
San Antonio
Liberty Hill
Cheyenne, Wyo.

Jarena Lee

Philadelphia
Middletown
Cecil City, Md.
Downington
Dutch Hill, L.I.
Stanton Mills
Snow Hill
Beaver Dams
Hillsborough
Greensborough
Cecil Cross
Hales' Mills
10 miles from Centreville
Philadelphia
Weston, Pa.
Lancaster, Pa.
Columbia
York
York Haven
Harrisburg, Pa.
Carlisle, Pa.
Shippensburg
Chambersburg
Norristown
Reading, Pa.
Littleton Morris's
Pottsgrove
Lewistown, Del.
Georgetown
Trenton
Princeton
Baltimore
Mount Ephraim, N.J.
N.Y.
Albany
Niagara
Buffalo
8 miles from Fort George
Buffalo Village
Westtown
West Chester
Fredericktown, Md.
Wheeling
Washington
Mt. Pleasant
Sinclairsville
Cap-teen
Barnsborough
Zanesville
West Zanesville
New-Lancaster
Columbus
Chillicothe
Cincinnati
Williamsport
Dayton
Wilkes-Barre
Hagerstown
Salem, N.J.
Bridgetown
Fair-field
Port Elizabeth
Norristown
New-Brunswick
Rahway
Asberry, N.Y.
St. Georges, Del.
Frankford
St. Catharine
Hambleton
Dundas
Flamburg
Ammonsburg
Rochester
Canondagua
Ithaca
Bethel
Brooklyn, L.I.
Flushing
Del.
Bristol
Brunswick
Elicott's Mills

Springtown
Blaketown, N.J.
Greenwich
Port Elizabeth
Goshen, Cape May
New Brunswick, N.Y.
New Hope
Attleboro
Ben Salem
Columbia
Pittsburg
Uniontown
Washington, Pa.
Waynesburg
Meconnoburg
Hambleton
Schuylkill
Marietta
Penningtonville
Burlington
Lawrenceville
New Haven
Rahway
Jamaica
Harvest traw
Hudson
Pittsfield
Catskill
Troy
Smithboro

NOTES

Preface

1. Mary R. Beard, *Woman as Force in History* (New York: Macmillan, 1946); and Gerda Lerner, *The Majority Finds Its Past* (New York: Oxford Univ. Press, 1979).

Introduction

1. Rose Norman, "The Representation of Religious Experience in Nineteenth-Century American Women's Autobiography," *Listening: Journal of Religion and Culture* 28, no. 2 (spring 1993): 132.
2. Estelle C. Jelinek, *The Tradition of Women's Autobiography* (Boston: Twayne Publishers, 1986), 97. Susie C. Stanley, *Wesleyan/Holiness Women Clergy* (Portland, Ore.: Western Evangelical Seminary, 1994), 7–14. Robert E. Sayre, "The Proper Study: Autobiographies in American Studies," in *The American Autobiography,* ed. Albert E. Stone, 11–30 (Englewood Cliffs, N.J.: Prentice-Hall, 1981).
3. In a selected list of women's autobiographies, Sidonie Smith and Julia Watson included the writings of Julia Foote, Zilpha Elaw, and Jarena Lee. Sidonie Smith and Julia Watson, eds., *Women, Autobiography, Theory* (Madison: Univ. of Wisconsin Press, 1998), 477–84. While Amanda Smith is missing from their list, her writings have received attention from autobiographical theorists such as Elizabeth Elkin Grammer ("'A Pen in His Hand': A Pen in Her Hand. Autobiographies by Female Itinerant Evangelists in Nineteenth-Century America" [Ph.D. diss., Univ. of Virginia, 1995]); and Rosetta Renae Haynes ("Radical Spiritual Motherhood: The Construction of Black Female Subjectivity in Nineteenth-Century African-American Women's Spiritual Autobiographies" [Ph.D. diss., Cornell Univ., 1996]). William L. Andrews, ed., *Sisters of the Spirit* (Bloomington: Indiana Univ. Press, 1986). See also Henry Louis Gates Jr., ed. *Spiritual Narratives* (New York: Oxford Univ. Press, 1988); and Amanda Smith, *An Autobiography* (Chicago: Meyer & Brothers, Publishers, 1893; reprint, New York: Garland Publishing, 1987). Another reprint of Amanda Smith's autobiography was published by Oxford University Press in 1988. Jarena Lee's autobiography was reprinted in 1984. See also Frances Smith Foster, "Neither Auction Block nor Pedestal: 'The Life and Religious Experience of Jarena Lee, A Coloured Lady,'" in *The*

Female Autograph, ed. Domna C. Stanton, 126–51 (Chicago: Univ. of Chicago Press, 1984).

4. Deborah E. McDowell, "New Directions for Black Feminist Criticism," in *The New Feminist Criticism,* ed. Elaine Showalter (New York: Pantheon Books, 1985), 186.
5. Phoebe Davidson, "Workings of the Spirit: Religious Impulse in Selected Autobiographies of American Women" (Ph.D. diss., Rutgers State Univ. of New Jersey, 1991), 294.
6. Several of the autobiographies have been reprinted. The Church of the Nazarene reprinted Cagle's autobiography. Reprints of Sarah Smith's, Van Cott's, Hannah Whitall Smith's, and Palmer's autobiographies, as well as Jennie Smith's *From Baca to Beulah,* have been published.
7. There are no articles on autobiography in *Methodist History* or *Wesleyan Theological Journal* other than Susie C. Stanley's "'Tell Me the Old, Old Story': Analysis of Autobiographies by Holiness Women," *Wesleyan Theological Journal* 29, nos. 1 and 2 (spring–fall 1994): 7–22. Gregory Schneider has explored the concept of the self within Methodism but has not examined any of the narratives I am analyzing. A. Gregory Schneider, *The Way of the Cross Leads Home* (Bloomington: Indiana Univ. Press, 1993). He did consult approximately twenty autobiographies of male Methodist preachers.
8. Brenda E. Brasher, *Godly Women* (Piscataway, N.J.: Rutgers Univ. Press, 1998), 62, 199.
9. Jackson W. Carroll, Barbara Hargrove, and Adair T. Lummis, *Women of the Cloth* (San Francisco: Harper & Row, 1983), 2.
10. However, the numbers did grow dramatically in mainline denominations. By 1986, Jacquet reported 7,628 women clergy in the mainline denominations, while the Wesleyan/Holiness number had remained steady at 4,176. Constant H. Jacquet Jr., *Women Ministers in 1986 and 1977* (New York: National Council of Churches, 1988), 5–6.
11. Sociologists Laura R. Olson, Sue E. S. Crawford, and James L. Guth repeated this error when they focused on mainline Protestant women clergy. They claimed this was "almost out of necessity" since "many American religious traditions, most notably the Catholic Church and most of evangelical Protestantism, do not ordain women at all." By ignoring the thousands of Wesleyan/Holiness (and Pentecostal) women clergy, the researchers' conclusions are skewed and are definitely not representative of women clergy as a whole. Laura R. Olson, Sue E. S. Crawford, and James L. Guth, "Changing Issue Agendas of Women Clergy," *Journal of the Scientific Study of Religion* 39, no. 2 (June 2000): 141.
12. Barbara Brown Zikmund, Adair T. Lummis, and Patricia Mei Yin Chang, *Clergy Women* (Louisville: Westminster John Knox Press, 1998), 137. The Wesleyan/Holiness denominations included were Church of God (Anderson, Ind.), Church of the Nazarene, Free Methodist Church, and The Wesleyan Church.
13. Norman H. Murdoch, "Female Ministry in the Thought and Work of Catherine Booth," *Church History* 53 (Sept. 1984): 349. Diana Winston, *Red-Hot and Righteous* (Cambridge, Mass.: Harvard Univ. Press, 1999), 183. Abbie C.

Mills, *Grace and Glory* (Los Angeles: By the author, 1907), 188. Elizabeth R. Wheaton, *Prisons and Prayer; or, A Labor of Love* (Tabor, Iowa: M. Kelley, [1906]), 308. Sarah A. Cooke, *The Handmaiden of the Lord, or Wayside Sketches* (Chicago: T. B. Arnold, 1896), 315, 345. Julia A. Shellhamer, *Trials and Triumphs of a Minister's Wife* (Atlanta: Repairer Publishing, 1923), 222. Martha A. Lee, *Mother Lee's Experience in Fifteen Years' Rescue Work* (Omaha, Nebr.: By the author, 1906), 92. Florence Roberts, *Fifteen Years with the Outcast* (Anderson, Ind.: Gospel Trumpet, 1912), 189, 292, 306, 356. [Emma] and L. [Lloyd] P. Ray, *Twice Sold, Twice Ransomed* (Chicago: Free Methodist Publishing House, 1926), 143.

14. Women listed by Mills in *Grace* included Sister Sparks Wheeler (116, 117), Cassie Smith (31, 117, 148), Sarah Smiley (31), Grace Weiser Davis (117), Mrs. Bottome (117), Lizzie Boyd (117), Nettie Van Name (117), Lida Kenney (96, 117), Lois Smith (148), Sister Van Holtz (161), Lizzie Sharp (237), Mrs. Robinson (83), Sister Clara Boyd (96), Sister Shay (97), Sister Morrow (115) "and others" (31, 117).
15. Mills, *Grace,* 67, 176, 214, 223, 237; see also 54, 96, 117, 192 for other references to Lizzie Smith. Perhaps Lizzie Smith is the married name of Lizzie Boyd since Mills recorded at Mountain Lake Park in 1887 that "the evening service was conducted by the sisters" Lizzie Smith and Clara Boyd (*Grace,* 96). Mills, *Grace,* 83, 115. Dora Dudley also knew Montgomery, who later became affiliated with the Pentecostal movement (*Beulah,* rev. and enlarged ed. (Grand Rapids, Mich.: By the author, 1896), 38). Amanda Smith, *Autobiography,* 169. Jennie Smith, *From Baca to Beulah, Sequel to "Valley of Baca"* (Philadelphia: Garrigues Brothers, 1880), 227. S. [Susan] N. [Norris] Fitkin, *Grace Much More Abounding* (Kansas City, Mo.: Nazarene Publishing House, n.d.), n.p.
16. Robert Folkenflik, ed., *The Culture of Autobiography: Constructions of Self-Representation* (Stanford: Stanford Univ. Press, 1993), 1; quoted in Diane Bjorklund, *Interpreting the Self* (Chicago: Univ. of Chicago Press, 1998), 211. "The Martyrdom of Saints Perpetua and Felicitas," in *The Acts of the Christian Martyrs,* trans. Herbert Musurillo (Oxford: Clarendon Press, 1972), 108–31.
17. Felicity Nussbaum, *The Autobiographical Subject* (Baltimore: Johns Hopkins Univ. Press, 1989), 160.
18. Catherine A. Brekus, *Female Preaching in America, Strangers and Pilgrims, 1740–1845* (Chapel Hill: Univ. of North Carolina Press, 1998), 257.
19. Margo Culley, "Women's Vernacular Literature: Teaching the Mother Tongue," in *Women's Personal Narratives,* ed. Leonore Hoffman and Margo Culley (New York: Modern Language Association of America, 1985), 16. Florence Roberts, *Fifteen Years,* 25. A few other authors did acknowledge literary shortcomings in their autobiographies. See also Amanda Smith, *Autobiography,* 505; and Zilpha Elaw, *Memoirs of the Life, Religious Experience, Ministerial Travels and Labours of Mrs. Zilpha Elaw, an American Female of Color* (London: By the author, 1846); reprint, *Sisters of the Spirit,* ed. William L. Andrews (Bloomington, Ind.: Indiana Univ. Press,. 1986), 57.
20. "Martyrdom of Saints Perpetua and Felicitas," 127.

21. They worked at the Marion, Indiana, camp meeting in 1878 and again at Churubasko, Michigan, in 1879. D. S. Warner, *Journal of D. S. Warner* Tms (photocopy), 345, 380. The journal only covers 1872–79, so there is a possibility they also may have worked together during a period of time not documented in his journal. While Foote's narrative was published in 1879, the last dated references to ministry in her book were in the early 1850s. Bettye Collier-Thomas has contributed to the information regarding Foote's later years in *Daughters of Thunder* (San Francisco: Jossey-Bass, 1997).
22. Hannah Whitall Smith, *My Spiritual Autobiography or How I Discovered the Unselfishness of God* (New York: Fleming H. Revell, 1903), 19.
23. Mary Fletcher, *The Life of Mrs. Mary Fletcher, Consort and Relict of the Rev. John Fletcher, Vicar of Madeley, Salop,* comp. and ed. Henry Moore (London: Conference-Office, 1818), xv, 93, 287. Unfortunately, according to a conversation with Paul Chilcote, Moore exercised his editorial pen in deleting a significant portion of her journal.
24. Mary Lee Cagle, *Life and Work of Mary Lee Cagle* (Kansas City, Mo.: Nazarene Publishing House, 1928), 23, 91.
25. Katherine Clay Bassard, *Spiritual Interrogations* (Princeton: Princeton Univ. Press, 1999), 88. Alma White, *Looking Back from Beulah* (Denver: Pentecostal Union, 1902; reprint, Zarephath, N.J.: Pillar of Fire, 1951); and Alma White, *The Story of My Life and the Pillar of Fire,* 6 vols. (Zarephath, N.J.: Pillar of Fire, 1919–34).
26. Ray, *Twice Sold,* 54–59.
27. Cagle, *Life and Work,* preface; and Mary Still Adams, *Autobiography of Mary Still Adams or, "In God We Trust"* (Los Angeles: Buckingham Bros., Printers, 1893), 286.
28. This was true for Sarah Cooke, Jarena Lee, Jennie Smith, Amanda Smith, and Emma Ray.

Chapter 1

1. John Wesley, *Plain Account of Christian Perfection* (London: Wesleyan Conference Office, 1872; reprint, Kansas City, Mo.: Beacon Hill Press of Kansas City, 1966), 31, 30, 61, 62, 90, 29, 94, 34, 50. For the continuing debate over Wesley's emphasis, see Randy L. Maddox, *Responsible Grace* (Nashville: Kingswood Books, 1994); and Kenneth J. Collins, *A Real Christian: The Life of John Wesley* (Nashville: Abingdon Press, 1999).
2. Wesley, *Plain Account,* 59, 79, 41, 45, 86, 61, 99. For several instances, see Wesley, *Plain Account,* 19, 37, 55, 118. I have quoted from the King James Version of the Bible since this was the version accessible to Wesleyan/Holiness women.
3. John Peters, *Christian Perfection and American Methodism* (Grand Rapids, Mich.: Francis Asbury Press of Zondervan Publishing House, 1985), 88.
4. Palmer's role in American Christian history was forgotten until Timothy L. Smith stressed her importance in *Revivalism and Social Reform in Mid-Nineteenth Century America* (New York: Abingdon Press, 1957; reprint

with new title, *Revivalism and Social Reform: American Protestantism on the Eve of the Civil War* (Baltimore: Johns Hopkins Univ. Press, 1980). For information on her life and ministry, see Harold E. Raser, *Phoebe Palmer* (Lewiston, N.Y.: Edwin Mellon Press, 1987); and Charles Edward White, *Beauty of Holiness* (Grand Rapids, Mich.: Asbury Press of Zondervan Publishing House, 1986). Thomas C. Oden, ed., *Phoebe Palmer* (New York: Paulist Press, 1988), 7. Phoebe Palmer, *The Way of Holiness* (50th American ed., 1867; reprint, Salem, Ohio: Schmul Publishing, 1988).

5. Douglas M. Strong has documented the political activity of Wesleyan Methodists in their quest to end slavery in *Perfectionist Politics, Religion and Politics* (Syracuse: Syracuse Univ. Press, 1999).
6. Lucy Drake Osborn, *Heavenly Pearls Set in a Life* (New York: Fleming H. Revell, 1893), 27; and Emma M. Whittemore, *Mother Whittemore's Records of Modern Miracles* (Toronto: Missions of Biblical Education, 1931), 22. Abbie C. Mills, *Quiet Hallelujahs* (Boston: McDonald & Gill, 1886), 210, 222.
7. Palmer, *Way of Holiness,* 23, 82. When there is no biblical reference for a verse quoted by an author (as in the first quotation from Palmer), I have not attempted to supply it. In some cases, it is impossible to determine the precise verse, given the paraphrase. In other instances, the author could be referring to one of several similar verses.
8. "Meditations on the Happiness of Heaven," *Western Christian Monitor,* June 1816, 245; quoted in Schneider, *Way of the Cross,* 50.
9. Schneider, *Way of the Cross,* 182, 116. Janet S. Everhart, "Maggie Newton Van Cott: The Methodist Episcopal Church Considers the Question of Women Clergy," *Women in New Worlds,* ed. Rosemary Skinner Keller, Louise L. Queen, and Hilah F. Thomas (Nashville: Abingdon, 1982), 303, 309–10. Schneider, *Way of the Cross,* 207.
10. While my purpose is not to trace the view of self among all holiness writers and theologians, one example will be representative. Lyrics to holiness hymns rather than systematic theologies have often been credited with conveying holiness theology. D. S. Warner, founder of the Church of God (Anderson, Ind.), penned the hymn "Fill Me with Thy Spirit, Lord." One of the verses reads, "Fill me with thy perfect Love / Naught of self would I retain. / Losing all Thy love to prove / Lord, I count a happy gain." *Worship the Lord* (Anderson, Ind.: Warner Press, 1989), No. 269.
11. Richard Hughes, "Christian Primitivism as Perfectionism: From Anabaptists to Pentecostals," in *Reaching Beyond,* ed. Stanley Burgess (Peabody, Mass.: Hendrickson, 1986), 213–55. For a brief discussion of egalitarian primitivism, see Susie C. Stanley, "'Bumping' into Modernity: Primitive/Modern Tensions in the Wesleyan/Holiness Movement," in *The Primitive Church in the Modern World,* ed. Richard T. Hughes (Urbana, Ill.: Univ. of Illinois Press, 1995), 128–29.
12. Mary Cole, *Trials and Triumphs of Faith* (Anderson, Ind.: Gospel Trumpet, 1914), 86–87. Julia Foote, *A Brand Plucked from the Fire* (Cleveland, Ohio: By the author, 1879); reprint, *Sisters of the Spirit,* ed. William L. Andrews (Bloomington, Ind.: Indiana Univ. Press, 1986), 208.

13. Elaine C. Huber, *Women and the Authority of Inspiration* (Lanham, Md.: Univ. Press of America, 1985), 128, 7–8. She also spoke of Spirit-filled empowerment (*Women,* 127), but she did not note the emphasis on the authority of inspiration or prophetic authority within the Wesleyan/Holiness movement.
14. Carolyn Walker Bynum, *Jesus as Mother* (Berkeley: Univ. of California Press, 1982), 261–62; quoted in Kate P. Crawford Galea, "'Anchored Behind the Veil': Mystical Vision as a Possible Source of Authority in the Ministry of Phoebe Palmer," *Methodist History* 31:4 (July 1993): 243.
15. Quoted in Richard Wheatley, *The Life and Letters of Mrs. Phoebe Palmer* (New York: W. C. Palmer, Publisher, 1881; reprint, New York: Garland Publishing, Inc., 1984), 631–32.
16. Luther Lee, "Woman's Right to Preach the Gospel," in *Five Sermons and a Tract,* ed. Donald W. Dayton (Chicago: Holrad House, 1975), 91. B. T. Roberts, *Ordaining Women* (Rochester: Earnest Christian Publishing House, 1891; reprint, Indianapolis: Light and Life Press, 1992), 103. Roberts acknowledged the move from prophetic to priestly authority within the church: "In the primitive Christian Church, when the ministers became proud and aspiring, and assumed priestly prerogatives, they assigned to women a lower place in the Christian ministry; and finally, as they apostatized more fully, they dropped her from the ministry altogether" (*Ordaining Women,* 27). Roberts's book remains one of the best apologies for women in ministry.
17. B. T. Roberts, *Ordaining Women,* 96. The Free Methodist Church rejected Roberts's radical primitivism and limited women's leadership. Thus, they were an exception within the Wesleyan/Holiness movement. The General Conference of 1874 licensed women as evangelists, recognizing them as lay preachers. Roberts's book resulted from the refusal of the General Conference in 1890 to ordain women. In 1911, women were granted limited ordination, but it was not until 1974 that women achieved the right to assume senior leadership positions in the denomination.
18. Judy Veenker, "Culture Clash: Asserting the Bible's Authority, Southern Baptists Say Pastors Must Be Male," *Christianity Today,* 10 July 2000, 19.
19. Margo Culley, "What a Piece of Work Is 'Woman'! An Introduction," in *American Women's Autobiography,* ed. Margo Culley (Madison: Univ. of Wisconsin Press, 1992), 9. Ann Taves, "Self and God in the Early Published Memoirs of New England Women," in *American Women's Autobiography,* ed. Margo Culley (Madison: Univ. of Wisconsin Press, 1992), 59.
20. Luther Lee, "Woman's Right," 83. Phoebe Palmer, *The Promise of the Father; or, A Neglected Specialty of the Last Days* (Boston: Henry V. Degen, 1859; reprint, Salem, Ohio: Schmul Publishers, n.d.). Catherine Booth, *Female Ministry* (London: n.p., 1859; reprint, New York: Salvation Army Supplies Printing and Publishing Dept., 1975), 10, 16. B. T. Roberts, *Ordaining Women,* 104. W. B. Godbey, *Woman Preacher* (Louisville, Ky.: Pentecostal Publishing, 1891), 13.

21. B. T. Roberts, *Ordaining Women,* 7. E. E. Shellhamer, *The Ups and Downs of a Pioneer Preacher* (Atlanta: Repairer Publishing Co., 1914), 77.
22. Carolyn G. Heilbrun, *Writing a Woman's Life* (New York: Ballantine Books, 1988), 23.
23. Elizabeth Johnson, *Friends of God and Prophets* (New York: Continuum, 1998), 208.
24. Sandra Lipsitz Bem, *The Lenses of Gender* (New Haven: Yale Univ. Press, 1993), 5, 46–47. Alma White, "Man and Woman Created Equal," *Woman's Chains,* May–June 1940, 6.
25. Julia Swindells, *The Uses of Autobiography* (London: Taylor & Francis, 1995), 213.
26. Carla A. Peterson, *"Doers of the Word"* (New York: Oxford Univ. Press, 1995), 56. Nellie Y. McKay, "Nineteenth-Century Black Women's Spiritual Autobiographies: Religious Faith and Self-Empowerment," in *Interpreting Women's Lives,* ed. Personal Narratives Group (Bloomington: Indiana Univ. Press, 1989), 150.
27. Kimberly Rae Connor, *Conversions and Visions in the Writings of African American Women* (Knoxville: Univ. of Tennessee Press, 1994), 20, 26, 46, 35, 39.
28. McKay, "Nineteenth-Century," 141. Jarena Lee, *Religious Experience and Journal of Mrs. Jarena Lee, Giving an Account of Her Call to Preach the Gospel* (Philadelphia: By the author, 1849), 19.
29. Amanda Smith, *Autobiography,* 248, 117, 198. Elaw, *Memoirs,* 85.
30. Sue E. Houchins, introduction to *Spiritual Narratives,* ed. H. L. Gates Jr. (New York: Oxford Univ. Press, 1988), xl.
31. Ibid., xxxii.
32. Ibid., xxxiii, xxxv.
33. Andrews, introduction to *Sisters of the Spirit,* 4, 14.
34. Susie C. Stanley, "'Tell Me the Old, Old Story,'" 7–22; Susie C. Stanley, "Empowered Foremothers: Wesleyan/Holiness Women Speak to Today's Christian Feminists," *Wesleyan Theological Journal* 24 (1989): 103–16; Susie C. Stanley, "What Sanctification Means to Me: 'Holiness Is Power,'" in *Sanctification* (Anderson, Ind.: Anderson University School of Theology, 1989),17–24; and Susie C. Stanley, "The Promise Fulfilled: Women's Ministries in the Wesleyan/Holiness Movement," in *Religious Institutions and Women's Leadership* (Columbia: Univ. of South Carolina Press, 1996), 139–57.
35. Virginia Lieson Brereton, *From Sin to Salvation* (Bloomington: Indiana Univ. Press, 1991), 67, 93, 29. Van Cott labeled the experience to which Brereton referred as "that *fullness* which God has promised" and proceeded to quote verses from Acts 2 (Maggie Newton Van Cott, *The Harvest and the Reaper* [New York: N. Tibbals & Sons, Publishers, 1876], 67). Van Cott had documented her conversion earlier when she reported that she "was soundly powerfully converted" (*Harvest and Reaper,* 54). Rosemary Skinner Keller makes the same mistake of equating conversion and sanctification. In

a chapter analyzing the conversions of five Methodist women, Keller defined sanctification as an ongoing process begun at conversion: "Sanctification points to the new life of the Christian, which is begun in conversion and continues throughout one's life as it is nurtured in spiritual growth" (Rosemary Skinner Keller, "Conversions and Their Consequences: Women's Ministry and Leadership in the United Methodist Tradition," in *Religious Institutions and Women's Leadership,* ed. Catherine Wessinger [Columbia, S.C.: Univ. of South Carolina Press, 1996], 102–3). She does this even though she recognized that Amanda Smith's experience of entire sanctification was a subsequent experience following conversion (*Conversions,* 108).

36. Cole, *Trials and Triumphs,* 191.
37. Brereton, *From Sin to Salvation,* 67.
38 J. Gordon Melton, "Emma Curtis Hopkins: A Feminist of the 1880s and Mother of New Thought," in *Women's Leadership in Marginal Religions,* ed. Catherine Wessinger (Urbana: Univ. of Illinois Press, 1993), 90. Liz Stanley, *The Auto/biographical I* (Manchester: Manchester Univ. Press, 1992), 114 (Liz Stanley is not related to the author). Davidson, "Workings of the Spirit," 277.
39. Annette Kolodny, "Dancing through the Minefield: Some Observations on the Theory, Practice, and Politics of a Feminist Literary Criticism," in *The New Feminist Criticism,* ed. Elaine Showalter (New York: Pantheon Books, 1985), 161.
40. Julia Watson and Sidonie Smith, "Introduction: De/Colonization and the Politics of Discourse in Women's Autobiographical Practices," in *De/Colonizing the Subject,* ed. Sidonie Smith and Julia Watson (Minneapolis: Univ. of Minnesota Press, 1992), xiv. Grammer, "Pen in His Hand," 25.
41. Personal Narratives Group, "Origins," in *Interpreting Women's Lives,* ed. Personal Narratives Group (Bloomington: Indiana Univ. Press, 1989), 4.
42. Elaine Showalter, "Feminist Criticism in the Wilderness," in *The New Feminist Criticism,* ed. Elaine Showalter (New York: Pantheon Books, 1985), 244. Palmer, *Way of Holiness,* 64.
43. Barbara Welter, *Dimity Convictions* (Athens: Ohio Univ. Press, 1976), 21–41. Three other traits of the "true woman" were piety, submission, and purity.
44. Shirley J. Yee, *Black Women Abolitionists* (Knoxville: Univ. of Tennessee Press, 1992), 44.
45. Bem, *Lenses of Gender,* 2, 81, 5; see also 46–49.
46. Liz Stanley, *Auto/biographical I,* 243.
47. Ibid., 105, 108. Sarah M. Grimké, *Letters on the Equality of the Sexes and the Condition of Woman* (Boston: Isaac Knapp, 1838; reprint, New York: Source Book Press, 1970), 60. Elizabeth Wilson, *A Scriptural View of Woman's Rights and Duties* (Philadelphia: Wm. S. Young, 1849), 35. Liz Stanley, *Auto/biographical I,* 109.
48. The term is Bem's (*Lenses of Gender,* 167).
49. Janet Wilson James, "Women in American Religious History: An Overview," in *Women in American Religion,* ed. Janet Wilson James (Philadelphia: Univ. of Pennsylvania Press, 1980), 21. Phoebe Palmer and Catherine Booth were other Wesleyan/Holiness women whom Wilson James classified as "traditionalists."

50. Quoted in Catherine A. Brekus, "'Let Your Women Keep Silence in the Churches': Female Preaching and Evangelical Religion in America, 1740–1845" (Ph.D. diss., Yale Univ., 1993), 294.
51. Nussbaum, *Autobiographical Subject,* xiv.
52. Sidonie Smith, *A Poetics of Women's Autobiography* (Bloomington: Indiana Univ. Press, 1987), 48. Jo-Ann Pilardi, *Simone de Beauvoir* (Westport, Conn.: Praeger, 1999), 57.
53. Wilson, *Scriptural View,* 280.
54. Palmer, *Way of Holiness,* 85, 33. Françoise Lionnet, *Autobiographical Voices* (Ithaca: Cornell Univ. Press, 1989), 5. Marjorie Procter-Smith, "'In the Line of the Female': Shakerism and Feminism," in *Women's Leadership in Marginal Religions,* ed. Catherine Wessinger (Urbana: Univ. of Illinois Press, 1993), 25.
55. Jelinek, *Tradition,* 107. Sidonie Smith, "Resisting the Gaze of Embodiment: Women's Autobiography in the Nineteenth Century," in *American Women's Autobiography,* ed. Margo Culley (Madison: Univ. of Wisconsin Press, 1992), 86. Jelinek, *Tradition,* 90, 94. For an example of a Wesleyan/Holiness woman's emphasis on her public career, see Alma White, *The Story of My Life and the Pillar of Fire* (Zarephath, N.J.: Pillar of Fire, 1935–43), 2:237, 4:208, 5:125–28, 146, 277, 284–85.
56. Elaine Showalter, *A Literature of Their Own* (Princeton: Princeton Univ. Press, 1977), 13; quoted in Nancy K. Miller, "Writing Fictions: Women's Autobiography in France," in *Life/lines,* ed. Bella Brodzki and Celeste Schenck (Ithaca: Cornell Univ. Press, 1988), 50.
57. William C. Spengemann, *The Forms of Autobiography Episodes in the History of a Literary Genre* (New Haven: Yale Univ. Press, 1980), xvi. James Olney, "Autobiography and the Cultural Moment: A Thematic, Historical, and Bibliographical Introduction," in *Autobiography,* ed. James Olney (Princeton: Princeton Univ. Press, 1980), 7. Estelle C. Jelinek, *Women's Autobiography* (Bloomington, Ind.: Indiana Univ. Press, 1980); and *The Female Autograph,* ed. Domna C. Stanton (Chicago: Univ. of Chicago Press, 1984). Laurie A. Finke, *Feminist Theory, Women's Writing* (Ithaca: Cornell Univ. Press, 1992), xii; quoted in Paul John Eakin, *American Autobiography* (Madison: Univ. of Wisconsin Press, 1991), 5.
58. Sidonie Smith, *Poetics,* 46. Lionnet, *Autobiographical Voices,* xi. Janel M. Mueller, "Autobiography of a New 'Creatur': Female Spirituality, Selfhood, and Authorship in 'The Book of Margery Kempe,'" in *The Female Autograph,* ed. Domna C. Stanton (Chicago: Univ. of Chicago Press, 1984), 69.
59. Liz Stanley, *Auto/biographical I,* 242–43. Nancy K. Miller, "Writing Fictions," 60. Bella Brodzki and Celeste Schenck, introduction to *Life/lines,* ed. Bella Brodzki and Celeste Schenck (Ithaca: Cornell Univ. Press, 1988), 1.
60. Grammer, "Pen in His Hand," 27–28.
61. Liz Stanley, *Auto/biographical I,* 246. Jelinek, *Tradition,* xi. Albert E. Stone, *Autobiographical Occasions and Original Acts* (Philadelphia: Univ. of Pennsylvania Press, 1982), 19.
62. Nussbaum, *Autobiographical Subject,* xii. Jill K. Conway, *When Memory Speaks* (New York: Alfred A. Knopf, 1998), 6. Sidonie Smith, *Poetics,* 10.

63. For one example, see Sheila M. Rothman, *Woman's Proper Place* (New York: Basic Books, 1978).
64. Sidonie Smith, "Resisting the Gaze," 85.
65. Linda Anderson, *Women and Autobiography in the Twentieth Century* (London: Prentice Hall, 1997), 4. Personal Narratives Group, "Truths," 264.
66. Nussbaum, *Autobiographical Subject,* xiv. Sayre, "Proper Study," 22.
67. Alistair Thomson, "Writing about Learning: Using Mass-Observation Educational Life-Histories to Explore Learning through Life," in *The Uses of Autobiography,* ed. Julia Swindells (London: Taylor & Francis, 1995), 163. Adrienne Rich, *Of Women Born* (London: Virago, 1874), n.p.; quoted in Anderson, *Women and Autobiography in the Twentieth Century,* 128.
68. Personal Narratives Group, "Conditions not of Her Own Making," 23. Nancy A. Hardesty, Lucille Sider Dayton, and Donald W. Dayton, "Women in the Holiness Movement: Feminism in the Evangelical Tradition," in *Women of Spirit,* ed. Rosemary Ruether and Eleanor McLaughlin (New York: Simon and Schuster, 1979). This chapter provides an excellent overview of the Wesleyan/Holiness movement and its affirmation of women preachers. The authors also outline six factors that account for the feminist thrust of the Wesleyan/Holiness movement. Randy Maddox, "Wesleyan Theology and the Christian Feminist Critique," *Wesleyan Theological Journal* 22, no. 1 (spring 1987): 107. The web site address for Wesleyan/Holiness Women Clergy, Intl., is www.messiah.edu/whwc.
69. Swindells, *Uses of Autobiography,* 10.
70 Kathryn K. Sklar, "Four Levels of Women's History," in *New Research on Women at the University of Michigan,* ed. Dorothy G. McGuigan (Ann Arbor: Univ. of Michigan, 1974), 8.

Chapter 2

1. Eleanor McLaughlin, "Women, Power, and the Pursuit of Holiness in Medieval Christianity," in *Women of Spirit,* ed. Rosemary Ruether and Eleanor McLaughlin (New York: Simon and Schuster, 1979), 102, 123.
2. Patricia A. Ward, "Madame Guyon in America: An Annotated Bibliography," *Bulletin of Bibliography* 52, no. 2 (June 1995): 107.
3. J. Agar Beet, *Holiness Symbolical and Real* (London: Robert Culley, 1910), 167–68; quoted in Melvin E. Dieter, *The Holiness Revival of the Nineteenth Century,* 2d ed. (Lanham, Md.: Scarecrow Press, 1996), 73. Darius Salter, *Spirit and Intellect* (Metuchen, N.J.: Scarecrow Press, 1986), 141.
4. John Wesley, *The Works of John Wesley,* CD-ROM (Franklin, Tenn.: Providence House Publishers, 1995), 3:409, 14:277, 278.
5. Patricia A. Ward, "Madame Guyon and Experiential Theology in America," *Church History* 67, no. 3 (Sept. 1998), 486. Salter, *Spirit and Intellect,* 12. Wheatley, *Life and Letters,* 560.
6. George [Scott] R. [Railton], *Salvation in the Convent under Madame Jeanne de la Mothe Guyon* (New York: Salvation Army, 1885), 32. B. T. Roberts, *Ordaining Women,* 41, 85.

7. Clara McLeister, "Madam Guyon," in *Men and Women of Deep Piety* (Atlanta: Repairer Publishing, 1920), 209, 213. J. O. McClurkan, "Madame Guyon," in *Chosen Vessels* (Nashville: Pentecostal Mission Publishing Co., 1901), 46, 50. Jennie Fowler Willing, "Madame Guyon the Mystic," *Guide to Holiness,* n.s. 71 (Dec. 1899): 188–89, 192, and n.s. 72 (Jan. 1900): 20, 21, 26. The first article in the series is unavailable. Ward, "Madame Guyon in America," 111, 108. Dieter, *Holiness Revival,* 48.
8. Hannah Whitall Smith, *My Spiritual Autobiography,* 232, 188. Lela G. McConnell, *Hitherto and Henceforth in the Kentucky Mountains; A Quarter of a Century of Adventures in Faith—The Year of Jubilee* (Lawson, Ky.: n.p., 1949), 172. Osborn, *Heavenly Pearls,* 248; and Shellhamer, *Trials and Triumphs,* 81. Cooke, *Handmaiden,* 49, 53, 65, 158, 197, 284, 45.
9. Lizzie E. Miller, *The True Way* (Los Angeles: By the author, 1895), 65. Osborn, *Heavenly Pearls,* 42, 92.
10. Patricia A. Ward, "Madame Guyon and the Democratization of Spirituality," *Papers of French Seventeenth Century Literature* 23, no. 45 (1996): 501–8. Jean Guyon, *The Autobiography of Madame Jean Guyon* (Philadelphia: National Publishing Association for the Promotion of Holiness, 1886), 151, 207. While this version, copyrighted by E. Jones, is an unacknowledged abridgement, I am quoting from it since it was accessible to and was most likely used by Wesleyan/Holiness women.
11. Guyon, *Autobiography,* 29, 31.
12. Ibid., 30, 134, 331, 66, 84, 78, 84–85, 31, 62.
13. Ibid., 29, 34, 19, 280.
14. Ibid., 58, 60.
15. Ibid., 65, 281, 325.
16. Ibid., 335, 205 (see also 334), 193, 204, 289, 291.
17. *John Wesley's Works,* 9:277. Following this critique, Wesley praised Guyon for her "depth of religion . . . heights of righteousness, and peace, and joy in the Holy Ghost!" He continued: "How few such instances do we find, of exalted love to God and our neighbour; of genuine humility; of invincible meekness, and unbounded resignation!" (277).
18. Guyon, *Autobiography,* 83, 123, 332, 123 80, 83.
19. Ibid., 201, 266, 241, 85, 179, 240.
20. Ibid., 241.
21. Ibid., 2, 170, 73, 123 (death of self); see also 71.
22. Ibid., 166, 209–10.
23. Ibid., 166, 188, 172–73 (quoting Gal. 2:20), 256, 240 (see also 71), 211, 210 (see also 188), 168 (see also 210). Wheatley, *Life and Letters,* 518. Osborn, *Heavenly Pearls,* 173. Jennie Smith, *Valley of Baca* (Cincinnati: Press of Jennings and Pye, 1876), 192; see also 237.
24. Guyon, *Autobiography,* 174. She also wrote, "I passed whole days without being able to pronounce one word, for the Lord was pleased to make me pass wholly into him by an entire internal transformation" (249). *Autobiography,* 175, 125.
25. Ibid., 175, 211.

26. Ibid., 175.
27. Elaw, *Memoirs,* 61. Guyon, *Autobiography,* 105, 140.
28. Guyon, *Autobiography,* 68.
29. Ibid., 69. She also spoke of the love of God in her heart (54, 65, 72).
30. Ibid., 23, 174, 233.
31. Ibid., 275, 340, 170.
32. Ibid., 146, 147.
33. Ibid., 178.
34. Ibid., 19, 121, 185.
35. Ibid., 188, 117.
36. Ibid., 248, 231, 248, 313.
37. Ibid., 171, 176, 179–80.
38. Ibid., 113, 124.
39. Ibid., 297, 263.
40. Ibid., 286, 205, 300, 312.
41. Ibid., 185, 273; see also 266.
42. Ibid., 273, 291, 258, 317.
43. Ibid., 249, 291, 331, 288.
44. Ibid., 278.
45. Ibid., 284, 283.
46. Ibid., 339. Guyon had begun her autobiography in 1682 (Marie-Florine Bruneau, *Women Mystics Confront the Modern World* [Albany: State Univ. of New York Press, 1998], 201). Guyon, *Autobiography,* 339.
47. Guyon, *Autobiography,* 326, 341; see also 336.
48. Ibid., 205, 272, 297.
49. Ibid., 256, 227, 323, 228.
50. Ibid., 293, 328.
51. Ibid., 336, 337.
52. Ibid., 341.
53. Ibid., 346, 340, 39, 319, 1.
54. Ibid., 140, 209.
55. Railton, *Salvation,* 28. Ward, "Madame Guyon and Experiential Theology," 484. Guyon, *Autobiography,* 343, 345. Railton, *Salvation,* 30.

Chapter 3

1. Lizzie E. Miller, *True Way,* 65.
2. Earl Kent Brown, *Women of Mr. Wesley's Methodism* (New York: Edwin Mellen Press, 1983), 109, 237. Some women engaged in both activities.
3. Jennie Smith, *Valley of Baca,* 151 (Rogers); Anna W. Prosser, *From Death To Life* (Buffalo: McGerald Publishing, 1901), 68 (Rogers); and Osborn, *Heavenly Pearls,* 49 (Fletcher). Cole, *Trials and Triumphs,* 68; Almira Losee, *Life Sketches* (New York: By the author, 1880), 47; and Cooke, *Handmaiden,* 37, 108, 45. Lizzie E. Miller, *True Way,* 17–18. Elaw, *Memoirs,* 144.

4. Jennie Fowler Willing, "Pentecostal Womanhood: Mary Fletcher," *Guide to Holiness* (Sept. 1900): 84. The series of articles on Fletcher extended from September through December 1900.
5. Phoebe Palmer, *Four Years in the Old World; Comprising the Travels, Incidents, and Evangelistic Labors of Dr. and Mrs. Palmer in England, Ireland, Scotland, and Wales* (New York: Foster & Palmer, Jr., 1867), 444. Raser, *Phoebe Palmer,* 248–49.
6. Nussbaum, *Autobiographical Subject,* 82. Palmer, *Promise of the Father,* 11. Palmer cited Fletcher's list of women in the Bible who spoke publicly. Later, in the same book, Palmer quoted information on Fletcher's life and affirmations of her ministry (*Promise,* 101–10). Jarena Lee, *Religious Experience,* 38. Cooke, *Handmaiden,* 176; she also listed Miss Barrett and Ann Cutler.
7. Heilbrun, *Writing,* 39. In another publication, she claimed Victorian women only had male models of autobiography available to them (Carolyn G. Heilbrun, "Non-Autobiographies of 'Privileged' Women: England and America," in *Life/lines,* ed. Bella Brodzki and Celeste Schenck [Ithaca: Cornell Univ. Press, 1988], 65).
8. Paul Chilcote reported: "Many of these early manuscript accounts are extant, and many more published in the pages of Wesley's *Arminian Magazine,* or reprinted from the magazine in collections such as Thomas Jackson's *Lives of the Early Methodist Preachers* (Paul Wesley Chilcote, *John Wesley and the Women Preachers of Early Methodism,* ATLA Monograph Series, No. 2 [Metuchen, N.J.: American Theological Library Association and Scarecrow Press, 1991], 3). See also Paul Wesley Chilcote, *Her Own Story* (Nashville: Kingswood Books, 2001).
9. Rebecca Larson, *Quaker Women* (Chapel Hill: Univ. of North Carolina Press, 1999), 63.
10. John Wesley, *The Letters of the Rev. John Wesley, A.M.,* 8 vols., ed. John Telford (London: Epworth Press, 1931), 4:133, 5:130. Chilcote, *John Wesley,* 142.
11. Joyce Quiring Erickson, "'Perfect Love': Achieving Sanctification as a Pattern of Desire in the Life Writings of Early Methodist Women," *Prose Studies* 20, no. 2 (Aug. 1997), 76. Quiring Erickson analyzes the journals of three women: Fletcher, Rogers, and Elizabeth Mortimer.
12. Brown, *Women,* 115. Fletcher, *Life,* 411. This was in reference to the deteriorating relationship between the priest of the Church of England and the Methodists in Madeley.
13. Fletcher, *Life,* 72, 26, 27–29. Hester Ann Rogers, *Life and Journal of Mrs. Hester Ann Rogers,* condensed and combined by Rev. E. Davies (Reading, Mass.: Holiness Book Concern, 1882), 106, 162. Fletcher, *Life,* 26–28. Rogers, *Life,* 45, 159. I chose this edition of Rogers's *Life* because it was printed by a Wesleyan/Holiness publisher, making it more likely that this was the edition women read. In the following citations from this source, I have indicated when the editor authored the information quoted.

14. Rogers, *Life,* 40, 42, 113, 48, 50, 124.
15. Ibid., 45, 80, 95, 153, 47, 93, 42.
16. Fletcher, *Life,* 29, 113, 283, 19, 340; see also 108, 323, and 415. The verse she quoted is Isaiah 1:25. Rogers, *Life,* 44. Both Rogers's and Fletcher's positions are consistent with Wesley, who promoted both views.
17. Rogers, *Life,* 159, 160; see also 44.
18. Fletcher, *Life,* 30, 75, 244, 155. Rogers, *Life,* 114, 50.
19. Fletcher, *Life,* 260, 354.
20. Ibid., 74. Rogers, *Life,* 50, 97, 157.
21. Fletcher, *Life,* 300. Guyon, *Autobiography,* 175. Fletcher, *Life,* 37, 159.
22. Brown, *Women,* 53.
23. Fletcher, *Life,* 38, 52, 18, 34, 42, 50, 42, 132, 41, 132, 75, 349.
24. Ibid., 16, 26, 37, 38, 95. Chilcote, *John Wesley,* 150. Chilcote listed Fletcher's sermons, texts, and where they were preached (318–19). He contended that she was "without any question one of the most prominent figures in Wesley's Methodism" (Paul Wesley Chilcote, "An Early Methodist Community of Women," *Methodist History* 38:4 [July 2000]: 219). Fletcher, *Life,* 95, 226, 276, 306.
25. Fletcher, *Life,* 105, 115–16. Chilcote identified this as "the most well-known description of the preaching of a woman in the Wesleyan revival" (*John Wesley,* 166). Fletcher, *Life,* 117, 119.
26. Fletcher, *Life,* 119. She engaged in 220 public meetings in 1777 alone (Chilcote, *John Wesley,* 169).
27. Nussbaum, *Autobiographical Subject,* 173. Unfortunately, Nussbaum did not list which autobiographies she consulted. See also Fletcher, *Life,* 116, 158, 233, 293, 301, 303, 76.
28. Fletcher, *Life,* 140, 30. She considered Fletcher as husband material on subsequent occasions (*Life,* 87, 91, 98). Fletcher, *Life,* 143–44. Brown quotes this (*Women,* 144). Fletcher, *Life,* 235.
29. Fletcher, *Life,* 407.
30. Rogers, *Life,* 83.
31. Ibid., 177, 24 (editorial comment), 29.
32. Ibid., 55–56, 121.
33. Ibid., 119 (editorial comment). Brown, *Women,* 50. Rogers, *Life,* 136–37 (editorial comment).
34. Cooke, *Handmaiden,* 108.

Chapter 4

1. Lela G. McConnell, *Rewarding Faith Plus Works* (n.p., 1962), 137. Emma Ray also recounted a chalk-talk using three hearts that introduced her to the doctrine of sanctification. Using a blackboard, the preachers depicted "the natural heart, the justified heart, and also the sanctified heart, illustrating by drawing three hearts and showing the fruit of each one" (Ray, *Twice Sold,* 60).
2. Maddox, *Responsible Grace,* 92; see also 120–21. Davidson, "Workings," 232.

3. Miller, *True Way,* 9. Osborn, *Heavenly Pearls,* 25.
4. Hannah Whitall Smith, *My Spiritual Autobiography,* 173 (see also 150), 84. Wheaton, *Prisons and Prayer,* 24; and Shellhamer, *Trials and Triumphs,* 15. See also Lela G. McConnell, *The Pauline Ministry in the Kentucky Mountains or A Brief Account of the Kentucky Mountain Holiness Association* (Louisville, Ky.: Pentecostal Publishing, [1942]), 12.
5. Miller, *True Way,* 10. Van Cott, *Harvest and Reaper,* 54. Fitkin, *Grace,* 7.
6. Cole, *Trials and Triumphs,* 38. Sarah Smith, *Life Sketches of Mother Sarah Smith* (Anderson, Ind.: Gospel Trumpet, 1902; reprint, Guthrie, Okla.: Faith Publishing House, n.d.), 4; and Cooke, *Handmaiden,* 18.
7. Mills, *Quiet,* 192; see also Kathryn Teresa Long, *The Revival of 1857–58* (New York: Oxford Univ. Press, 1998). Hannah Whitall Smith, *My Spiritual Autobiography,* 172–73.
8. Whittemore, *Mother Whittemore's Records,* 23.
9. Martha Lee, *Mother Lee's Experience,* 28. Mills, *Quiet,* 192. Ray, *Twice Sold,* 43.
10. Amanda Smith, *Autobiography,* 47. Losee, *Life Sketches,* 32. White, *Story,* 1:117, 144–45. Palmer, *Way of Holiness,* 50, 52.
11. Hannah Whitall Smith, *My Spiritual Autobiography,* 162, 180. Martha Lee, *Mother Lee's Experience,* 28; and Elaw, *Memoirs,* 56. Amanda Smith, *Autobiography,* 49. Fitkin, *Grace,* 7. Losee, *Life Sketches,* 52.
12. Florence Roberts, *Fifteen Years,* 16–18. White, *Story,* 1:151, 156, 157.
13. Cooke, *Handmaiden,* 18. Losee, *Life Sketches,* 32. Cole, *Trials and Triumphs,* 38.
14. Jarena Lee, *Religious Experience,* 5, 8. Cagle, *Life and Work,* 16. Lela McConnell, *Pauline*, 12. Hannah Whitall Smith, *My Spiritual Autobiography,* 173.
15. William Andrews was aware that these women viewed sanctification as a "second blessing," yet he mistakenly referred to sanctification as the "new birth." This has probably inadvertently caused confusion since "new birth" is a synonym for conversion (introduction to *Sisters of the Spirit,* 15). Elizabeth Elkin Grammer also erred by equating sanctification and conversion when she discussed Phoebe Palmer's description of sanctification and her altar theology ("Pen in His Hand," 113). Rosetta Renae Haynes also mistakenly equated the two experiences ("Radical Spiritual Motherhood," 50). Losee, *Life Sketches,* 75. White, *Story,* 5:354–55. Florence Roberts, *Fifteen Years,* 50. Fitkin, *Grace,* 34–35.
16. Hannah Whitall Smith, *My Spiritual Autobiography,* 261.
17. McConnell, *Hitherto,* 158. Ray, *Twice Sold,* 61.
18. Mills, *Quiet,* 202. Cooke, *Handmaiden,* 259; and Cole, *Trials and Triumphs,* 68. Jennie Smith, *Valley of Baca,* 151.
19. Palmer, *Way of Holiness,* 15, 22.
20. Losee, *Life Sketches,* 62–63.
21. Mills, *Grace,* 13. Palmer, *Way of Holiness,* 24. She advised others of the active role they must play in achieving sanctification; see 133, 139, 142.

Wesley, *Plain Account,* 10, 11, 13; and Rogers, *Life,* 82. Palmer, *Way of Holiness,* 43–45, 46.

22. David Bundy, "Visions of Sanctification: Themes of Orthodoxy in the Methodist, Holiness, and Pentecostal Traditions," unpublished paper, 15; quoted in Diane Cunningham Leclerc, "Original Sin and Sexual Difference: A Feminist Historical Theology of a Patristic, Wesleyan, and Holiness Doctrine" (Ph.D. diss., Drew Univ., 1998), 15. Rogers, *Life,* 95. Raser summarized other comparisons between the theology of Rogers and Palmer (*Phoebe Palmer,* 245–49).
23. Cooke, *Handmaiden,* 40, 259; and Dudley, *Beulah,* 62. Lela G. McConnell, *Faith Victorious in the Kentucky Mountains: The Story of Twenty-Two Years of Spirit-Filled Ministry* (Berne, Ind.: Economy Printing Concern, 1946), 20. She quoted John Wesley, "Faith automatically works when all is on the altar," but a search of his writings has failed to locate this sentence.
24. Adams, *Autobiography,* 67.
25. Jennie Smith, *Valley of Baca,* 156; Cole, *Trials and Triumphs,* 41. Mills, *Quiet,* 203. Osborn made a similar statement (*Heavenly Pearls,* 35). McConnell, *Rewarding,* 171. Sarah Smith also spoke of "my life, friends, and children" (*Life Sketches,* 8). Cooke, *Handmaiden,* 39. See also Mattie E. Perry, *Christ and Answered Prayer; Autobiography of Mattie E. Perry* (Cincinnati: By the Author, 1939), 35.
26. Palmer, *Way of Holiness,* 47, 143. McConnell, *Hitherto,* 172.
27. Palmer, *Way of Holiness,* 28, 46. Jane Dunning, *Brands from the Burning* (Chicago: Baker & Arnold, 1881), 22; and Prosser, *Death To Life,* 97. Foote, *Brand,* 234.
28. Losee, *Life Sketches,* 73–74. McConnell, *Pauline,* 18. Mills, *Quiet,* 202, 207, 203. See also Mills, where she speaks of being filled with the Holy Ghost (*Grace,* 17).
29. Palmer, *Way of Holiness,* 34, 77. John Wesley's colleague Rev. John Fletcher also stressed the necessity of testimony. Cole, *Trials and Triumphs,* 42. McConnell, *Hitherto,* 173. Cooke, *Handmaiden,* 258.
30. Miller, *True Way,* 21. Losee, *Life Sketches,* 58–59, 63, 74.
31. Fitkin, *Grace,* 34, 36. Shellhamer, *Trials and Triumphs,* 20–21. McConnell, *Pauline,* 18.
32. Palmer, *Way of Holiness,* 30–31. Sarah Smith, *Life Sketches,* 9. Jarena Lee, *Religious Experience,* 10.
33. Palmer, *Way of Holiness,* 28. Jennie Smith, *Valley of Baca,* 156. Osborn, *Heavenly Pearls,* 35. Mills, *Quiet,* 209. Fitkin, *Grace,* 36. White, *Story,* 2:206. Prosser, *Death To Life,* 97.
34. Hannah Whitall Smith, *My Spiritual Autobiography,* 287, 288.
35. Osborn, *Heavenly Pearls,* 35. Ray, *Twice Sold,* 63.
36. Wesley, *Plain Account,* 61. Shellhamer, *Trials and Triumphs,* 24. McConnell, *Faith,* 33. Osborn, *Heavenly Pearls,* 36. Ray, *Twice Sold,* 62–63.
37. Palmer, *Way of Holiness,* 31.
38. Wheaton, *Prisons and Prayer,* 25–26.

39. Fitkin, *Grace,* 36. Teresa of Avila, *The Life of Teresa of Jesus,* trans. and ed. E. Allison Peers (New York: Image Books Doubleday, 1991), 274–75.
40. Perry, *Christ and Answered Prayer,* 221. See also Foote, who spoke of "instantaneous sanctification" (*Brand,* 231). Cagle, *Life and Work,* 21. For the most part, Cagle wrote in the third person. Celia Bradshaw Winkle sought sanctification for four days (Celia Bradshaw Winkle, *The Preacher Girl* [St. Petersburg, Fla.: By the author, 1967], 21), while McConnell's search lasted eight days (*Pauline,* 18). Shellhamer took three weeks (*Trials and Triumphs,* 21), while Jarena Lee's search lasted three months (*Religious Experience,* 9). Sarah Smith, *Life Sketches,* 8; and White, *Story,* 1:410. Even though the search may have been extensive, once the conditions of consecration and faith were met, the experience itself was instantaneous.
41. Martha Lee, *Mother Lee's Experience,* 31. McConnell, *Hitherto,* 167; and McConnell, *Pauline,* 172. Palmer, *Way of Holiness,* 82.
42. White, *Story,* 1:412. Dunning, *Brands,* 52.
43. Mills, *Grace,* 145. Elaine Pagels documented the shift in the Christian view of human nature in *Adam, Eve, and the Serpent* (New York: Random House, 1988).
44. Cole, *Trials and Triumphs,* 42. Palmer, *Way of Holiness,* 43.
45. White was the exception in that she used Augustine's phrase "original sin" (*Story,* 2:113, 5:355). Some contemporary Wesleyan/Holiness adherents, including this author, find it hard to reconcile Augustine's doctrine of original sin or inbred sin with the current psychological understanding of the self and its construction. We reject Augustine's understanding of the doctrine of original sin and, instead, affirm the doctrine of deprivity. *Deprivity* refers to the relationship with God that we are deprived of as a result of sin. Leon Hynson, who holds this position, has addressed what happens to the self at sanctification: "Unlike much pathetic theology which speaks of the death of self, we accent not its death but its life. The crucifixion about which St. Paul speaks is the passing away of the autonomous 'I' which is succeeded by the renewed or living 'I.' 'I am crucified. I live.' (Galatians 2:20). The essential 'I' has never died; it has been deprived of its wholeness or fulness. The privation concept teaches that what I need is a renewed and completed essential self. This deprived self is made whole in the renewing of the Holy Spirit; when the righteousness of God, lost in the fall, is restored. Then my relationships are controlled by the 'anchored I' rather than by the autonomous 'I.' The incompleteness of the autonomous self is now swallowed in spiritual fulness." (Leon Hynson, "Original Sin as Privation: An Inquiry into a Theology of Sin and Sanctification," *Wesleyan Theological Journal* 22, no. 2 [fall 1987]: 76). The death of self as understood by sanctified women will be discussed below.
46. Mills, *Quiet,* 209; Losee, *Life Sketches,* 58; and Perry, *Christ and Answered Prayer,* 36. Miller, *True Way,* 22; and Jennie Smith, *Valley of Baca,* 157.
47. White, *Story,* 3:382. McConnell, *Faith,* 31. Foote, *Brand,* 218. Amanda Smith, *Autobiography,* 226, 423.
48. Shellhamer, *Trials and Triumphs,* 21.

49. Leclerc, "Original Sin," 202, 182. Palmer, *Way of Holiness,* 26, 82. Cooke, *Handmaiden,* 38. Shellhamer, *Trials and Triumphs,* 23–24.
50. Cooke, *Handmaiden,* 39. Prosser, *Death To Life,* 198. Foote, *Brand,* 230. Prosser, *Death To Life,* 199–200.
51. Dudley, *Beulah,* 58–59. Mills, *Quiet,* 222.
52. Osborn, *Heavenly Pearls,* 50–51. Perry, *Christ and Answered Prayer,* 78.
53. Losee, *Life Sketches,* 33. Van Cott, *Harvest and Reaper,* 133. Wheaton, *Prisons and Prayer,* 542–43. White, *Story,* 3:40, 1:110. Amanda Smith, *Autobiography,* 113. Rogers, *Life,* 22; and Fletcher, *Life,* 21–22.
54. Dudley, *Beulah,* 55. Cagle, *Life and Work,* 20.
55. Sarah Smith, *Life Sketches,* 28. Foote, *Brand,* 178. Shellhamer, *Trials and Triumphs,* 175. Dunning, *Brands,* 16. Florence Roberts also advised her readers to refrain from playing cards (*Fifteen Years,* 350). Losee, *Life Sketches,* 24; and Miller, *True Way,* 101. Florence Roberts, *Fifteen Years,* 434.
56. White, *Story,* 3:14.
57. Mary A. Glaser, *Wonderful Leadings* (Allentown, Pa.: Haines & Worman, Printers, 1893), 10. Osborn, *Heavenly Pearls,* 48.
58. Rogers, *Life,* 85. Palmer, *Way of Holiness,* 23. McConnell, *Hitherto,* 160–61. Mills, *Quiet,* 252; and Perry, *Christ and Answered Prayer,* 83–84.
59. McConnell, *Hitherto,* 167. McConnell, *Pauline,* 193–94. Prosser, *Death To Life,* 181, 182. She also referred to Gal. 2:20, where she equated "I" with the carnal nature (*Death To Life,* 186). *Death To Life,* 188, 181, 184–85, 187.
60. Wesley, *Plain Account,* 26. Foote, *Brand,* 187; McConnell, *Faith,* 32–33; Perry, *Christ and Answered Prayer,* 114–15; and Palmer, *Way of Holiness,* 23. Amanda Smith, *Autobiography,* 76, 103. Wheaton, *Prisons and Prayer,* 377; and Van Cott, *Harvest and Reaper,* 67. Glaser, *Wonderful,* 63; and Jennie Smith, *Valley of Baca,* 107.
61. Cooke, *Handmaiden,* 260. Glaser, *Wonderful,* 87. Miller, *True Way,* 22. Dudley, *Beulah,* 62. Osborn, *Heavenly Pearls,* 92.
62. Mills, *Grace,* 13. The verse quoted is Matt. 5:48. Mills, *Quiet,* 203. Mills, *Grace,* 13. Losee, *Life Sketches,* 58. Hannah Whitall Smith, *My Spiritual Autobiography,* 258–59.
63. Wesley, *Plain Account,* 24–25, 27, 36, 35, 36, 52–53, 54, 57, 82, 84.
64. Palmer, *Way of Holiness,* 88, 26.
65. Palmer, *Way of Holiness,* 40, 67, 89; see also 80, 110.
66. Mills, *Quiet,* 202. Hannah Whitall Smith, *My Spiritual Autobiography,* 267, 290.
67. Cooke, *Handmaiden,* 270, 316, 374–75. Ray, *Twice Sold,* 64, 102, 168.
68. Amanda Smith, *Autobiography,* 119–20. Osborn, *Heavenly Pearls,* 44. Ray, *Twice Sold,* 65, 96. McConnell, *Hitherto,* 174.
69. McConnell, *Pauline,* 184; Osborn, *Heavenly Pearls,* 29; Elaw, *Memoirs,* 114; Dunning, *Brands,* 52; and Mills, *Quiet,* 202. McConnell, *Pauline,* 184. Wesley, *Plain Account,* 37, 55, 81, 84, 50. McConnell, *Faith,* 148. Ray, *Twice Sold,* 305.
70. McConnell, *Hitherto,* 158. McConnell, *Faith,* 188. McConnell, *Hitherto,* 155. Foote, *Brand,* 232.

71. Palmer, *Promise of the Father,* 206. Palmer, *Four Years,* 33. *Guide to Holiness* 64 (1873): 24, quoted in White, *Beauty of Holiness,* 286. White, *Story,* 5:196. A. Gregory Schneider, "Objective Selves Versus Empowered Selves: The Conflict over Holiness in the Post–Civil War Methodist Episcopal Church," *Methodist History* 32, no. 4 (July 1994): 241, 247.
72. Mills, *Quiet,* 204. For more information on the relationship between sanctification and power, see Susie C. Stanley, "Empowered Foremothers: Wesleyan/Holiness Women Speak to Today's Christian Feminists," *Wesleyan Theological Journal* 24 (1989): 103–16; and Susie C. Stanley, "What Sanctification," 17–24. Losee, *Life Sketches,* 60, 74. Osborn, *Heavenly Pearls,* 42; see also 54. Prosser, *Death To Life,* 84, 106. Adams, *Autobiography,* 5.
73. Mills, *Quiet,* 222.
74. Donald W. Dayton traced Pentecostalism's reliance on Wesleyan/Holiness theology; see also Donald W. Dayton, *Theological Roots of Pentecostalism* (Peabody: Hendrickson Publishers, 1991). For example, see Mills, *Grace,* 63; and McConnell, *Hitherto,* 92. Palmer, *Way of Holiness,* 77. Cooke, *Handmaiden,* 115; see also 257. Mills, *Grace,* 208. Amanda Smith, *Autobiography,* 187.
75. McConnell, *Pauline,* 93. McConnell, *Faith,* 68. Palmer, *Way of Holiness,* 33; Miller, *True Way,* 42, 160; Amanda Smith, *Autobiography,* 340; Glaser, *Wonderful,* 43, 113; Jennie Smith, *Incidents and Experiences of a Railroad Evangelist* (Washington, D.C.: By the author, 1920), 160. McConnell, *Pauline,* 20. Jarena Lee, *Religious Experience,* 17. Emma Irick, *The King's Daughter* (Kansas City, Mo.: Pedestal Press, 1973), 19. McConnell, *Pauline,* 20.
76. Miller, *True Way,* 137, 126. Cagle, *Life and Work,* 59. McConnell, *Pauline,* 106, 93.
77. Palmer, *Way of Holiness,* 88. White, *Story,* 1:354. Shellhamer, *Trials and Triumphs,* 41.
78. Sarah Smith, *Life Sketches,* 9, 11, 26, 9.
79. Foote, *Brand,* 187. Amanda Smith, *Autobiography,* 111.
80. Losee, *Life Sketches,* 122, 80. Osborn, *Heavenly Pearls,* 44. Prosser, *Death To Life,* 48, 178; McConnell, *Hitherto,* 92; and McConnell, *Rewarding,* 11.
81. Amanda Smith, *Autobiography,* 80.
82. Glaser, *Wonderful,* 104. While Palmer is sometimes portrayed as being more ambivalent in her assertions of women's right to preach, she did insist, "Where church order is at variance with divine order, it were better to obey God than man" (*Promise of the Father,* vi). Cole, *Trials and Triumphs,* 191.
83. Galea, "Anchored Behind the Veil," 245, 242, 236.
84. Donald Mathews, "Evangelical America—The Methodist Ideology," in *Perspectives on American Methodism,* ed. Russell E. Richey, Kenneth E. Rowe, and Jean Miller Schmidt (Nashville: Kingswood-Abingdon, 1993), 30; quoted in Grammer, "Pen in His Hand," 287.

85. Haynes, "Radical Spiritual Motherhood," 133 (see also 49, 98), 49. She borrowed the term *radical egalitarianism* from William Andrews (introduction to *Sisters of the Spirit,* 20). Andrews also stressed the relationship between empowerment and sanctification for the African American women whose autobiographies he reprinted (Jarena Lee, Zilpha Elaw, and Julia Foote) in *Sisters of the Spirit* (14). Grammer, "Pen in His Hand," 132. Grammer considered Jarena Lee, Zilpha Elaw, Amanda Smith, and Julia Foote.
86. Katherine Clay Bassard, *Spiritual Interrogations* (Princeton: Princeton Univ. Press, 1999), 3–4. McKay, "Nineteenth-Century," 142.
87. Margaret Bendroth, review of "Anna Tilden: Unitarian Culture and the Problem of Self-Representation," in *Church History* 68, no. 1 (Mar. 1999): 218. Patricia Meyer Spacks, "Selves in Hiding," in *Women's Autobiography,* ed. Estelle C. Jelinek (Bloomington: Indiana Univ. Press, 1980), 131.
88. Schneider, "Objective Selves," 249. Brekus, *Female Preaching,* 181.
89. Jarena Lee, *Religious Experience,* 11.

Chapter 5

1. Liz Stanley, *Auto/biographical I,* 112; see also 113–14; and William L. Andrews, *To Tell a Free Story* (Urbana: Univ. of Illinois Press, 1986), 14.
2. Adams, *Autobiography,* 66–67, 5; see also Cooke, *Handmaiden,* 22.
3. Cooke, *Handmaiden,* 176. Shellhamer, *Trials and Triumphs,* 73.
4. Elaw, *Memoirs,* 67.
5. Cagle, *Life and Work,* 21. White, *Story,* 1:161.
6. For instance, see Cole, *Trials and Triumphs,* 51; and Jarena Lee, *Religious Experience,* 10. Cooke, *Handmaiden,* 34. Shellhamer, *Trials and Triumphs,* 14. Jennie Smith, *Baca to Beulah,* 63.
7. Elaw, *Memoirs,* 82, 77. Foote, *Brand,* 200.
8. Winkle, *Preacher Girl,* 23. Jarena Lee, *Religious Experience,* 10–11; and Jennie Smith, *Baca to Beulah,* 62. Osborn, *Heavenly Pearls,* 108. Lizzie E. Miller, *True Way,* 19–20.
9. Fitkin, *Grace,* 10–11.
10. Ray, *Twice Sold,* 145–46.
11. Glaser, *Wonderful,* 51, 54–55, 48, 117. Glaser believed that "sin always lies at the root of sickness" (*Wonderful,* 70). White believed that physical problems sometimes were a message from God trying to show her something (*Story,* 3:66).
12. Cagle, *Life and Work,* 24. White, *Story,* 1:403.
13. Adams, *Autobiography,* 99. Van Cott, *Harvest and Reaper,* 168, 171.
14. Cole, *Trials and Triumphs,* 51.
15. Ibid.
16. Cagle, *Life and Work,* 24, 21. Adams, *Autobiography,* 73.
17. Foote, *Brand,* 201. Lizzie E. Miller, *True Way,* 23–24; and Osborn, *Heavenly Pearls,* 108.

18. Elaw, *Memoirs,* 75. McConnell, *Faith,* 22. McConnell, *Pauline,* 37. Jarena Lee, *Religious Experience,* 11, 24.
19. Hannah Whitall Smith, *My Spiritual Autobiography,* 69. Irick, *King's Daughter,* 20. Cagle, *Life and Work,* 24; and Glaser, *Wonderful,* 143.
20. Mills, *Quiet,* 239; and Cagle, *Life and Work,* 21. God called McConnell in her early youth (*Faith,* 22). Shellhamer was thirteen (*Trials and Triumphs,* 14); and White was sixteen (*Story,* 1:161). Cole, *Trials and Triumphs,* 50–52, 54. Sarah Smith, *Life Sketches,* 15–17.
21. The groups who did ordain small numbers of women at this time were the Free Will Baptists, the United Brethren in Christ, the Christian Church, Unitarians, Universalists, and Congregationists.
22. White, *Story,* 1:161, 164. Cagle, *Life and Work,* 21.
23. Irick, *King's Daughter,* 20; and Shellhamer, *Trials and Triumphs,* 14.
24. Cynthia Grant Tucker, *Prophetic Sisterhood* (Boston: Beacon Press, 1990), 59. Mary Sumner Boyd," Women Preachers," *Woman Citizen* (Dec. 1920): 796, 802.
25. Prosser, *Death To Life,* 69. Van Cott, *Harvest and Reaper,* 206. Mills, *Grace,* 38. Mills, *Quiet,* 240. Losee, *Life Sketches,* 210, 9–10. McConnell, *Pauline,* 30, 45, 66.
26. Shellhamer, *Trials and Triumphs,* 74–76, 77, 78.
27. Ibid., 168, 169, 170.
28. Irick, *King's Daughter,* 20, 28, 44. The Pentecostal Church of the Nazarene changed its name to the Church of the Nazarene in 1919 to avoid confusion with the Pentecostal movement. Nazarenes do not speak in tongues, which is a key doctrine distinguishing the Pentecostal movement. Fitkin, *Grace,* 31, 46.
29. Osborn, *Heavenly Pearls,* 213.
30. Van Cott, *Harvest and Reaper,* 185, 186–87.
31. Wheaton, *Prisons and Prayer,* 142, 381.
32. She was ordained in 1899 by the New Testament Church of Christ, the coalition of churches she organized. Robert Stanley Ingersol, "Burden of Dissent: Mary Lee Cagle and the Southern Holiness Movement" (Ph.D. diss., Duke Univ., 1989), 187. Cagle, *Life and Work,* n.p.
33. Van Cott, *Harvest and Reaper,* 206–7, 219, 220–21.
34. Shellhamer, *Trials and Triumphs,* 62.
35. Sally Kempton, "Cutting Loose: A Private View of the Women's Uprising," in *The American Sisterhood,* ed. Wendy Martin (New York: Harper & Row, 1972), 352; quoted in Stone, *Autobiographical Occasions,* 197. Osborn, *Heavenly Pearls,* 77.
36. Jennie Smith, *Ramblings in Beulah Land: A Continuation of Experiences in the Life of Jennie Smith. No. 2* (Philadelphia: Garrigues Brothers, 1888), 138, 70. Jennie Smith, *Ramblings in Beulah Land: A Continuation of Experiences in the Life of Jennie Smith* (Philadelphia: Garrigues Brothers, 1886), 14–15.
37. Elizabeth Cady Stanton, Susan B. Anthony, and Matilda J. Gage, eds., *History of Woman Suffrage* (Rochester, N.Y.: Charles Mann, 1881), 1:70, 72.

38. White, *Story,* 4:121, 2:70 (see also 5:83), 5:108.
39. Lizzie E. Miller, *True Way,* 24.
40. Ray, *Twice Sold,* 46.
41. Van Cott, *Harvest and Reaper,* 312–13, 150–56, 155, 160.
42. Cagle, *Life and Work,* 28–29.
43. Losee, *Life Sketches,* 176, 9.
44. Osborn, *Heavenly Pearls,* 67, 118, 65–66, 66–67, 69, 70.
45. For two examples of his criticism of her sermon content, see White, *Story,* 1:429 and 2:64–65, 2:65, 2:218.
46. Florence Roberts, *Fifteen Years,* 44–46.
47. Osborn, *Heavenly Pearls,* 74. Prosser, *Death To Life,* 57.
48. White, *Story,* 2:217, 2:319, 5:64, 5:67.
49. Glaser, *Wonderful,* 81, 93, 96, 102, 135, 151.
50. Ibid., 79, 97, 98, 105, 120–21, 139, 79, 104 (see also 155), 102, 123, 138.
51. White, *Story,* 2:12, 14, 48, 73–74, 79, 80, 115.
52. Ibid., 2:116–17, 132, 133.
53. Cole, *Trials and Triumphs,* 124–25.
54. Elaw, *Memoirs,* 123. Foote, *Brand,* 212. See Jarena Lee for another example of an opponent who changed his mind (*Religious Experience,* 55).
55. Jennie Smith, *Incidents and Experiences,* 54. Cooke, *Handmaiden,* 129.
56. Adams, *Autobiography,* 147.
57. Cagle, *Life and Work,* 79–80, 72, 84–85. Jarena Lee, *Religious Experience,* 23. Cole, *Trials and Triumphs,* 106.
58. Van Cott, *Harvest and Reaper,* 167, 168.
59. Adams, *Autobiography,* 133.
60. Ibid., 150–51.
61. Ibid., 3, 132; see also 146.
62. Jarena Lee, *Religious Experience,* 18. Joycelyn K. Moody, "On the Road with God: Travel and Quest in Early Nineteenth-Century African American Holy Women's Narratives," *Religion and Literature* 27, no. 1 (spring 1995): 44. Irick, *King's Daughter,* 48, 26. Van Cott, *Harvest and Reaper,* 158, 164.
63. Osborn, *Heavenly Pearls,* 299.
64. White, *Story,* 2:101 (see also 2:102–3), 255, 257.
65. Shellhamer, *Trials and Triumphs,* 71, 72, 104, 105, 114, 121.
66. Ibid., 137, 139, 140–41.
67. Ibid., 68, 114.
68. Ibid., 219–22.
69. Mary G. Mason, "Dorothy Day and Women's Spiritual Autobiography," in *American Women's Autobiography,* ed. Margo Culley (Madison: Univ. of Wisconsin Press, 1992), 194, 212.
70. Lizzie E. Miller, *True Way,* 154–55. The woman's name is correctly spelled Miriam.
71. Hannah Whitall Smith, *My Spiritual Autobiography,* 118. Van Cott, *Harvest and Reaper,* 15.
72. Cooke, *Handmaiden,* 177, 175, 176.

73. Cagle, *Life and Work,* 172–73, 174. Joseph E. Coleson's *'Ezer Cenegdo* (Grantham, Pa.: Wesleyan/Holiness Women Clergy, 1996) outlines a Wesleyan/Holiness interpretation of Gen. 1–3.
74. Elaw, *Memoirs,* 61, 84.
75. Cagle, *Life and Work,* 61. Cole, *Trials and Triumphs,* 85–86. White, *Story,* 4:406; 5:54; see also 5:86, 108, 110, 125–28 (a newspaper account of two services), and 146.
76. Glaser, *Wonderful,* 145. Amanda Smith, *Autobiography,* 281. Irick, *King's Daughter,* 20.
77. Personal Narratives Group, "Origins," 8. Jarena Lee, *Religious Experience,* 38. Lizzie E. Miller, *True Way,* 62.
78. White, *Story,* 2:30, 237. Cooke, *Handmaiden,* 34.
79. Losee, *Life Sketches,* 64–67, 105.
80. Cole, *Trials and Triumphs,* 52.
81. Jarena Lee, *Religious Experience,* 55.
82. White, *Story,* 5:132.
83. Dudley, *Beulah,* 51. Grammer, "Pen in His Hand," 10. White, *Story,* 3:238.
84. Glaser, *Wonderful,* 96. Amanda Smith, *Autobiography,* 204, 200. Mills, *Grace,* 37. Wheaton, *Prisons and Prayer,* 332.
85. Losee, *Life Sketches,* 210.
86. Foote, *Brand,* 206, 208, 206–7. Collier-Thomas, *Daughters of Thunder,* 59.
87. Dudley, *Beulah,* 51. Jarena Lee, *Religious Experience,* 11–12. Osborn, *Heavenly Pearls,* 139. Jennie Smith, *Ramblings No. 2,* 57.
88. Van Cott, *Harvest and Reaper,* 326. While other women rarely attributed their scriptural views on women preaching to others, Van Cott sprinkled her chapter with numerous direct quotations. Jarena Lee and Mary Lee Cagle were among other exceptions. Lee quoted Adam Clarke (c. 1760–1832) once (*Religious Experience,* 23), while Cagle referred to him six times (*Life and Work,* 162, 174). Cagle also mentioned William Godbey, who had authored a pamphlet (*Woman Preacher*) in support of women preachers.
89. White, *Story,* 3:236–37. White was probably quoting from an editorial, "Woman's Ministry," which she had written for one of her periodicals in January 1911. She mentioned the editorial prior to these comments. Cole, *Trials and Triumphs,* 85–87; Cooke, *Handmaiden,* 174–77; and Cagle, *Life and Work,* 160–76. White sprinkled references throughout her autobiography (*Story,* 2:237, 4:208, 5:125–28, 146, 277, 284–85). Shellhamer, *Trials and Triumphs,* "A Word to Women," 192–93; and Cooke, *Handmaiden,* "Shall Women Preach the Gospel?" 174–77. Alma White, *Woman's Ministry* (London: Pillar of Fire, [1921]). Palmer, *Promise of the Father.* Wesleyan/Holiness women preachers not included in this study also published biblical defenses. See also Booth, *Female Ministry;* Fannie McDowell Hunter, *Women Preachers* (Dallas, Tex.: Berachah Printing, 1905); and Annie May Fisher, *Woman's Right to Preach: A Sermon Reported as Delivered at Chilton, Texas* (San Antonio: By the author, 1903). Wesleyan/Holiness men who supported women

preachers by authoring defenses were B. T. Roberts, *Ordaining Women;* Godbey, *Woman Preacher;* and Luther Lee, "Woman's Right."

90. Cagle, *Life and Work,* 161. Dudley, *Beulah,* 51. Osborn, *Heavenly Pearls,* 70.
91. White, *Story,* 5:128; Van Cott, *Harvest and Reaper,* 326–28, 333; and Shellhamer, *Trials and Triumphs,* 192. Van Cott, *Harvest and Reaper,* 327. Shellhamer, *Trials and Triumphs,* 193. Cooke, *Handmaiden,* 175. See also Shellhamer, *Trials and Triumphs,* 192.
92. Jarena Lee, *Religious Experience,* 23.
93. White, *Story,* 5:127–28. See also Van Cott, *Harvest and Reaper,* 333. Cagle, *Life and Work,* 163.
94. Dudley, *Beulah,* 51. Shellhamer, *Trials and Triumphs,* 192. White, *Story,* 3:336. Cooke, *Handmaiden,* 174. Van Cott, *Harvest and Reaper,* 337. Cagle, *Life and Work,* 169. Losee, *Life Sketches,* 213. Jarena Lee, *Religious Experience,* 11. Shellhamer, *Trials and Triumphs,* 193, 189–90. Cagle, *Life and Work,* 168. See also Losee, *Life Sketches,* 213.
95. Cooke, *Handmaiden,* 174. Cole, *Trials and Triumphs,* 86. Cagle, *Life and Work,* 161, 169–71. White, *Story,* 3:236. Glaser, *Wonderful,* 61. This was the only scriptural defense that Glaser provided. Cole, *Trials and Triumphs,* 86. Cagle, *Life and Work,* 161. Foote, *Brand,* 208, 222. White, *Story,* 2:237, 3:236, 5:127. Glaser, *Wonderful,* 62. Van Cott, *Harvest and Reaper,* 328–29 (quoting Adam Clarke), 337. Cagle, *Life and Work,* 170 (quoting Adam Clarke). Cooke, *Handmaiden,* 174.
96. Losee, *Life Sketches,* 210. McConnell, *Pauline,* 40. Amanda Smith, *Autobiography,* 321.
97. Cole, *Trials and Triumphs,* 87. Elaw, *Memoirs,* 124. Foote, *Brand,* 209. Van Cott, *Harvest and Reaper,* 334. Cagle, *Life and Work,* 166–67. Van Cott, *Harvest and Reaper,* 334–35. Foote, *Brand,* 209. Cagle, *Life and Work,* 167. Cole, *Trials and Triumphs,* 87. Foote, *Brand,* 209. Cooke, *Handmaiden,* 174. Van Cott, *Harvest and Reaper,* 333, 335. Elaw, *Memoirs,* 124. Van Cott, *Harvest and Reaper,* 335. Elaw and Van Cott neglected to mention three other women whose names appear in Romans 16: Julia, Mary, and Persis.
98. Foote, *Brand,* 209. White, *Story,* 4:208. Cooke, *Handmaiden,* 175. Van Cott, *Harvest and Reaper,* 333. Cagle, *Life and Work,* 163.
99. White, *Story,* 4:208–9. See also Elaw, *Memoirs,* 124.
100. Foote, *Brand,* 209. Cagle, *Life and Work,* 166.
101. Dudley, *Beulah,* 51. Foote, *Brand,* 209. Jarena Lee, *Religious Experiences,* 77. Van Cott, *Harvest and Reaper,* 331. White, *Story,* 5:285. Cagle, *Life and Work,* 171. Foote, *Brand,* 209.
102. Van Cott, *Harvest and Reaper,* 329. White, *Story,* 3:237, 4:208; see also 5:127, 284. Cagle, *Life and Work,* 175 (drawing on Adam Clarke).
103. Elaw, *Memoirs,* 124.
104. Cole, *Trials and Triumphs,* 86. Foote, *Brand,* 209. Van Cott, *Harvest and Reaper,* 330. Cagle, *Life and Work,* 162. Cole, *Trials and Triumphs,* 86. Cooke, *Handmaiden,* 175. White, *Story,* 3:237 (see also 5:284), 4:208.

Cagle, *Life and Work,* 165. Van Cott, *Harvest and Reaper,* 330. Cagle, *Life and Work,* 174.

105. Cole, *Trials and Triumphs,* 85. White, *Story,* 2:97. Cooke, *Handmaiden,* 175. Foote, *Brand,* 227.
106. Van Cott, *Harvest and Reaper,* 337. White, *Story,* 5:128, 3:236–37, 4:209.

Chapter 6

1. Leigh Gilmore, *Autobiographics* (Ithaca: Cornell Univ. Press, 1994), 18.
2. Irick, *King's Daughter,* 65, 38.
3. Osborn, *Heavenly Pearls,* 107, 115, 116. Lizzie E. Miller, *True Way,* 141.
4. Mills, *Grace,* 42, 125, 134, 141, 151, 66, 116, 83, 59–60, 62.
5. Ibid., 179. Perry, *Christ and Answered Prayer,* 37. Losee, *Life Sketches,* 168.
6. Amanda Smith, *Autobiography,* 174–75.
7. Ibid., 167, 210.
8. Ibid., 184.
9. Ibid., 205–8, 210–11.
10. Ibid., 116.
11. White, *Story,* 2:116. White's involvement with the Ku Klux Klan raises questions regarding racism. Here, her motivation, like that of many Methodist, Baptist, and Disciples of Christ clergy who were also active in the KKK, was anti-Catholicism. For further discussion of White's affiliation with the KKK, see Susie C. Stanley, *Feminist Pillar of Fire* (Cleveland, Ohio: Pilgrim Press, 1993), 85–98.
12. Amanda Smith, *Autobiography,* 116–17.
13. Ray, *Twice Sold,* 29. Cooke, *Handmaiden,* 234–35. Jarena Lee, *Religious Experience,* 45.
14. Ray, *Twice Sold,* 316–17.
15. For example, see J. Deotis Roberts, *Liberation and Reconciliation,* rev. ed. (Maryknoll: Orbis Books, 1994).
16. Amanda Smith, *Autobiography,* 174.
17. Lizzie E. Miller, *True Way,* 49.
18. Cagle, *Life and Work,* 31, 82. She also reported conducting camp meetings at Roby, Texas, and Snyder (*Life and Work,* 57, 103). *Life and Work,* 85.
19. Cole, *Trials and Triumphs,* 188–89.
20. Ibid., 190.
21. Ibid., 175, 183, 186, 193, 260, 186.
22. Losee, *Life Sketches,* 178–79.
23. Jarena Lee, *Religious Experience,* 44–45, 28, 47, 58, 78.
24. Ibid., 78. Irick, *King's Daughter,* 33. Osborn, *Heavenly Pearls,* 100. Lizzie E. Miller, *True Way,* 129.
25. Mills, *Grace,* 96. Jennie Smith, *Ramblings,* 11. Wesleyan/Holiness magazines advertised other camp meetings under the leadership of women. *Guide to Holiness* magazine in 1880 reported the Woman's Holiness

Camp Meeting at Mount Tabor, New Jersey. Sister Foote preached while she, Sister Lizzie M. Boyd, and Mrs. Dr. Keller "discoursed" at the love feast. The magazine informed its readers: "The word at each service was in the demonstration of the Spirit and with power . . . Effective altar work was conducted after each sermon, and there were seekers of both pardon and purity" ("Revival Miscellany," *Guide to Holiness* 76 [Aug. 1880]: 56). A notice in the *Advocate of Bible Holiness* in 1882 advertised "A Holiness Campmeeting, led primarily by women of the various Christian denominations who believe in entire sanctification as a distinct work" (Quoted in Dieter, *Holiness Revival,* 69).

26. Ray, *Twice Sold,* 68, 72. She mentioned Mother Starett by name (*Twice Sold,* 172). Florence Roberts, *Fifteen Years,* 259; see also 62.
27. Wheaton, *Prisons and Prayer,* 241–42. Wheaton opposed capital punishment because "it does not stop crime" (*Prisons and Prayer,* 156).
28. Ibid., 215, 399, preface, 332.
29. Jennie Smith, *Baca to Beulah,* 25, 148. Jennie Smith, *Incidents and Experiences,* 5.
30. Jennie Smith, *Incidents and Experiences,* 5. Jennie Smith, *Ramblings No. 2,* 42, 40.
31. Jennie Smith, *Ramblings No. 2,* 12–13, 39, 42, 85, 93. Jennie Smith, *Incidents and Experiences,* 12, 41, 92, 108–9, 155, 12, 155, 172, 108, 162, 41.
32. Jennie Smith, *Incidents and Experiences,* 9, 19.
33. Jennie Smith, *Ramblings No. 2,* 117. Jennie Smith, *Incidents and Experiences,* 99, 153.
34. Jennie Smith, *Incidents and Experiences,* 9.
35. Ibid., 128, 162, 90, 172.
36. Maude H. Kahl, *His Guiding Hand* (Overland Park, Kans.: Herald and Banner Press, 1970), 108; Florence Roberts, *Fifteen Years,* 155; and Cooke, *Handmaiden,* 76. Ray, *Twice Sold,* 143, 157.
37. Shellhamer, *Trials and Triumphs,* 29–30, 95–99.
38. Cagle, *Life and Work,* 110–11.
39. Wheaton, *Prisons and Prayer,* 340–42.
40. Ibid., 343–45.
41. Mills, *Quiet,* 241. Van Cott, *Harvest and Reaper,* 198. Dudley, *Beulah,* 81, 84, 91.
42. Cole, *Trials and Triumphs,* 118; and Perry, *Christ and Answered Prayer,* 201. Mills, *Quiet,* 242–43. Osborn, *Heavenly Pearls,* 112–13.
43. Florence Roberts, *Fifteen Years,* 306.
44. For example, see Amanda Smith, *Autobiography,* 156–57.
45. Van Cott, *Harvest and Reaper,* 206, 209, 222. Jarena Lee, *Religious Experience,* 51, 46; see also 77 and 82 for statistics in subsequent years.
46. Perry, *Christ and Answered Prayer,* 217, 57, 266.
47. Ray, *Twice Sold,* 184.
48. Irick, *King's Daughter,* 52. Shellhamer, *Trials and Triumphs,* 154–55.
49. Cagle, *Life and Work,* 101. Shellhamer, *Trials and Triumphs,* 108.

50. Sarah Smith, *Life Sketches,* 10. Lizzie E. Miller, *True Way,* 75. Osborn, *Heavenly Pearls,* 113. Wheaton, *Prisons and Prayer,* 307. Cole, *Trials and Triumphs,* 269–70. Foote, *Brand,* 215. Cagle, *Life and Work,* 50. Ray, *Twice Sold,* 152. McConnell, *Pauline,* 196. Mills, *Grace,* 137.
51. Mills, *Grace,* 102. Shellhamer, *Trials and Triumphs,* 146.
52. Elaw, *Memoirs,* 133.
53. Amanda Smith, *Autobiography,* 117–18.
54. Foote, *Brand,* 215.
55. Ibid., 218, 224.
56. Irick, *King's Daughter,* 24–25. Fitkin, *Grace,* 38–39. Shellhamer, *Trials and Triumphs,* 57, 167.
57. Cole, *Trials and Triumphs,* 205, 220, 152. Perry, *Christ and Answered Prayer,* 56–57.
58. McConnell, *Pauline,* 196. Cole, *Trials and Triumphs,* 156, 159, 165, 105, 274. Kahl, *His Guiding Hand,* 200–202. McConnell, *Pauline,* 42. Winkle, *Preacher Girl,* 32. Cooke, *Handmaiden,* 219. Foote, *Brand,* 211.
59. Wheaton, *Prisons and Prayer,* 307, 308, 213, 295, 517–23, 25, 187.
60. Jennie Smith, *Baca to Beulah,* 326. Van Cott, *Harvest and Reaper,* 230. Cagle, *Life and Work,* 62. Adams, *Autobiography,* 116, 122, 137, 174.
61. Lizzie E. Miller, *True Way,* 148–49. Mills, *Grace,* 86–87, 121; and Mills, *Quiet,* 247.
62. Elaw, *Memoirs,* 83, 101. Foote, *Brand,* 222. Jarena Lee, *Religious Experience,* 20, 27, 30, 35, 37.
63. Perry, *Christ and Answered Prayer,* 58–59.
64. Kahl, *His Guiding Hand,* 71–72.
65. Ibid., 92, 100–101, 115.
66. Lizzie E. Miller, *True Way,* 142–43.
67. Shellhamer, *Trials and Triumphs,* 115–16, 122.
68. Irick, *King's Daughter,* 33, 35, 42, 46.
69. Kahl, *His Guiding Hand,* 89, 207, 222.
70. Ibid., 231, 210, 218–34, 240, 245, 250–51.
71. Shellhamer, *Trials and Triumphs,* 104, 114, 105, 131.
72. Irick, *King's Daughter,* 55, 58, 56, 58.
73. Cagle, *Life and Work,* 22.
74. Ibid., 29, 39, 63, 51.
75. Ibid., 45, 46, 68, 70, 82, 107, 103, 51, 117, 106.
76. Ibid., 89. Even though she entitled a chapter "Beginning of a Holiness Organization on the Plains," she only devoted one paragraph to the organization of her churches.
77. Cagle, *Life and Work,* 109. The official name of her coalition of churches was the New Testament Church of Christ. This group merged with the Independent Holiness Church of Christ to become the Holiness Church of Christ in 1905. The Holiness Church of Christ then merged with the Pentecostal Church of the Nazarene in 1908. The "Pentecostal" in the church title was later dropped. Timothy L. Smith, *Called unto Holiness* (Kansas

City, Mo.: Nazarene Publishing House, 1962), 159, 169, 171. Cagle, *Life and Work,* 127, 133, 147–48, 131, 158.

78. White, *Story,* 1:426, 2:160, 2:126, 2:363–64, 4:218.
79. One of the first Christian leaders to realize the evangelistic potential of the radio, White purchased a radio station in Denver in 1927. There were sixty-one branches, including a work in London, England, at the time of her death ("Fundamentalist Pillar," *Time,* 8 July 1946, 73).
80. Lee Casey, "Bishop White of Denver—A Cromwell in Skirts," *Denver Rocky Mountain News,* 28 June 1946.
81. McConnell, *Pauline,* 26, 28, 44, 61, 62, 110, 158.
82. Ibid., 66, 197, 52, 10, 110.
83. McConnell, *Rewarding,* 13, 112, 17.
84. McConnell, *Pauline,* 184–85. Lela G. McConnell, *The Power of Prayer Plus Faith* (n.p., 1952), 112. McConnell, *Pauline,* 184.

Chapter 7

1. Perry, *Christ and Answered Prayer,* 46–50. Mary Alice Tenney, *Blueprint for a Christian World* (Winona Lake, Ind.: Light and Life Press, 1953), 234. Leon O. Hynson reached the same conclusion. See also *To Reform the Nation* (Grand Rapids, Mich.: Francis Asbury Press of Zondervan Publishing House, 1984), 10, 140.
2. Several authors have corroborated the involvement of holiness adherents in social reform and social transformation. For instance, Mary Alice Tenney, a Free Methodist scholar, traced the roots of social holiness to John Wesley's equal interest in both evangelism and social ministry. Tenney documented early Methodism's adoption of Wesley's vision of "a society where the principles of Christianity worked as leaven to create a new order" (*Blueprint,* 236). Timothy L. Smith introduced the relationship between the Wesleyan/Holiness movement and social reform to the broader academic community in his groundbreaking *Revivalism and Social Reform in Mid-Nineteenth Century America.* While Norris Magnuson used the terms *Evangelical welfare* and *gospel welfare,* he primarily documented the work of holiness denominations and individuals (*Salvation in the Slums,* ATLA Series, no. 10 [Metuchen, N. J.: Scarecrow Press, 1977], ix, x, xii). Douglas M. Strong in *Perfectionist Politics* documented the role of the Wesleyan Methodist Connection (now known as The Wesleyan Church), a Wesleyan/Holiness denomination, in antislavery and women's rights efforts prior to the Civil War.
3. Walter Rauschenbusch, *A Theology for the Social Gospel* (New York: Macmillan, 1917; reprint, Nashville: Abingdon, 1978), 131. Hynson, *Reform the Nation,* 56.
4. Ray, *Twice Sold,* 305. Palmer, *Way of Holiness,* 124, 148.
5. Dunning, *Brands,* 251–52.
6. Ray, *Twice Sold,* 209, 74, 228. Hynson, *Reform the Nation,* 96.

7. Adams, *Autobiography,* 60–61, 77, 140, 80, 137; see also 78, 92, 138, 139, 284.
8. Florence Roberts, *Fifteen Years,* 369. Ray, *Twice Sold,* 198, 70–71, 122, 148, 150, 143, 201. Witteman's husband was one of her assistants.
9. Ronald J. Sider, *One-Sided Christianity?* (Grand Rapids, Mich.: Zondervan Publishing House, and San Francisco: HarperSanFrancisco, 1993), 165.
10. Ibid., 139–40.
11. Dunning, *Brands,* 58; and Prosser, *Death To Life,* 73. Kahl, *His Guiding Hand,* 70; and Osborn, *Heavenly Pearls,* 102. Dunning, *Brands,* 8, 27, 72, 74, 77, 28, 29. Once, a man received a bed prior to hearing the gospel (*Brands,* 65). Whittemore, *Mother Whittemore's Records,* 156, 165.
12. Whittemore, *Mother Whittemore's Records,* 155.
13. Ibid., 156.
14. Prosser, *Death To Life,* 73. Dunning, *Brands,* 100. Whittemore, *Mother Whittemore's Records,* 157–58.
15. Lizzie E. Miller, *True Way,* 99, 107, 181. Mills, *Grace,* 232. Wheaton, *Prisons and Prayer,* 146; and Cooke, *Handmaiden,* 168.
16. Losee, *Life Sketches,* 193, 204, 205.
17. Dunning, *Brands,* 245, 116, 252, 7, 124–25. Amanda Smith mentioned this home in her narrative (*Autobiography,* 112).
18. Dunning, *Brands,* 57. For examples, see 74–79, 91–95, 95–98, 224–26.
19. Prosser, *Death To Life,* 72, 74, 138. After embracing holiness, A. B. Simpson, a Presbyterian minister, founded the Christian Alliance and the Evangelical Missionary Alliance in 1887, which merged later to become the Christian and Missionary Alliance. The church does not fit neatly into the Wesleyan/Holiness movement because of its Reformed theology. The group also sponsored Emma Whittemore's first Door of Hope, which will be discussed below. Martha Lee, *Mother Lee's Experience,* 44, 47, 91, 92, 101, 104, 107, 101, 104, 56, 137, 185, 187, 191.
20. Florence Roberts, *Fifteen Years,* 83, 89, 91–92, 59–60, 225. Cole, *Trials and Triumphs,* 228–29. Shellhamer, *Trials and Triumphs,* 61.
21. Whittemore, *Mother Whittemore's Records,* 41, 48, 61, 62. Lizzie Miller shared Whittemore's viewpoint: "My sympathies were soon enlisted in behalf of these poor fallen creatures, who were a constant prey to sin and crime" (*True Way,* 30). Miller condemned those who led young women into vice: "If there is one thing blacker than another, in this life of vice and crime, it is that of enticing young and helpless girls into degradation and disgrace" (*True Way,* 34).
22. Whittemore, *Mother Whittemore's Records,* 120, 63–64, 59–60, 233, 226, 268.
23. Ibid., 282.
24. Ibid., 238, 236–37.
25. Martha Lee, *Mother Lee's Experience,* preface, 196, 149–50, 156, 123–25, 129.
26. Jennie Smith, *Baca to Beulah,* 285. Jennie Smith, *Ramblings,* 149–51.
27. Florence Roberts, *Fifteen Years,* 52–53, 226–27.
28. Ibid., 228, 143, 145, 206, 261.

29. Martha Lee, *Mother Lee's Experience,* 59.
30. Whittemore, *Mother Whittemore's Records,* 258.
31. Ibid., 184.
32. Florence Roberts, *Fifteen Years,* 342; see also 63. Martha Lee, *Mother Lee's Experience,* 64.
33. Hannah Whitall Smith, *My Spiritual Autobiography,* 82. For Smith's involvement, see Elizabeth Cady Stanton, Susan B. Anthony, and Matilda Joslyn Gage, eds., *History of Woman Suffrage* (Rochester, N.Y.: Charles Mann, 1885), 3:230. White, *Story,* 4:243, 369, 237.
34. White, *Story,* 5:132–33, 314.
35. Ibid., 4:237; 5:32, 86, 136, 273, 229; 4:370.
36. White, *Story,* 4:236–37; 5:329, 108. Inez Haynes Irwin, "The Equal Rights Amendment: Why the Woman's Party Is for It," *Good Housekeeping,* Mar. 1924, 18. *New York Times,* 11 Sept. 1920, quoted in Margory Nelson, "Ladies in the Streets: A Sociological Analysis of the National Woman's Party, 1910–1930" (Ph.D. diss., State Univ. of New York at Buffalo, 1976), 150. White, *Story,* 5:108.
37. White, *Story,* 5:304; see also 5:329.
38. Ibid., 5:304, 132.
39. Ibid., 5:329.
40. [Eliza Daniel] Stewart, *Memories of the Crusade* (Columbus, Ohio: William Hubbart; reprint, New York: Arno Press, 1972), 86. Carol C. Mattingly quoted several references to Pentecost and the reliance on the Holy Spirit's power in *Well-Tempered Women* (Carbondale: Southern Illinois Univ. Press, 1998), 47, 49, 50. Stewart, *Memories,* 40. Losee, *Life Sketches,* 217. Stewart, *Memories,* 150, 201.
41. Foote, *Brand,* 174. Van Cott, *Harvest and Reaper,* 108, 217. Adams, *Autobiography,* 69, 176. Perry, *Christ and Answered Prayer,* 165.
42. Surprisingly, a discussion of women clergy is missing from a recent book on W.C.T.U. rhetoric. The only woman preacher mentioned is Amanda Smith (Mattingly, *Well-Tempered Women,* 93). Mills, *Grace,* 217, 223. Prosser, *From Death To Life,* 44–46.
43. Ray, *Twice Sold,* 67, 113. Dudley, *Beulah,* 18. Wheaton, *Prisons and Prayer,* 201.
44. Jennie Smith, *Valley of Baca,* 218. Jennie Smith, *Baca to Beulah,* 209, 300; and Jennie Smith, *Ramblings,* 49. Jennie Smith, *Incidents and Experiences,* 151. Jennie Smith, *Ramblings No. 2,* 48, 86, 146. Jennie Smith, *Baca to Beulah,* 342. Jennie Smith, *Incidents and Experiences,* 168.
45. Lizzie E. Miller, *True Way,* 26, 50, 163, 137–41.
46. Martha Lee, *Mother Lee's Experience,* 63. Wheaton, *Prisons and Prayer,* 340, 404.
47. Florence Roberts, *Fifteen Years,* 442, 426, 422; see also 448.
48. Jennie Smith, *Baca to Beulah,* 269. See also Jennie Smith, *Ramblings No. 2,* 16.
49. Jarena Lee, *Religious Experiences,* 82, 90.

50. Amanda Smith, *Autobiography,* 17. Ray, *Twice Sold,* 15. Foote, *Brand,* 166. Ray, *Twice Sold,* 15. Foote, *Brand,* 184.
51. Ray, *Twice Sold,* 146. Lizzie E. Miller, *True Way,* 52. Dunning, *Brands,* 93.
52. Van Cott, *Harvest and Reaper,* 115–18.
53. Foote, *Brand,* 222.
54. Amanda Smith, *Autobiography,* 112–15.
55. Ibid.
56. Ibid., 119.
57. Ibid., 196–98.

Chapter 8

1. Domna C. Stanton, "Autogynography: Is the Subject Different?" in *The Female Autograph,* ed. Domna C. Stanton (Chicago: Univ. of Chicago Press, 1984), 14. Sidonie Smith, *Poetics,* 44.
2. Personal Narratives Group, "Origins," 11.
3. Leah D. Hewitt, *Autobiographical Tightropes* (Lincoln: Univ. of Nebraska Press, 1990), 3; and Margo Culley, "What a Piece of Work," 9. Hewitt, *Autobiographical Tightropes,* 3. Sidonie Smith, "Resisting the Gaze," 85. See also Sidonie Smith, *Poetics,* 44; and Nancy K. Miller, "Writing Fictions," 50.
4. Davidson, "Workings of the Spirit," 5. Adams, *Autobiography,* 3.
5. Adams, *Autobiography,* 3. Michel Foucault, "What Is an Author?" in *Language, Counter-Memory, Practice,* trans. Donald F. Bouchard and Sherry Simon (Ithaca: Cornell Univ. Press, 1977), 138.
6. Foucault, "What Is an Author?" 118, 138. Katherine R. Goodman, "Elisabeth to Meta: Epistolary Autobiography and the Postulation of the Self," in *Life/lines,* ed. Bella Brodzki and Celeste Schenck (Ithaca: Cornell Univ. Press, 1988), 308. See also Brodzki and Schenck, introduction to *Life/lines,* 14. Liz Stanley, *Auto/biographical I,* 16–17. Domna Stanton, "Autogynography," 16–17.
7. Hilary Hinds, *God's Englishwomen* (Manchester: Manchester Univ. Press, 1996), 18, 86. See 81–87 for a summary of the death of the author debate.
8. Ann D. Gordon, "The Political Is the Personal: Two Autobiographies of Woman Suffragists," in *American Women's Autobiography,* ed. Margo Culley (Madison: Univ. of Wisconsin Press, 1992), 111.
9. Sidonie Smith, *Poetics,* 49. White, *Story,* 5:126–27. Brekus, *Female Preaching,* 178.
10. Florence Roberts, *Fifteen Years,* 441.
11. Jelinek, *Tradition,* ix, xiii. For a similar description, see Jelinek, *Women's Autobiography,* 17.
12. Brekus, *Female Preaching,* 171.
13. Jelinek, *Tradition,* xiii. Jelinek, *Women's Autobiography,* xii. Liz Stanley, *Auto/Biographical I,* 247. Gilmore, *Autobiographies,* 11.
14. Brodzki and Schenck, introduction to *Life/lines,* 9. Mary Jean Green, "Structures of Liberation: Female Experience and Autobiographical Form in Quebec," in *Life/lines,* 189. McConnell, *Faith,* 187. Jennie Smith, *Baca to*

Beulah, 148. She also mentioned hearing her sing at Cincinnati in 1876 (*Baca to Beulah,* 25). Mills, *Grace,* 97, 147, 31, 94, 87, 172. Osborn, *Heavenly Pearls,* 137. Ingersol documented this network in "Burden of Dissent."

15. Cole, *Trials and Triumphs,* 147, 151, 270, 273.
16. Nellie Y. McKay, "Race, Gender, and Cultural Context in Zora Neale Hurston's *Dust Tracks on a Road,*" in *Life/lines,* 175–76.
17. Mary G. Mason, "The Other Voice: Autobiographies of Women Writers," in *Life/lines,* 22, 41.
18. Lois J. Fowler and David H. Fowler, *Revelations of Self* (Albany: State Univ. of New York Press, 1990), xxiii.
19. Brekus, *Female Preaching,* 174. Hinds, *God's Englishwomen,* 89–99. Amy Oden, *In Her Words* (Nashville: Abingdon, 1994), 13. Amanda Smith, *Autobiography,* 144, 505. Sarah Smith, *Life Sketches,* 21.
20. Elaw, *Memoirs,* 70. Moody, "On the Road," 44.
21. Haynes, "Radical Spiritual Motherhood," 3; see also Connor, *Conversions,* 44.
22. Grammer, "Pen in His Hand," 265.
23. Martha Lee, *Mother Lee's Experience,* preface.
24. Jennie Smith, *Valley of Baca,* 171; Losee, *Life Sketches,* preface; Cagle, *Life and Work,* preface; and Winkle, *Preacher Girl,* preface. Adams, *Autobiography,* 195–96. Irick, *King's Daughter,* foreword and acknowledgments. Jennie Smith, *Valley of Baca,* 187, 197. Jennie Smith, *Baca to Beulah,* 320. Jarena Lee, *Religious Experience,* 77, 97. Cooke, *Handmaiden,* 5; and L. B. Kent, introduction to Cooke, *Handmaiden,* 7–11.
25. Lizzie E. Miller, *True Way,* 9.
26. White, *Story,* 2:84–85.
27. Ray, *Twice Sold,* preface. Amanda Smith, *Autobiography,* preface. The verses she quoted are 2 Cor. 8:11 and Isa. 49:13.
28. McConnell, *Power,* preface. Adams, *Autobiography,* 241. Shellhamer, *Trials and Triumphs,* preface.
29. Wheaton, *Prisons and Prayer,* preface. Sarah Smith, *Life Sketches,* 3, 21, 32.
30. Adams, *Autobiography,* 212. Cole, *Trials and Triumphs,* 21. Jarena Lee, *Religious Experience,* 21. Foote, *Brand,* 172, 168. Shellhamer, *Trials and Triumphs,* 175. Adams, *Autobiography,* 213. Perry, *Christ and Answered Prayer,* 62.
31. Foote, *Brand,* 174. Florence Roberts, *Fifteen Years,* 110, 140, 227, 296.
32. McConnell, *Hitherto,* 54, 106. Jennie Smith, *Ramblings,* 23.
33. Jennie Smith, *Baca to Beulah,* 24. For examples, see Jennie Smith, *Ramblings,* 142; *Ramblings No. 2,* 76 ("So, dear reader, if the eye of an *unsaved soul* is resting upon these lines, we beseech of you, as though sitting at your side talking face to face, don't put off this one thing needful.") Jennie Smith, *Incidents,* 194.
34. Mills, *Grace,* 220, 231. Adams, *Autobiography,* 257. Jarena Lee, *Religious Experience,* 76. She also wrote, "I feel the unction from on high, while I

hold my pen" (*Religious Experience,* 79). Kahl, *His Guiding Hand,* preface. Losee, *Life Sketches,* preface; and Florence Roberts, *Fifteen Years,* 25.

35. Adams, *Autobiography,* 271; see also 3–4, 257. Glaser, *Wonderful,* 10, 74, 92; see also 110, 113. Foote, *Brand,* 223. Perry, *Christ and Answered Prayer,* 48. Jarena Lee, *Religious Experience,* 31. Sarah Smith, *Life Sketches,* 19.
36. McConnell, *Power,* 86. McConnell, *Hitherto,* 157. McConnell, *Rewarding,* 170. Mills, *Grace,* preface. Lizzie E. Miller, *True Way,* preface. Florence Roberts, *Fifteen Years,* 50.
37. McConnell, *Hitherto,* 56. See also McConnell, *Faith,* 11.
38. Jennie Smith, *Incidents and Experiences,* 114.
39. Dudley, *Beulah,* preface. Losee, *Life Sketches,* preface. Losee's book covers her ministry prior to working with Mormons. Jennie Smith, *Incidents and Experiences,* 194. Jennie Smith, *Baca to Beulah,* 17.
40. Jarena Lee, *Religious Experience,* 77, 79, 85.
41. Wheaton, *Prisons and Prayer,* preface. Irick, *King's Daughter,* foreword. Osborn, *Heavenly Pearls,* preface.
42. Cole, *Trials and Triumphs,* 70, 282, 299, 70, 238.
43. Amanda Smith, *Autobiography,* 505–6. Foote, *Brand,* 227.
44. Camp Meeting of the National Association of the Church of God, West Middlesex, Pa., 9 Aug. 1999.

SOURCES CITED

Autobiographies

Adams, Mary Still. *Autobiography of Mary Still Adams or, "In God We Trust."* Los Angeles: Buckingham Bros., Printers, 1893.

Cagle, Mary Lee. *Life and Work of Mary Lee Cagle: An Autobiography.* Kansas City, Mo.: Nazarene Publishing House, 1928.

Cole, Mary. *Trials and Triumphs of Faith.* Anderson, Ind.: Gospel Trumpet, 1914.

Cooke, Sarah A. *The Handmaiden of the Lord, or Wayside Sketches.* Chicago: T. B. Arnold, 1896.

Dudley, Dora A. *Beulah: or, Some of the Fruits of One Consecrated Life.* Rev. and enlarged ed. Grand Rapids, Mich.: By the author, 1896.

Dunning, Jane. *Brands from the Burning: An Account of a Work among the Sick and Destitute in Connection with Providence Mission, New York City.* Chicago: Baker & Arnold, 1881.

Elaw, Zilpha. *Memoirs of the Life, Religious Experience, Ministerial Travels and Labours of Mrs. Zilpha Elaw, an American Female of Color: Together with Some Account of the Great Religious Revivals in America.* London: By the author, 1846. Reprint, *Sisters of the Spirit: Three Black Women's Autobiographies of the Nineteenth Century.* Ed. William L. Andrews. Bloomington, Ind.: Indiana Univ. Press, 1986.

Fitkin, S. [Susan] N. [Norris]. *Grace Much More Abounding: A Story of the Triumphs of Redeeming Grace During Two Score Years in the Master's Service.* Kansas City, Mo.: Nazarene Publishing House, n.d.

Fletcher, Mary. *The Life of Mrs. Mary Fletcher, Consort and Relict of the Rev. John Fletcher, Vicar of Madeley, Salop: Compiled from her Journal and Other Authentic Documents.* Comp. and ed. Henry Moore. London: Conference-Office, 1818.

Foote, Julia. *A Brand Plucked from the Fire: An Autobiographical Sketch.* Cleveland, Ohio: By the author, 1879. Reprint, *Sisters of the Spirit: Three Black Women's Autobiographies of the Nineteenth Century.* Ed. William L. Andrews. Bloomington, Ind.: Indiana Univ. Press, 1986.

Glaser, Mary A. *Wonderful Leadings.* Allentown, Pa.: Haines & Worman, Printers, 1893.

Guyon, Jean. *The Autobiography of Madame Jean Guyon.* Philadelphia: National Publishing Association for the Promotion of Holiness, 1886.

Irick, Emma. *The King's Daughter.* Kansas City, Mo.: Pedestal Press, 1973.

Kahl, Maude H. *His Guiding Hand: An Autobiography.* Overland Park, Kans.: Herald and Banner Press, 1970.

Lee, Jarena. *Religious Experience and Journal of Mrs. Jarena Lee, Giving an Account of Her Call to Preach the Gospel.* Philadelphia: By the author, 1849.

Lee, Martha A. *Mother Lee's Experience in Fifteen Years' Rescue Work: With Thrilling Incidents of Her Life.* Omaha, Nebr.: By the author, 1906.

Losee, Almira. *Life Sketches: Being Narrations of Scenes Occurring in the Labours of Almira Losee.* New York: By the author, 1880.

McConnell, Lela G. *Faith Victorious in the Kentucky Mountains: The Story of Twenty-Two Years of Spirit-Filled Ministry.* Berne, Ind.: Economy Printing Concern, 1946.

———. *Hitherto and Henceforth in the Kentucky Mountains; A Quarter of a Century of Adventures in Faith—The Year of Jubilee.* Lawson, Ky.: n.p., 1949.

———. *The Pauline Ministry in the Kentucky Mountains or A Brief Account of the Kentucky Mountain Holiness Association.* Louisville, Ky.: Pentecostal Publishing, [1942].

———. *The Power of Prayer Plus Faith.* n.p., 1952.

———. *Rewarding Faith Plus Works.* n.p., 1962.

Miller, Lizzie E. *The True Way: Life and Evangelical Work of Lizzie E. Miller (of Fairview, West Va.) Written by Herself.* Los Angeles: By the author, 1895.

Mills, Abbie C. *Grace and Glory.* Los Angeles: By the author, 1907.

———. *Quiet Hallelujahs.* Boston: McDonald & Gill, 1886.

Osborn, Lucy Drake. *Heavenly Pearls Set in a Life: A Record of Experiences and Labors in America, India and Australia.* New York: Fleming H. Revell, 1893.

Palmer, Phoebe. *The Way of Holiness: Notes by the Way.* 50th American ed., 1867. Reprint, Salem, Ohio: Schmul Publishing, 1988.

Perry, Mattie E. *Christ and Answered Prayer; Autobiography of Mattie E. Perry.* Cincinnati: By the author, 1939.

Prosser, Anna W. *From Death To Life: An Autobiography.* Buffalo: McGerald Publishing, 1901.

Ray, [Emma], and L. [Lloyd] P. *Twice Sold, Twice Ransomed: Autobiography of Mr. and Mrs. L. P. Ray.* Chicago: Free Methodist Publishing House, 1926.

Roberts, Florence. *Fifteen Years with the Outcast.* Anderson, Ind.: Gospel Trumpet, 1912.

Rogers, Hester Ann. *Life and Journal of Mrs. Hester Ann Rogers.* Condensed and combined by Rev. E. Davies. Reading, Mass.: Holiness Book Concern, 1882.

Shellhamer, Julia A. *Trials and Triumphs of a Minister's Wife.* Atlanta: Repairer Publishing, 1923.

Smith, Amanda. *An Autobiography: The Story of the Lord's Dealings with Mrs. Amanda Smith, The Colored Evangelist.* Chicago: Meyer & Brother, Publishers, 1893. Reprint, New York: Garland Publishing, 1987.

Smith, Hannah Whitall. *My Spiritual Autobiography or How I Discovered the Unselfishness of God.* New York: Fleming H. Revell, 1903.

Smith, Jennie. *From Baca to Beulah, Sequel to "Valley of Baca."* Philadelphia: Garrigues Brothers, 1880.

———. *Incidents and Experiences of a Railroad Evangelist.* Washington, D.C.: By the author, 1920.

———. *Ramblings in Beulah Land: A Continuation of Experiences in the Life of Jennie Smith.* Philadelphia: Garrigues Brothers, 1886.

———. *Ramblings in Beulah Land: A Continuation of Experiences in the Life of Jennie Smith. No. 2.* Philadelphia: Garrigues Brothers, 1888.

———. *Valley of Baca: A Record of Suffering and Triumph.* Cincinnati: Press of Jennings and Pye, 1876.

Smith, Sarah. *Life Sketches of Mother Sarah Smith: "A Mother in Israel."* Anderson, Ind.: Gospel Trumpet, 1902. Reprint, Guthrie, Okla.: Faith Publishing House, n.d.

Van Cott, Maggie Newton. *The Harvest and the Reaper: Reminiscences of Revival Work of Mrs. Maggie N. Van Cott: The First Lady Licensed to Preach in the Methodist Episcopal Church in the United States.* New York: N. Tibbals & Sons, Publishers, 1876.

Wheaton, Elizabeth R. *Prisons and Prayer; or, A Labor of Love.* Tabor, Iowa: M. Kelley, [1906].

White, Alma. *The Story of My Life and the Pillar of Fire.* 5 vols. Zarephath, N.J.: Pillar of Fire, 1935–43.

Whittemore, Emma M. *Mother Whittemore's Records of Modern Miracles.* Toronto: Missions of Biblical Education, 1931.

Winkle, Celia Bradshaw. *The Preacher Girl: A Thrilling Story.* St. Petersburg, Fla.: By the author, 1967.

Other Sources

Anderson, Linda. *Women and Autobiography in the Twentieth Century: Remembered Futures.* London: Prentice Hall, 1997.

Andrews, William L., ed. *Sisters of the Spirit: Three Black Women's Autobiographies of the Nineteenth Century.* Bloomington: Indiana Univ. Press, 1986.

———. *To Tell a Free Story: The First Century of Afro-American Autobiography, 1760–1865.* Urbana: Univ. of Illinois Press, 1986.

Bassard, Katherine Clay. *Spiritual Interrogations: Culture, Gender and Community in Early African American Women's Writing.* Princeton: Princeton Univ. Press, 1999.

Beard, Mary R. *Woman as Force in History: A Study in Traditions and Realities.* New York: Macmillan, 1946.

Bem, Sandra Lipsitz. *The Lenses of Gender: Transforming the Debate on Sexual Equality.* New Haven: Yale Univ. Press, 1993.

Bendroth, Margaret. Review of *Anna Tilden: Unitarian Culture and the Problem of Self-Representation,* in *Church History* 68, no.1 (Mar. 1999): 217–19.

Bjorklund, Diane. *Interpreting the Self: Two Hundred Years of American Autobiography.* Chicago: Univ. of Chicago Press, 1998.

Booth, Catherine. *Female Ministry: Woman's Right to Preach the Gospel.* London: n.p., 1859. Reprint, New York: Salvation Army Supplies Printing and Publishing Dept., 1975.

Boyd, Mary Sumner. "Women Preachers." *Woman Citizen* (Dec. 1920): 794–96, 802.

Brasher, Brenda E. *Godly Women: Fundamentalism and Female Power.* New Brunswick, N.J.: Rutgers Univ. Press, 1998.

Brekus, Catherine A. *Female Preaching in America, Strangers and Pilgrims, 1740–1845.* Chapel Hill: Univ. of North Carolina Press, 1998.

———. "'Let Your Women Keep Silence in the Churches': Female Preaching and Evangelical Religion in America, 1740–1845." Ph.D. diss., Yale Univ., 1993.

Brereton, Virginia Lieson. *From Sin to Salvation: Stories of Women's Conversion, 1800 to the Present.* Bloomington, Ind.: Indiana Univ. Press, 1991.

Brodzki, Bella, and Celeste Schenck. Introduction to *Life/lines: Theorizing Women's Autobiography,* ed. Bella Brodzki and Celeste Schenck, 1–15. Ithaca: Cornell Univ. Press, 1988.

Brown, Earl Kent. *Women of Mr. Wesley's Methodism.* New York: Edwin Mellen Press, 1983.

Bruneau, Marie-Florine. *Women Mystics Confront the Modern World: Marie de l'Incarnation (1599–1672) and Madame Guyon (1648–1717).* Albany: State Univ. of New York Press, 1998.

Bynum, Carolyn Walker. *Jesus as Mother.* Berkeley: Univ. of California Press, 1982.

Carroll, Jackson W., Barbara Hargrove, and Adair T. Lummis. *Women of the Cloth: A New Opportunity for the Churches.* San Francisco: Harper & Row, 1983.

Chilcote, Paul Wesley. "An Early Methodist Community of Women." *Methodist History* 38, no. 4 (July 2000): 219–31.

———. *John Wesley and the Women Preachers of Early Methodism.* ATLA Monograph Series, No. 25. Metuchen, N.J.: American Theological Library Association and Scarecrow Press, 1991.

Coleson, Joseph E. *'Ezer Cenegdo: A Power Like Him, Facing Him as Equal.* Grantham, Pa.: Wesleyan/Holiness Women Clergy, 1996.

Collier-Thomas, Bettye. *Daughters of Thunder: Black Women Preachers and Their Sermons, 1850–1979.* San Francisco: Jossey-Bass Publishers, 1997.

Collins, Kenneth J. *A Real Christian: The Life of John Wesley.* Nashville: Abingdon Press, 1999.

Connor, Kimberly Rae. *Conversions and Visions in the Writings of African-American Women.* Knoxville: Univ. of Tennessee Press, 1994.

Conway, Jill K. *When Memory Speaks: Reflections on Autobiography.* New York: Alfred A. Knopf, 1998.

Culley, Margo. "What a Piece of Work Is 'Woman'! An Introduction." In *American Women's Autobiography: Fea(s)ts of Memory,* ed. Margo Culley, 3–31. Madison: Univ. of Wisconsin Press, 1992.

———. "Women's Vernacular Literature: Teaching the Mother Tongue." In *Women's Personal Narratives: Essays in Criticism and Pedagogy,* ed. Leonore Hoffman and Margo Culley, 9–17. New York: Modern Language Association of America, 1985.

Davidson, Phebe. "Workings of the Spirit: Religious Impulse in Selected Autobiographies of American Women." Ph.D. diss., Rutgers State Univ. of New Jersey, 1991.

Dayton, Donald W. *Theological Roots of Pentecostalism.* Peabody: Hendrickson Publishers, 1991.

Dieter, Melvin E. *The Holiness Revival of the Nineteenth Century.* 2d ed. Lanham, Md.: Scarecrow Press, 1996.

Eakin, Paul John. *American Autobiography: Retrospect and Prospect.* Madison: Univ. of Wisconsin Press, 1991.

Erickson, Joyce Quiring. "'Perfect Love': Achieving Sanctification as a Pattern of Desire in the Life Writings of Early Methodist Women." *Prose Studies* 20, no. 2 (Aug. 1997): 72–89.

Everhart, Janet S. "Maggie Newton Van Cott: The Methodist Episcopal Church Considers the Question of Women Clergy." In *Women in New Worlds,* ed. Rosemary Skinner Keller, Louise L. Queen, and Hilah F. Thomas, 300–317. Nashville: Abingdon, 1982.

Finke, Laurie A. *Feminist Theory, Women's Writing.* Ithaca: Cornell Univ. Press, 1992.

Foster, Frances Smith. "Neither Auction Block nor Pedestal: 'The Life and Religious Experience of Jarena Lee, A Coloured Lady.'" In *The Female Autograph: Theory and Practice of Autobiography from the Tenth to the Twentieth Century,* ed. Domna C. Stanton, 126–51. Chicago: Univ. of Chicago Press, 1984.

Foucault, Michel. "What Is an Author?" In *Language, Counter-Memory, Practice: Selected Essays and Interviews.* Trans. Donald F. Bouchard and Sherry Simon, 113–38. Ithaca: Cornell Univ. Press, 1977.

Fowler, Lois J., and David H. Fowler. *Revelations of Self: American Women in Autobiography.* Albany: State Univ. of New York Press, 1990.

"Fundamentalist Pillar." *Time,* 8 July 1946, 73.

Galea, Kate P. Crawford. "'Anchored behind the Veil': Mystical Vision as a Possible Source of Authority in the Ministry of Phoebe Palmer." *Methodist History* 31, no. 4 (July 1993): 236–47.

Gilmore, Leigh. *Autobiographies: A Feminist Theory of Women's Self-Representation.* Ithaca: Cornell Univ. Press, 1994.

Godbey, W. B. *Woman Preacher.* Louisville, Ky.: Pentecostal Publishing, 1891.

Goodman, Katherine R. "Elisabeth to Meta: Epistolary Autobiography and the Postulation of the Self." In *Life/lines: Theorizing Women's Autobiography,* ed. Bella Brodzki and Celeste Schenck, 1–15. Ithaca: Cornell Univ. Press, 1988.

Gordon, Ann D. "The Political Is the Personal: Two Autobiographies of Woman Suffragists." In *American Women's Autobiography,* ed. Margo Culley, 111–27. Madison: Univ. of Wisconsin Press, 1992.

Grammer. Elizabeth Elkin. "'A Pen in His Hand': A Pen in Her Hand Autobiographies by Female Itinerant Evangelists in Nineteenth-Century America." Ph.D. diss., Univ. of Virginia, 1995.

Green, Mary Jean. "Structures of Liberation: Female Experience and Autobiographical Form in Quebec." In *Life/lines: Theorizing Women's Autobiography,* ed. Bella Brodzki and Celeste Schenck, 189–99. Ithaca: Cornell Univ. Press, 1988.

Grimké, Sarah M. *Letters on the Equality of the Sexes and the Condition of Woman.* Boston: Isaac Knapp, 1838. Reprint, New York: Source Book Press, 1970.

Hardesty, Nancy A., Lucille Sider Dayton, and Donald W. Dayton. "Women in the Holiness Movement: Feminism in the Evangelical Tradition." In *Women of Spirit: Female Leadership in the Jewish and Christian Traditions,* ed. Rosemary Ruether and Eleanor McLaughlin, 225–54. New York: Simon and Schuster, 1979.

Haynes, Rosetta Renae. "Radical Spiritual Motherhood: The Construction of Black Female Subjectivity in Nineteenth-Century African-American Women's Spiritual Autobiographies." Ph.D. diss., Cornell Univ., 1996.

Heilbrun, Carolyn G. "Non-Autobiographies of 'Privileged' Women: England and America." In *Life/lines: Theorizing Women's Autobiography,* ed. Bella Brodzki and Celeste Schenck, 62–76. Ithaca: Cornell Univ. Press, 1988.

———. *Writing a Woman's Life.* New York: Ballantine Books, 1988.

Hewitt, Leah. D. *Autobiographical Tightropes.* Lincoln: Univ. of Nebraska Press, 1990.

Hinds, Hilary. *God's Englishwomen.* Manchester: Manchester Univ. Press, 1996.

Houchins, Sue E. Introduction to *Spiritual Narratives: Maria W. Stewart, Jarena Lee, Julia Foote, and Virginia W. Broughton,* ed. Henry Lewis Gates Jr., xxix–xliv. New York: Oxford Univ. Press, 1988.

Huber, Elaine C. *Women and the Authority of Inspiration: A Reexamination of Two Prophetic Movements From a Contemporary Feminist Perspective.* Lanham, Md.: Univ. Press of America, 1985.

Hughes, Richard. "Christian Primitivism as Perfectionism: From Anabaptists to Pentecostals." In *Reaching Beyond,* ed. Stanley Burgess, 213–55. Peabody, Mass.: Hendrickson, 1986.

Hynson, Leon O. "Original Sin as Privation: An Inquiry into a Theology of Sin and Sanctification." *Wesleyan Theological Journal* 22, no. 2 (fall 1987): 65–83.

———. *To Reform the Nation: Theological Foundations of Wesley's Ethics.* Grand Rapids, Mich.: Francis Asbury Press of Zondervan Publishing House, 1984.

Ingersol, Robert Stanley. "Burden of Dissent: Mary Lee Cagle and the Southern Holiness Movement." Ph.D. diss., Duke Univ., 1989.

Irwin, Inez Haynes. "The Equal Rights Amendment: Why the Woman's Party Is for It." *Good Housekeeping,* Mar. 1924, 18.

Jacquet, Jr., Constant H. *Women Ministers in 1986 and 1977: A Ten Year Review.* New York: National Council of Churches, 1988.

James, Janet Wilson. "Women in American Religious History: An Overview." In *Women in American Religion,* ed. Janet Wilson James, 1–25. Philadelphia: Univ. of Pennsylvania Press, 1980.

Jelinek, Estelle C. *Women's Autobiography: Essays in Criticism.* Bloomington, Ind.: Indiana Univ. Press, 1980.

———. *The Tradition of Women's Autobiography: From Antiquity to the Present.* Boston: Twayne Publishers, 1986.

Johnson, Elizabeth. *Friends of God and Prophets.* New York: Continuum, 1998.

Keller, Rosemary Skinner. "Conversions and Their Consequences: Women's Ministry and Leadership in the United Methodist Tradition." In *Religious Institutions and Women's Leadership: New Roles inside the Mainstream,* ed. Catherine Wessinger, 101–23. Columbia, S.C.: Univ. of South Carolina Press, 1996.

Kolodny, Annette. "Dancing through the Minefield: Some Observations on the Theory, Practice, and Politics of a Feminist Literary Criticism." In *The New Feminist Criticism,* ed. Elaine Showalter, 144–67. New York: Pantheon Books, 1985.

Larson, Rebecca. *Quaker Women: Preaching and Prophesying in the Colonies and Abroad, 1700–1775.* Chapel Hill: Univ. of North Carolina Press, 1999.

Leclerc, Diane Cunningham. "Original Sin and Sexual Difference: A Feminist Historical Theology of a Patristic, Wesleyan, and Holiness Doctrine." Ph.D. diss., Drew Univ., 1998.

Lee, Luther. "Woman's Right to Preach the Gospel." In *Five Sermons and a Tract,* ed. Donald W. Dayton, 77–100. Chicago: Holrad House, 1975.

Lerner, Gerda. *The Majority Finds Its Past: Placing Women in History.* New York: Oxford Univ. Press, 1979.

Lionnet, Françoise. *Autobiographical Voices: Race, Gender, Self-Portraiture.* Ithaca: Cornell Univ. Press, 1989.

Long, Kathryn Teresa. *The Revival of 1857–58: Interpreting an American Religious Awakening.* New York: Oxford Univ. Press, 1998.

Maddox, Randy L. *Responsible Grace: John Wesley's Practical Theology.* Nashville: Kingswood Books, 1994.

———. "Wesleyan Theology and the Christian Feminist Critique." *Wesleyan Theological Journal* 22, no. 1 (spring 1987): 101–11.

Magnuson, Norris. *Salvation in the Slums.* ATLA Series, no. 10. Metuchen, N. J.: Scarecrow Press, 1977.

"The Martyrdom of Saints Perpetua and Felicitas." In *The Acts of the Christian Martyrs.* Trans. Herbert Musurillo, 107–31. Oxford: Clarendon Press, 1972.

Mason, Mary G. "Dorothy Day and Women's Spiritual Autobiography." In *American Women's Autobiography: Fea(s)ts of Memory,* ed. Margo Culley, 185–217. Madison: Univ. of Wisconsin Press, 1992.

———. "The Other Voice: Autobiographies of Women Writers." In *Life/lines: Theorizing Women's Autobiography,* ed. Bella Brodzki and Celeste Schenck, 19–44. Ithaca: Cornell Univ. Press, 1988.

Mattingly, Carol C. *Well-Tempered Women: Nineteenth-Century Temperance Rhetoric.* Carbondale: Southern Illinois Univ. Press, 1998.

McClurkan, J. O. "Madame Guyon." In *Chosen Vessels.* Nashville: Pentecostal Mission Publishing, 1901.

McDowell, Deborah E. "New Directions for Black Feminist Criticism." In *The New Feminist Criticism,* ed. Elaine Showalter, 186–99. New York: Pantheon Books, 1985.

McKay, Nellie Y. "Nineteenth-Century Black Women's Spiritual Autobiographies: Religious Faith and Self-Empowerment." In *Interpreting Women's Lives: Feminist Theory and Personal Narratives,* ed. Personal Narratives Group, 139–54. Bloomington, Ind.: Indiana Univ. Press, 1989.

———. "Race, Gender, and Cultural Context in Zora Neale Hurston's *Dust Tracks on a Road.*" In *Life/lines: Theorizing Women's Autobiography*, ed. Bella Brodzki and Celeste Schenck, 175–88. Ithaca: Cornell Univ. Press, 1988.

McLaughlin, Eleanor L. "Women, Power and the Pursuit of Holiness in Medieval Christianity." In *Women of Spirit: Female Leadership in the Jewish and Christian Traditions,* ed. Rosemary Ruether and Eleanor McLaughlin, 100–130. New York: Simon and Schuster, 1979.

McLeister, Clara. "Madam Guyon." In *Men and Women of Deep Piety.* Atlanta: Repairer Publishing, 1920.

Melton, J. Gordon. "Emma Curtis Hopkins: A Feminist of the 1880s and Mother of New Thought." In *Women's Leadership in Marginal Religions,* ed. Catherine Wessinger, 88–101. Urbana: Univ. of Illinois Press, 1993.

Miller, Nancy K. "Writing Fictions: Women's Autobiography in France." In *Life/lines: Theorizing Women's Autobiography,* ed. Bella Brodzki and Celeste Schenck, 45–61. Ithaca: Cornell Univ. Press, 1988.

Moody, Joycelyn K. "On the Road with God: Travel and Quest in Early Nineteenth-Century African American Holy Women's Narratives." *Religion and Literature* 27, no. 1 (spring 1995): 35–51.

Mueller, Janel M. "Autobiography of a New 'Creatur': Female Spirituality, Selfhood, and Authorship in 'The Book of Margery Kempe.'" In *The Female Autograph: Theory and Practice of Autobiography from the Tenth to the Twentieth Century,* ed. Domna C. Stanton, 57–69. Chicago: Univ. of Chicago Press, 1984.

Murdoch, Norman H. "Female Ministry in the Thought and Work of Catherine Booth." *Church History* 53 (Sept. 1984): 348–62.

Nelson, Margory. "Ladies in the Streets: A Sociological Analysis of the National Woman's Party, 1910–1930." Ph.D. diss., State Univ. of New York at Buffalo, 1976.

Norman, Rose. "The Representation of Religious Experience in Nineteenth-Century American Women's Autobiography." *Listening: Journal of Religion and Culture* 28, no. 2 (spring 1993): 128–40.

Nussbaum, Felicity. *The Autobiographical Subject: Gender and Ideology in Eighteenth-Century England.* Baltimore: Johns Hopkins Univ. Press, 1989.

Oden, Amy. *In Her Words: Women's Writings in the History of Christian Thought.* Nashville: Abingdon, 1994.

Oden, Thomas C. *Phoebe Palmer: Selected Writings.* New York: Paulist Press, 1988.

Olney, James. "Autobiography and the Cultural Moment: A Thematic, Historical, and Bibliographical Introduction." In *Autobiography: Essays Theoretical and Critical,* ed. James Olney, 3–27. Princeton: Princeton Univ. Press, 1980.

Olson, Laura R., Sue E. S. Crawford, and James L. Guth. "Changing Issue Agendas of Women Clergy." *Journal of the Scientific Study of Religion* 39, no. 2 (June 2000): 140–53.

Pagels, Elaine. *Adam, Eve, and the Serpent.* New York: Random House, 1988.

Palmer, Phoebe. *Four Years in the Old World; Comprising the Travels, Incidents, and Evangelistic Labors of Dr. and Mrs. Palmer in England, Ireland, Scotland, and Wales.* New York: Foster & Palmer, Jr., 1867.

———. *The Promise of the Father; or, A Neglected Specialty of the Last Days.* Boston: Henry V. Degen, 1859. Reprint, Salem, Ohio: Schmul Publishers, n.d.

Personal Narratives Group. "'Conditions not of Her Own Making.'" In *Interpreting Women's Lives,* ed. Personal Narratives Group, 19–23. Bloomington: Indiana Univ. Press, 1989.

———. "Origins." In *Interpreting Women's Lives,* ed. Personal Narratives Group, 3–15. Bloomington: Indiana Univ. Press, 1989.

———. "Truths." In *Interpreting Women's Lives,* ed. Personal Narratives Group, 261–64. Bloomington: Indiana Univ. Press, 1989.

Peters, John. *Christian Perfection and American Methodism.* Grand Rapids, Mich.: Francis Asbury Press of Zondervan Publishing House, 1985.

Peterson, Carla L. *"Doers of the Word": African-American Women Speakers and Writers in the North (1830–1880).* New York: Oxford Univ. Press, 1995.

Pilardi, Jo-Ann. *Simone de Beauvoir.* Westport, Conn.: Praeger, 1999.

Procter-Smith, Marjorie. "'In the Line of the Female': Shakerism and Feminism." In *Women's Leadership in Marginal Religions,* ed. Catherine Wessinger, 23–40. Urbana: Univ. of Illinois Press, 1993.

R. [Railton], George [Scott]. *Salvation in the Convent under Madame Jeanne de la Mothe Guyon.* New York: Salvation Army, 1885.

Raser, Harold E. *Phoebe Palmer: Her Life and Thought.* Lewiston: Edwin Mellen Press, 1987.

Rauschenbusch, Walter. *A Theology for the Social Gospel.* Macmillan, 1917. Reprint, Nashville: Abingdon, 1978.

"Revival Miscellany." *Guide to Holiness* 76 (Aug. 1880): 56.

Roberts, B. T. *Ordaining Women.* Rochester: Earnest Christian Publishing House, 1891. Reprint, Indianapolis: Light and Life Press, 1992.

Roberts, Deotis J. *Liberation and Reconciliation: A Black Theology.* Rev. ed. Maryknoll: Orbis Books, 1994.

Rothman, Sheila M. *Woman's Proper Place.* New York: Basic Books, 1978.

Salter, Darius L. *Spirit and Intellect: Thomas Upham's Holiness Theology.* Metuchen, N.J.: Scarecrow Press, 1986.

Sayre, Robert E. "The Proper Study: Autobiographies in American Studies." In *The American Autobiography,* ed. Albert E. Stone, 11–30. Englewood Cliffs, N. J.: Prentice-Hall, 1981.

Schneider, A. Gregory. "Objective Selves versus Empowered Selves: The Conflict over Holiness in the Post–Civil War Methodist Episcopal Church." *Methodist History* 32, no. 4 (July 1994): 237–49.

———. *The Way of the Cross Leads Home.* Bloomington: Indiana Univ. Press. 1993.

Scott, Karen. "St. Catherine of Siena, 'Apostola.'" *Church History* 61, no. 1 (Mar. 1992): 34–46.

Shellhamer, E. E. *The Ups and Downs of a Pioneer Preacher.* Atlanta: Repairer Publishing, 1914.

Showalter, Elaine. "Feminist Criticism in the Wilderness." In *The New Feminist Criticism,* ed. Elaine Showalter, 243–70. New York: Pantheon Books, 1985.

Sider, Ronald J. *One-Sided Christianity? Uniting the Church to Heal a Lost and Broken World.* Grand Rapids, Mich.: Zondervan Publishing House and San Francisco: Harper, 1993.

Sklar, Kathryn K. "Four Levels of Women's History." In *New Research on Women at the University of Michigan,* ed. Dorothy G. McGuigan, 7–10. Ann Arbor: Univ. of Michigan, 1974.

Smith, Sidonie. *A Poetics of Women's Autobiography: Marginality and the Fictions of Self-Representation.* Bloomington, Ind.: Indiana Univ. Press, 1987.

———. "Resisting the Gaze of Embodiment: Women's Autobiography in the Nineteenth Century." In *American Women's Autobiography,* ed. Margo Culley, 75–110. Madison: Univ. of Wisconsin Press, 1992.

Smith, Sidonie, and Julia Watson, eds. *Women, Autobiography, Theory.* Madison: Univ. of Wisconsin Press, 1998.

Smith, Timothy L. *Called unto Holiness: The Story of the Nazarenes: The Formative Years.* Kansas City, Mo.: Nazarene Publishing House, 1962.

———. *Revivalism and Social Reform in Mid-Nineteenth Century America.* New York: Abingdon Press, 1957. Reprint with new title *Revivalism and Social Reform: American Protestantism on the Eve of the Civil War*. Baltimore: Johns Hopkins Univ. Press, 1980.

Spacks, Patricia Meyer. "Selves in Hiding." In *Women's Autobiography: Essays in Criticism,* ed. Estelle C. Jelinek, 112–32. Bloomington: Indiana Univ. Press, 1980.

Spengemann, William C. *The Forms of Autobiography Episodes in the History of a Literary Genre.* New Haven: Yale Univ. Press, 1980.

Stanley, Liz. *The Auto/biographical I: The Theory and Practice of Feminist Auto/Biography.* Manchester: Manchester Univ. Press, 1992.

Stanley, Susie C. "'Bumping' into Modernity: Primitive/Modern Tensions in the Wesleyan/Holiness Movement." In *The Primitive Church in the Modern World,* ed. Richard T. Hughes, 139–57. Urbana, Ill.: Univ. of Illinois Press, 1995.

———. "Empowered Foremothers: Wesleyan/Holiness Women Speak to Today's Christian Feminists." *Wesleyan Theological Journal* 24 (1989): 103–16.

———. *Feminist Pillar of Fire: The Life of Alma White.* Cleveland, Ohio: Pilgrim Press, 1993.

———. "The Promise Fulfilled: Women's Ministries in the Wesleyan/Holiness Movement." In *Religious Institutions and Women's Leadership: New Roles inside the Mainstream,* ed. Catherine Wessinger, 139–57. Columbia: Univ. of South Carolina Press, 1996.

———. "'Tell Me the Old Old Story': An Analysis of Autobiographies by Holiness Women." *Wesleyan Theological Journal* 29, nos. 1 and 2 (spring–fall 1994): 7–22.

———. *Wesleyan/Holiness Women Clergy: A Bibliography.* Portland, Ore.: Western Evangelical Seminary, 1994.

———. "What Sanctification Means to Me: 'Holiness Is Power.'" In *Sanctification: Discussion Papers in Preparation for the Fourth International Dialogue on Doctrinal Issues,* 17–24. Anderson, Ind.: Anderson Univ. School of Theology, 1989.

Stanton, Domna C. "Autogynography: Is the Subject Different?" In *The Female Autograph,* ed. Domna C. Stanton, 3–20. Chicago: Univ. of Chicago Press, 1984.

Stanton, Elizabeth Cady, Susan B. Anthony, and Matilda J. Gage, eds. *History of Woman Suffrage,* vols. 1 and 3. Rochester, N.Y.: Charles Mann, 1881, 1885.

Stewart, [Eliza Daniel]. *Memories of the Crusade.* Columbus, Ohio, 1889: William Hubbart. Reprint, New York: Arno Press, 1972.

Stone, Albert E. *Autobiographical Occasions and Original Acts.* Philadelphia: Univ. of Pennsylvania Press, 1982.

Strong, Douglas M. *Perfectionist Politics: Abolitionism and the Religious Tensions of American Democracy.* Religion and Politics. Syracuse: Syracuse Univ. Press, 1999.

Swindells, Julia. *The Uses of Autobiography.* London: Taylor & Francis, 1995.

Taves, Ann. "Self and God in the Early Published Memoirs of New England Women." In *American Women's Autobiography,* ed. Margo Culley, 57–74. Madison: Univ. of Wisconsin Press, 1992.

Tenney, Mary Alice. *Blueprint for a Christian World.* Winona Lake, Ind.: Light and Life Press, 1953.

Teresa of Avila. *The Life of Teresa of Jesus: The Autobiography of Teresa of Avila.* Trans. and ed. E. Allison Peers. New York: Image Books Doubleday, 1991.

Thomson, Alistair. "Writing about Learning: Using Mass-Observation Educational Life-Histories to Explore Learning through Life." In *The Uses of Autobiography,* ed. Julia Swindells, 163–76. London: Taylor & Francis, 1995.

Tucker, Cynthia Grant. *Prophetic Sisterhood: Liberal Women Ministers of the Frontier.* Boston: Beacon Press, 1990.

Veenker, Judy. "Culture Clash: Asserting the Bible's Authority, Southern Baptists Say Pastors Must Be Male." *Christianity Today,* 10 July 2000, 19.

Ward, Patricia A. "Madame Guyon and Experiential Theology in America." *Church History* 67, no. 3 (Sept. 1998): 484–98.

———. "Madame Guyon and the Democratization of Spirituality." *Papers of French Seventeenth Century Literature* 23, no. 45 (1996): 501–8.

———. "Madame Guyon in America: An Annotated Bibliography." *Bulletin of Bibliography* 52, no. 2 (June 1995): 107–11.

Warner, Daniel Sydney. "Journal of D. S. Warner." Tms. (photocopy).

Watson, Julia, and Sidonie Smith. "Introduction: De/Colonization and the Politics of Discourse in Women's Autobiographical Practices." In *De/Colonizing the Subject,* ed. Sidonie Smith and Julia Watson, xiii–xxxi. Minneapolis: Univ. of Minnesota Press, 1992.

Welter, Barbara. *Dimity Convictions.* Athens: Ohio Univ. Press, 1976.

Wesley, John. *The Letters of the Rev. John Wesley, A. M.* Ed. John Telford. London: Epworth Press, 1931.

———. *Plain Account of Christian Perfection.* London: Wesleyan Conference Office, 1872. Reprint, Kansas City, Mo.: Beacon Hill Press of Kansas City, 1966.

———. *The Works of John Wesley,* vol. 3, CD-ROM. Franklin, Tenn.: Providence House Publishers, 1995.

Wheatley, Richard. *The Life and Letters of Mrs. Phoebe Palmer.* New York: W. C. Palmer, Publisher, 1881. Reprint, New York: Garland Publishing, 1984.

White, Alma. "Man and Woman Created Equal." *Woman's Chains* (May–June 1940): 6.

———. "Shall Woman Occupy Her Place?" *Woman's Chains* (Jan.–Feb. 1926): 5.

———. *Woman's Ministry.* London: Pillar of Fire, [1921].

White, Charles Edward. *The Beauty of Holiness: Phoebe Palmer as Theologian, Revivalist, Feminist, and Humanitarian.* Grand Rapids, Mich.: Francis Asbury Press of Zondervan Publishing House, 1986.

Willing, J.[Jennie] Fowler. "Madame Guyon the Mystic." *Guide to Holiness,* n.s., 71 (Dec. 1899): 188, 189; and n.s., 72 (Jan. 1900): 20, 21, 26.

———. "Pentecostal Womanhood: Mary Fletcher." *Guide to Holiness.* (Sept. 1900): 84.

Wilson, Elizabeth. *A Scriptural View of Woman's Rights and Duties.* Philadelphia: Wm. S. Young, 1849.

Winston, Diana. *Red-Hot and Righteous: The Urban Religion of The Salvation Army.* Cambridge, Mass.: Harvard Univ. Press, 1999.

Worship the Lord. Anderson, Ind.: Warner Press, 1989.

Yee, Shirley J. *Black Women Abolitionists: A Study in Activism, 1828–1860.* Knoxville: Univ. of Tennessee Press, 1992.

Zikmund, Barbara Brown, Adair T. Lummis, and Patricia Mei Yin Chang. *Clergy Women: An Uphill Calling.* Louisville, Ky.: Westminster John Knox Press, 1998.

INDEX

Holy Boldness was designed and typeset on a Macintosh computer system using QuarkXPress software. The text is set in Garamond ITC and the chapter openings are set in Gill Sans. This book was designed by Cheryl Carrington, typeset by Kimberly Scarbrough, and manufactured by Thomson-Shore, Inc.